KU-342-430

Contents

Figures and Tables   vii

Introduction   ix

I. Methods

1. Student Teams-Achievement Divisions
   Robert E. Slavin   3

2. Team Assisted Individualization and Cooperative
   Integrated Reading and Composition
   Robert E. Slavin and Nancy A. Madden   20

3. Pieces of the Puzzle: The Jigsaw Method
   Judy Clarke   34

4. Learning Together
   David W. Johnson and Roger T. Johnson   51

5. Structuring Academic Controversy
   David W. Johnson and Roger T. Johnson   66

6. Complex Instruction: Higher-Order Thinking in
   Heterogeneous Classrooms
   *Elizabeth G. Cohen, Rachel A. Lotan, Jennifer A.
   Whitcomb, Maria V. Balderrama, Ruth Cossey, and
   Patricia E. Swanson*   82

7. Group Investigation in the Cooperative Classroom
   Yael Sharan and Shlomo Sharan   97

8. The Structural Approach: Six Keys to Cooperative
   Learning
   Spencer Kagan and Miguel Kagan   115

II. Applications

9. CDP Cooperative Learning: Working Together to
   Construct Social, Ethical, and Intellectual Understanding
   *Marilyn Watson, Daniel Solomon, Stefan Dasho, Peter
   Shwartz, and Sylvia Kendzior*   137

10. Creating "Thought-Full" Classrooms: Fostering Cognitive
    Literacy via Cooperative Learning and Integrated
    Strategies Instruction
    Edwin S. Ellis and R. Kevin Feldman   157

11. Teaching and Learning the Language Arts with
    Cooperative Learning Methods
    Aryeh Wohl and Esther Klein-Wohl   177

12. An Integrated Groupwork Model for the Second-
    Language Classroom
    Yael Bejarano   193

13. Cooperative Learning and Postmodern Approaches to
    Teaching Literature
    Mark Brubacher and Ryder Payne   212

14. Cooperative Learning and Science
    Sharon J. Sherman   226

15. Cooperative Learning to Support Thinking, Reasoning,
    and Communicating in Mathematics
    Laurel Robertson, Neil Davidson, and Roberta L. Dees   245

16. Cooperative Learning and Computers
    Mary Male   267

III. Implementation

17. Creating a Community Context for Cooperative Learning
    Liana Nan Graves   283

18. Facilitating Teachers' Power through Collaboration: Implementing Cooperative Learning in Elementary Schools

Rachel Hertz-Lazarowitz and Margarita Calderón   300

19. Cooperative Learning and School Organization: A Theoretical and Practical Perspective

Shlomo Sharan and Hanna Shachar   318

20. Cooperative Learning and the Teacher

Shlomo Sharan   336

Selected Bibliography   349

Author Index   353

Subject Index   359

About the Editor and Contributors   371

Figures and Tables

FIGURES

1.1.	Team Summary Sheet	9
1.2.	Assigning Students to Teams	10
1.3.	Quiz Score Sheet (STAD and Jigsaw II)	15
1.4.	Quiz Score Sheet (STAD and Jigsaw II) after the First Quiz	16
1.5.	Team Summary Sheet after the First Quiz	17
4.1.	Cooperative Learning	53
4.2.	Cooperative School Organizational Structure	61
6.1.	Activity Card	92
8.1.	Element-based Activity	121
8.2.	Structure-based Activity	122
8.3.	Overview of Theoretical Constructs	126
10.1.	Cognitive Processing and Corresponding Cognitive Literacy Strategy Steps	161
10.2.	Writing Version of the Cognitive Literacy Strategy	162
10.3.	A Graphic Organizer	163
10.4.	Main Ideas and Supporting Points on a Graphic Organizer	165
10.5.	Sample of Writing about Bald Eagles	166
10.6.	Summary of ISI Instructional Stages, General Purpose, and Examples	167

12.1. An Integrated Groupwork Model for the Second-Language
       Classroom   194
12.2. The Content Component in the IGM   196
12.3. The Process Component in the IGM   201
14.1. Team Word Web   236
14.2. Sequence Chain   237
14.3. Energy Forms Attribute Wheel   238
15.1. Example of a Class Chart   250
18.1. Professional Development Model   301
18.2. Teacher Researchers: Empowerment for Stages 1–5   314
19.1. Classroom and School Organizational Features with Low
       versus High Levels of Participation in Decision Making 320

TABLES

5.1. Comparison of Instructional Methods   69
5.2. Nature of Instructional Methods   70
8.1. Team Discussion versus Three-Step Interview   117
8.2. Overview of Selected Structures   120
8.3. Overview of Selected Lesson Designs   124
8.4. Design Elements of Selected Lesson Designs   125

Introduction

The chapters in this volume provide readers with a broad picture of cooperative learning methods today. Included are descriptions of the main generic methods, applications of cooperative learning to various subject matter domains, and chapters dealing with the implementation of cooperative learning in the schools and the problems it confronts.

In light of the decision to encompass all of these topics, it was unrealistic to strive for comprehensiveness within the confines of this volume. One obvious omission is the application of cooperative learning to the social studies, although examples of cooperative learning in social studies are found in several chapters in this book. Apart from the constraints of space, two handbooks on cooperative learning stressing the social studies were prepared more or less at the same time as this volume (Pedersen & Digby, 1995; Stahl, 1993). Therefore, a single chapter on that subject in this volume seemed to be an unnecessary duplication of effort, as well as too limited in scope to constitute a contribution. Nor could any one set of chapters on the application of cooperative learning ever be definitive. The applications presented here are illustrations of how one might use cooperative learning in different subject-matter domains. Many other illustrations now in use could not be presented here, and new approaches are constantly evolving.

The "new wave" of cooperative learning appeared in the early seventies—following the pioneering work of John Dewey, and later of Alice Miel and Herbert Thelen in the 1950s. Yet, the challenges of teacher education for employing cooperative learning methods and implementing them in the schools still remain. Cooperative learning seems to have become, or is on the road to becoming, an integral part of the instructional repertoire of many elementary school teachers. However, it is not yet widely taught in university teacher education programs, and its impact on classroom organization and procedures in secondary schools has yet to be noticed. Nor has cooperative learning at the high school level been explored sufficiently in systematic research.

Investigators of the school change process and its tribulations warned several decades ago that essential changes in elementary schools were more likely to succeed than in secondary schools. That observation remains valid for cooperative learning to this day. Clearly, in terms of adopting fundamental innovations, the secondary school is a mighty fortress that, even in the face of seemingly powerful efforts to introduce change, proves singularly resistant. The paradigm shift in instruction that is frequently observable in the elementary grades thus far has not met with much success in high schools.

Over the course of the past three decades, it became increasingly apparent to the proponents and investigators of cooperative learning that adoption and institutionalization of these approaches to instruction required system-wide changes in school organization and functioning. Instructional change could not be accomplished if change agents, whoever they may be, focus on retraining individual teachers who would attempt to introduce the new methods into their classrooms. Innovative teaching demanded much organizational and collegial coordination and support. Teachers working in isolation could not sustain it. Genuine school change requires more than "tinkering" with the teaching methods used in one or two classrooms. Introduction of cooperative learning into classroom teaching on a systematic basis qualifies as genuine school change that entails a relatively broad restructuring of the school's mode of operation. The need for a system-wide approach to the dissemination of cooperative learning and other innovations is explained in the present volume as well as in other recent publications (Brody & Davidson, 1998; Sarason, 1990, 1998; Sharan, Shachar & Levine, 1999; Sharan & Sharan, 1991; Slavin, Madden, Dolan & Wasik, 1996). High schools consist of many sub-systems included within the larger organization. One of the reasons (though certainly not the only one) why cooperative learning has been adopted in so few high schools is due to their relatively complex organization, by comparison to elementary schools, and to the challenges this complexity poses for change agents, both internal and external. Accomplishing the system-wide changes in high schools needed to accommodate an instructional change such as cooperative learning is a formidable task.

The structure of this volume was planned with systems theory in mind, just as cooperative learning itself displays some of the critical features of social systems. Cooperative learning transforms the classroom from a collection of individuals to a network of groups. That alone alters the social structure of the classroom from one of being an audience (collection of students) focused for long periods of time on the performer on the stage (teacher), to a social system comprised of interacting parts. This micro-system, in turn, is embedded in a larger system (the school) whose component parts (staff members and administrators) must interact in ways that facilitate and sustain the interaction occurring in the restructured classroom. Without such interaction among teachers and administrators for planning, coordinating, problem solving and decision making, cooperative learning is unlikely to survive over the long run. Innovative methods of instruction cannot survive if they are treated as entities with a life of their own independent of the organizational setting in which they are employed. To ignore the environment of a given system or subsystem is to invite rapid entropy or even disaster, as students of modern organizational theory have known for quite some time. Hence, this volume treats classroom teaching at length, but chapters 17 to 19 and the concluding section of chapter 20, focus on what must be done to have cooperative learning adopted by the school as a social system.

A topic not addressed in this volume is how the school-wide use of cooperative learning relates to the macro-system, namely to the wider community. On many occasions when the editor of this volume and colleagues served as consultants in secondary schools, teachers and administrators were often apprehensive about how parents would react to the marked change in classroom teaching method with the introduction of cooperative learning. Teachers feared that parents would object to cooperative learning for a variety of reasons—such as how their children would compete with others later in their schooling when their classes now stressed cooperation—and would pressure principals and teachers to abandon the innovation. Educators in schools also expressed concern about how central-office supervisors would relate to the adoption of instructional changes required by cooperative learning. It appeared to some that the policies of the wider school system might conflict with the goals and methods of cooperative learning. These latter topics and others of similar nature await serious treatment by educators and researchers.

Still another feature of the school-community relationship is the opportunities for life-related learning offered by the many settings found in the community. Most schools do not avail themselves of these opportunities for enriching their resources for teaching and learning because they perceive academic learning as a process that takes place within the area delimited by the walls of the school building (Sarason, 1983, 1996; Sharan, Shachar & Levine, 1999). Perhaps future volumes on cooperative learning will expand the horizons of these approaches to instruction to encompass the notion of the community as a site for learning by cooperative teams of students.

The first part of this volume presents eight generic methods of cooperative learning that can be applied to a wide variety of subject matter or used in the teaching of an integrated or multidisciplinary curriculum. The sequence in which these chapters appear was determined by the decision as to where the particular method should be placed on three different scales. First, what is the degree of change from traditional instructional conditions, in the classroom and in the school environment, required for the implementation of the specific cooperative learning method? Second, what is the degree of change from traditional instructional behavior and teaching role? The descriptions of the two poles of this scale would be: Do teachers continue to present information verbally to students for extended periods of time as part of the lesson, or are students engaged in asking questions and seeking information in a variety of sources in order to solve problems? Third, to what extent does the method entail alteration of existing curricular materials? Is the worksheet- and textbook-centered approach still viable with this method? As it turned out, almost all of the methods were judged to require a considerable degree of curricular redesign, so that the third scale could not discriminate between the different methods, and the sequencing of the chapters in the "Methods" part is based almost exclusively on the first two scales.

The reader will quickly notice that not all of the authors of cooperative learning methods recommend similar procedures for classroom implementation. Indeed, some authors explicitly take exception to practices that are part of the routine procedures of other methods. The title "cooperative learning method" does not imply uniformity in thought or procedures for all of the methods, and no attempt was made to reconcile the differences. However, what should not be overlooked is the fact that, given the diversity of the authors of these chapters and the different parts of the world in which they have worked trying to copy with different educational problems, the degree of agreement between them is quite remarkable.

The part called "Applications" opens with two chapters that focus on the contribution of cooperative learning to psychological functioning and development, namely, moral judgment and behavior (chapter 9) and cognitive and metacognitive functioning in learning (chapter 10). These are followed by three chapters on language arts (chapters 11, 12, and 13) and three on science, math, and computers (chapters 14, 15, and 16).

The third and last part is devoted to the teachers and to the implementation of cooperative learning at the level of the school as an organizational unit. Indeed, the role of teachers figures in most of the chapters throughout this volume. Like all instructional methods, the appeal of cooperative learning methods and their effects on students are a function of how they are mastered and managed by teachers and schools. Even the most brilliantly designed instructional method cannot circumvent the competence of the teachers and the impact of the school environment. Teachers' multiple roles in the classroom and in the school are at the heart of the practice of cooperative learning.

It is hoped that this volume will convey the message that cooperative learning can make a significant contribution to teaching and learning in schools, but that promise is far from being realized at this time. Schools and teachers have yet to receive the professional assistance and training necessary for changing the prevailing traditional forms of teaching. In this time of widespread debate about educational reform, more attention must be paid to the topics raised in this volume regarding classroom instruction and its schoolwide organizational requirements.

Yael Sharan deserves a special vote of gratitude for her tireless efforts in helping to edit this volume. She prevented the task from assuming overwhelming proportions, and her unmatched attention to detail led to many improvements in the text. Thanks too are due to Robert Slavin and James McPartland at the Center for Research on Effective Schooling at the Johns Hopkins University, where a six-month sabbatical provided much-needed support at a critical stage in the preparation of this volume.

REFERENCES

Brody, C. & Davidson, N. (Eds.)(1998). *Professional development for cooperative learning: Issues and approaches*. Albany, NY: State University of New York Press.

Pedersen, J. & Digby, A. (Eds.)(1995). *Secondary schools and cooperative learning: Theories, models and strategies*. New York: Garland Publishing.

Sarason, S. (1983). *Schooling in America: Scapegoat and salvation*. New York: The Free Press.

Sarason, S. (1990). *The predictable failure of educational reform*. San Francisco: Jossey-Bass.

Sarason, S. (1996). *Revisiting "The culture of the school and the problem of change."* New York: Teachers College Press.

Sarason, S. (1998). *Political leadership and educational failure*. San Francisco: Jossey-Bass.

Sharan, S., Shachar, H. & Levine, T. (1999). *The innovative school: Organization and instruction*. Westport, CT: Bergin & Garvey.

Sharan, S. & Sharan, Y. (1991). Cooperative learning: Changing teachers' instructional methods. In N. Wyner (Ed.), *Current perspectives on the culture of schools*. Boston: Brookline Books, 143–164.

Slavin, R., Madden, N., Dolan, L., & Wasik, B. (1996). *Every child, every school: Success for all*. Thousand Oaks, CA: Corwin Press.

Stahl, R. (Ed.)(1993). *Cooperative learning in the social studies: A handbook for teachers*. Menlo Park, CA: Addison-Wesley.

PART I
Methods

1

Student Teams-Achievement Divisions

Robert E. Slavin

This chapter describes Student Teams-Achievement Divisions (STAD), one of a set of instructional techniques developed and researched at Johns Hopkins University collectively known as Student Team Learning. These techniques are based on the idea of having students work in cooperative learning teams to learn academic objectives. Student Team Learning techniques are not one-time activities designed to liven up the classroom from time to time, but are alternatives to traditional instruction that can be used as permanent means of organizing the classroom to effectively teach a wide variety of subjects. Student Team Learning methods share with other cooperative learning methods the idea that students work together to learn and are responsible for their own as well as others' learning. However, Student Team Learning methods emphasize the use of team goals and team success, which can only be achieved if all members of the team learn the objectives being taught. That is, in Student Team Learning, the students' tasks are not to *do* something as a team, but to *learn* something as a team, where the team's work is not done until all team members have mastered the material being studied.

There are three concepts that are central to all Student Team Learning methods: team rewards, individual accountability, and equal opportunities for success. In all of these methods, teams may earn certificates or other rewards if they achieve above a designated criterion. Note that the teams are not in competition; all (or none) of the teams may achieve the criterion in a given week. *Individual accountability* refers to the fact that in all Student Team Learning methods, the team's success depends on the individual learning of all team members. This focuses the activity of the team members on tutoring one another and making sure that everyone on the team is ready for a quiz or other assessment that students will take without teammate help. *Equal opportunities for success* means that what students contribute to their teams is based on their improvement over their own past performance. This ensures that high, average, and low achievers are equally challenged to do their best, and the contributions of all team members will be valued.

Research on cooperative learning methods (Slavin, 1990) has indicated that team rewards and individual accountability are essential elements for effects of cooperation on basic skills achievement. It is not enough to simply tell students to work together. Further, there is good reason to believe that if students are rewarded for doing better than they have in the past, then they will be more motivated to achieve than if they are rewarded based on their performance in comparison to others, because rewards for improvement make success neither too difficult nor too easy for students to achieve (Slavin, 1980).

STUDENT TEAMS-ACHIEVEMENT DIVISIONS: OVERVIEW

Student Teams-Achievement Divisions (STAD) is the most extensively researched of all cooperative learning methods (see Slavin, 1990). It is also very adaptable—it has been used in mathematics, science, social studies, English, industrial arts, and many other subjects, and at levels from second grade to college.

In STAD, students are assigned to four-member learning teams that are mixed in performance level, sex, and ethnicity. The teacher presents a lesson, and then students work within their teams to make sure that all team members have mastered the lesson. Finally, all students take individual quizzes on the material, at which time they may not help one another. Students' quiz scores are compared to their own past averages, and points are awarded based on the degree to which students can meet or exceed their own earlier performance. These points are then summed to form team scores, and teams that meet certain criteria may earn certificates or other rewards. The whole cycle of activities, from teacher presentation to team practice to quiz, usually takes three to five class periods. STAD is most appropriate for teaching well-defined objectives, such as mathematical computations and applications, language usage and mechanics, geography and map skills, and science concepts.

The main idea behind STAD is to motivate students to encourage and help each other master skills presented by the teacher. If students want their team to earn team rewards, they must help their teammates to learn the material. They must encourage their teammates to do their best, expressing norms that learning is important, valuable, and fun. Students are allowed to work together after the teacher's lesson, but may not help each other with quizzes, so every student must know the material (individual accountability). Students may work in pairs and compare answers, discuss any discrepancies, and help each other with any roadblocks, they may discuss approaches to solving problems, or they may quiz each other on the content they are studying. They teach their teammates and assess their strengths and weaknesses to help them succeed on the quizzes. Since team scores are based on students' improvement over their own past records (equal opportunities for success), any student can be the team "star" in a given week, either by scoring well above his or her past record or by getting a perfect paper, which always produces a maximum score regardless of students' past averages.

STAD is a generic method of organizing the classroom rather than a comprehensive method of teaching any particular subject; teachers use their own lessons and other materials. Worksheets and quizzes are available for most school subjects for grades three through nine (see "Resources" at the end of this chapter), but most teachers use their own materials to supplement or replace these materials.

RESEARCH ON STAD

The principal goal of Student Team Learning is to accelerate the achievement of all students. The Student Team Learning methods have been thoroughly evaluated and have been consistently found to be effective in well-controlled studies in regular public schools (see Slavin, 1990). These studies have taken place in urban, rural, and suburban schools over periods of four to thirty weeks, at grade levels from three to twelve. Of twenty-two studies of STAD in grades three through twelve, seventeen found significantly higher achievement for this method than for traditional instruction, and five found no differences. For example, Slavin and Karweit (1984) used STAD over an entire school year in inner-city ninth-grade mathematics classes. Student performance on a standardized mathematics test increased significantly more than in either a mastery learning group or a control group using the same materials. Substantial differences favoring STAD have been found in such diverse subjects as social studies (e.g., Allen & VanSickle, 1984), language arts (e.g., Slavin & Oickle, 1981), science (Okebukola, 1985), and industrial arts (Perrault, 1982), as well as in other studies of mathematics (e.g., Sherman & Thomas, 1986). Effects have been positive for high, average, and low achievers.

Student Team Learning methods have had positive effects on many important outcomes in addition to achievement. One of these is race relations. Several studies have found that these methods increased the number of friendships between black and white students (Slavin, 1985). One of the STAD studies (Slavin, 1979) found that these positive effects continued into the following school year, when students were no longer in the junior high school classes in which they had experienced the program.

Studies of STAD have documented significant gains in student self-esteem, liking of class, attendance, and behavior (Slavin, 1990). Student Team Learning methods are often used in classes containing mainstreamed students with academic handicaps and have been effective both for improving these students' achievement and behavior and for increasing their acceptance by their classmates (Slavin, 1990).

USING STUDENT TEAMS-ACHIEVEMENT DIVISIONS IN THE CLASSROOM

The remainder of this chapter presents a guide to the use of Student Teams-Achievement Divisions (STAD). For information on training and materials for STAD and other Student Team Learning methods, see "Resources" at the end of the chapter.

Overview

STAD is made up of five major components: class presentations, teams, quizzes, individual improvement scores, and team recognition.

Class Presentations

Material in STAD is initially introduced in a class presentation. This is most often a lecture-discussion conducted by the teacher, but could include audiovisual presentations. Class presentations in STAD differ from usual teaching only in that they must be clearly focused on the STAD unit. In this way, students realize that they must pay careful attention during the class presentation, because doing so will help them to do well on the quizzes, and their quiz scores determine their team scores.

Teams

Teams are composed of four or five students who represent a cross-section of the class in academic performance, sex, and race or ethnicity. The major function of the team is to prepare its members to do well on the quizzes. After the teacher presents the material, the team meets to study worksheets or other material. The worksheets may be materials obtained from the Johns Hopkins Team Learning Project (see "Resources" at the end of the chapter), or they may be teacher-made. Most often, the study takes the form of students discussing problems together, comparing answers, and correcting any misconceptions if teammates make mistakes.

The team is the most important feature of STAD. At every point, emphasis is placed on team members doing their best for the team, and on the team doing its best to help its members. The team provides the peer support for academic performance that is important for effects on learning, but it also provides the mutual concern and respect that are important for effects on such outcomes as intergroup relations, self-esteem, and acceptance of mainstreamed students.

Quizzes

After one to two periods of teacher presentation and one to two periods of team practice, the students take individual quizzes. Students are not permitted to help one another during the quizzes. This makes sure that every student is individually responsible for knowing the material.

Individual Improvement Scores

The idea behind the individual improvement scores is to give each student a performance goal that the student can reach, but only if he or she works harder and performs better than in the past. Any student can contribute maximum points to his or her team in this scoring system, but no student can do so without showing definite improvement over past performance. Each student is given a "base" score, derived from the student's average performance on similar quizzes. Then students earn points for their teams based on how much their quiz scores exceed their base scores.

Team Recognition

Teams may earn certificates or other rewards if their average scores exceed a certain criterion. Students' team scores may also be used to determine up to five bonus points toward their grades. Certificates for teams that meet high standards of performance, newsletter recognition, bulletin-board displays, special privileges, small prizes, or other rewards emphasize the idea that doing well as a team is important.

Preparing to Use STAD

Materials

STAD can be used with curriculum materials specifically designed for Student Team Learning and distributed by the Johns Hopkins Team Learning Project, or it can be used with teacher-made materials. As of this writing, Johns Hopkins materials are available in mathematics for grades two through ten, language arts for grades three through eight, junior high school life and physical science, and other topics.

However, it is quite easy to make your own materials. Simply make a worksheet, a worksheet answer sheet, and a quiz for each unit you plan to teach. Each unit should occupy three to five days of instruction.

Assigning Students to Teams

A team in STAD is a group of four or five students who represent a cross-section of the class in past performance, race or ethnicity, and sex.

That is, a four-person team in a class that is one-half male, one-half female, three-quarters white, and one-quarter minority might have two boys and two girls and three white students and one minority student. The team would also have a high performer, a low performer, and two average performers. Of course, "high performer" is a relative term; it means high for the class, not necessarily high compared to national norms.

Students are assigned to teams by the teacher, rather than by choosing teams themselves, because students tend to choose others like themselves. You may take likes, dislikes, and "deadly combinations" of students into account in your assignments, but do not let students choose their own teams. Instead, follow these steps:

1. *Make copies of Team Summary Sheets.* Before you begin to assign students to teams, you will need to make one copy of a Team Summary Sheet (Figure 1.1) for every four students in your class.

2. *Rank students.* On a sheet of paper, rank the students in your class from highest to lowest in past performance. Use whatever information you have to do this—test scores are best, grades are good, but your own judgment is fine. Exact rankings are not critical.

3. *Decide on the number of teams.* Each team should have four members if possible. To decide how many teams you will have, divide the number of students in the class by four. If the number is divisible by four, the quotient will be the number of four-member teams you should have. For example, if there are thirty-two students in the class, you would have eight teams with four members each. If the division is uneven, the remainder will be one, two, or three. You will then have one, two, or three teams composed of five members. For example, if there are thirty students in your class, you would have seven teams; five would have four members and two would have five members.

4. *Assign students to teams.* When you are assigning students to teams, balance the teams so that (*a*) each team is composed of students whose performance levels range from low to average to high, and (*b*) the average performance level of all the teams in the class is about equal. To assign students to teams, use your list of students ranked by performance. Assign team letters to each student. For example, in an eight-team class you would use the letters *A* through *H*. Start at the top of your list with the letter *A*; continue lettering toward the middle. When you get to the last team letter, continue lettering in the opposite order. For example, if you were using the letters *A* to *H* (as in Figure 1.2), the eighth and ninth students would be assigned to team H, the tenth to team G, the next to team F, and so on. When you get back to letter *A*, stop and repeat the process from the bottom up, again starting and ending with the letter *A*.

   Notice that two of the students (17 and 18) in Figure 1.2 are not assigned at this point. They will be added to teams as fifth members, but first the teams should be checked for ethnicity and sex balance. If, for example, one-fourth of the class is black, approximately one student on each team should be black. If the teams you have made based on performance ranking are not evenly divided on both ethnicity and sex (they will hardly ever be balanced on the first try),

Figure 1.1
Team Summary Sheet

Team Name _____

LOGO

Team Summary Sheet

Team Members										Totals
Total Team Score										
Team Average *										
Team Award										

1-003.1

*Team Average = Total Team Score/Number of Team Members
Source: Slavin, 1986.

you should change team assignments by trading students of the same approximate performance level but of different ethnicity or sex between teams until a balance is achieved.

5. *Fill out Team Summary Sheets.* After you have finished assigning all students to teams, fill in the names of the students on each team on your Team Summary Sheets (Figure 1.1), leaving the team name blank.

6. *Determine initial base scores.* Base scores represent students' average scores on past quizzes. If you are starting STAD after you have given three or more

Figure 1.2
Assigning Students to Teams

	Rank Order	Team Name
High-Performing Students	1	A
	2	B
	3	C
	4	D
	5	E
	6	F
	7	G
	8	H
Average-Performing Students	9	H
	10	G
	11	F
	12	E
	13	D
	14	C
	15	B
	16	A
	17	
	18	
	19	A
	20	B
	21	C
	22	D
	23	E
	24	F
	25	G
	26	H
Students	27	H
	28	G
	29	F
	30	E
	31	D
	32	C
	33	B
	34	A

Source: Slavin, 1986.

quizzes, use students' average quiz scores as base scores. Otherwise, use students' final grades from the previous year, as follows:

Last Year's Grade

Initial Base Score

—A—90——A – /B + —85——B—80——B – /C + —75——C—70——C – /D + —65——D or F—60——

Getting Started

• Teach your first lesson (one to two periods).
• Announce team assignments and have students move their desks together to make team tables. Tell students that they will be working in teams for several weeks and may earn certificates or other rewards based on their team's total performance. Allow students ten minutes to decide on a team name.
• Let students study worksheets in their teams (one to two periods).
• Give the first quiz.

The first week of STAD is the hardest, but most students will settle into the pattern by the second week. Some students may complain about the teams to which they were assigned, but almost all students find a way to get along with their teammates by the second week. Do not change team assignments after you have announced them except under extreme circumstances, because it is partly students' realization that they will be in their team for several weeks that gets them to work on getting along with their teammates instead of complaining about them.

Schedule of Activities

STAD consists of a regular cycle of instructional activities, as follows:

Teach. Present the lesson.

Team study. Students work on worksheets in their teams to master the material.

Test. Students take individual quizzes.

Team recognition. Team scores are computed based on team members' improvement scores, and certificates or other recognition are given to high-scoring teams.

These activities are described in detail below.

Teach

Time: One to two class periods.

Main idea: Present the lesson.

Materials needed: Your lesson plan.

Each lesson in STAD begins with a class presentation. In your lesson, stress the following (adapted from Good, Grouws, & Ebmeier, 1983):

- Tell students what they are about to learn and why it is important. Arouse student curiosity with a puzzling demonstration, real-life problem, or other means.
- Briefly review any prerequisite skills or information.
- Stick close to the objectives that you will test.
- Focus on meaning, not memorization.
- Actively demonstrate concepts or skills, using visual aids, manipulatives, and many examples.
- Frequently assess student comprehension by asking many questions.
- Have all students work problems or examples or prepare answers to your questions.
- Call on students at random so that they will never know whom you might ask a question—this makes all students prepare themselves to answer.
- Do not give long class assignments at this point; have students work one or two problems or examples or prepare one or two answers, then give them feedback.
- Always explain why an answer is correct or incorrect unless it is obvious.
- Move rapidly from concept to concept as soon as students have grasped the main idea.
- Maintain momentum by eliminating interruptions, asking many questions, and moving rapidly through the lesson.

Team Study

Time: One to two class periods.

Main idea: Students study worksheets in their teams.

Materials needed: Two worksheets for every team; two answer sheets for every team.

During team study, the team members' tasks are to master the material you presented in your lesson and to help their teammates master the material. Students have worksheets and answer sheets they can use to practice the skill being taught and to assess themselves and their teammates. Only two copies of the worksheets and answer sheets are given to each team in order to force teammates to work together, but if some students prefer to work alone or want their own copies, you may make additional copies available. During team study, stress the following:

- Have teammates move their desks together or move to team tables.
- Hand out worksheets and answer sheets (two of each per team) with a minimum of fuss.
- Tell students to work together in pairs or threes. If they are working problems, each student in a pair or three should work the problem and then check with his

or her partner(s). If anyone missed a question, his or her teammates have a responsibility to explain it. If students are working on short-answer questions, they may quiz each other, with partners taking turns holding the answer sheet or attempting to answer the questions.

- Emphasize to students that they are not finished studying until they are sure their teammates will make 100% on the quiz.
- Make sure that students understand that the worksheets are for studying—not for filling out and handing in. That is why it is important for students to have the answer sheets to check themselves and their teammates as they study.
- Have students explain answers to one another instead of just checking each other against the answer sheet.
- When students have questions, have them ask a teammate before asking you.
- While students are working in teams, circulate through the class, praising teams that are working well, sitting in with each team to hear how they are doing, and so on.

Quiz

Time: One-half to one class period.

Main idea: Individual quiz.

Material needed: One quiz per student.

- Distribute the quiz and give students adequate time to complete it. Do not let students work together on the quiz; at this point students must show what they have learned as individuals. Have students move their desks apart if this is possible.
- Either allow students to exchange papers with members of other teams, or collect the quizzes to score after class. Have the quizzes scored and team scores figured in time for the next class if at all possible.

Team Recognition

Main idea: Figure individual improvement scores and team scores and award certificates or other team rewards.

Figuring Individual and Team Scores

As soon as possible after each quiz, you should figure individual improvement scores and team scores and award certificates or other rewards to high-scoring teams. If at all possible, the announcement of team scores should be made in the first period after the quiz. This makes the connection between doing well and receiving recognition clear to students, which increases their motivation to do their best.

Improvement points: Students earn points for their teams based on the degree to which their quiz scores (percent correct) exceed their base scores, as follows:

Quiz score more than 10 points below base score: 0.

Quiz score 10 points below to 1 point below base score: 10.

Quiz score base score to 10 points above base score: 20.

Quiz score more than 10 points above base score: 30.

Perfect paper (regardless of base score): 30.

Figuring improvement points is not at all difficult, and when you get used to it, it will take only a few minutes. The purpose of base scores and improvement points is to make it possible for all students to bring maximum points to their teams, whatever their level of past performance. Students understand that it is fair that each student should be compared to his or her own level of past performance, as all students enter class with different levels of skills and experience in the subject that is being taught. If record keeping is a problem, you may have students figure their own improvement points in class or recruit volunteers to help you after class.

Put the points you have calculated on each student's quiz as follows: base score = 83; quiz score = 90; improvement points = 20. For your own records, you may wish to put this information on a quiz score sheet (see Figures 1.3 and 1.4). Put the improvement points on students' Team Summary Sheets (see Figure 1.5).

Team scores: To figure team scores, put each student's improvement points on the appropriate Team Summary Sheet and divide by the number of team members who were present, rounding off any fractions (.5 is rounded up) (see Figure 1.5). Note that team scores depend on improvement scores rather than on raw scores on the quiz.

Recognizing Team Accomplishments

There are two levels of awards given based on average team scores. These are as follows: "greatteam," 18–22; "superteam," 23 or higher. Note that all teams can achieve the awards; teams are not in competition with one another.

You should provide some sort of recognition or reward for achieving at the greatteam or superteam level. Attractive certificates to each team member may be used, with a large, fancy certificate (8 1/2″ × 11″) for superteams and a smaller one for greatteams. Many teachers make bulletin-board displays listing the week's superteams and greatteams or displaying Polaroid pictures of the successful teams. Others prepare one-page newsletters, give students special buttons to wear, or let superteams and greatteams line up first for recess or receive other special privileges. Use your imagination and creativity and vary rewards from time to time; it is more important that you are excited about students' accomplishments than that you give large rewards.

Figure 1.3
Quiz Score Sheet (STAD and Jigsaw II)

Student	Date: Quiz: Base Score	Quiz Score	Improvement Points	Date: Quiz: Quiz Score	Improvement Points	Date: Quiz: Quiz Score	Improvement Points	New Base

Source: Slavin, 1986.

Figure 1.4
Quiz Score Sheet (STAD and Jigsaw II) after the First Quiz

Student	Date: May 23 Quiz: Addition with Regrouping			Date: Quiz:			Date: Quiz:		
	Base Score	Quiz Score	Improvement Points	Base Score	Quiz Score	Improvement Points	Base Score	Quiz Score	Improvement Points
Sara A.	90	100	30						
Tom B.	90	100	30						
Ursula C.	90	82	10						
Danielle D.	85	74	0						
Eddie E.	85	98	30						
Natasha F.	85	82	10						
Travis G.	80	67	0						
Tammy H.	80	91	30						
Edgar I.	75	79	20						
Andy J.	75	76	20						
Mary K.	70	91	30						
Stan L.	65	82	30						
Alvin M.	65	70	20						
Carol N.	60	62	20						
Harold S.	55	46	10						
Jack E.	55	40	0						

Source: Slavin, 1986.

Figure 1.5
Team Summary Sheet after the First Quiz

TEAM NAME **Fantastic Four**

TEAM MEMBERS	1	2	3	4	5	6	7	8	9	10	11	12	13	14
Sara A.	30													
Eddie E.	30													
Edgar I.	20													
Carol N.	20													
TOTAL TEAM SCORE	100													
TEAM AVERAGE	25													
TEAM AWARD	Superteam													

*Team Average = Total Team Score ÷ Number of Team Members.
Source: Slavin, 1986.

Returning the First Set of Quizzes

When you return the first set of quizzes (with the base scores, quiz scores, and improvement points) to the students, you will need to explain the improvement-point system. In your explanation, emphasize the following:

1. The main purpose of the improvement-point system is to give everyone a minimum score to try to beat and to set that minimum score based on past performance so that all students will have an equal chance to be successful if they do their best academically.

2. The second purpose of the improvement-point system is to make students realize that the scores of everyone on their team are important—that all members of the team can earn maximum improvement points if they do their best.

3. The improvement-point system is fair because everyone is competing only with himself or herself—trying to improve his or her own performance—regardless of what the rest of the class does.

Recomputing Base Scores

Every marking period (or more frequently, if you like), recompute students' average quiz scores on all quizzes and assign students new base scores.

Changing Teams

After five or six weeks of STAD, reassign students to new teams. This gives students who were on low-scoring teams a new chance, allows students to work with other classmates, and keeps the program fresh.

Grading

When it comes time to give students report-card grades, the grades should be based on the students' actual quiz scores, not their improvement points or team scores. If you wish, you might make the students' team scores a part of their grades (for example, you might award up to five bonus points for being on a superteam). If your school gives separate grades for effort, you might use team and/or improvement scores to determine the effort grades.

Resources

Teacher's manuals, materials, and training are available from the Center for Social Organization of Schools, The Johns Hopkins University, Baltimore, Maryland.

NOTE

Figures 1.1 through 1.5 are from R. E. Slavin *Using Student Team Learning* (3rd edition, 1986), pp. 80, 16, 81, 20, 21.

This chapter is adapted from R. E. Slavin (1986). It was written under a grant from the Office of Educational Research and Improvement, U.S. Department of Education (No. OERI-R-117-R90002). The opinions expressed are those of the author and do not necessarily represent OERI policy.

REFERENCES

Allen, W. H., & VanSickle, R. L. (1984). Learning teams and low achievers. *Social Education, 48,* 60–64.

Good, T., Grouws, D., & Ebmeier, H. (1983). *Active mathematics teaching.* New York: Longman.

Okebukola, P. A. (1985). The relative effectiveness of cooperative and competitive interaction techniques in strengthening students' performance in science classes. *Science Education, 69,* 501–509.

Perrault, R. (1982). *An experimental comparison of cooperative learning to non-cooperative learning and their effects on cognitive achievement in junior high industrial arts laboratories.* Unpublished doctoral dissertation, University of Maryland.

Sherman, L. W., & Thomas, M. (1986). Mathematics achievement in cooperative versus individualistic goal-structured high school classrooms. *Journal of Educational Research, 79,* 169–172.

Slavin, R. E. (1979). Effects of biracial learning teams on cross-racial friendships. *Journal of Educational Psychology, 71,* 381–387.

Slavin, R. E. (1980). Effects of individual learning expectations on student achievement. *Journal of Educational Psychology, 72,* 520–524.

Slavin, R. E. (1985). Cooperative learning: Applying contact theory in desegregated schools. *Journal of Social Issues, 41*(3), 45–62.

Slavin, R. E. (1986). *Using student team learning* (3rd ed.). Baltimore, MD: Johns Hopkins University, Center for Social Organization of Schools.

Slavin, R. E. (1990). *Cooperative learning: Theory, research, and practice.* Englewood Cliffs, NJ: Prentice Hall.

Slavin, R. E., & Karweit, N. L. (1984). Mastery learning and student teams: A factorial experiment in urban general mathematics classes. *American Educational Research Journal, 21,* 725–736.

Slavin, R. E., & Oickle, E. (1981). Effects of cooperative learning teams on student achievement and race relations: Treatment by race interactions. *Sociology of Education, 54,* 174–180.

2

Team Assisted Individualization and Cooperative Integrated Reading and Composition

Robert E. Slavin and Nancy A. Madden

Development and research on the forms of cooperative learning most widely used today began in the early 1970s. With few exceptions, the early developers of cooperative learning methods were social psychologists applying psychology to education. None of them came from any particular curriculum field. Not surprisingly, then, the methods that were first developed—Student Teams-Achievement Divisions (STAD), Teams-Games-Tournaments (TGT), Jigsaw, Group Investigation, and the Johnsons' methods—were all curriculum-free, broadly applicable teaching methods. Then and now, a cooperative learning workshop can be presented to teachers of grades K–12 and subjects from math to social studies to industrial arts, and everyone will go home with methods they can apply in their classrooms. Indeed, one of the greatest strengths of cooperative learning is its adaptability to many instructional uses.

Yet while it is an important contribution to have methods that can be used for many purposes, it is also probably true that methods appropriate for all uses are not optimal for any particular subject and grade level. No one would suggest that identical teaching methods would be appropriate for math, for reading, for writing, and for other subjects.

At Johns Hopkins University, the authors and colleagues developed and evaluated cooperative learning programs designed specifically for particular subjects and grade levels. We had several critical objectives. First, we wanted to use what had been learned about cooperative learning to try to solve fundamental problems of instruction, such as accommodating individual differences in reading and math. In particular, we wanted to design programs that could be used in very heterogeneous classes to reduce the need for special education or tracking. Second, we wanted to design cooperative learning programs capable of being used all year, not just from time to time as part of teachers' bags of tricks. Third, we wanted to incorporate knowledge about curriculum- and domain-specific learning into our cooperative approaches, such as teaching of story grammar and summarization in reading or writing process in writing.

The programs we developed, Team Assisted Individualization (TAI) in mathematics and Cooperative Integrated Reading and Composition (CIRC), are well researched and are among the most effective cooperative learning methods. This chapter describes TAI and CIRC and the research that has been done on them.

TEAM ASSISTED INDIVIDUALIZATION

The first comprehensive cooperative learning model we developed and researched was Team Assisted Individualization–Mathematics, a program that combines cooperative learning with individualized instruction to meet the needs of diverse classrooms (Slavin, 1985b). TAI was developed for several reasons. First, we hoped that TAI would provide a means of combining the motivational power and peer assistance of cooperative learning with an individualized instructional program capable of giving all students materials appropriate to their levels of skill in mathematics and allowing them to proceed through these materials at their own rates. Second, we developed TAI to apply cooperative learning techniques to solve many of the problems of individualized instruction. In the 1960s, individualized instruction and related methods were expected to revolutionize instruction, especially in mathematics. However, reviews of the research on these instructional methods in mathematics have consistently concluded that they are no more effective than traditional instruction (e.g., Miller, 1976; Horak, 1981). Several problems inherent to programmed instruction have been cited as contributing to these disappointing findings. Among these are too much time spent on management rather than on teaching, too little incentive for students to progress rapidly through the programmed materials, and an excessive reliance on written instruction rather than instruction from a teacher. We felt that by combining programmed instruction with cooperative learning and turning most of the management functions (e.g., scoring answers, locating and filing materials, keeping records, assigning new work) over to the students themselves, these problems could be solved. If students could handle most of the checking and management, the teacher would be free to teach individuals and small, homogeneous teaching groups. Students working in learning teams toward a cooperative goal could help one another study, provide instant feedback to one another, and encourage one another to proceed rapidly and accurately through the materials.

Finally, TAI was developed as a means of producing the well-documented social effects characteristic of cooperative learning (Slavin, 1990) while meeting diverse needs. Our principal concern here was with mainstreaming. It was felt that mainstreaming of academically handicapped students in mathematics was limited by a feeling on the part of regular-class teachers that they were unprepared to accommodate the instructional needs of these students (Gickling & Theobald, 1975). Further, studies of attitudes toward academically handicapped students consistently find that these students are not well accepted by their nonhandicapped classmates (Gottlieb & Leyser, 1981). Since cooperative learning methods have had positive effects on social relations of all kinds, and specifically on relationships between handicapped and nonhandicapped students, we felt that the best possible mathematics program for the mainstreamed classroom would be one that combined cooperative learning with individualized instruction (see Madden & Slavin, 1983). More recently, a move in many districts away from tracking toward heterogeneous classes (Oakes, 1992) has increased the need for effective programs able to accommodate mathematics instruction to diverse needs.

Principal Features of TAI

TAI is primarily designed for grades three through six, but has also been used at higher grade levels (up to the community college level) for groups of students not ready for a full algebra course. It is almost always used without aides, volunteers, or other assistance. The principal elements of TAI are as follows (adapted from Slavin, Leavey, & Madden, 1986):

Teams

Students are assigned to four- to five-member teams. Each team consists of a mix of high, average, and low achievers, boys and girls, and students of any ethnic groups in the class. Every eight weeks, students are reassigned to new teams.

Placement Test

Students are pretested at the beginning of the program on mathematics operations. They are placed at the appropriate point in the individualized program based on their performance on the placement test.

Curriculum Materials

Following instruction from the teacher (see the following section "Teaching Groups"), students work in their teams on self-instructional curriculum materials covering addition, subtraction, multiplication, division, numeration, decimals, fractions, word problems, statistics, and algebra. Word problems are emphasized throughout the materials. The units are in the form of books. Each unit has the following parts:

- A guide page that reviews the teacher's lesson, explaining the skill to be mastered and giving a step-by-step method of solving the problems.
- Several skill practice pages, each consisting of sixteen problems. Each skill practice page introduces a subskill that leads to a final mastery of the entire skill.
- Two parallel sets of ten items, formative tests A and B.
- A unit test of fifteen items.
- Answer sheets for the skill practice pages and formative tests (located at the back of student books) and answers for unit tests (located in a separate "monitor book").

Teaching Groups

Every day, the teacher teaches lessons to small groups of students drawn from the heterogeneous teams who are at the same point in the curriculum. Teachers use specific concept lessons provided as part of the program. The purpose of these sessions is to introduce major concepts to the students. Teachers make extensive use of manipulatives, diagrams, and demonstrations. The lessons are designed to help students understand the connection between the mathematics they are doing and familiar, real-life problems. While the teacher works with a teaching group, the other students continue to work in their teams on their self-instructional units. This direct instruction to teaching groups is made possible by the fact that students take responsibility for almost all checking, materials handling, and routing.

Team Study Method

Following the placement test, the students are given a starting place in the sequence of mathematics units. They work on their units in their teams, using the following steps:

1. Students locate their units within their books and read the guide page, asking teammates or the teacher for help if necessary. Then the students begin with the first skill practice page in their unit.

2. Each student works the first four problems on his or her own skill practice page and then has a teammate check the answers against an answer sheet printed upside down at the back of each student book. If all four are correct, the student may go on to the next skill practice page. If any are incorrect, the student must try the next four problems, and so on, until he or she gets one block of four problems correct. If they run into difficulties at this stage, the students are encouraged to ask for help within their teams before asking the teacher for help.

3. When a student gets four in a row on the last skill practice page, he or she takes Formative Test A, a ten-item quiz that resembles the last skill practice page. Students work alone on the test until they are finished. A teammate scores the formative test. If the student gets eight or more of the ten problems correct, the teammate signs the student's paper to indicate that the student is certified

by the team to take the unit test. If the student does not get eight correct (this is rare), the teacher is called in to respond to any problems the student is having. The teacher diagnoses the student's problem, briefly reteaches the skill, and then may ask the student to work again on certain skill practice items. The student then takes Formative Test B, a second ten-item test comparable in content and difficulty to Formative Test A.

4. When a student passes Formative Test A or B, he or she takes the test paper to a student monitor from a different team to get the appropriate unit test. The student then completes the unit test, and the monitor scores it. Two different students serve as monitors each day. If the student gets at least twelve items correct (out of fifteen), the monitor posts the score on the student's Team Summary Sheet. Otherwise, the test is given to the teacher, who meets with the student to diagnose and remedy the student's problems. Again, because students have already shown mastery on the skill practice pages and formative tests, it is very rare that they fail a unit test.

Team Scores and Team Recognition

At the end of each week, the teacher computes a team score. This score is based on the average number of units covered by each team member and the accuracy of the unit tests. Criteria are established for team performance. A high criterion is set for a team to be a "superteam," a moderate criterion is established for a team to be a "greatteam," and a minimum criterion is set for a team to be a "goodteam." The teams meeting the "superteam" and "greatteam" criteria receive attractive certificates.

Facts Tests

Twice each week, the students are given three-minute facts tests (usually multiplication or division facts). The students are given fact sheets to study at home to prepare for these tests.

Whole-Class Units

After every three weeks, the teacher stops the individualized program and spends a week teaching lessons to the entire class covering such skills as geometry, measurement, sets, and problem-solving strategies. Students work together as a total team on such units, as in Student Teams-Achievement Divisions (see chapter 1).

Research on TAI

Seven field experiments have been conducted to evaluate the effects of TAI on student achievement, attitudes, and behavior (see Slavin, 1985b). Academic achievement outcomes were assessed in six of the seven studies. In five of these, TAI students significantly exceeded control students on standardized (CTBS or CAT) Math Computations scales. Similar effects were found for Concepts and Applications in only one of the four studies in which this variable was assessed, but in all four studies, means for Concepts and Applications favored the TAI group. In the five studies in which the treatment effects for Computations were statistically significant, they were also quite large; on average, TAI classes gained twice as many grade equivalents as did control students. Effects of TAI were equally positive for high, average, and low achievers, and for academically handicapped as well as nonhandicapped students. Positive effects of TAI have also been found on such outcomes as self-concept in math, liking of math class, classroom behavior, race relations, and acceptance of mainstreamed academically handicapped students. One additional study of TAI was conducted as part of a study of the "cooperative school," described later in this chapter.

COOPERATIVE INTEGRATED READING AND COMPOSITION

Following the success of the TAI mathematics program, we turned our development efforts toward reading and writing/language arts, the two subjects that, with mathematics, constitute the core of the elementary school program. Because these subjects are very different from mathematics, our approach to applying cooperative learning to reading and writing was very different from our approach to mathematics. For one thing, reading, writing, and language arts subsume a set of subskills that each demand different approaches. For example, optimal procedures for teaching reading comprehension or vocabulary would certainly be different from those for teaching decoding, spelling, writing, or language mechanics.

The program we ultimately developed and researched is called Cooperative Integrated Reading and Composition (CIRC) (Madden, Slavin, & Stevens, 1986). The overall development plan focused on using cooperative learning as a vehicle by which to introduce practices identified in recent research on reading and writing into routine classroom practice, and to embed cooperative learning within the fabric of the elementary reading and writing program. The major elements of CIRC are presented in the following section (see Stevens, Madden, Slavin, & Farnish, 1987).

Principal Features of CIRC

The CIRC program consists of three principal elements: basal-related activities, direct instruction in reading comprehension, and integrated language arts/writing. In all of these activities, students work in heterogeneous learning teams.

Reading Groups

In classes using reading groups, students are assigned to two or three reading groups (eight to fifteen students per group) according to their reading level, as determined by their teachers. In other classes, students are grouped heterogeneously.

Teams

Students are assigned to pairs (or triads) within their reading groups (if any). The pairs are then assigned to teams composed of partnerships from two different reading groups. For example, a team might be composed of two students from the top reading group and two from the low group. Mainstreamed academically handicapped and remedial reading (e.g., Chapter 1) students are distributed among the teams.

Many of the activities within the teams are done in pairs, while others involve the whole team; even during pair activities, however, the other pair is available for assistance and encouragement. Most of the time, the teams work independently of the teacher, while the teacher either teaches reading groups drawn from the various teams or works with individuals.

Students' scores on all quizzes, compositions, and book reports are contributed to form a team score. Teams that meet an average criterion of 90% on all activities in a given week are designated "superteams" and receive attractive certificates; those that meet an average criterion of 80–89% are designated "greatteams" and receive less elaborate certificates.

Story-related Activities

Students use their regular basal readers or novels. Stories are introduced and discussed in teacher-led reading groups that meet for approximately twenty minutes each day. During these sessions, teachers set a purpose for reading, introduce new vocabulary, review old vocabulary, discuss the story after students have read it, and so on. Presentation methods for each segment of the lesson are structured. For example, teachers are taught to use a vocabulary-presentation procedure that requires a demonstration of understanding of word meaning by each individual, a review of methods of word attack, oral reading of vocabulary to achieve automaticity, and use of the meanings of the vocabulary words to help introduce the content of the story. Story discussions are structured to emphasize such skills as making and supporting predictions about the story and understanding major structural components of the story (e.g., problem and solution in a narrative).

After stories are introduced, students are given a series of activities to do in their teams when they are not working with the teacher in a reading group. The sequence of activities is as follows:

1. *Partner reading:* Students read the story silently first and then take turns reading the story aloud with their partners, alternating readers after each paragraph. As his or her partner reads, the listener follows along and corrects any errors the reader makes.

2. *Story structure and story-related writing:* Students are given questions related to each narrative story emphasizing the story grammar (characters, settings, problem, and problem solutions). Halfway through the story, they are instructed to stop reading and to identify the characters, the setting, and the problem in the story, and to predict how the problem will be resolved. At the end of the story, students respond to the story as a whole and write a few paragraphs on a topic related to the story (for example, they might be asked to write a different ending to the story).

3. *Words out loud:* Students are given a list of new or difficult words used in the story that they must be able to read correctly in any order without hesitating or stumbling. These words are presented by the teacher in the reading group, and then students practice their lists with their partners or other teammates until they can read them smoothly.

4. *Word meaning:* Students are given a list of story words that are new in their speaking vocabularies and asked to look them up in a dictionary, paraphrase the definition, and write a sentence for each that shows the meaning of the word (e.g., "An *octopus* grabbed the swimmer with its eight long legs," not "I have an *octopus*").

5. *Story retell:* After reading the story and discussing it in their reading groups, students summarize the main points of the story to their partners. The partners have a list of essential story elements that they use to check the completeness of the story summaries.

6. *Spelling:* Students pretest one another on a list of spelling words each week and then work over the course of the week to help one another master the list. Students use a "disappearing list" strategy in which they make new lists of missed words after each assessment until the list disappears and they can go back to the full list, repeating the process as many times as necessary.

Partner Checking

After students complete each of the story-related activities, their partners initial a student assignment form indicating that they have completed and/ or achieved criterion on that task. Students are given daily expectations as to the number of activities to be completed, but they can go at their own rate and complete the activities earlier if they wish, creating additional time for independent reading (discussed later).

Tests

At the end of three class periods, students are given a comprehension test on the story, are asked to write meaningful sentences for each vocabulary word, and are asked to read the word list aloud to the teacher.

Students are not permitted to help one another on these tests. The test scores and evaluations of the story-related writing are major components of students' weekly team scores.

Direct Instruction in Reading Comprehension

One day each week, students receive direct instruction from the teacher in reading comprehension skills such as identifying main ideas, drawing conclusions, and comparing and contrasting ideas. A special step-by-step curriculum was designed for this purpose. After each lesson, students work on reading comprehension worksheets and/or games as a whole team, first gaining consensus on one set of worksheet items, then practicing independently, assessing one another's work, and discussing any remaining problems on a second set of items.

Independent Reading

A library of trade books is established in each class. Every evening, students are asked to read a trade book of their choice for at least twenty minutes. Parents initial forms indicating that students have read for the required time, and students contribute points to their teams if they submit a completed form each week. Students complete at least one book report every two weeks, for which they also receive team points. They present their reports at "book club" sessions in which they try to interest their classmates in taking home the book themselves. Independent reading and book reports replace all other homework in reading and language arts. If students complete their basal-related activities or other activities early, they may also read their independent reading books in class.

Integrated Language Arts and Writing

During language arts periods, teachers use a specific language arts/writing curriculum especially developed for the program. Students work on language arts in the same teams as in reading. During three one-hour sessions each week, students participate in a writer's workshop (Graves, 1983), writing at their own pace on topics of their choice. Teachers present ten-minute minilessons at the beginning of each period on writing process, style, or mechanics, for example, brainstorming for topics, conducting a peer revision conference, eliminating run-on sentences, or using quotations. Students spend the main part of the period planning, drafting, revising, editing, and publishing their writing. Informal and formal peer and teacher conferences are held during this time. Ten minutes at the end of the hour are reserved for sharing and "celebration" of student writing. Teacher-directed lessons on specific aspects of writing, such as organizing a narrative or a descriptive paragraph, using specific sensory words in a description, and ensuring noun-verb agreement, are conducted during two periods each week, and students practice and master these skills in their teams.

Involvement of Special-Education Resource Teachers and Reading Teachers

One key concern in the design of the CIRC program was to fully integrate the activities of special-education resource teachers and remedial reading teachers with those of the regular classroom teachers. "Remedial reading" refers here both to Chapter 1 reading programs and to district-funded remedial programs, which are organized similarly to Chapter 1 programs. This integration was done differently in the two evaluations of the full CIRC program. In the twelve-week pilot study (Madden, Stevens, & Slavin, 1986), resource and remedial reading teachers removed students from their reading classes for part or all of the reading period and implemented the CIRC program in separate areas. However, in a twenty-four-week full-scale evaluation (Stevens, Madden, Slavin, & Farnish, 1987; Madden, Stevens & Slavin, 1986), the schools involved scheduled resource and remedial reading pullouts at times other than reading or language arts/writing periods. Special and remedial reading teachers attended the CIRC training sessions but did not use CIRC methods or materials in their pullout programs, except that they occasionally helped students with problems they were encountering in the CIRC program being used in the regular class.

Research on CIRC

As of this writing, three studies have evaluated the impact of the full CIRC program. The first study (Madden, Stevens, & Slavin, 1986; Stevens et al. 1987) evaluated the full CIRC program over a twelve-week period. Overall, the effects of the CIRC program on student achievement were quite positive. CIRC classes gained 30% to 36% of a grade equivalent more than control students in reading comprehension and reading vocabulary, 52% of a grade equivalent more than control students in language expression, 25% of a grade equivalent more in language mechanics, and 72% of a grade equivalent more in spelling. On writing samples, CIRC students outperformed control students on ratings of organization, ideas, and mechanics. The effects of CIRC were equal for students at all levels of prior achievement, high, average, and low.

The second study (Stevens et al., 1987) was designed to evaluate the CIRC program in third- and fourth-grade classes over a full school year, incorporating changes suggested by the experience of the pilot study. For the total samples involved, the results of the second study were even more positive than those of the first study. On California Achievement Test reading comprehension, language expression, and language mechanics scales, CIRC students gained significantly more than control students, averaging gains of almost two-thirds of a grade equivalent more than control students. Differences of 20% of a grade equivalent on reading vocabulary were not significant, however. On writing samples, CIRC students again outperformed control students on organization, ideas, and mechanics ratings. The second study added informal reading inventories as measures of students' oral reading skills. CIRC students scored significantly higher than control students on word recognition, word analysis, fluency, error rate, and grade-placement measures of the Durrell Informal Reading Inventory, with effect sizes ranging from 44% to 64% of a standard deviation. As in the first study, the CIRC program produced equal gains for students initially high, average, and low in reading skills, although mainstreamed academically handicapped students made particularly impressive gains (Slavin, Stevens, & Madden, 1988). The third evaluation of CIRC was conducted as part of a broader study of the cooperative school, described in the next section.

The Cooperative School

The most recent study of CIRC and TAI (Stevens & Slavin, 1992) was one in which the two programs were evaluated together, along with other elements of school and classroom organization. This was a two-year study of the "cooperative school."

Two schools in a Baltimore suburb implemented a program in which all students in grades two through six experienced CIRC in reading, writing, and language arts, TAI in math, and (in many cases) STAD in social studies and/or science. In addition, teachers engaged in peer coaching, cooperative planning, site-based management, and active parent involvement programs. Academically handicapped students were mainstreamed in regular classrooms all day, and special-education teachers teamed with regular classroom teachers during reading and math periods to help low achievers. The special-education students were distributed among the various teams but were taught by the special-education teachers during teaching-group times.

The two schools were compared to matched control schools on district-administered California Achievement Tests. Significant differences (controlling for pretests) were found on Reading Vocabulary, Reading Comprehension, Language Expression, and Math Computations scales, but only nonsignificant trends in the same direction were found for Language Mechanics and Math Applications. The reading and language findings may be primarily interpreted as effects of CIRC, while the math effects may be interpreted as effects of TAI. Significant and particularly large effects were found on the same measures (plus Math Applications) for the special-education subsample. In addition, a separate analysis for very high achievers (those in the top 10% and 5% of their schools) also found substantial positive effects on the same outcomes (Slavin, 1991).

The cooperative-school study provided several important findings. First, it demonstrated that cooperative learning could be used effectively over an extended period (two years) for most of students' instructional days. It added evidence to earlier studies (Slavin, Madden, & Leavey, 1984; Slavin, Stevens, & Madden, 1988) indicating positive effects of CIRC and TAI on the achievement of mainstreamed academically handicapped students and provided evidence that these methods are equally effective for highly able students. Perhaps most important, the cooperative-school study showed that cooperative learning can serve as a basis for fundamental reform of curriculum, instruction, and school organization in the elementary grades.

CONCLUSION

Research on TAI and CIRC has clearly supported the idea that complex, comprehensive approaches that combine cooperative learning with other instructional elements can be effective in increasing the achievement of all students in heterogeneous classes. They demonstrate that cooperative learning programs can be used as the primary instructional method in reading, writing, and mathematics, not just as an additional strategy to add to teachers' repertoires.

One important possibility opened up by the development of TAI and CIRC is the use of cooperative learning as the unifying element of school reform. These methods are critical elements of the cooperative school (Slavin, 1987), a school-level change model that incorporates widespread use of cooperative learning, peer coaching, comprehensive mainstreaming, teacher involvement in decision making, and other elements.

Equally important is the opportunity presented by comprehensive cooperative learning models to serve as a vehicle for introducing into routine classroom use developments from the fields of curriculum and educational psychology. Cooperative learning provides a structure within which it is possible to incorporate identification of story elements, prediction, summarization, direct instruction in reading comprehension, and integration of reading and writing within the reading period. It provides a structure capable of enhancing the effectiveness and practicality of writing-process methods, or of adapting instruction to individual needs in mathematics. In this way, cooperative learning can be seen as not only an innovation in itself, but also as a catalyst for other needed changes in curriculum and instruction.

If educational methods are to have the capacity to make major changes in student achievement, they will have to address many elements of classroom organization and instruction at the same time. TAI and CIRC are two examples of what the future may hold in applying the best knowledge we have to improving instructional methodology.

NOTE

This chapter is adapted from Slavin, Madden, & Stevens (1989/90). It was written under a grant from the Office of Educational Research and Improvement, U.S. Department of Education (No. OERI-R-117-R90002). Any opinions expressed are those of the authors and do not represent OERI policy.

REFERENCES

Gickling, E., & Theobald, J. (1975). Mainstreaming: Affect or effect. *Journal of Special Education, 9,* 317–328.

Gottlieb, J., & Leyser, Y. (1981). Friendship between mentally retarded and non-retarded children. In S. Asher & J. Gottman (Eds.), *The development of children's friendships.* Cambridge: Cambridge University Press.

Graves, D. (1983). *Writing: Teachers and children at work.* Exeter, NH: Heinemann.

Horak, V. M. (1981). A meta-analysis of research findings on individualized instruction in mathematics. *Journal of Educational Research, 74,* 249–253.

Madden, N. A., & Slavin, R. E. (1983). Cooperative learning and social acceptance of mainstreamed academically handicapped students. *Journal of Special Education, 17,* 171–182.

Madden, N. A., Slavin, R. E., & Stevens, R. J. (1986). *Cooperative Integrated Reading and Composition: Teacher's manual.* Baltimore, MD: Johns Hopkins University, Center for Research on Elementary and Middle Schools.

Madden, N. A., Stevens, R. J., & Slavin, R. E. (1986). *Reading instruction in the mainstream: A cooperative learning approach* (Technical Report No. 5). Baltimore, MD: Johns Hopkins University, Center for Research on Elementary and Middle Schools.

Miller, R. L. (1976). Individualized instruction in mathematics: A review of research. *Mathematics Teacher, 69,* 345–351.

Oakes, J. (1992). Can tracking research inform practice? Technical, normative, and political considerations. *Educational Researcher, 21*(4), 12–21.

Slavin, R. E. (1985a). Cooperative learning: Applying contact theory in desegregated schools. *Journal of Social Issues, 41*(3), 45–62.

Slavin, R. E. (1985b). Team Assisted Individualization: Combining cooperative learning and individualized instruction in mathematics. In R. E. Slavin, S. Sharan, S. Kagan, R. Hertz-Lazarowitz, C. Webb, & R. Schmuck (Eds.), *Learning to cooperate, cooperating to learn* (pp. 177–209). New York: Plenum Press.

Slavin, R. E. (1986). *Using student team learning* (3rd ed.). Baltimore, MD: Johns Hopkins University, Center for Research on Elementary and Middle Schools.

Slavin, R. E. (1987). Cooperative learning and the cooperative school. *Educational Leadership, 45*(3), 7–13.

Slavin, R. E. (1989). Cooperative learning and student achievement. In R. E. Slavin (Ed.), *School and classroom organization.* Hillsdale, NJ: Lawrence Erlbaum Associates.

Slavin, R. E. (1990). *Cooperative learning: Theory, research, and practice.* Englewood Cliffs, NJ: Prentice Hall.

Slavin, R. E. (1991). Are cooperative learning and untracking harmful to the gifted? *Educational Leadership, 48*(6), 68–71.

Slavin, R. E., Leavey, M. B., & Madden, N. A. (1986). *Team Accelerated Instruction—Mathematics.* Watertown, MA: Mastery Education Corporation.

Slavin, R. E., Madden, N. A., & Leavey, M. (1984). Effects of Team Assisted Individualization on the mathematics achievement of academically handicapped and non-handicapped students. *Journal of Educational Psychology, 76,* 813–819.

Slavin, R. E., Madden, N. A., & Stevens, R. J. (1989/90). Cooperative learning models for the 3 R's. *Educational Leadership, 47*(4), 22–28.

Slavin, R. E., Stevens, R. J., & Madden, N. A. (1988). Accommodating student diversity in reading and writing instruction: A cooperative learning approach. *Remedial and Special Education, 9*(1), 60–66.

Stevens, R. J., Madden, N. A., Slavin, R. E., & Farnish, A. M. (1987). Cooperative Integrated Reading and Composition: Two field experiments. *Reading Research Quarterly, 22,* 433–454.

Stevens, R. J., & Slavin, R. E. (1992). *The cooperative elementary school: Effects on students' achievement, attitudes, and social relations.* Baltimore, MD: Johns Hopkins University, Center for Research on Effective Schooling for Disadvantaged Students.

3

Pieces of the Puzzle: The Jigsaw Method

Judy Clarke

This chapter introduces and explores the Jigsaw approach. The first section introduces the naturalness of a reconstituted group format, outlines the four generic stages of a Jigsaw grouping, and provides a brief background. The second and third sections explore two different models of the Jigsaw approach. The last section examines possible problems and explores potential solutions.

NATURAL INTERDEPENDENCE

Groups share two kinds of interdependence in living or working together. They depend upon one another to achieve tasks—members of effective groups bring together diverse strengths, interests, expertise, experience, knowledge, perspectives, and personalities to reach goals that surpass those that can be achieved by individual members. They also depend upon one another for personal and social support. Interpersonal support is the "salve" of an effective group. It is also required if people are going to be able to work together to solve problems. Task interdependence and interpersonal interdependence are at the heart of all successful groups—friendship groups, family groups, work teams, community groups, volunteer associations, and sports teams.

Across the world, there is a growing use of heterogeneous work teams, usually through cross-role representation, to draw upon the resources of varied specialists within the workplace. Such cross-role teams can create "break the mold" solutions because of the synergy that comes from combining a diversity of thinking and perspectives. All employees, board members, owners, and perhaps clients are acknowledged as valued participants in the ongoing organizational tasks of finding and solving problems.

The use of the reconstituted work groups in classrooms, such as in the Jigsaw approach, is based on the same principles of interdependence that operate in the cross-role teams in the workplace. Class members bring their personal abilities and ways of thinking and working, as well as specialized knowledge, to analogous cross-role work groups. The Jigsaw approach was developed as one way to help build a classroom as a community of learners where all students are valued.

In 1972, in Austin, Texas, a team of administrators, teachers, and researchers initiated a six-year project to find a way of restructuring the teaching and learning process to develop equity of participation and outcomes for all children in desegregated classrooms. At the heart of their work was a passionate desire to reduce the competitive ethos in classrooms that created an artificial reward economy where some students "won" and many "lost." The team experimented to create and research a process that made it imperative that the students treat each other as resources. First, they structured the learning process so that individual competitiveness was incompatible with success, and second, they made certain that success could occur only after students cooperated. Out of their work came the use of reconstituted groups, which they called the Jigsaw classroom (Aronson, et al., 1978). Since then, the Jigsaw approach has evolved and spread into classrooms and into the staff-development activities of many diverse workplaces around the world.

In this approach, students work together in small groups where they must rely on each other. Each group member becomes "specialized" in subject matter and thereby possesses critical information to contribute to classmates. Cooperation and mutual trust become valuable and necessary to academic achievement. Although the Jigsaw approach has been very flexibly applied with limitless variations, there are four generic stages in the process.

Stage 1: Introduction

The teacher organizes the class into heterogeneous "home" groups, for example:

Home Group A: Avi, Nada, Sudir, Lara

Home Group B: Nayoung, Emil, Tovinder, Nikki

Next the teacher introduces a topic, text, information, or material to the class and helps the students to understand why they are studying this topic, how it fits with what they have done before, and what they will study in the future. It is important in this stage that the students become interested in what they are studying (Reid, Forrestal, & Cook, 1989). The teacher explains how student learning will be assessed throughout the learning experience. Many teachers also provide a rationale for the value of the small-group process for this particular learning experience. Each member in the home group is given, or selects, a part of the subject matter to be explored.

Stage 2: Focused Exploration

Students reorganize to form focus groups. Members of each focus group work together to learn about a specific topic/perspective:

Focus Group 1: Avi & Nayoung

Focus Group 2: Nada & Emil

Focus Group 3: Sudir & Tovinder

Focus Group 4: Lara & Nikki

During this stage, students need encouragement to think out loud in order to clarify their ideas and build understanding together. Sometimes teachers also encourage exploratory writing where students jot down the main ideas they are working on to help them clarify and focus their thinking. Teachers may also provide a guided set of questions to help students explore the ideas in their assigned material.

Stage 3: Reporting and Reshaping

Students return to their home groups to take turns describing the ideas generated in their focus groups. During the reporting stage, group members are encouraged to pose questions and discuss ideas in depth. Often as students work through understanding each other's part, they begin to re-shape their understanding of the whole.

Stage 4: Integration and Evaluation

The teacher may design an individual, small-group, or whole-class activity where students can actively integrate their learning. For example, students may carry out a demonstration task in their home groups. The teacher will ask questions to help students reflect on how they worked together and what they might do the same or differently the next time they work together.

The original idea of naming the process of reconstituted groups as "Jigsaw" came from the metaphor of putting together the pieces of a puzzle to create a whole picture. Since Aronson and his team first published their approach in 1978, several versions have evolved (Sharan, Hare, Webb, & Hertz-Lazarowitz, 1980; Slavin et al., 1985).

Robert Slavin and his colleagues at Johns Hopkins University designated Aronson's model as Jigsaw I and created Jigsaw II (1986, 1990). This version differs from Aronson's in two fundamental ways: in the outcomes for the process and in the way in which interdependence is structured. The Jigsaw II process requires students to revisit narrative material through the lens of different perspectives to deepen conceptual understanding of significant themes, frameworks, or central ideas.

The second fundamental difference in Slavin's approach is his approach to assessment combined with the use of an extrinsic reward structure. Home groups are established as "teams" comprised of a heterogeneous mix of students by current performance level (high, middle, low). Students teach each other and take individual quizzes that cover all the topics or themes. Individual quiz scores are compiled into a team score. Improvement scoring is used to help low performers' gains make a weighted contribution to the team. Winning teams are highlighted in a newsletter or on a class bulletin board. Thus interdependence is fostered by building a competitive spirit between teams and encouraging cooperation among team members in order to advance the collective team score (Slavin, 1990).

Kagan (1990) outlined several variations within the four generic stages of Jigsaw that provide additional support to individual students and strengthen the coaching possibilities in the second stage of the Jigsaw process. Kagan also suggested other structures for reconstituted groups.

In Australia, Jo-Anne Reid, Peter Forrestal, and Jonathan Cook developed a flexible approach to reconstituted groups that allows for several different possible recombinations, mainly for presenting work completed in home groups (1989). These educators were the first to clearly articulate and link stages in the learning process (moving from information toward understanding) with the four generic steps of Jigsaw.

ONE APPROACH TO JIGSAW

This section provides three illustrations of one model of Jigsaw where students work to specialize in subject matter and bring understandings back to their home group. Although the examples in this section resemble earlier versions of Jigsaw, in particular, Aronson's approach (1978), there are significant differences that are described at the end of each example.

Example 1: Using Visual Information

The first example is a structured-partner Jigsaw applicable across the curriculum. With adaptations, this activity can be used with students aged six years through adult. Because of the structured format, demonstrations by the teacher, and the potential for key visuals, this activity supports second-language learners, especially when these students are paired up with first-language speakers.

Stage 1: Introduction

As part of an introduction to a unit or theme, for example, on change, the teacher has collected interesting and colorful pictures from magazines, calendars, and posters. As a way of engaging the students' interest in the topic of change, the teacher places students in pairs and asks them to think about a change they have made in their own lives. The teacher provides a few questions to help students think through their experience. The students talk in pairs first and then combine with another pair to share their experiences in a group of four.

The teacher shows a slide of an interesting picture on a screen and leads students through a structured set of questions to help them draw ideas from the graphic information. Students turn to work with their original partner to talk through the guided questions. These questions model a format that students will use in stage two of this Jigsaw activity.

Stage 2: Focused Exploration

Next the teacher hands each group of four two different pictures. Each pair takes one of the pictures and moves apart from their group. They work through the following guided format:[1]

Using Visual Information: A Guided Discussion Sheet for Pairs

Together

    Look at the picture.

    What do you think is happening?

    What do you think is the main topic?

Partner One

    Talk to your partner about who, where, what is happening, and why.

Partner Two

    Talk to your partner about interesting details you see.

Together

    Talk to develop some questions.

    Talk to create a list of the most important ideas in this picture. You may wish to create a quick flowchart or word web.

Stage 3: Reporting and Reshaping

Pairs return to form their group of four and take turns talking about the ideas about change that they have been developing as they explored their pictures.

Stage 4: Integration and Evaluation

The teacher conducts a whole-class discussion using nonprompted questioning to draw out and discuss main themes regarding the topic of change. Nonprompted questioning involves randomly appointing any student to speak rather than calling upon volunteers. Students work once more in pairs to reexamine their picture to revise their original thinking in the light of the group discussion. The teacher asks for volunteers to explain how their thinking changed as a result of hearing the ideas of others in the class.

This Jigsaw activity promotes a natural kind of interdependence through three modifications: the extensive use of pairs, a structured-partner format, and the opportunity to revise original thinking after listening to whole-class discussion. Students work closely with a partner throughout the activity and also meet with another pair as a group of four a few times to consult. For many students, a pair is a large enough group at the beginning of learning to work together. Alternatively, using pairs can provide a change of pace and often some relief from the challenges of working in fours or fives. Pairs also maximize the access to talking time for all students in the class. Many students will experience success in working with just one other person and grow naturally to understand the value of working with others.

Furthermore, to strengthen the potential success of partner work, this Jigsaw activity uses a guided format (a set of directed questions) to help the partners take turns in talking about the picture they are exploring. In most situations, the teacher will have introduced this format several times with the whole class, demonstrating with students practicing in pairs, coaching each other through the turn-taking process.

In the fourth stage, after the class discussion, students work again with their original partner to revise their thinking based on the input of others in the class. This is another way of highlighting the value of interdependence. The message here is strong: We can change and enrich our thinking after being exposed to the ideas of others.

Finally, the teacher is using this Jigsaw activity to learn about what students already think about change, to capture their interest in the topic, and to lay ground for future work. This ongoing informal teacher observation and data collection become the basis for the assessment of student learning. The teacher may make supportive and inquiring interventions to assist students in solving problems; the teacher may jot notes on a tracking sheet in response to specific students; the teacher may ask partners to discuss how well they worked together and what they may do differently next time; and the teacher might ask the class to discuss the value of listening to others' ideas in enriching personal understandings.

Interdependence is fostered very naturally throughout this Jigsaw process. Most of the time students work in pairs face-to-face through a turn-taking process, with the teacher observing and making gentle interventions when needed.

Example 2: Problems in Working Together

The following example is applicable across the curriculum and helps students, aged ten through adult, to consider how to deal with problems in working together cooperatively. This Jigsaw activity resembles earlier versions of Jigsaw, notably Aronson's original model, with students working on separate "pieces" and bringing them together. There are three main variations: students work in home groups that are base groups—places where they meet regularly for peer support and coaching; the content for the Jigsaw material is generated by the students; and the self-evaluation in the fourth stage leads students to set goals and make plans for future learning.

Stage 1: Introduction

The students in a tenth-grade class have been assigned to work in groups of four as base groups for peer support and tutoring. They meet daily in base groups at the beginning of class. One day the teacher asks each base group to identify problems students experience when working cooperatively. After a brief period generating ideas in the small groups, they work as a whole class to sort the problems into three categories: group dynamics—isolation, roles, unequal contribution, achieving consensus, and lack of responsibility; task completion—absenteeism, avoidance, not understanding, product versus process, not completing, reflection, and evaluation; and social skills—put-downs, arguing, domination, communication, and making judgments.

Each base group selects one problem and writes up a brief case study to illustrate the problem. The class selects for further investigation four of the case studies that are closely related to current difficulties groups are experiencing. In base groups, each member chooses one of the four cases to explore further in a focus group.

Group Dynamics—Isolation

A group has been assigned a cooperative problem-solving task. It has been instructed that all members are to make a meaningful and positive contribution, but one member of the group seems to have a great deal of difficulty fitting into the group. She feels that the other members do not listen to or accept the suggestions that she makes. She feels left out and isolated. What could you do?

Task Completion—Not Completing Work

Your group has been assigned a task to complete cooperatively. A deadline has been given for completion of the work, and all members are aware of this date. There is an attempt to organize the task by the members, but as the due date gets closer, the group realizes that the work is not likely to be completed on time. What could you do?

Social Skills—Arguing

While working on an assignment in a group, you realize that the members of your group are challenging each other's ideas. At the beginning, this seemed to be fun and there was a lot of lively discussion, but now things have taken a change for the worse. Members are arguing and seem to be more interested in winning the argument than in cooperating. What could you do?

Social Skills—Put-downs

Your group has been assigned a brainstorming task to complete cooperatively. Each member is encouraged to contribute ideas without fear of ridicule or judgment from the rest of the group. One member offers an idea that is immediately followed by "What a stupid thing to say!" The offended member announces that she is not going to give any more ideas and then proceeds to turn away from the other members. What could you do?

Stage 2: Focused Exploration

In focus groups, the students use a decision-making model that the class has learned: They develop criteria for a good decision, generate alternative solutions, and consider and weigh consequences. Last, each group selects decisions that meet their criteria.

Stage 3: Reporting and Reshaping

Students return to their base groups to present potential decisions. Each student reports and responds to questions.

Stage 4: Integration and Evaluation

The teacher asks students to write a one-page reflection sheet. She or he asks them to identify one problem that concerns them personally and give reasons for their concern. Students individually write out a plan for what they might do the next time the problem occurs, with alternative backup plans in case their first decision does not work.

Students share their writing in base groups and file their one-page reflection in the base-group binder. They will revisit the sheets in two weeks to discuss and write about how their decisions are working and what they might change if the problem recurs. The teacher reminds them daily to look for opportunities to apply their decisions.

This kind of Jigsaw activity, applied as a process to identify, define, explore, and solve problems, can be used with groups such as a school staff, representative student body, volunteer boards, or corporate orga-nizations. It is limitless in opportunities for application. Additionally, the individual goal-setting and monitoring process can be integrated into many situations. As a rule, members of most groups can make personal decisions about how to act differently in the future.

Example 3: Staff-Development Jigsaw

This staff-development activity will help teachers consolidate their un-derstanding of the Jigsaw process. It is applicable to teachers in all discipline areas and across all levels in education.

Stage 1: Introduction

The staff-development leader helps participants to form groups of four and engage in an introductory activity. The leader introduces four focus topics, and each group member selects one and moves to find a partner with the same topic.

Stage 2: Focused Exploration

Task sheets have been developed for each topic to guide the teachers' discussions.

Topic 1: Introduction to the Jigsaw Approach

Please read the first section of this chapter, called "Natural Interde-pendence," and work with your partner to list the important ideas you have learned/relearned about the Jigsaw approach. Save the idea that you find most important for last.

What's Important about the Jigsaw Approach

1. _____

2. _____

3. _____

4. _____

5. _____

One idea that I find really important is:

_____

Topic 2: Three Examples of One Approach to Jigsaw

Please read through the second section of this chapter, called "One Approach to Jigsaw." Work with your partner to complete the following three tasks before returning to your home group:

1. Discuss how this model of Jigsaw works.
2. Identify one example you like. Describe how you might adapt the example for use in your teaching.
3. Explain one or two of the ways these examples are modified to strengthen interdependence among students. Select ways you might use or adapt.

Topic 3: Two Examples of Another Approach to Jigsaw

Please read through the third section of this chapter, called "Another Approach to Jigsaw." Work with your partner to complete the following three tasks before returning to your home group:

1. Discuss how this model of Jigsaw works.
2. Identify one example you like. Describe how you might adapt the example for use in your teaching.
3. Explain one or two of the ways these examples are modified to strengthen interdependence among students. Select ways you might use or adapt.

Topic 4: Problems and Potential Solutions

First you will work with your partner to accomplish the tasks identified in the next paragraph. After fifteen minutes of working with your partner, the group leader will be meeting with all participants who are working on topic 4 to raise and discuss other concerns.

Please read through the last section of this chapter, called "Problems and Potential Solutions." There are three parts to your task when you return to your home group. Briefly outline each problem: the pressure of accountability; fairness with assessment and evaluation; and contrived interdependence. Stop after each problem to describe one or two suggestions from the text and encourage discussion in your home group to elicit alternative solutions. Discuss other concerns and solutions raised in the meeting with the group leader.

Stage 3: Reporting and Reshaping

The teachers meet in their home groups to report on their task assignments. There is a logical progression to the reporting order, from topic 1 through to topic 4, and therefore the group member with topic 4 is asked to help move the group along to complete all four reports.

Stage 4: Integration and Evaluation

The group leader helps participants to debrief the process they just experienced. For example, the leader may record "thoughts" and "feelings" participants experienced throughout the Jigsaw process themselves and continue with a general discussion period. Teachers can meet in interest groups (by age level or subject area) to plan a Jigsaw activity for their students.

This example resembles earlier versions of Jigsaw by dividing up the textual material. Task sheets help to focus discussion in pairs during the second stage, which maximizes each participant's access to discussion and exploration.

The Jigsaw approach is useful in all areas of staff development as a way to actively involve participants. There are innumerable resources that can be used as material for the focus topics to engage teachers (and parents) in active learning and teaching: case studies, community and business talks, curriculum units, student presentations, professional readings, research reports, separate workshops (as in conference Jigsaws), simulations, student learning portfolios, videos, and so on.

ANOTHER APPROACH TO JIGSAW

In this alternative model of Jigsaw, during the first stage, the class shares a learning experience in which its members gain a "whole" understanding of subject matter. They may work in small home groups, receive direct instruction, and also work independently. After the class members have completed the learning experience, they will move into focus groups to explore in greater depth what they have learned by examining different perspectives and issues. Although the examples in this section resemble Slavin's Jigsaw II (1990), there are significant differences that are described at the end of each example.

Example 1: Character Study

This Jigsaw activity is applicable in humanities/English curriculum areas. With adaptations it can be used with students aged eight through adult.

Stage 1: Introduction

The students have read a novel or play and worked throughout the study in small groups of four. The teacher asks each group member to select one character for deeper exploration. For example, in Shakespeare's play, *Julius Caesar*, students may choose one of the following four: Caesar, Anthony, Brutus, and Cassius. In the case of White's novel, *Charlotte's Web,* students may select among Charlotte, Wilbur, Fern, and Mr. Arable. Once students have selected a character to explore, each group member pairs up with another student in the classroom who has selected the same character.

Stage 2: Focused Exploration

The teacher asks partners to select five questions from a list to explore their character. With *Julius Caesar,* the following kinds of questions would stimulate a deeper understanding of the four characters: Who is the real Caesar (or Brutus, Anthony, or Cassius): hero, villain, or both? Compare your character's private self with his public self. List shortcomings of your character and support your ideas with examples. Describe the character's strengths and provide evidence. Is your character a different person to different people? Explain. Did your character deserve his fate? Why? Younger students, exploring characters in *Charlotte's Web,* may design word webs and include sketches to portray their understanding of their character as a real person.

After working in pairs to explore their character, partners meet with another pair studying the same character and work together as a foursome to generate a shared understanding and also to define areas worthy of debate.

Stage 3: Reporting and Reshaping

Each member returns to his or her home group to report on his or her character. Others in the group ask questions and pose challenges.

Stage 4: Integration and Evaluation

The teacher has prepared a modern problem and explained that students will work in their home groups to figure out what the four characters might do faced with that problem. Briefly, group members return to their "character" pair to consider what their character's thinking might be. Home groups re-form and are responsible for discussing how the four characters would interact in the problem situation and for developing a plot line. Each group will be sending one of its group members as a representative to a small fishbowl panel to report its story so the class can hear all the various plots that have been developed.

This example varies most from previous versions of Jigsaw during the fourth stage of integration and evaluation. Students are asked to apply their learning to a new problem. They have the opportunity to consult once more with their "character" partner and then work in their home group of four to solve the new problem "in role." Also built into this variation of the Jigsaw process is an opportunity for all home groups to learn from one another through a representative fishbowl panel report.

Example 2: Excursions

This Jigsaw applies across the curriculum and is appropriate for those aged six years through adult.

Stage 1: Introduction

Students have taken a field trip to a historic village, a high-tech computer company, an outdoor overnight experience, or a farm, a museum, or some other point of interest. They are organized in groups of four for the excursion. Upon return, each member of the group of four is going to carry out a specialized activity.

Stages 2 and 3

There are many kinds of activities that enhance the learning that takes place before and during an excursion. Following are a few examples.

Overnight Excursion

Groups of four create a magazine report of their trip. Each home group selects a theme for its issue (animal life, plant life, outdoor activities, habitats). Each member will work in a focus group to specialize in one kind of writing and to develop an individual piece. Four kinds of writing might include narrative, expository, journalistic, and humorous (cartooning, comic strips). When the members return to their home group, they will work together on the format, layout, graphics, and publication of their magazine.

Visit to a Farm

Students work in focus groups to research four aspects of farm life (technology used on the farm, the production of flour from seed to market, the composting process, and the change in farm production over the past fifty years). They meet in home groups to pool their information in order to create a chart or poster.

Visit to a Replicated Pioneer Village

On the visit to the village, the students toured in their home groups of four. Each member of the group selected a different topic to explore on the trip: ways pioneer life is different from today; ways it is similar today; pioneer occupations; and buildings in a pioneer village. The home-group members help one another with their specialized tasks. When they return to class, students meet with others in the class who specialized in the same topics. Home-group members meet to report on the four topics.

Stage 4: Integration and Evaluation

In this stage, teachers provide an activity for students to integrate and demonstrate their understandings. Home groups may create a magazine or design posters or charts, or individuals may write an illustrated essay.

This type of Jigsaw can require students to prepare a group or individual product to integrate and demonstrate their learning. Furthermore, there is a wide range of possible abilities, skills, and talents required by the open-ended activities. Students can be involved in the planning, carrying out, and evaluation of the learning activities to create a more student-centered experience.

This third section of the chapter has described ways of structuring the Jigsaw process to enable students to enrich and deepen their understanding of subject matter. The last section considers three possible problems and potential solutions in carrying out the Jigsaw process.

PROBLEMS AND POTENTIAL SOLUTIONS

The Pressure of Accountability

The design of the Jigsaw process ensures that all students in the class are responsible for learning and for teaching what they have learned to others. For some students, this may create an overwhelming sense of pressure to perform when they return to their home group in the third stage of the Jigsaw. Students may worry about their second-language communication skills, learning difficulties, or social status, blocking their ability to contribute in their home group.

There are many possible ways to support students to counter the potential undue pressure of accountability. Following are some strategies.

Peer Support

Students may be "twinned" in the home group, so that two home-group members move off together into the focus group and return together to the home group. It is important that the students share the work in both the focus group and the home group. Another way of building peer support when students work in pairs on the focus task is to ask them to combine with another pair working on the same topic before moving back to the home group to share and compare their ideas.

Task Specialization

If the tasks in the focus groups are differentiated so that they require different kinds of abilities, it is possible for teachers to tailor the task in the focus groups to draw upon the strengths of individual students who may be at risk. One focus group might work with a computer software package rather than with text reference materials.

Open-ended Tasks

If the tasks have many valid approaches and many valid solutions, then students can feel much more comfortable. During the work of the focus group, there will be less pressure to come to a convergent closure. They will also feel more self-possessed when they bring back the ideas of their focus group to their home group because there is no one solution or one correct response.

Pencils and Task Sheets versus No Pencils

Depending on the nature of the task in the focus groups, it may relieve pressure to ask students to jot notes during their focus-group discussion. Notes can give students support when they are reporting to the home group. Sometimes teachers design task sheets to help the focus group to organize its work.

On the other hand, being free to engage in discussion during the focus group without taking notes can feel much more involving and less pressured. This difference may sometimes depend on the nature of the task and sometimes on the learning style of individual students.

Fairness with Assessment and Evaluation

Assessment and evaluation are challenging for teachers with all student learning. However, with cooperative learning, the issues of assessing group product and group process provide additional concerns. Following are some ways of dealing with these concerns.

Summative Evaluation of Individual Learning

The Jigsaw process can be used to enhance individual learning. During the fourth stage, students can create an individual product to express what they have learned throughout the process of working, teaching, and learning from others. The teacher can write or make anecdotal comments as well as assigning a grade. The students can also be involved by writing constructive anecdotal comments. This summative evaluation can include supportive comments in response to the student's personal and social development in learning to work with others.

Formative Evaluation of Individual Learning

Throughout the Jigsaw process, the teacher may ask students to reflect individually, or as a group, on how they are working together—both in terms of the academic learning and in terms of how the group is functioning. This periodic pausing to make sense of what is happening (to discuss ways to organize the task, ways to focus the group, and ways to disagree in a constructive way, and to consider ways of encouraging others to contribute) assists individual personal, social, and academic development. It helps students to understand what is required to work productively and requires them to set goals and to assess their own progress. Throughout the Jigsaw process, teachers can meet with groups and may collect samples of work in progress (hard copy, on disk, on video, or on audiotape).

Assigning marks or grades to personal and social development is counterproductive because it may teach self-serving shrewdness and promote competition within the class. Numbers or letters do not provide specific information for growth. A mark of 6 out of a possible 10 for listening is significantly indeterminate data to describe a student's attitudes, skills, and knowledge about listening and is unhelpful in giving the student support and direction. Constructive anecdotal comments and discussion guide students with detailed understandings of their own development and growth and also provide them with information for focused and manageable goals for future work in groups.

Grading Group Products

When students have sufficient skills to work together to create a group product, the teacher can recognize both individual contributions and the collective work of the group. In the example of the home group that has created a magazine as a collective product, the teacher may assign 70% of the grade to judge individual contributions and 30% of the grade to value the way in which the group planned the format and organized its individual pieces to produce a single product.

Assessing and Evaluating without Grades/Marks

There are many ways to assess learning without assigning numbers or grades. Teachers can hold conferences with groups and with individual students. Students can keep portfolios and use journals to track their own development. Using the Jigsaw approach to help students deepen their understanding of subject matter will contribute significantly to their overall learning and affect their individual performance on assessment tasks.

Contrived Interdependence

Artificially created interdependence is a problem in cooperative learning in many approaches, not just with Jigsaw. For the Jigsaw approach to be a meaningful learning experience, not just a way of organizing students to teach by rote in pieces, students need to believe in the worth of their own contribution and in the worth of the contributions of others. These beliefs develop over time when students are involved in relevant, stimulating, rich activities with many ways of contributing and participating. Students need to become absorbed in open-ended and challenging activities that require them to articulate their thinking, listen to others' ideas, consider new evidence, and synthesize and apply information.

NOTE

1. This set of guided questions is adapted from a structured pair activity developed by Gib Goodfellow, the Toronto Board of Education, Ontario, Canada.

REFERENCES

Aronson, E., Blaney, N., Stephan, C., Sikes, J., & Snapp, M. (1978). *The Jigsaw classroom.* Beverly Hills, CA: Sage Publications.

Kagan, S. (1990). *Cooperative learning: Resources for teachers.* San Juan Capistrano, CA: Resources for Teachers.

Reid, J., Forrestal, P., & Cook, J. (1989). *Small group learning in the classroom.* Concord, Ontario: Irwin Publishing.

Sharan, S., Hare, P., Webb, C. D., & Hertz-Lazarowitz, R. (Eds.). (1980). *Cooperation in education.* Provo, UT: Brigham Young University Press.

Slavin, R. E. (1986). *Using Student Team Learning* (3rd ed.). Baltimore, MD: Johns Hopkins University, Center for Research on Elementary and Middle Schools.

Slavin, R. E. (1990). *Cooperative learning: Theory, research, and practice.* Englewood Cliffs, NJ: Prentice Hall.

Slavin, R., Sharan, S., Kagan, S., Hertz-Lazarowitz, R., Webb, C., & Schmuck, R. (Eds.). (1985). *Learning to cooperate, cooperating to learn.* New York: Plenum Press.

4

Learning Together

David W. Johnson and Roger T. Johnson

USING COOPERATIVE LEARNING

The Learning Together approach to cooperative learning should include all of the following elements: (*a*) Three types of cooperative learning procedures should be used in an integrative way. These three types are formal cooperative learning, informal cooperative learning, and cooperative base groups. (*b*) Each cooperative lesson or activity should include the essential components that make cooperation work, namely, positive interdependence, face-to-face promotive interaction, individual accountability, social skills, and group processing. (*c*) The repetitive, routine lessons as well as classroom routines should be cooperative (cooperative learning structures). (*d*) The organizational structure of schools should be changed from a competitive/individualistic mass-production structure to a cooperative team-based structure (the cooperative school) (Johnson & Johnson, 1989b; Johnson, Johnson, & Holubec, 1991, 1992; Johnson, Johnson, & Smith, 1991). Teachers then use cooperative learning enough to reach a routine-use level of competence, participate regularly in colleague support-group meetings to discuss how to improve their lessons, and meet in small groups to participate in school-based decision making.

The Learning Together approach to cooperative learning was developed from the interaction among theory, research, and practice in a five-step process. First came a review that synthesized the results of research on cooperative learning to determine the current state of knowledge in the area (Johnson, 1970; Johnson & Johnson, 1974, 1983, 1989a; Johnson, Maruyama, Johnson Nelson, & Skon, 1981; Johnson, Johnson, & Maruyama, 1983). Second, a series of theoretical models was formulated based on the results of the previous research and the theorizing of Morton Deutsch (1949, 1962). Third, we conducted a program of research to validate our theory. Fourth, based on the theory supported by the research, a series of procedures was devised for teachers (and administrators). Fifth, school districts in many countries were trained to implement cooperative learning. The plan of implementation was built from earlier work in organizational change and innovation in education (Johnson, 1970; Miles, 1964; Watson, 1967; Watson & Johnson, 1972). The result of these stages of development was that answers could be provided to a series of questions:

1. What are the ways cooperative learning may be used in the classroom?
2. What are the key elements that make cooperation work?
3. What is the organizational context in which cooperative learning will flourish?
4. What is the process of gaining expertise in using and implementing cooperative learning?
5. What are the outcomes that may be expected from using cooperative learning at the student level and cooperative teams at the school and district levels?

INTEGRATED USE OF TYPES OF COOPERATIVE LEARNING

Cooperative learning may be used in various ways (Figure 4.1). They include formal cooperative learning, informal cooperative learning, cooperative base groups, and cooperative structures. *Formal cooperative learning* is students working together, for one class period to several weeks, to achieve shared learning goals and to complete specific tasks and assignments. These assignments include decision making or problem solving, completing a curriculum unit, writing a report, conducting a survey or experiment, reading a chapter or reference book, learning vocabulary, or answering questions at the end of the chapter (Johnson, Johnson, & Holubec, 1990, 1991). Any course requirement or assignment may be reformulated to be cooperative. In formal cooperative learning groups, teachers do the following:

1. *Specify the objectives for the lesson*: In every lesson there should be an academic objective specifying the concepts and strategies to be learned and a social skills objective specifying the interpersonal or small-group skill to be used and mastered during the lesson.
2. *Make a number of preinstructional decisions*: A teacher has to decide on the size of groups, the method of assigning students to groups, the roles students will be assigned, the materials needed to conduct the lesson, and the way the room will be arranged.
3. *Explain the task and the positive interdependence*: A teacher clearly defines the assignment, teaches the required concepts and strategies, specifies the positive

Figure 4.1
Cooperative Learning

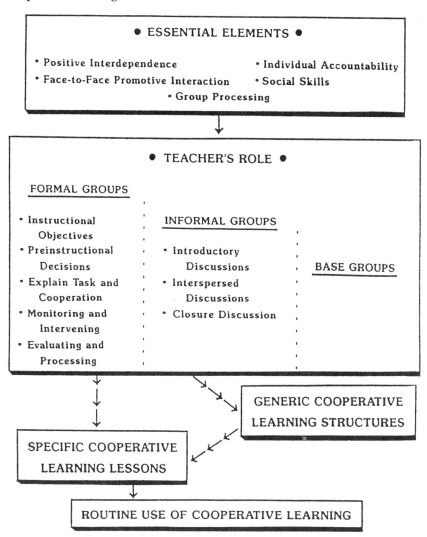

interdependence and individual accountability, gives the criteria for success, and explains the expected social skills to be engaged in.

4. *Monitor students' learning and intervene within the groups to provide task assistance or to increase students' interpersonal and group skills*: A teacher systematically observes and collects data on each group as it works. When it is needed, the teacher intervenes to assist students in completing the task accurately and in working together effectively.

5. *Evaluate students' learning and help students process how well their groups func-*
   tioned: Students' learning is carefully assessed and their performances are evaluated. Members of the learning groups then process how effectively they have
   been working together.

Informal cooperative learning consists of having students work together
to achieve a joint learning goal in temporary, ad hoc groups that last from
a few minutes to one class period (Johnson, Johnson, & Holubec, 1992;
Johnson, Johnson, & Smith, 1991). During a lecture, demonstration, or
film, these groups can be used to focus student attention on the material
to be learned, set a mood conducive to learning, help set expectations as
to what will be covered in a class session, ensure that students cognitively
process the material being taught, and provide closure to an instructional
session. During direct teaching, the instructional challenge for the teacher
is to ensure that students do the intellectual work of organizing material,
explaining it, summarizing it, and integrating it into existing conceptual
structures. Informal cooperative learning groups are often organized so
that students engage in three- to five-minute focused discussions before
and after a lecture and two- to three-minute turn-to-your-partner discussions interspersed throughout a lecture.

Cooperative base groups are long-term, heterogeneous cooperative
learning groups with stable membership (Johnson, Johnson, & Holubec,
1992; Johnson, Johnson, & Smith, 1991). The purposes of the base group
are to give the support, help, encouragement, and assistance each member
needs to make academic progress (attend class, complete all assignments,
learn) and develop cognitively and socially in healthy ways. Base groups
meet daily in elementary school and twice a week in secondary school (or
whenever the class meets). They are permanent (lasting from one to several
years) and provide the long-term caring peer relationships necessary to
influence members consistently to work hard in school. They formally meet
to discuss the academic progress of each member, provide help and assistance to each other, and verify that each member is completing assignments
and progressing satisfactorily through the academic program. Base groups
may also be responsible for letting absent group members know what went
on in class when they miss a session. Informally, members interact every
day within and between classes, discussing assignments and helping each
other with homework. The use of base groups tends to improve attendance,
to personalize the work required and the school experience, and to improve
the quality and quantity of learning. The larger the class or school and the
more complex and difficult the subject matter, the more important it is to
have base groups. Base groups are also helpful in structuring homerooms
and when a teacher meets with a number of advisees.

Cooperative learning structures are standard cooperative procedures for
conducting generic, repetitive lessons and managing classroom routines

(Johnson & Johnson, 1991; Johnson, Johnson, & Holubec, 1991). They are used to organize course routines and generic lessons that repeat over and over again. These repetitive cooperative lessons provide a base on which the cooperative classroom may be built. Some examples are checking homework, preparing for and reviewing a test, drill-review of facts and events, reading of textbooks and reference materials, writing reports and essays, giving presentations, learning vocabulary, learning concepts, doing projects such as surveys, and problem solving. Each of these instructional activities may be done cooperatively and, once planned and conducted several times, will become an automatic activity in the classroom. They may also be used in combination to form an overall lesson.

The *routine-use level of teacher competence* is the ability to structure cooperative learning situations automatically without conscious thought or planning. Any lesson in any subject area with any set of curriculum materials may be reflexively structured to be cooperative as an automatic habit pattern. Cooperative learning can then be used long-term with fidelity.

An example of the integrated use of the types of cooperative learning is as follows. Students arrive at school in the morning and meet in their base groups to welcome each other, complete a self-disclosure task (such as "What is each member's favorite television show?"), check each student's homework to make sure all members understand the academic material and are prepared for the day, and tell each other to have a great day. The teacher then begins a lesson on world interdependence. The teacher has a series of objects and wants students to identify all the countries involved in creating the objects. To help students cognitively organize in advance what they know about the world economy, the teacher uses informal cooperative learning by asking students to turn to the person seated next to them and identify the seven continents and one product that is produced in each continent. They have four minutes to do so.

Formal cooperative learning is now used in the lesson. The objectives for the lesson are for students to learn about global economic interdependence and to improve their skill in encouraging each other's participation. The teacher has the thirty students count off from one to ten to form triads randomly. They sit so they can either face each other or face the teacher. The teacher hands out the objects, which include a silk shirt with plastic buttons, a cup of tea (a saucer and cup with a tea bag and a lump of sugar in it), and a Walkman and earphones (with a cassette tape of a Nashville star) made by Philips (a European company). She assigns members of each triad the roles of hypothesizer (who hypothesizes about the number of products in each item and where they came from), a reference guide (who looks up each hypothesized country in the book to see what products it exports), and a recorder. After each item the roles are rotated so that each student fulfills each role once.

The teacher introduces world economic interdependence by noting the following facts:

1. A hand-held calculator most often consists of electronic chips from the United States, is assembled in Singapore or Indonesia, is placed in a steel housing from India, and is stamped with a label "Made in Japan" (the trees and chemicals from which the paper and ink in the label are made are all processed elsewhere, and the plastic in the keys and body is all made elsewhere) on arrival in Yokohama.
2. Modern hotels in Saudi Arabia are built with room modules made in Brazil, construction labor from South Korea, and management from the United States.
3. The global economic interdependence is almost beyond imagining.

The teacher then assigns the academic task of identifying how many countries contributed to the production of each object. She establishes positive goal interdependence by stating that it is a cooperative assignment, and, therefore, all members of the group must agree on an answer before it is recorded, and all members must be able to explain each of the group's answers. The criterion for success is to hand in a correctly completed report form and for each member to score 90% or better on the test to be given the next day on world economic interdependence.

She establishes positive reward interdependence by stating that if the record sheet is accurate, each member will receive 15 points, and if all members of the group achieve 90% or better on the test, each member will receive 5 bonus points. Individual accountability is established by the roles assigned and the individual test. In addition, the teacher will observe each group to make sure that all students are participating and learning. The teacher informs students that the expected social skill to be used by all students is encouraging each other's participation. She defines the skill and has each student practice it twice before the lesson begins.

While students work in their groups, the teacher monitors by systematically observing each group and intervening to provide academic assistance and help in using the interpersonal and small-group skills required to work together effectively. At the end of the lesson, the groups hand in their report forms to be evaluated and process how well they worked together by identifying three things members did to help the group achieve and one thing that could be added to improve their group next time.

Next, the teacher uses a generic cooperative lesson structure to teach vocabulary. Studying vocabulary words is a routine that occurs every week in this class. The teacher instructs students to move into their vocabulary pairs, take the vocabulary words identified in the world interdependence lesson, and for each word (a) write down what they think the word means, (b) look it up in the text and write down its official definition, (c) write a sentence in which the word is used, and (d) learn how to spell the word.

When they have done that for each word, the pair is to make up a story in which all of the words are used. Pairs then exchange stories and carefully determine whether all the words are used appropriately and spelled correctly. If not, the two pairs discuss the word until everyone is clear about what it means and how it should be used.

The teacher uses informal cooperative learning to provide closure to the lesson by asking students to meet with a person from another group, write out four conclusions they derived from the lesson, and circle the one they believed was the most important. At the end of the school day, the cooperative base groups meet to review what students believe is the most important thing they have learned during the day, what homework has been assigned, and what help each member needs to complete the homework, and to tell each other to have a fun afternoon and evening.

ESSENTIAL COMPONENTS: WHAT MAKES COOPERATION WORK

Mastering the use of formal and informal cooperative learning procedures, routine cooperative structures, and cooperative base groups requires an understanding of and ability to implement the components essential for a cooperative effort. Teachers need to master the essential elements of cooperation for at least two reasons. First, teachers need to tailor cooperative learning to their unique instructional needs, circumstances, curricula, subject areas, and students. Second, teachers need to diagnose the problems some students may have in working together and intervene to increase the effectiveness of the student learning groups.

Simply placing students in groups and telling them to work together does not in and of itself result in cooperative efforts. There are many ways in which group efforts may go wrong. Seating students together can result in competition at close quarters or individualistic efforts with talking. The essential elements of cooperation need to be understood if teachers are to be trained to implement cooperative learning successfully. Teachers need enough training and practice on the essential elements of cooperation to become educational engineers who can take their existing lessons, curricula, and courses and structure them cooperatively.

When teachers have real expertise in using cooperative learning, they will structure five essential components into instructional activities (Johnson & Johnson, 1989a; Johnson, Johnson, & Holubec, 1990). Well-structured cooperative learning lessons are differentiated from poorly structured ones on the basis of these elements. These essential elements, furthermore, should be carefully structured within all levels of cooperative efforts. Each learning group is a cooperative effort, but so is the class as a whole, the teaching team, the school, and the school district. The five essential elements are as follows:

1. *Positive interdependence:* Positive interdependence is the perception that you are linked with others in such a way that you cannot succeed unless they do (and vice versa), that is, their work benefits you and your work benefits them. It promotes a situation in which students work together in small groups to maximize the learning of all members, sharing their resources, providing mutual support, and celebrating their joint success. Positive interdependence is the heart of cooperative learning. Students must believe that they sink or swim together. Within every cooperative lesson, positive goal interdependence must be established through mutual learning goals (learn the assigned material and make sure that all members of your group learn the assigned material). In order to strengthen positive interdependence, joint rewards (if all members of your group score 90% correct or better on the test, each will receive 5 bonus points), divided resources (giving each group member a part of the total information required to complete an assignment), and complementary roles (reader, checker, encourager, elaborator) may also be used. For a learning situation to be cooperative, students must perceive that they are positively interdependent with other members of their learning group.

2. *Face-to-face promotive interaction:* Once teachers establish positive interdependence, they need to maximize the opportunity for students to promote each other's success by helping, assisting, supporting, encouraging, and praising each other's efforts to learn. There are cognitive activities and interpersonal dynamics that only occur when students get involved in promoting each other's learning. These include orally explaining how to solve problems, discussing the nature of the concepts being learned, teaching one's knowledge to classmates, and connecting present with past learning. Accountability to peers, ability to influence each other's reasoning and conclusions, social modeling, social support, and interpersonal rewards all increase as the face-to-face interaction among group members increases. In addition, the verbal and nonverbal responses of other group members provide important information concerning a student's performance. Silent students are uninvolved students who are not contributing to the learning of others as well as themselves. Promoting each other's success results in both higher achievement and in getting to know each other on a personal as well as a professional level. To obtain meaningful face-to-face interaction, the size of groups needs to be small (two to four members).

3. *Individual accountability:* Individual accountability exists when the performance of each individual student is assessed and the results are given back to the group and the individual. It is important that the group members know who needs more assistance, support, and encouragement in completing the assignment. It is also important that group members know that they cannot "hitchhike" on the work of others. The purpose of cooperative learning groups is to make each member a stronger individual in his or her own right. Students learn together so that they can subsequently perform more highly as individuals. To ensure that each member is strengthened, students are held individually accountable to do their share of the work. Common ways to structure individual accountability include (*a*) giving an individual test to each student, (*b*) randomly selecting one student's product to represent the entire group, or (*c*) having each student explain what he or she has learned to a classmate.

4. *Social skills:* Contributing to the success of a cooperative effort requires inter-personal and small-group skills. Placing socially unskilled individuals in a group and telling them to cooperate does not guarantee that they will be able to do so effectively. Persons must be taught the social skills for high-quality cooperation and be motivated to use them. Leadership, decision-making, trust-building, communication, and conflict-management skills have to be taught just as purposefully and precisely as academic skills. Procedures and strategies for teaching students social skills may be found in Johnson (1990) and D. W. Johnson and F. Johnson (1991).

5. *Group processing:* Group processing exists when group members discuss how well they are achieving their goals and maintaining effective working relationships. Groups need to describe what member actions are helpful and unhelpful and make decisions about what behaviors to continue or change. Students must also be given the time and procedures for analyzing how well their learning groups are functioning and the extent to which students are employing their social skills to help all group members to achieve and to maintain effective working relationships within the group. Such processing (*a*) enables learning groups to focus on group maintenance, (*b*) facilitates the learning of social skills, (*c*) ensures that members receive feedback on their participation, and (*d*) reminds students to practice collaborative skills consistently. Some of the keys to successful processing are allowing sufficient time for it to take place, making it specific rather than vague, maintaining student involvement in processing, reminding students to use their social skills while they process, and ensuring that clear expectations as to the purpose of processing have been communicated.

In order to effectively use cooperative learning, teachers must understand the nature of cooperation and the essential components of a well-structured cooperative lesson. Understanding what positive interdependence, promotive interaction, individual accountability, social skills, and group processing are and developing skills in structuring them allow teachers to adapt cooperative learning to their unique circumstances and to fine-tune their use of cooperative learning to solve problems students are having in working together. Conceptual understanding and skillful use of cooperative learning are two sides of the coin of expertise. Theory is the cutting edge of practice. It is the development of conceptual understanding of how to teach that allows true teaching genius to be expressed. The complexity and promise of conceptual understanding of cooperative learning make fidelity in implementing the elements of cooperative learning essential. Once the essential elements are clearly understood and mastered, teachers can fine-tune and adapt cooperative learning to their specific circumstances, needs, and students.

THE COOPERATIVE SCHOOL

The issue of cooperation among students is part of a larger issue of the organizational structure of schools. For decades, business and industrial organizations have functioned as "mass-production" organizations that divided work into small component parts performed by individuals who worked separately from and, in many cases, in competition with peers. Personnel were considered to be interchangeable parts in the organizational machine.

Most schools have also been structured as mass-manufacturing organizations. Teachers work alone, in their own rooms, with their own sets of students, and with their own sets of curriculum materials. Students can be assigned to any teacher because teachers are interchangeable parts in the education machine, and, conversely, teachers can be given any student to teach. Schools need to change from a mass-production competitive/individualistic organizational structure to a high-performance, cooperative, team-based organizational structure (see Johnson & Johnson, 1989b). The new organizational structure is generally known as "the cooperative school" (Figure 4.2).

In a cooperative school, students work primarily in cooperative learning groups, teachers and building staff work in cooperative teams, and district administrators work in cooperative teams. The organizational structures of the classroom, school, and district are then congruent. Each level of cooperative teams supports and enhances the other levels.

A cooperative school structure begins in the classroom with the use of cooperative learning the majority of the time. Cooperative learning is used to increase student achievement, create more positive relationships among students, and generally improve students' psychological well-being (Johnson & Johnson, 1989a). A secondary effect is that using cooperative learning in the classroom affects teachers' attitudes and competencies concerning collaborating with colleagues. Teachers typically cannot promote isolation and competition among students all day and be collaborative with colleagues. What is promoted in the instructional situations tends to dominate relationships among staff members.

The second level in creating a cooperative school is to form collegial support groups, task forces, and ad hoc decision-making groups within the school (Johnson & Johnson, 1989b). The use of cooperation to structure faculty and staff work involves (a) collegial support groups, (b) school-based decision making, and (c) faculty meetings. Just as the heart of the classroom is cooperative learning, the heart of the school is the collegial support group. Collegial support groups are small cooperative groups whose purpose is to increase teachers' instructional expertise and success. The focus is on improving instruction in general and increasing members' expertise in using cooperative learning in particular. A collegial support group consists of two to five teachers who have the goal of improving each other's instructional expertise and promoting each other's professional growth (Johnson & Johnson, 1989b). Collegial support groups should be small, and members should be heterogeneous. Collegial support groups

Figure 4.2
Cooperative School Organizational Structure

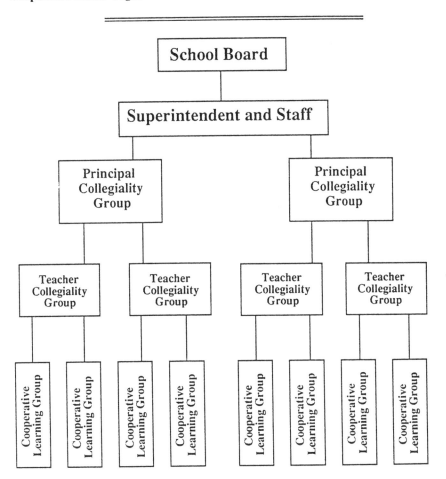

are first and foremost safe places where (*a*) members like to be, (*b*) there is support, caring, concern, laughter, camaraderie, and celebration, and (*c*) the primary goal of improving each other's competence in using cooperative learning is never obscured. The purpose of this collegial support group is for members to work jointly to improve continuously each other's expertise in using cooperative learning procedures, or, in other words, to

1. provide the help, assistance, support, and encouragement each member needs to gain as high a level of expertise in using cooperative learning procedures as possible;

2. serve as an informal support group for sharing, letting off steam, and discussing problems connected with implementing cooperative learning procedures;

3. serve as a base for teachers experienced in the use of cooperative learning procedures to teach other teachers how to structure and manage lessons cooperatively; and

4. create a setting in which camaraderie and shared success occur and are celebrated.

A school-based decision-making program may be created through the use of two types of cooperative teams. First, a task force considers a school problem and proposes a solution to the faculty as a whole. The faculty is then divided into ad hoc decision-making groups and considers whether to accept or modify the proposal. The decisions made by the ad hoc groups are summarized, and the entire faculty then decides on the action to be taken to solve the problem. More specifically, task forces plan and implement solutions to schoolwide issues and problems such as curriculum adoptions and lunchroom behavior. Task forces diagnose a problem, gather data about the causes and extent of the problem, consider a variety of alternative solutions, make conclusions, and present a recommendation to the faculty as a whole. Ad hoc decision-making groups are used during faculty meetings to involve all staff members in important school decisions. Ad hoc decision-making groups are part of a small-group/large-group procedure in which staff members listen to a recommendation, are assigned to small groups, meet to consider the recommendation, report to the entire faculty their decision, and then participate in a whole-faculty decision as to what the course of action should be. The use of these three types of faculty cooperative teams tends to increase teacher productivity, morale, and professional self-esteem.

Faculty meetings represent a microcosm of what administrators think that the school should be. If administrators use a competitive/individualistic format of lecture, whole-class discussion, and individual worksheets in faculty meetings, they have made a powerful statement about the way they want their faculty to teach. The clearest modeling of cooperative procedures in the school may be in faculty meetings and other meetings structured by the school administration. Formal and informal cooperative groups, cooperative base groups, and repetitive structures can be used within faculty meetings just as they can be used within the classroom. This process is simply a matter of engineering and practice.

The third level in creating a cooperative school is to implement administrative cooperative teams within the district (Johnson & Johnson, 1989b). Administrators are organized into collegial support groups to increase their administrative expertise and success. Administrative task forces, shared decision making, and cooperative procedures may dominate at the district level as much as at the school level. If administrators compete to see who is the best administrator in the district, they are unlikely to be able to promote cooperation among staff members of the school. The more the district and school personnel work in cooperative teams, the easier it will be for teachers to use cooperative learning, and vice versa.

Cooperation is more than an instructional procedure. It is a basic shift in organizational structure that extends from the classroom through the superintendent's office. Cooperative learning will not flourish in a mass-production, competitive, and individualistic organizational structure. There needs to be a congruent cooperative structure throughout all organizational levels of the school and school district.

GAINING EXPERTISE IN USING COOPERATIVE LEARNING

Gaining expertise in using cooperative learning in the classroom and cooperative teams in the school and district takes at least one lifetime. Expertise is reflected in a person's proficiency, adroitness, competence, and skill in structuring cooperative efforts. Cooperation takes more expertise than do competitive or individualistic efforts, because it involves dealing with other people as well as dealing with the demands of the task. Expertise, furthermore, focuses attention on the transfer of what is learned within training sessions to the workplace and the long-term maintenance of new procedures throughout the person's career. Approaches to training in cooperative learning may be ordered on a continuum from direct, prescriptive approaches (prepackaged lessons, curricula, strategies, and activities that are used in a lock-step prescribed manner) to conceptual, adaptive approaches (using general conceptual models to tailor cooperative learning specifically for a teacher's circumstances, students, and needs). Teachers must be engineers with cooperative learning, not technicians. Technicians are trained in how to teach packaged lessons, curricula, and strategies in a lock-step (step 1, step 2, step 3) prescribed manner, without really understanding what cooperation is or what makes it work. An engineer conceptually understands cooperative learning and, therefore, can adapt it to his or her specific teaching circumstances, students, and curricula and repair it when it breaks down.

The conceptual approach is used in all technological arts and crafts. An engineer designing a bridge, for example, applies validated theory to the unique problems imposed by the need for a bridge of a certain length, to carry specific loads, from a bank of one unique geological character to a bank of another unique geological character, in an area with specific winds, temperatures, and susceptibility to earthquakes. A conceptual approach requires teachers to engage in the same process by (*a*) learning a conceptualization of essential components of cooperative learning and (*b*) applying that conceptual model to their unique teaching situations, circumstances, students, and instructional needs. Each teacher has to adapt and refine cooperative learning to fit his or her idiosyncratic situation. Each class may require a different adaptation in order to maximize the effectiveness of cooperative learning. Understanding the essential elements allows teachers to (*a*) think metacognitively about cooperative learning, (*b*) create any number of lessons, strategies, and activities, and (*c*) achieve the goals of developing enough expertise to

1. take any lesson in any subject area and structure it cooperatively;
2. practice and practice the use of cooperative learning until they are at a routine/integrated level of use and implement cooperative learning at least 60% of the time in their classrooms;
3. describe precisely what they are doing and why they are doing it in order to (*a*) communicate to others the nature of cooperative learning and (*b*) teach colleagues how to implement cooperative learning in their classrooms and settings; and
4. apply the principles of cooperation to other settings, such as collegial relationships and faculty meetings.

Such expertise is usually gained through a progressive-refinement procedure of (*a*) teaching a cooperative lesson, (*b*) assessing how well it went, (*c*) reflecting on how it could have been taught better, and then (*d*) teaching an improved cooperative lesson, assessing how well it went, and so forth. Teachers thus gain experience in an incremental step-by-step manner. This process is greatly enhanced by collegial support groups. Gaining expertise in using cooperative learning is in itself a cooperative process that requires a team effort. Collegial support groups encourage and assist teachers in a long-term, multiyear effort to improve continually their competence in using cooperative learning (Johnson & Johnson, 1989b). With only a moderately difficult teaching strategy, for example, teachers may require from twenty to thirty hours of instruction in its theory, fifteen to twenty demonstrations using it with different students and subjects, and an additional ten to fifteen coaching sessions to attain higher-level skills. For a more difficult teaching strategy like cooperative learning, several years of training and support may be needed to ensure that teachers master it.

REFERENCES

Deutsch, M. (1949). A theory of cooperation and competition. *Human Relations,* 2, 129–152.

Deutsch, M. (1962). Cooperation and trust: Some theoretical notes. In M. Jones (Ed.), *Nebraska symposium on motivation* (pp. 275–319). Lincoln: University of Nebraska Press.

Johnson, D. W. (1970). *The social psychology of education.* New York: Holt, Rinehart, & Winston.

Johnson, D. W. (1979). *Educational psychology.* Englewood Cliffs, NJ: Prentice Hall.

Johnson, D. W. (1990). *Reaching out: Interpersonal effectiveness and self-actualization* (4th ed.). Englewood Cliffs, NJ: Prentice Hall.

Johnson, D. W., & Johnson, F. (1991). *Joining together: Group theory and group skills* (4th ed.). Englewood Cliffs, NJ: Prentice Hall.

Johnson, D. W., & Johnson, R. (1974). Instructional goal structure: Cooperative, competition, or individualistic. *Review of Educational Research, 44,* 213–240.

Johnson, D. W., & Johnson, R. (1983). The socialization and achievement crises: Are cooperative learning experiences the solution? *Applied Social Psychology Annual, 4,* 119–164.

Johnson, D. W., & Johnson, R. (1985). Impact of classroom organization and instructional methods on the effectiveness of mainstreaming. In C. Meisel (Ed.), *Mainstreaming handicapped children: Outcomes, controversies, and new directions* (pp. 215–250). Hillsdale, NJ: Lawrence Erlbaum Associates.

Johnson, D. W., & Johnson, R. (1989a). *Cooperation and competition: Theory and research.* Edina, MN: Interaction Book Company.

Johnson, D. W., & Johnson, R. (1989b). *Leading the cooperative school.* Edina, MN: Interaction Book Company.

Johnson, D. W., & Johnson, R. (1991). *Cooperative learning lesson structures.* Edina, MN: Interaction Book Company.

Johnson, D. W., Johnson, R., & Holubec, E. (1990). *Circles of learning: Cooperation in the classroom* (3rd ed.). Edina, MN: Interaction Book Company.

Johnson, D. W., Johnson, R., & Holubec, E. (1991). *Cooperation in the classroom* (4th ed.). Edina, MN: Interaction Book Company.

Johnson, D. W., Johnson, R., & Holubec, E. (1992). *Advanced cooperative learning* (2nd ed.). Edina, MN: Interaction Book Company.

Johnson, D. W., Johnson, R., & Smith, K. (1991). *Active learning: Cooperation in the college classroom.* Edina, MN: Interaction Book Company.

Johnson, D., Johnson, R., & Maruyama, G. (1983). Interdependence and interpersonal attraction among heterogeneous and homogeneous individuals: A theoretical formulation and a meta-analysis of the research. *Review of Educational Research, 53,* 5–54.

Johnson, D., Maruyama, G., Johnson, R., Nelson, D., & Skon, L. (1981). Effects of cooperative, competitive, and individualistic goal structures on achievement: A meta-analysis. *Psychology Bulletin, 89,* 47–62.

Miles, M. (Ed.). (1964). *Innovation in education.* New York: Teachers College Press.

Watson, G. (Ed.). (1967). *Concepts for social change.* Washington, DC: National Training Laboratories.

Watson, G., & Johnson, D. W. (1972). *Social psychology: Issues and insights* (2nd ed.). Philadelphia: Lippincott.

5

Structuring Academic Controversy

David W. Johnson and Roger T. Johnson

Have you learned lessons only of
those who admired you, and were tender
with you, and stood aside for you?

Have you not learned great lessons
from those who braced themselves
against you, and disputed the passage
with you?

Walt Whitman, 1860

COOPERATION AND CONFLICT

Conflict is frequent and probably inevitable within cooperative efforts. As diverse individuals and groups work together, their interdependence creates conflicts. Within a cooperative effort, participants often disagree and argue with each other. The more participants care about their mutual goals, and the more they care about each other, the more frequently they will disagree, and the more intense their disagreement may be. The absence of conflict within a cooperative endeavor may indicate apathy toward the task and each other. When two students must agree on the answer to a math problem, for example, conflicts are possible if one student says that the answer is eleven and the other student says that the answer is fourteen. Such intellectual conflicts are not only inevitable, they are highly desirable and are one of the major reasons why cooperative learning promotes higher achievement, higher-level reasoning, greater retention, and greater creativity than do competitive or individualistic learning.

Conflicts can only be managed constructively within a cooperative context. When participants are in competition with each other, they will go for the win rather than a constructive resolution of the conflict. It is only when participants clarify their mutual goals and long-term relationship that a constructive resolution to conflicts is sought. Thus, if conflicts are to be managed competently, cooperation must be established and the long-term working relationship must be perceived to be of more importance than the short-term issue. If students, for example, are to learn how to deal with their conflicts in helpful and beneficial ways, the classroom and school must be cooperative enterprises.

Many people are very uncomfortable in conflict situations. In many schools and classrooms, conflicts are suppressed and avoided in a mistaken belief that the absence of conflict is "good." Educators who are "conflict-avoiders" have forgotten what John Dewey tried to make clear in his book *Human Nature and Conduct* (1922):

Conflict is the gadfly of thought. It stirs us to observation and memory. It instigates invention. It shocks us out of sheep-like passivity, and sets us at noting and contriving. . . . conflict is the 'sine qua non' of reflection and ingenuity.

Within cooperative learning groups, intellectual conflict should be encouraged and nurtured, rather than suppressed or avoided. Educators must understand what controversy is, how students benefit from it, how intellectual conflicts create academic benefits, what the key elements are that make controversy work, and the teacher's role in structuring and managing academic controversies (Johnson, 1970, 1979; Johnson & Johnson, 1979, 1987, 1989; Johnson, Johnson & Smith, 1986).

THE NATURE OF CONTROVERSY

Controversy exists when one student's ideas, information, conclusions, theories, and opinions are incompatible with those of another, and the two seek to reach an agreement. Controversies are resolved by engaging in deliberate discourse aimed at synthesizing novel solutions. When controversies are structured, participants are required to research and prepare a position; rehearse orally the relevant information; advocate a position; teach their knowledge to peers; analyze, critically evaluate, and rebut information; reason both deductively and inductively; take the perspectives of others; and synthesize and integrate information into factual and judgmental conclusions that are summarized into a joint position to which all sides can agree.

Structured academic controversies are most often contrasted with individualistic learning, debate, and concurrence seeking. For instance, students can work independently with their own set of materials at their own pace (individualistic learning). Or students can appoint a judge and then debate the different positions with the expectation that the judge will determine who presented the better position (debate). Finally, students can inhibit discussion to avoid any disagreement and compromise quickly to reach a consensus while they discuss the issue (concurrence seeking). Concurrence seeking is close to the groupthink concept of Janis (1982) in which members of a decision-making group set aside their doubts and misgivings about whatever policy is favored by the emerging consensus so as to be able to concur with the other members. The underlying motivation of groupthink is the strong desire to preserve the harmonious atmosphere of the group on which each member has become dependent for coping with the stresses of external crises and for maintaining self-esteem.

A key to the effectiveness of conflict procedures for promoting learning is the mixture of cooperative and competitive elements within the procedure (Table 5.1). The greater the cooperative elements and the less the competitive elements, the more constructive the conflict (Deutsch, 1973). Cooperative elements alone, however, do not ensure maximal productivity. There has to be both cooperation and conflict. Thus controversy is characterized by both positive goal and resource interdependence as well as by conflict. Debate has positive resource interdependence, negative goal interdependence, and conflict. Within concurrence seeking there is only positive goal interdependence, and within individualistic learning situations there is neither interdependence nor intellectual conflict (Table 5.2).

An example of an academic controversy is as follows. In an English literature class, students are considering the issue of civil disobedience. They learn that in the civil rights movement in the United States, individuals broke the law to gain equal rights for minorities. In numerous instances, such as in the civil rights and antiwar movements, individuals wrestle with the issue of breaking the law to redress a social injustice. In order to study the role of civil disobedience in a democracy, students are placed in cooperative learning groups of four members. The group is then divided into two pairs. One pair is given the assignment of making the best case possible for the constructiveness of civil disobedience in a democracy. The other pair is given the assignment of making the best case possible for the destructiveness of civil disobedience in a democracy. In the resulting conflict, students draw from such sources as the Declaration of Independence by Thomas Jefferson, *Civil Disobedience* by Henry David Thoreau, *Speech at Cooper Union, New York* by Abraham Lincoln, and *Letter from Birmingham Jail* by Martin Luther King, Jr., to challenge each other's reasoning and analyses concerning when civil disobedience is, and is not, constructive.

This unit would typically take five class periods to conduct. During the first class period, each pair develops its position and plans how to present the best case possible to the other pair. Near the end of the period, pairs

Table 5.1
Comparison of Instructional Methods

Controversy	Debate	Concurrence-Seeking	Individualistic
Categorizing and Organizing information To Derive Conclusions	Categorizing and Organizing information To Derive Conclusions	Categorizing and Organizing information To Derive Conclusions	Categorizing and Organizing information To Derive Conclusions
Presenting, Advocating, Elaborating Position And Rationale	Presenting, Advocating, Elaborating Position And Rationale	Active Presentation Of Position	No Oral Statement Of Positions
Being Challenged By Opposing Views	Being Challenged By Opposing Views	Quick Compromise To One View	Presence Of Only One View
Conceptual Conflict And Uncertainty About The Correctness Of Own Views	Conceptual Conflict And Uncertainty About The Correctness Of Own Views	High Certainty About The Correctness Of Own Views	High Certainty About The Correctness Of Own Views
Epistemic Curiosity And Perspective Taking	Epistemic Curiosity	No Epistemic Curiosity	No Epistemic Curiosity
Reconceptualization, Synthesis, Integration	Closed-Minded Adherence To Own Point Of View	Closed-Minded Adherence To Own Point Of View	Closed-Minded Adherence To Own Point Of View
High Achievement, Positive Relationships, Psychological Health/Social Competences	Moderate Achievement, Relationships, Psychological Health	Low Achievement, Relationships, Psychological Health	Low Achievement, Relationships, Psychological Health

Table 5.2
Nature of Instructional Methods

	Controversy	Debate	Concurrence Seeking	Individualistic
Positive Goal Interdependence	Yes	No	Yes	No
Positive Resource Interdependence	Yes	Yes	No	No
Negative Goal Interdependence	No	Yes	No	No
Conflict	Yes	Yes	No	No

are encouraged to compare notes with pairs from other groups who represent the same position. During the second class period, each pair makes its presentation. Each member of the pair has to participate in the presentation. Members of the opposing pair are encouraged to take notes and listen carefully. During the third class period, the group members discuss the issue following a set of rules to help them criticize ideas without criticizing people, differentiate the two positions, and assess the degree of evidence and logic supporting each position. During the fourth period, the pairs (a) reverse perspectives and present each other's positions and (b) drop all advocacy and begin developing a group report that synthesizes the best evidence and reasoning from both sides. During the fifth period, (a) the report is finalized (the teacher evaluates reports on the quality of the writing, the logical presentation of evidence, and the oral presentation of the report to the class), (b) the group's conclusions are presented to the class (all four members of the group are required to participate orally in the presentation), (c) students each take an individual test, and if every member of the group achieves up to criterion, they all receive bonus points, and (d) the group processes how well it worked together and how it could do even better next time.

Such intellectual "disputed passages" create numerous benefits for students when they (a) occur within cooperative learning groups and (b) are carefully structured to ensure that students manage them constructively. As Thomas Jefferson noted, "Difference of opinion leads to inquiry, and inquiry to truth."

However, many teachers are reluctant to spark disagreements in the classroom. Teachers often suppress students' academic disagreements and consequently miss out on valuable opportunities to capture students' attention and enhance learning.

HOW STUDENTS BENEFIT

When students interact, conflicts among their ideas, conclusions, theories, information, perspectives, opinions, and preferences are inevitable. Teachers who capitalize on these differences find that academic conflicts can yield highly constructive dividends. The outcomes of controversy may be grouped into three broad outcomes: achievement, positive interpersonal relationships, and psychological health and social competence. Controversy can also be fun, enjoyable, and exciting.

Achievement and Retention

Compared with concurrence seeking, debate, and individualistic efforts, controversy tends to result in greater mastery and retention of the subject matter being studied as well as greater ability to generalize the principles learned to a wider variety of situations. In a meta-analysis of the available research, Johnson and Johnson (1989) found that controversy produced higher achievement and retention than did debate (effect size = 0.77), individualistic learning (effect size = 0.65), and concurrence seeking (effect size = 0.42). The dozens of studies conducted indicate that students who participate in an academic controversy recall more correct information, are better able to transfer learning to new situations, use more complex and higher-level reasoning strategies in recalling and transferring information learned, and are better able to generalize the principles they learned to a wider variety of situations.

Quality of Problem Solving

If students are to become citizens capable of making reasoned judgments about the complex problems facing society, they must learn to use the higher-level reasoning and critical thinking processes involved in effective problem solving. To do so, students must enter empathetically into the arguments of both sides of the issue, ensure that the strongest possible case is made for each side, and arrive at a synthesis based on rational, probabilistic thought. Participating in structured controversy teaches students of all ages how to find high-quality solutions to complex problems. Compared with concurrence seeking, debate, and individualistic efforts, controversy tends to result in higher-quality decisions and solutions to complex problems for which different viewpoints can plausibly be developed.

An interesting question concerning controversy and problem solving is what happens when erroneous information is presented by participants. Simply, can the advocacy of two conflicting but wrong solutions to a problem create a correct one? The value of the controversy process lies not so much in the correctness of an opposing position as in the attention and thought processes it induces. More cognitive processing may take place when individuals are exposed to more than one point of view, even if the point of view is incorrect. A number of studies with both adults and children have found significant gains in performance when erroneous information is presented by one or both sides in a controversy (Ames & Murray, 1982).

Creativity

Compared with concurrence seeking, debate, and individualistic efforts, controversy tends to result in more frequent creative insights into the issues being discussed and more creative synthesis combining both perspectives (Johnson & Johnson, 1989). Controversy increases the number of ideas, the quality of ideas, the creation of original ideas, the use of a wider range of ideas, originality, the use of more varied strategies, and the number of creative, imaginative, novel solutions. Studies further demonstrated that controversy encouraged group members to dig into a problem, raise issues, and settle them in ways that showed the benefits of a wide range of ideas being used, as well as resulting in a high degree of emotional involvement in and commitment to solving the problems the group was working on.

Exchange of Expertise

Compared with concurrence seeking, debate, and individualistic efforts, controversy tends to result in greater exchange of expertise (Johnson & Johnson, 1989). Students often know different information and theories, make different assumptions, and have different opinions. Within any cooperative learning group, students with a wide variety of expertise and perspectives are told to work together to maximize each member's learning. Many times students study different parts of an assignment and are expected to share their expertise with the other members of their group. Conflict among their ideas, information, opinions, preferences, theories, conclusions, and perspectives is inevitable. Yet such controversies are typically avoided or managed destructively. Having the skills to manage the controversies constructively and knowing the procedures for exchanging information and perspective among individuals with differing expertise are essential for maximal learning and growth.

Task Involvement

John Milton, in *Doctrine and Discipline,* stated, "Where there is much desire to learn, there of necessity will be much arguing, much writing, many opinions; for opinion in good men is but knowledge in the making." Making knowledge through disagreement does arouse emotions and increases involvement. Compared with concurrence seeking, debate, and individualistic efforts, controversy tends to result in greater task involvement, reflected in greater emotional commitment to solving the problem, greater enjoyment of the process, and more feelings of stimulation and enjoyment (Johnson & Johnson, 1989). *Task involvement* refers to the quality and quantity of the physical and psychological energy that individuals invest in their efforts to achieve. Task involvement is reflected in the attitudes participants have toward the task and toward the controversy experience. Individuals who engaged in controversies tended to like the task and procedure better and generally had more positive attitudes toward the experience than did individuals who engaged in concurrence-seeking discussions, individualistic efforts, or debate.

Interpersonal Attraction among Participants

It is often assumed that the presence of controversy within a group will lead to difficulties in establishing good interpersonal relations and will promote negative attitudes toward fellow group members, and it is also often assumed that arguing leads to rejection, divisiveness, and hostility among peers (Collins, 1970). Within controversy and debate there are elements of disagreement, argumentation, and rebuttal that could result in individuals disliking each other and could create difficulties in establishing good relationships. On the other hand, conflicts have been hypothesized potentially to create positive relationships among participants (Deutsch, 1962; Johnson, 1970). The evidence indicates that controversy promotes greater liking and social support among participants than does debate, concurrence seeking, no controversy, or individualistic efforts (Johnson & Johnson, 1989).

Psychological Health and Social Competence

There are a number of components of psychological health that are strengthened by participating in academic controversies (Johnson & Johnson, 1989). Compared with concurrence seeking, debate, and individualistic efforts, controversy tends to result in higher academic self-esteem and greater perspective-taking accuracy. Being able to manage disagreements and conflicts constructively enables individuals to cope with the stresses involved in interacting with a variety of other people.

THE PROCESS OF CONTROVERSY

> Since the general or prevailing opinion on any subject is rarely or never the whole truth, it is only by the collision of adverse opinion that the remainder of the truth has any chance of being supplied.
> John Stuart Mill

The hypothesis that intellectual challenge promotes higher-level reasoning, critical thinking, and metacognitive thought is derived from a number of premises:

1. When individuals are presented with a problem or decision, they have an initial conclusion based on categorizing and organizing incomplete information, their limited experiences, and their specific perspective.

2. When individuals present their conclusion and its rationale to others, they engage in cognitive rehearsal, deepen their understanding of their position, and discover higher-level reasoning strategies.

3. When individuals are confronted by other people with different conclusions based on other people's information, experiences, and perspectives, they can become uncertain as to the correctness of their views. A state of conceptual conflict or disequilibrium is aroused.

4. Uncertainty, conceptual conflict, and disequilibrium motivate an active search for more information, new experiences, and a more adequate cognitive perspective and reasoning process in hopes of resolving the uncertainty. Berlyne (1965) called this active search "epistemic curiosity." Divergent attention and thought are stimulated.

5. By adapting their cognitive perspective and reasoning through understanding and accommodating the perspective and reasoning of others, individuals derive a new, reconceptualized, and reorganized conclusion. Novel solutions and decisions are detected that are, on balance, qualitatively better.

Each of these premises is discussed here.

Step 1: Organizing Information and Deriving Conclusions

In order to make high-quality decisions, individuals have to think of the proper alternatives, do a good job of evaluating them, and choose the most promising one. When individuals are presented with a problem or decision, they have an initial conclusion based on categorizing and organizing incomplete information, their limited experiences, and their specific perspective. Individuals organize their current knowledge and experiences, within the framework of their perspective, into a conceptual framework from which they can derive a conclusion (through the use of inductive and deductive logic). The conceptual frameworks formed, however, often lead to inaccurate conclusions because of the limitations of perspective, one's expectations and mental set at the time, a tendency to give one's dominant response to the situation, or fixation on the first seemingly satisfactory solution generated.

Step 2: Presenting and Advocating Positions

Most students get few opportunities to present and advocate a position. Within a controversy, students present and advocate positions to others who, in turn, are advocating opposing positions. *Advocacy* may be defined as the presenting of a position and providing reasons why others should adopt it. Decisions and conclusions are then reached through a process of argument and counterargument aimed at persuading others to adopt, modify, or drop positions. Advocating a position and defending it against refutation require engaging in considerable cognitive rehearsal and elaboration, increased understanding of the position, and the discovery of higher-level reasoning processes. Disagreements within a group have been found to provide a greater amount of information and variety of facts as well as changes in the salience of known information.

Step 3: Being Challenged by Opposing Views

In controversy, individuals' conclusions are challenged by the advocates of opposing positions. Members critically analyze each other's positions in attempts to discern weaknesses and strengths. They attempt to refute opposing positions while rebutting the attacks on their position. At the same time, they are aware that they need to learn the information being presented and understand the perspective of the other group members.

The direct evidence indicates that individuals engaged in controversy are motivated to know the others' positions and to develop understanding and appreciation of them (Johnson & Johnson, 1989). Hearing opposing views being advocated, furthermore, stimulates new cognitive analysis and frees individuals to create alternative and original conclusions. When contrary information is not clearly relevant to completing the task at hand, it may be ignored, discounted, or perceived in biased ways in favor of supporting evidence. When individuals realize, however, that they are accountable for knowing the contrary information some time in the near future, they will tend to learn it. Even being confronted with an erroneous point of view can result in more divergent thinking and the generation of novel and more cognitively advanced solutions.

Step 4: Conceptual Conflict and Uncertainty

Hearing other alternatives being advocated, having one's position criticized and refuted, and being challenged by information that is incompatible with and does not fit with one's conclusions leads to conceptual conflict and uncertainty. The greater the disagreement among group members, the more frequently disagreement occurs, the greater the number of people disagreeing with a person's position, the more competitive the context of the controversy, and the more affronted the person feels, the greater the conceptual conflict and uncertainty the person experiences (Johnson & Johnson, 1989).

When faced with intellectual opposition within a cooperative context, students will ask each other for more information. Conceptual conflict motivates an active search for more information (a process called epistemic curiosity) in hopes of resolving the uncertainty. Indices of epistemic curiosity of individuals include actively (*a*) searching for more information, (*b*) seeking to understand opposing positions and rationales, and (*c*) attempting to view the situation from opposing perspectives.

Step 5: Reconceptualization, Synthesis, Integration

When overt controversy is structured within a problem-solving, decision-making, or learning group by identifying alternatives and assigning members to advocate the best case for each alternative, the purpose is not to choose the best alternative. The purpose is to create a synthesis of the best reasoning and conclusions from all the various alternatives. Synthesizing occurs when individuals integrate a number of different ideas and facts into a single position. It is the intellectual bringing together of ideas and facts and engaging in inductive reasoning by restating a large amount of information into a conclusion or summary. Synthesizing is a creative process involving seeing new patterns within a body of evidence, viewing the issue from a variety of perspectives, and generating a number of optional ways of integrating the evidence. This requires probabilistic (i.e., knowledge is available only in degrees of certainty) rather than dualistic (i.e., there is only right and wrong, and authority should not be questioned) or relativistic (i.e., authorities are seen as sometimes right, but right and wrong depend on your perspective) thinking. The dual purposes of synthesis are to arrive at the best possible decision or solution and to find a position that all group members can agree on and commit themselves to. There is evidence that controversy leads to accuracy of perspective taking, incorporation of others' information and reasoning into one's own position, attitude and position change, and transition to higher stages of cognitive reasoning, all of which contribute to the quality of individuals' reconceptualization, synthesis, and integration.

KEY ELEMENTS FOR MAKING CONTROVERSY CONSTRUCTIVE

Although controversies can operate in a beneficial way, they will not do so under all conditions. As with all types of conflicts, the potential for either constructive or destructive outcomes is present in a controversy. Whether there are positive or negative consequences depends on the conditions under which controversy occurs and the way in which it is managed. These key elements are as follows (Johnson & Johnson, 1979, 1989, 1992):

1. *A cooperative context:* Communication of information is far more complete, accurate, encouraged, and utilized in a cooperative context than in a competitive context. Controversy in a cooperative context promotes open-minded listening

to the opposing position, while in a competitive context, controversy promotes a closed-minded orientation in which individuals are unwilling to make concessions to the opponent's viewpoint and refuse to incorporate any of the opponent's viewpoint into their own position.

2. *Heterogeneous participants:* Heterogeneity among individuals leads to potential controversy and to more diverse interaction patterns and resources for achievement and problem solving.

3. *Relevant information distributed among participants:* The more information individuals have about an issue, the more successful their problem solving.

4. *Social skills:* In order for controversies to be managed constructively, individuals need a number of conflict-management skills, such as disagreeing with each other's ideas while confirming each other's personal competence, and seeing the issue from a number of perspectives.

5. *Rational argument:* Rational argumentation includes generating ideas, collecting and organizing relevant information, using inductive and deductive logic, and making tentative conclusions based on current understanding.

STRUCTURING ACADEMIC CONTROVERSIES

Structure the Academic Task

The task must be structured (1) cooperatively and (2) so that there are at least two well-documented positions (e.g., pro and con). The choice of topic depends on the interests of the instructor and the purposes of the course.

Prepare Instructional Materials

Prepare the instructional materials so that group members know what position they have been assigned and where they can find supporting information. The following materials are needed for each position:

1. A clear description of the group's task
2. A description of the phases of the controversy procedure and the interpersonal and small-group skills to be used during each phase
3. A definition of the position to be advocated, with a summary of the key arguments supporting the position
4. Resource materials (including a bibliography) to provide evidence for the elaboration of the arguments supporting the position to be advocated

Structure the Controversy

The principal requirements for a successful structured controversy are a cooperative context, skillful group members, and heterogeneity of group membership. These are structured as follows:

1. Assign students to heterogeneous groups of four. Divide each group into two pairs. A high reader and a low reader may be assigned to each pair. The responsibility of the pair is to get to know the information supporting its assigned position and to prepare a presentation and a series of persuasive arguments to use in the discussion with the opposing pair.

2. Assign pro and con positions to the pairs and give students supporting materials to read and study. A bibliography of further sources of information may also be given. A section of resource materials may be set up in the library.

3. Structure positive interdependence by highlighting (a) the cooperative goals (ensuring that all group members reach a consensus on the issue, master all the information relevant to both sides of the issue [measured by a test], and participate in writing a quality group report and making a presentation to the class) and (b) resource interdependence (materials are jigsawed within the group); and reward interdependence (bonus points are given to members if all of them learn the basic information contained in the two positions and score well on the test).

4. Structure individual accountability by ensuring that each student participates in preparing the assigned position, presenting the position, discussing the issue, reversing perspectives, preparing the report, presenting the report, and taking an individual test on the material.

Conduct the Controversy

1. Assign each pair the following tasks:
   a. Learning their position and its supporting arguments and information
   b. Researching all information relevant to their position
   c. Giving the opposing pair any information found supporting the opposing position
   d. Preparing a persuasive presentation to be given to the other pair
   e. Preparing a series of persuasive arguments to be used in the discussion with the opposing pair

   Pairs research and prepare their positions, presentations, and arguments. Students are given the following instructions:

   Plan with your partner how to advocate your position effectively. Read the materials supporting your position. Find more information in the library reference books to support your position. Plan a persuasive presentation. Make sure you and your partner master the information supporting your assigned position and present it in a persuasive and complete way so that the other group members will comprehend and learn the information.

2. Have each pair present its position to the other. Presentations should involve more than one medium and persuasively advocate the best case for the position. There is no arguing during this time. Students should listen carefully to the opposing position. Students are told:

As a pair, present your position forcefully and persuasively. Listen carefully and learn the opposing position. Take notes, and clarify anything you do not understand.

3. Have students openly discuss the issue by freely exchanging their information and ideas. For higher-level reasoning and critical thinking to occur, it is necessary to probe and push each other's conclusions. Students ask for data to support each other's statements, clarify rationales, and show why their position is a rational one. Students evaluate critically the opposing position and its rationale, defend their own positions, and compare the strengths and weaknesses of the two positions. Students refute the claims being made by the opposing pair and rebut the attacks on their own position. Students are to follow the specific rules for constructive controversy. Students should also take careful notes on and thoroughly learn the opposing position. Sometimes a "time-out" period needs to be provided so that pairs can caucus and prepare new arguments. Teachers encourage more spirited arguing, take sides when a pair is in trouble, play devil's advocate, ask one group to observe another group engaging in a spirited argument, and generally stir up the discussions. Students are instructed:

Argue forcefully and persuasively for your position, presenting as many facts as you can to support your point of view. Listen critically to the opposing pair's position, asking them for the facts that support their viewpoint, and then present counterarguments. Remember that this is a complex issue, and you need to know both sides to write a good report.

4. Have the pairs reverse perspectives and positions by presenting the opposing position as sincerely and forcefully as they can. It helps to have the pairs change chairs. They can use their own notes, but may not see the materials developed by the opposing pair. Students' instructions are:

Working as a pair, present the opposing pair's position as if you were they. Be as sincere and forceful as you can. Add any new facts you know. Elaborate their position by relating it to other information you have previously learned.

5. Have the group members drop their advocacy and reach a decision by consensus. Then they do the following:

   a. The group members write a group report that includes their joint position and the supporting evidence and rationale. Often the resulting position is a third perspective or synthesis that is more rational than the two assigned. All group members sign the report, indicating that they agree with it, can explain its content, and consider it ready to be evaluated.

   b. The group members take a test on both positions. If all members score above the preset criteria of excellence, each receives five bonus points.

   c. The group members process how well the group functioned and how their performance may be improved during the next controversy. Teachers may wish to structure the group processing to highlight the specific conflict-management skills students need to master.

Students are instructed:

Summarize and synthesize the best arguments for both points of view. Reach consensus on a position that is supported by the facts. Change your mind only when the facts and the rationale clearly indicate that you should do so. Write your report with the supporting evidence and rationale for your synthesis that your group has agreed on. When you are certain the report is as good as you can make it, sign it. Organize your report to present it to your entire class.

Teach Students Conflict Skills

No matter how carefully teachers structure controversies, if students do not have the interpersonal and small-group skills to manage conflicts constructively, the controversy will not produce its potential effects. The social skills emphasized are those involved in systematically advocating an intellectual position and evaluating and criticizing the position advocated by others, as well as the skills involved in synthesis and consensual decision making. Students should be taught the skills of (*a*) focusing on the mutual goal of coming to the best decision possible, not on winning, (*b*) confirming others' competence while disagreeing with their positions and challenging their reasoning (being critical of ideas, not people), (*c*) separating others' personal worth from criticism of their ideas, (*d*) listening to everyone's ideas, even if one does not agree with them, (*e*) first bringing out all the ideas and facts supporting both sides (differentiating the differences between positions) and then trying to put them together in a way that makes sense (integration of ideas), (*f*) taking the opposing perspective in order to understand both sides of the issue, (*g*) changing one's mind when the evidence clearly indicates that one should, (*h*) paraphrasing what someone has said if it is not clear, (*i*) emphasizing rationality in seeking the best possible answer, given the available data, and (*j*) following the golden rule of conflict (act toward your opponents as you would have them act toward you).

REFERENCES

Ames, G., & Murray, F. (1982). When two wrongs make a right: Promoting cognitive change by social conflict. *Developmental Psychology, 18,* 894–897.

Berlyne, D. (1965). Curiosity and education. In J. Krumboltz (Ed.), *Learning and the educational process.* Chicago: Rand McNally, 67–89.

Collins, B. (1970). *Social psychology.* Reading, MA: Addison-Wesley.

Deutsch, M. (1962). Cooperation and trust: Some theoretical notes. In M. Jones (Ed.), *Nebraska symposium on motivation* (pp. 275–319). Lincoln: University of Nebraska Press.

Deutsch, M. (1973). *The resolution of conflict.* New Haven, CT: Yale University Press.

Dewey, J. (1922). *Human nature and conduct.* New York: Henry Holt and Co.

Janis, I. (1982). *Groupthink: Psychological studies of policy decisions and fiascoes.* Boston: Houghton Mifflin.

Johnson, D. W. (1970). *Social psychology of education.* Edina, MN: Interaction Book Company.

Johnson, D. W. (1979). *Educational psychology*. Englewood Cliffs, NJ: Prentice Hall.

Johnson, D. W. (1980). Group processes: Influences of student-student interaction on school outcomes. In J. McMillan (Ed.), *The social psychology of school learning*. New York: Academic Press.

Johnson, D. W. (1990). *Reaching out: Interpersonal effectiveness and self-actualization* (4th ed.). Englewood Cliffs, NJ: Prentice Hall.

Johnson D. W., & Johnson, F. (1991). *Joining together: Group theory and group skills* (4th ed.). Englewood Cliffs, NJ: Prentice Hall.

Johnson, D. W., & Johnson, R. (1979). Conflict in the classroom: Controversy and learning. *Review of Educational Research, 49,* 51–61.

Johnson, D. W., & Johnson, R. (1987). *Learning together and alone*. Englewood Cliffs, NJ: Prentice Hall.

Johnson, D. W., & Johnson, R. (1989). *Cooperation and competition: Theory and research*. Edina, MN: Interaction Book Company.

Johnson, D. W., & Johnson, R. (1992). *Creative controversy: Intellectual challenge in the classroom*. Edina, MN: Interaction Book Company.

Johnson, D. W., Johnson, R., & Smith, K. (1986). Academic conflict among students: Controversy and learning. In R. Feldman (Ed.), *The social psychology of education*. Cambridge: Cambridge University Press, 199–231.

6

Complex Instruction: Higher-Order Thinking in Heterogeneous Classrooms

Elizabeth G. Cohen, Rachel A. Lotan,
Jennifer A. Whitcomb, Maria V. Balderrama,
Ruth Cossey, and Patricia E. Swanson

Students at Washington Middle School are members of over twenty different ethnic groups and come from a wide range of economic backgrounds. They represent the full spectrum of percentile rankings on standardized achievement tests. To capitalize on this diversity and to minimize the number of students who may get lost in the system, the school community has taken bold steps. Classes have been detracked, and teachers use Complex Instruction, designed to develop higher-order thinking in academically heterogeneous classrooms.

Ms. Wilson teaches mathematics at Washington Middle School. Her classes fully reflect the diversity of the student body. She uses a curriculum that challenges each of her students in its demand for mathematical reasoning. Terry, Kiante, Alicia, and Robbie are working on the Mathematical Tug-of-War,[1] an activity that involves functional relationships, inequalities, and equivalence. First, the group read a story about two tug-of-war matches involving giant frogs, athletic grandmas, and a frisky kangaroo. In the story, the students found that an even tug-of-war is five grandmas of equal strength pulling against four giant frogs, also of equal strength. Another even match results when the kangaroo pulls against two grandmas and a giant frog. The group's task is threefold: (*a*) to use characters from the story to create a tricky tug-of-war match that would not come out even, (*b*) to provide a written account of two different ways to verify mathematically which side would win the tug-of-war it had created, and (*c*) to make a poster that presents its tug-of-war as a problem for others to solve.

Ms. Wilson approaches the group. She is particularly concerned about

Terry, who is doodling different tugs-of-war with kangaroos, grandmas, and frogs. As usual, Terry seems withdrawn, excluded from the animated conversation among the other members of her group. Kiante, Alicia, and Robbie like the match they came up with. Kiante solved the problem using fractions and is making the case for this approach. Alicia used percentages and is arguing for her method. Robbie is demanding that they help him understand both approaches.

Ms. Wilson: I see that you found two different ways to solve your problem match. How will you decide if your solution and approaches make sense, and how are you going to help everyone in the group understand the solutions?

Kiante: Me and Alicia did the work and we know that the side with the two grandmas and kangaroo will beat the side with one grandma and four frogs. Alicia is going to show us how she figured it out after I explain how I got my answer.

Ms. Wilson: That sounds like a good plan. How will you make sure everybody in your group understands?

Alicia: Well, I'm the facilitator, so I'll make sure that everybody listens to everybody else. Then Terry can start drawing the picture.

Terry: Ms. Wilson, I think that actually the side with the grandma and four frogs might win. In my picture, these four frogs are like five grandmas, so this side has like six grandmas. (Terry points to her drawing.) This side will win because . . . see, the other side with the two grandmas and a kangaroo is like two grandmas and two more grandmas and a frog . . . 'cause the kangaroo is with the frog and two more grandmas. Look, at my picture.

Ms. Wilson: Group, please pay attention to Terry's solution. Terry reasoned out the problem through visual representations of the characters. She has an alternative approach to solve the match with visual substitution, and her argument that the frogs and grandma might win has merit.

Ms. Wilson stepped into this group because she had detected that a status problem was operating. In this academically heterogeneous classroom, unequal participation rates during groupwork lead to unequal learning. Students like Kiante and Alicia are thriving, while students like Terry might be losing ground. Fortunately, three components necessary to address the status problem are operating in Ms. Wilson's classroom: (*a*) a management system that frees Ms. Wilson from directly supervising students, (*b*) a multiple-abilities curriculum that fosters the development of higher-order thinking skills, and (*c*) specific attempts made by Ms. Wilson to treat the status problem. These components form the three legs of the Complex Instruction stool. In the following sections of this chapter, we describe these three components and address the ways in which school-level support and staff development enhance the implementation of Complex Instruction.

TREATING STATUS PROBLEMS IN COMPLEX INSTRUCTION

Ms. Wilson viewed cooperative learning as an appropriate and promising instructional strategy for her academically and linguistically diverse classrooms. When students are involved in cooperative learning, they interact and use one another as resources. Those who do not read or speak the language of instruction may get help from their peers. They have greater access to understanding than they might during traditional teacher-directed instruction. Peer interaction increases interest and engagement in the task and provides a strong potential for learning.

These assertions, however, mask an instructional dilemma inherent in groupwork: that of unequal influence on, and participation in, the task, a dilemma illustrated in the case of Terry. This problem is rooted in the students' perceptions of themselves and each other.

Expectation states theory (Berger, Cohen, & Zelditch, 1972) describes how status characteristics come to affect interaction and influence in group situations. A status characteristic is an agreed-upon social ranking where everyone feels that it is better to have a high rank than a low rank. Status characteristics may be diffuse, based upon general social distinctions such as race and gender; or they may be specific, based upon perceived ability relevant to a specific task. Reading ability is an example of a specific status characteristic operating in the classroom.

According to the theory, status characteristics of individuals become a basis for the groups' expectations for competence of the individual. Status problems are the result of differing expectations for competence: low expectations for low-status students, and high expectations for high-status students. These expectations for competence are held by teachers, by classmates, and by the students themselves. Students who lack traditional academic skills or proficiency in the language of instruction or who are social isolates are too often perceived as low-status students. When low-status students are in groups, they barely participate, are often ignored, and frequently are not given a share of the materials or a turn at the activity. When this occurs, we recognize a status problem (Cohen, 1986, chap. 3).

When students are given a new cooperative task, these expectations are activated and become self-fulfilling even if the task does not require traditional academic abilities. Students who are expected to be good at school talk more, have greater access to the materials, and are more influential in group discussions. Their ideas are adopted by the group, often regardless of their quality. Simultaneously, students who are perceived to be poor at schoolwork or who are unpopular are given few opportunities to participate, and their ideas are poorly evaluated and often ignored. Had Ms. Wilson not stepped in, the students in Terry's group would not have benefitted from Terry's insights. Sometimes, low-status students are literally "elbowed out"; they can't even get their hands on the materials. Their problems are often compounded by frustrated teachers who attribute the off-task behavior of low-status students to lack of motivation.

Status problems can lead to learning problems. Research on Complex Instruction has shown that the rate of interaction in the group is a strong predictor of learning gains. Individuals who test below grade level especially benefit from talking with members of the group. As high-status students interact more in the group, they learn more from the task; as low-status students interact less, they in turn learn less (Cohen, 1984). Paradoxically, in a setting designed to promote equity, the rich get richer while the poor get poorer. Complex Instruction offers two strategies to treat status problems in the classroom: (a) the multiple-abilities status treatment and (b) assigning competence to low-status students.

The Multiple-Abilities Treatment

How can we reap the benefits of cooperative learning while minimizing the problem of unequal access and learning for low-status students? One answer lies in widening our own and the students' conception of what it means to be "smart." The multiple-abilities treatment is grounded in a multiple-abilities curriculum and based on the teacher's public recognition of a wealth of intellectual abilities that are relevant and valued in the classroom and in daily life. For instance, consider some of the numerous abilities needed to complete the Mathematical Tug-of-War task: organizing information, using and understanding multiple representations of a mathematical situation, and justifying an argument.

Rather than assuming that all students can be ranked along a single dimension of ability, we need instead to consider different kinds of intellectual ability. Students will have different strengths and weaknesses among these multiple abilities. For example, the highly verbal student may have difficulty with tasks that require spatial and visual ability. Likewise, the student who scores poorly on vocabulary tests may be an astute scientific observer. This view of ability is compatible with recent work in psychology that suggests that intelligence is multidimensional (Gardner, 1983; Sternberg, 1985).

In Complex Instruction, a multiple-abilities treatment typically occurs during orientation to the day's work in groups. The teacher starts by naming the different skills and abilities necessary for successful completion of an activity and then establishes the link or relevance of these abilities to the task. Depending on the task, she or he might discuss such specific visual spatial abilities as diagramming mathematical concepts, expressing an idea as a cartoon, or creating a three-dimensional model. A challenging multiple-abilities task calls for reasoning abilities such as hypothesizing, estimating, analyzing problems logically, figuring out how something works mechanically, or translating a musical or visual message into words. In an effective multiple-abilities treatment, students become convinced that the task in which they are about to engage is fundamentally different from traditional classroom tasks because it relies on many different kinds of intellectual abilities.

The next goal is to create a mixed set of expectations for each student approaching the task. By this we mean explicitly telling the students, "No one will have all the abilities necessary to do this task, but everyone will have some of the abilities." Herein lies the premise of Complex Instruction: Each individual brings valuable and different abilities to the task. All are needed to succeed. This message is not a simplistic "Cooperate because it is the nice thing to do." Rather, it is "Cooperate because you need each other."

When successful, the multiple-abilities treatment leaves each student thinking, "I may not have all the abilities, nobody does, but I certainly have some of them. I have something to contribute to this task." The teacher can raise new expectations for the competence of low-status students and help students to understand that, like all human beings, high-status students have their strengths and weaknesses as well.

Assigning Competence to Low-Status Students

Unfortunately, the status order in the classroom is deeply ingrained. Even with the multiple-abilities treatment, it is difficult to change students' notions about who is competent and who is expected to fail. While research has shown that a multiple-abilities orientation can help to equalize interaction between high- and low-status students (Cohen, Lotan, & Catanzarite, 1990), a second treatment shows even stronger potential to boost the participation of low-status students.

Assigning competence is a public statement that specifically recognizes the intellectual contribution different students make to the groupwork task. Teachers can assign competence to any student in the classroom, but we recommend especially focusing attention on low-status students. When Ms. Wilson told the group to listen to Terry because she had reasoned out the problem through visual substitutions, she was assigning competence to Terry.

Assigning competence is a positive evaluation. It relies on the teacher's power as a legitimate source of evaluation. Students are likely to believe the teacher's opinion. In order to change the expectations students hold for themselves and each other, assigning competence must be *public* so that the student's classmates hear it. It is important to remember that we are not just trying to raise one student's self-concept, but are attempting to raise the group's expectations for that student. Assigning competence must be *specific* so that the student and the group know exactly what he or she did well. Finally, it must make the intellectual ability demonstrated by the student *relevant* to the work of the group.

Assigning competence has the potential to increase expectations for competence of low-status students and to increase their rate of interaction. It is strongest when it is made on the spot during groupwork; however, many teachers find it easier to take notes on students' contributions and assign competence later, during wrap-up or orientation the next day.

Assigning competence validates the message of the multiple-abilities orientation. The teacher is, in essence, demonstrating to the students that they each have intellectual abilities that are highly esteemed in society, such as planning, organizing, creating, performing, reasoning, or inventing. She or he does so by specifically tying students' performance in the group to such a valued intellectual ability. For students, the evidence of their expertise is their own performance. It is irrefutable.

Public recognition means that other students know that the teacher thinks that this student is competent in a particular skill or ability. Emphasizing the relevance of this skill or ability to the task will raise expectations even more powerfully. It will make it more likely that the group will talk to that student. When low-status students have access to the interaction, they also have greater access to learning.

TRANSFORMING THE CLASSROOM FOR COMPLEX INSTRUCTION

In Complex Instruction, treatment of status problems takes place in the context of a transformed classroom; there is a special management system, and the curricular materials are designed to enable students to excel using multiple intellectual abilities. This transformation is evident in Ms. Wilson's classroom. Her students used cooperative norms and a set of roles that helped get their job done. In addition, the group was working on a multiple-abilities task that emphasized higher-order thinking.

The Classroom-Management System

Ms. Wilson's class typically has up to six or seven different groups of four or five students, with each group working on a different task simultaneously. Because the tasks are uncertain and open-ended, it becomes necessary to delegate authority to the students. When the teacher delegates authority, students talk with each other to find out what they should be doing and how to solve the challenging problems they have been assigned. Otherwise, the students will constantly run to the teacher for help.

Delegation of authority occurs through (*a*) use of an activity card with instructions for the task and individual reports to be completed by each member of the group, (*b*) the development of a set of cooperative norms guiding student behavior, and (c) a set of procedural roles that helps the group get its work done.

The Activity Card and Individual Report

So that the teacher does not have to go from one group to the next telling each one what to do, she or he transfers her or his authority and assigns tasks through written instructions on an activity card (Figure 6.1). Instructions can be written in English and in other languages used in the classroom; they can include visuals that depict the tasks for those students who have difficulty reading. With an activity card, the students can work on their own to decide what and how they are to do their work. They can use each other as resources. Students also complete an individual report at their learning stations to ensure individual accountability.

Developing Cooperative Norms

As with other models of cooperative learning, Complex Instruction stresses preparation of students for the new behaviors needed for working in small groups. If students come to feel that they ought to behave in these new ways, they will teach, reinforce, and enforce cooperative behaviors with their peers. When this happens, the teacher has successfully developed a new set of norms (written or unwritten rules for how one ought to behave) that will do much to control behavior in desirable ways. The two central norms that Complex Instruction uses as basic rules of the classroom are the following: (a) "You have the right to ask anyone else in your group for assistance," and (b) "You have the duty to assist anyone in your group who asks for help."

Cooperative behaviors do not develop overnight. Before starting group-work, students need to learn these behaviors and to practice them in selected skill-building activities (see Cohen, 1986, chap. 5, for more details). During groupwork, it is essential to observe how well students are doing in cooperative behaviors. They will need feedback and will benefit from discussion on how to use these norms in specific situations. Feedback can be addressed both to individuals and to groups, but it must be specific so that it makes clear to the students which behaviors the teacher saw or failed to see.

Use of Student Roles

Delegation of authority is supported by giving each student a procedural role to play. The most widely used roles are facilitator, materials manager, recorder/reporter, safety officer, and harmonizer. It is important to rotate these roles so that everyone gets a chance to play every role. Each role is designed to help the group function and work together more efficiently. Many of these roles are roles the teacher plays in the whole-class setting. Instead of asking the students "to mind their own business," as in the conventional classroom, in groupwork, we are asking the students to mind each other's business.

The roles selected depend on the age of the student and the nature of the task. However, we always use the facilitator, who sees to it that all get the help they need. Even a second grader can be taught to play this important role successfully. The facilitator makes sure that somebody reads the activity card, that all the group members participate, and that the group turns to the teacher only if no one knows the answer. Through the use of the facilitator role, the group takes responsibility for its own behavior rather than constantly turning to the teacher for assistance and mediation.

The roles are designed to encourage interaction and discussion and to take care of the business of the group. They do not represent a division of labor that permits people to split off from the group to do their job. For example, the reporters are directed to discuss their report with the group rather than prepare it individually.

It is not enough to assign roles; roles must be developed at all grade levels. To do so, teachers discuss with their students effective strategies for acting out these roles, insist that students play their roles, and try not to let the most dominant students take away roles (such as facilitator or reporter) from the quiet students.

Role of the Teacher

The teacher's role changes dramatically when students are engaged in groupwork. One of her or his major functions is to encourage and stimulate student interaction concerning the task. According to research on Complex Instruction, the more that students talk and work together, the more they learn (Cohen, Lotan, & Leechor, 1989). Therefore, teachers will want to see as many students as possible at any given moment engaged in task-related discussion while at the learning stations. Based on data from numerous classrooms, we found that it is highly desirable to have more than 35% of the students interact at any one time.

How are students persuaded to interact? Part of this job is done by intrinsically interesting, engaging, and rich tasks that require students to exchange ideas and materials. Having a facilitator also helps to foster interaction. Just as important, the teacher avoids hovering over the groups and giving them detailed directions and extensive information while they are at work. Our research has shown that direct instruction through verbal presentations and directions by the teacher cuts down on the amount of students' talking and working together, and thus on favorable learning outcomes. Recall how Ms. Wilson carefully took stock of the Tug-of-War group before she stepped in, and while in the group, she stayed the minimum time, stimulating the group to interact and to retain intellectual ownership of the problem.

Teachers who use this management system often say to us, "I feel like

I've been done out of a job. The students do very well without me." Not exactly. This management system frees the teacher to play a more sophisticated instructional role: First, while students are at learning stations, she or he devotes time to asking higher-order questions, extending the group's thinking on its activities, and taking care of status problems. Second, during orientation and wrap-up (at the beginning and end of the lesson), the teacher provides information, summarizes, makes connections, and frames the overall lesson.

Delegating authority does not mean giving up control of the classroom. In Complex Instruction, we insist on both group and individual accountability. The group is responsible for seeing to it that its members remain engaged and complete their work. Individuals are held accountable to play their roles and to complete an individual report based on the group's discussion, experiment, or discovery. The individual reports provide each student an opportunity to demonstrate what he or she has learned in the activity.

Designing Curriculum for Complex Instruction

In Complex Instruction classrooms, promoting equal access to information and fostering higher-order thinking is paramount. To do so requires specialized curricula. We use the following criteria when creating curricula for groupwork or when adapting existing materials to follow the Complex Instruction model: (a) we organize activities around a central concept or "big idea," (b) activities are open-ended and uncertain, and (c) we ensure that students use multiple intellectual abilities to complete tasks.

Thematic Organization of Units

To foster conceptual understanding of content material, we organize Complex Instruction units around a central concept, theme, or "big idea." Students encounter this concept or idea in different contexts; thus they have multiple opportunities to grapple with the material. When we are deciding on the conceptual content of a unit, we draw upon the fundamental principles and methods of a discipline. For instance, a seventh-grade unit on the Reformation is organized around the question often debated in history and political science, "How do you challenge the authority of an institution?" Students rotate through different group activities that address this question. One activity focuses on the role art and political cartoons play in forming and reforming public opinion; one on the role individuals, like Martin Luther, play in catalyzing change; and another on the role the printing press or the media play in spreading ideas. Student learning goes well beyond the facts and dates of the Reformation; indeed, students learn how a combination of factors reshape people's ideas and lead them to seek reform. Studying this question as it applies to the specific situation of the

Reformation prepares students both to ask and to respond thoughtfully to the same issue as it applies in other situations, such as the American Revolution or the 1989 student rebellion in China.

Uncertain or Open-ended Tasks

In Complex Instruction, learning tasks are open-ended in two ways: in their solution as well as in the process by which students arrive at the solution. For example, for the Tug-of-War task, the number of legitimate solutions is virtually unlimited. With respect to process, each group decides which and how many characters to include and how to structure an unequal match. There is no answer sheet here for the teacher.

Open-ended and inherently uncertain tasks increase the need for interaction since students draw upon each other's expertise and repertoire of problem-solving strategies. Given the intellectual heterogeneity of the students in the group, these repertoires are rich and varied. When working with Complex Instruction activities, we encourage students to explore alternative solutions, communicate their thoughts effectively, justify their arguments, and examine issues from different perspectives. These are the processes that contribute to the development of higher-order thinking and to other desired outcomes of learning.

A good example of an open-ended task is an activity found in *Finding Out/Descubrimiento* (DeAvila & Duncan, 1982), an English-Spanish math and science curriculum for the elementary grades[2]. To learn about measurement, students are asked first to estimate and then to measure different body parts of a big inflatable dinosaur. The most interesting conversations occur when second graders figure out where exactly the waist of a dinosaur is. Wouldn't a belly button be the irrefutable indicator? Furthermore, how does one measure something round with nothing but a ruler and some yarn?

Multiple Abilities

Multiple-abilities tasks are a necessary condition for successful status treatments. For example, in our integrated social studies and language arts unit for middle grades "How do historians know about the Crusades?" we have attempted to incorporate many intellectual abilities. Students rotate among different tasks to learn how historians examine texts, artifacts, and the music and art of the period to make sense of historical events. In the first type of task, students examine visual representations of historical artifacts: photos and a floor plan of the ruins of a castle built by the Crusaders in Syria (see Figure 6.1). Students analyze the pictures, hypothesize about the architectural strengths and weaknesses of the castle, and speculate why the Crusaders might have chosen that particular location. Next, the students design and build a three-dimensional model of a fortress that will protect their group from enemy invaders. Designing this

Figure 6.1
Activity Card

```
                                            Unit:  CRUSADES


             HOW DO HISTORIANS KNOW ABOUT THE CRUSADES?

                           Activity 1:
            Crusader Castle, Crac des Chevaliers, Syria, 12 C
                          Activity Card

    Historians often turn to art, architecture, and craftwork of
    the period they are studying for clues about how people
    lived and what they wanted to remember.

    As a team, look carefully at the photographs of Crac des
    Chevaliers and discuss the questions below.

        1.   Why would the Crusaders build a castle?

        2.   What does the architecture of this castle (the
             floor plan and interior/exterior structures) tell
             you about how warfare was conducted in the
             medieval times?

        3.   If you lived inside this castle, how would you
             defend it against enemy attacks?

        4.   If you were an enemy invader, how would you plan
             your attack of this castle?

        5.   What do you think were the roles of men and women
             inside the castle?  What were the roles of
             children?

                       *         *         *


    Design and build a castle or a fortress to protect your
    group from adverse forces.  Present your castle to the
    class.

    Copyright:  Program for Complex Instruction/Stanford University School of Education
```

model requires careful planning, mechanical ingenuity, and translating a two-dimensional sketch into a three-dimensional model, each an intellectual ability.

In the second type of task, students listen to medieval ballads, identify musical instruments, and describe the mood and the message of the songs. Among the intellectual abilities students use in these tasks are hearing or creating melodies and rhythmic patterns, appreciating musical expressions, and understanding how a song's melody and its lyrics play off one another.

The third type of task relies on understanding textual sources such as excerpts from Pope Urban II's speech calling the masses to join the Crusades and eyewitness accounts of the siege of Jerusalem. After thorough analysis of the text, students translate the verbal messages into different media: They create a mural or dramatize the siege from the Muslim point of view. These activities require a host of intellectual abilities: understanding sophisticated texts, detecting sources of bias, being empathetic, relating a single textual passage to the larger scheme of events, and translating the message of the text into nonverbal forms.

TRANSFORMING THE SCHOOL FOR COMPLEX INSTRUCTION

How long does it take to develop expertise in Complex Instruction? A long time. We do not see staff development as presenting a one- or two-day workshop and then abandoning teachers to the complexities of working within a radically different classroom structure. We envision a learning process involving the development of conceptual understanding, practice in applying new knowledge, and ongoing feedback and support at the school.

Staff Development

Groupwork is an instructional context that asks as much problem solving, intellectual flexibility, and creativity from the teacher as it does from the students. A teacher's conceptual understanding of the theory and principles underlying Complex Instruction is related to the quality of implementation in the classroom. Teachers who understand why they are delegating authority to the groups or how status problems come to affect interaction and learning are able to solve problems and adapt instructional strategies to meet the needs of their students. What kind of staff development prepares the teacher for this process?

Preparation for employing Complex Instruction involves participation in a yearlong program that provides teachers with the theoretical understanding and practical experience necessary to maintain high-quality implementation. Teachers attend a two-week summer seminar. During the first week, teachers learn the theory and apply its principles to classroom practice. They analyze vignettes of classroom situations, solve problems concerning appropriate teacher interventions in dysfunctional groups, and work in teams to study the curriculum and prepare to teach a lesson. During the second week, teachers participate in a practicum. They present a Complex Instruction lesson to a class of school-aged students. Systematic observations of student behaviors are made, along with the quality of teacher-student interaction. Videotapes of the lessons provide specific feedback to the teachers. They also observe one another during the practicum and learn how to use observation instruments during groupwork.

During the school year, we follow the teachers into their classrooms to provide feedback. A sound feedback process is built on an adequate sample of observations and grounded in clear criteria and standards. These criteria and standards are derived from the theoretical base that underlies Complex Instruction. At least three observations serve as the basis for calculating the average rates of students who talk and work together at learning centers and the types of teacher interaction we observe. The percentage of the teacher's speech acts that are focused on group management, questioning, and treating status is also calculated. These data are used to construct bar charts to provide a visual and specific framework that allows teachers to step back and assess their lessons. For example, if the bar chart shows that the average rate of talking and working together is less than 35%, or that most of the teacher's speech acts are focused around getting the students through the task, we work with the teacher, discussing strategies for using the system of norms and roles more effectively. We strive for three feedback meetings per teacher because there is evidence to the effect that the number of such meetings is positively related to the development of teachers' conceptual understanding as well as to the quality of classroom implementation.

Teachers return to Stanford for two days midyear. On the first day, we go into more depth on the treatment of status problems, probably the most challenging component of Complex Instruction. In small groups, teachers reflect on the status structure in their own classrooms and practice using status treatments. Another full day is devoted to curriculum adaptation and development, allowing teachers to capitalize on their subject-matter expertise and expand their use of Complex Instruction.

School-Level Support for Complex Instruction

Our collective experience, supported by the extensive research we have conducted in elementary schools, has taught us that teachers and administrators must collaborate to support successful implementation of Complex Instruction. Restructuring the classroom demands school-level support.

The implementation of multiple-abilities curricula requires resources beyond the classroom. For example, manipulatives are central to the hands-on, multimedia activities described earlier. Buying, storing, and replacing consumable materials necessitates allocation and coordination of resources such as staff time and money. It is unlikely that an isolated teacher will be able to collect and organize the materials alone. An instructional assistant, a resource teacher, or a team of teachers needs to be given time to work on this task. Some principals have set aside a room exclusively for storing materials and have allocated staff time for coordination and maintenance of the materials.

When implementing Complex Instruction, teachers, like their students, benefit when they talk and work together. Team meetings provide teachers with an opportunity to exchange information and ideas about specific units or activities. For example, teachers' discussions range from practical concerns about safety to conceptual topics such as mainstreaming special-education students or developing a science orientation to the lesson. Repeatedly, teachers have reported to us that having opportunities to discuss such issues with colleagues is extremely helpful. The Meeting Tamer, a simple instrument used to structure meetings, is often used by teachers to keep themselves on task and to use meeting time efficiently. We also found that when teachers had the opportunity to visit each other's classrooms and provide systematic feedback to one another, the quality of implementation was maintained over time.

Teacher collaboration differs somewhat between elementary and secondary schools. For example, subject specialization at the secondary level suggests that teachers who implement Complex Instruction collaborate at three different levels: within their subject areas, at the grade level, and in schoolwide teams.

Successful principals also need to buffer teachers from competing demands, such as additional innovative programs that may jeopardize successful implementation of Complex Instruction. Some principals have resolved this dilemma by making Complex Instruction a schoolwide priority and by working closely with teachers. When principals send a clear message to teachers that they expect them to implement Complex Instruction, teachers implement more frequently and maintain a higher quality of implementation. With sufficient staff development and school-level support, the Complex Instruction model of cooperative learning can realize its goals.

NOTES

1. A Mathematical Tug-of-War comes from a Complex Instruction unit called Getting Started; it has been adapted from an activity by the same name created by Marilyn Burns.

2. This curriculum is commercially available from the Santillana Publishing Company.

REFERENCES

Berger, J., Cohen, B. P., & Zelditch, M. (1972). Status characteristics and social interaction. *American Sociological Review*, 37, 241–255.

Cohen, E. G. (1984). Talking and working together: Status, interaction, and learning. In P. Peterson, L. C. Wilkinson, & M. Hallinan (Eds.), *The social context of instruction: Group organization and group processes.* New York: Academic Press.

Cohen, E. G. (1986). *Designing groupwork: Strategies for the heterogeneous classroom.* New York: Teachers College Press.

Cohen, E. G., Lotan, R. A., & Catanzarite, L. (1990). Treating status problems in the cooperative classroom. In S. Sharan (Ed.), *Cooperative learning: Theory and research* (pp. 205–229). New York: Praeger.

Cohen, E. G., Lotan, R. A., & Leechor, C. (1989). Can classrooms learn? *Sociology of Education, 62,* 75–94.

DeAvila, E. A., & Duncan, S. (1982). *Finding out/Descubrimiento.* San Rafael, CA: Linguametrics Group.

Gardner, H. (1983). *Frames of mind.* New York: Basic Books.

Sternberg, R. J. (1985). *Beyond IQ: A triarchic theory of human intelligence.* Cambridge: Cambridge University Press.

7

Group Investigation in the Cooperative Classroom

Yael Sharan and Shlomo Sharan

Educators are seeking ways to reduce the hegemony of recitation-presentation teaching methods based on "a series of unrelated teacher questions that require convergent factual answers and student display of (presumably) known information" (Tharp & Gallimore, 1988, p. 14). Cooperative learning methods provide an alternative to this model of teaching. They strive to create a setting responsive to students' questions and productions and offer a variety of ways of increasing active student participation in the learning process. Some cooperative learning methods call for more teacher direction than others, but all of them enable students to interact in varying degrees and talk about what they think, know, and feel about what they are learning. In addition, when students study together in small groups, they help each other and, at the same time, develop self-direction and responsibility for their learning.

Incorporating cooperative learning methods in their instructional repertoire requires teachers to change their traditional roles as transmitters of information. As they become more confident in the role of guiding and facilitating cooperative learning, teachers adopt more diverse and complex cooperative procedures. When they feel that their students are used to working together to achieve academic goals, they can introduce Group Investigation. Investigating in groups calls for students to use all the interpersonal and study skills acquired in other cooperative learning methods and to apply them to the planning of specific learning goals. Students also cooperate in carrying out their investigation and in planning how to integrate and present their findings, and, together with the teacher, they collaborate in evaluating their academic and interpersonal efforts (Joyce &

Weil, 1986; Sharan & Hertz-Lazarowitz, 1980; Sharan & Sharan, 1992; Thelen, 1981).

In this chapter, we describe the Group Investigation model of cooperative learning and show how teachers and students can implement it successfully in their classrooms. To understand the goals and procedures of this model, we begin by exploring the four basic components that serve as its foundation.

FOUR BASIC FEATURES OF GROUP INVESTIGATION

The unique character of Group Investigation lies in the integration of four basic features: investigation, interaction, interpretation, and intrinsic motivation (Sharan & Sharan, 1992). We elaborate on each of them in order to highlight their respective contributions to this model of cooperative learning, even though in practice they do not appear separately or sequentially.

Investigation

Investigation, the first of the four components of Group Investigation, refers to the general orientation toward learning adopted by the teacher and the students. When the classroom is carrying out a Group Investigation project, it becomes an "inquiring community," and each student is an investigator who coordinates his or her inquiry with the class's common purpose. Thus, in Thelen's (1981) words, the class is both an inquiring community and a community of inquirers.

The investigation begins when the teacher poses a challenging, multifaceted problem to the class. In the course of their search for answers to the problem, students construct the knowledge they acquire, rather than having it presented to them prepackaged by the teacher. The process of investigation emphasizes students' initiative, as evidenced by the questions they pose, by the sources they find, and by the answers they formulate. Students seek out information and ideas in cooperation with their peers and combine it with the opinions, information, ideas, interests, and experiences that each one brings to the task. Together they forge their information and ideas into new knowledge through a process of interpretation, as we shall see in the next section.

Group Investigation has its roots in John Dewey's philosophy of education (Archambault, 1974; Sharan, 1990; Sharan & Sharan, 1992). Dewey believed that meaningful learning proceeds through the steps of scientific inquiry, whereby students experience how knowledge is generated. This method is applicable to almost all branches of human knowledge and is not limited to those subjects typically labeled "science." In Dewey's view, investigation of any subject can incorporate the essential features of the scientific method and thus can educate students in the spirit and method of scientific inquiry. Teachers and students give voice to this idea when they report that Group Investigation helps students "learn how to learn."

Following Dewey, Thelen (1981) presented a teaching model that creates an actively inquiring classroom. The model is based on six stages, or "activities," selected so that students investigate issues that are of interest to them as individuals and as members of society, and that are, at the same time, compatible with the class's common purpose. Thelen knew well that teachers and students who participate in group work have to prepare for this role and learn basic principles of how to function as members of a small investigating group. The patterns of interaction among peers, as well as among students and teachers, are crucial to the successful implementation of Group Investigation.

Interaction

As noted earlier, Group Investigation takes place in a classroom that is organized as an inquiring community, providing a social context for learning. Contact, talk, mutual assistance, and support among students in small groups are part and parcel of the process of Group Investigation. At each stage of the investigation, students have ample opportunities for interaction: They discuss the plan of their inquiry; they examine a variety of sources and exchange ideas and information; they decide together how to summarize and integrate their findings; and they plan how to present their findings to their classmates.

Effective interaction in small groups requires the acquisition of basic teamwork and discussion skills. To this end, Group Investigation (together with other cooperative learning methods) benefits from the basic principles and procedures for the design and management of task-oriented groups, as developed by Kurt Lewin and his followers in the group dynamics movement (Schmuck & Schmuck, 1992). Over the years, cooperative learning methods have generated and refined a large repertoire of exercises and activities that enable students to acquire and practice effective interaction in groups (Graves & Graves, 1990; Kagan, 1992).

Interaction among students is essential to Group Investigation. It is the vehicle by which students encourage one another, elaborate on one another's ideas, help each other focus their attention on the task, and even confront one another's ideas with opposing points of view. Intellectual and social interaction are the means by which students rework their personal knowledge in light of the new knowledge gathered by the group in the course of the investigation (Thelen, 1981). Extensive classroom-based research documents how the interaction that takes place throughout a Group Investigation project effectively fosters positive interethnic relations, perceptions, and attitudes in the heterogeneous classroom (Sharan & Sharan, 1992).

Interpretation

While students conduct their inquiry individually, in pairs, and in small groups, they gather a great deal of information from a variety of sources. At regular intervals they meet with other members of their group to exchange information and ideas. Together they attempt to make sense of what their inquiry has yielded. Interpretation of their combined findings is a process of negotiation between each student's personal knowledge and the new knowledge acquired, and between each student and the ideas and information contributed by other members of the group. In this context, interpretation is a social-intellectual process par excellence.

Facilitating the process of interpretation through group interaction is consistent with Dewey's and Thelen's view of education, as well as with the constructivist approach to cognition, as developed by Piaget and his followers (Sigel & Cocking, 1977). This approach to understanding human thought processes asserts that individuals build their notions of reality out of their experiences, feelings, and information, and that these constructions form knowledge. Group Investigation provides students with the opportunity to interact with others who have investigated different aspects of the same general topic, and who contribute different perspectives on that topic. The cooperative interpretation of information gathered by group members promotes their ability to organize, confirm, and consolidate their findings and thus to make sense of them.

Intrinsic Motivation

Group Investigation motivates students to take an active role in determining what and how they will learn. It invites them to make individual and joint choices and decisions based on the questions they ask and the problems they seek to investigate. The guidelines they set are the ones they act upon, so that they have a great deal of control over their learning. For a while they share in initiating events in their lives in school and are therefore willing to invest greater effort in learning than when they are constantly told what and how to learn (Sharan & Shaulov, 1990).

By inviting students to relate the problems they set out to investigate to their own curiosity, experiences, and feelings, Group Investigation heightens their personal interest in seeking the information they need. Their investigation draws additional motivating power from their interaction with one another. Many cooperative learning methods are based on shared responsibility and interaction among group members. Group Investigation in particular increases the opportunity to capitalize on the drive and positive interdependence that develop when students study together.

GROUP INVESTIGATION

All four features of Group Investigation—investigation, interaction, interpretation, and intrinsic motivation—are combined in the six stages of the model:

Stage 1: Class determines subtopics and organizes into research groups.

Stage 2: Groups plan their investigations.

Stage 3: Groups carry out their investigations.

Stage 4: Groups plan their presentations.

Stage 5: Groups make their presentations.

Stage 6: Teacher and students evaluate their projects.

How does the learning process unfold in each stage of Group Investigation? How can the teacher integrate the four basic components of Group Investigation while guiding the investigation of the general problem set before the class?

Stage 1: Class Determines Subtopics and Organizes into Research Groups

Presenting the General Problem

The teacher presents the class with a broad, multifaceted problem that has no single right answer. The problem is most often a part of the curriculum, although it may also stem from a timely issue or from the students' interest in a particular topic. It is best to phrase the issue as a problem rather than as a general statement, so as to set the tone for inquiry and somewhat define the scope of the investigation. Another factor to consider when choosing the problem is its relevance to the students' lives in and out of school. Directly or indirectly, the investigation strives to increase the students' ability to understand the world around them.

Variety of Resources

Presenting the general problem does not in and of itself stimulate the students' interest in inquiry. For a week or two before the onset of the investigation, the teacher displays a variety of resource materials and invites the class to examine them. Books, magazines, stamps, pictures, maps, catalogs, slides, videotapes, and newspapers are some of the materials that may be displayed. Perhaps a lecture on the general problem is appropriate, or an exploratory discussion during which basic terms are clarified. Sometimes the teacher will choose to arouse the students' curiosity by taking them to see a particular site, by showing slides or a film, or by conducting a library search.

Employing any or several of these ways of introducing the general problem demonstrates to the students that information is indeed available from many sources at different levels and of different types. Every student should be able to find material appropriate to his or her interests, reading level, and preferred mode of learning. The variety of material is also intended to help students begin to see what is familiar to them about the problem as well as what is unknown to them. On the wall above the area where materials are displayed, the teacher posts one instruction: "Look through all the material. What do you know about the topic? What would you like to know about it?"

Generating Questions

After the initial exploration, students are ready to formulate and select various questions for inquiry. The teacher writes the general problem on the board and invites students to say what they would like to investigate in order to understand it better. Everyone will ask a question if the teacher encourages diverse reactions and accepts all contributions. The cooperative planning of the study questions can proceed in one of three ways (Sharan & Sharan, 1992):

- *Individually:* Each student writes down those questions that he or she would like to investigate. After ten or fifteen minutes, the teacher invites students to tell the class what they wrote and writes each suggestion on the board.

- *Buzz groups:* Students meet in groups of four or five and take turns voicing their ideas about what to investigate. Recorders in each group write down all the questions and then share them with the class, either by writing them on the board or handing their lists to the teacher.

- *Individuals, pairs, quartets:* This procedure allows for each student to think alone as well as to benefit from the exchange of thoughts with others. At each step, students compare their lists of questions and compile a single list. The final list is handed to the teacher.

Determining Subtopics

The next step in this stage is to make all the questions available to the whole class. The questions can be posted on the wall, photocopied and distributed to each student, or written on the board. Now students sort the questions into categories. This can be done by adapting one of the three methods outlined in the section on generating questions. The categories the class determines become the subtopics for separate groups to investigate.

Forming Interest Groups

The titles of the subtopics are displayed before the class and present tangible evidence of their planning. Now each student signs up to investigate the subtopic that best reflects his or her interest. Groups are generally formed on the basis of common interest in a specific subtopic. The teacher may wish to limit the number of students in a group to four or five. If a large number of students sign up for one particular subtopic, it is possible to form two or three groups that will investigate it. If the subsequent investigation reflects the combined interests and abilities of all group members, then each group will produce a unique product.

The learning process and the teacher's role in stage 1 are summarized as follows:

Learning Process	**Teacher's Role**
Exploring options	Leading exploratory discussions
Connecting personal knowledge to the problem	Providing initial materials
	Facilitating awareness of interest in problem
Generating questions	
Sorting questions	Coordinating organization of investigation
Determining subtopics	
Choosing subtopic for investigation	

Stage 2: Groups Plan Their Investigations

Students join their respective research groups and focus their attention on the cooperative planning of the questions they will seek to answer. Group members have three main responsibilities:

1. To choose the questions they will seek to answer.
2. To determine the resources they need.
3. To divide the work and assign roles.

Group members discuss their ideas, interests, and views about the scope of their joint inquiry. They use the list of questions generated by the class as their base and choose those questions they feel best reflect their specific interests in the subtopic. As their planning proceeds, they add a few questions and reject a few, all the while clarifying what it is they want to investigate.

Cooperative planning at this stage enables each student to choose the method of investigation that best suits him or her. One may prefer to interview people; another may enjoy reading reference material; another may feel most comfortable with visual material. Some students may feel that they learn best when they build something, draw diagrams, or see for themselves the actual context of the problem. In the course of their planning discussions, groups take into account their members' varied tendencies and preferences and, accordingly, divide the parts of the investigation among themselves.

The Teacher's role

The teacher circulates among the groups and offers help to those who need it. Members of one group may be unhappy with their original plan. Instead of insisting that they stick to a plan that is uninteresting to them, the teacher discusses alternatives and helps them redirect their goal. Another group may have planned to tackle too many questions, and another, too few. Again, the teacher can help group members formulate more realistic plans.

It is also the teacher's responsibility to help groups choose appropriate resources (see the section on preparing for a Group Investigation project later in this chapter). Perhaps the teacher knows of someone who can meet with a group and provide information or a point of view not available in books. Or maybe the teacher will suggest an article or book not ordinarily accessible to group members. The teacher's guidance in choosing material is especially necessary for slow readers and for students for whom English is a second language (Olsen, 1992).

The interaction among students at this stage determines the choices and decisions that shape their investigation. The more practice students have in planning their investigation, the more it will reflect the unique interests and choices of group members. A class's first attempt at Group Investigation may yield very few questions that may hardly seem worthwhile pursuing. It is important, nevertheless, to accept even a small number of questions and use them as the basis for carrying out all the stages of the process. In this way the teacher keeps the implied promise to base the investigation on the students' questions. No doubt they will be encouraged to be more forthcoming when they are given another opportunity to plan an investigation project.

The learning process and the teacher's role in stage 2 may be summarized as follows:

Learning Process	Teacher's Role
Cooperative planning	Helping groups formulate realistic plans
Generating questions	Helping maintain cooperative norms

Learning Process	Teacher's Role
Clarifying thoughts with groupmates	Helping groups locate appropriate resources
Anticipating what they will study	
Choosing relevant sources	
Deciding what to investigate	
Assigning roles	

Stage 3: Groups Carry Out Their Investigations

In this stage, which may last several class periods, each group carries out its plans. Singly or in pairs, group members

- locate information from a variety of sources;
- organize and record the data;
- report their findings to their groupmates;
- discuss and analyze their findings;
- determine if they need more information; and
- interpret and integrate their findings.

Students are encouraged to locate the information they require from as wide a variety of sources as possible: textbooks, experiments, reference books, pamphlets, magazines, maps, stamps, films, videotapes, and other materials. Other sources of information are sites such as museums, historical buildings, and parks, and, of course, experts on the subject.

In some cases, teachers may ask all groups to include a particular chapter or article in their list of sources, or they may suggest that all groups visit a site together or meet with the same expert, despite the differences in subtopics. Sometimes teachers choose to have all groups learn some basic facts about the general topic. A convenient way to do this is to prepare a learning station with the relevant material and have all groups work there in turn.

The questions that groups decided upon in stage 2 guide them as they locate information. In any one period, a variety of investigating activities may be going on simultaneously. Some students may be reading in the classroom or in the school library; others may be conducting an experiment; a few may be viewing a videotape or summarizing data received from an interview; others may be discussing their interpretation of some interim findings, while the teacher meets with yet another group. Students take notes as they gather information, photocopy a few relevant pages, tape an interview, or otherwise record their findings.

Whether students investigate their particular aspect of the subtopic individually or in pairs, they will benefit from discussing the material with other group members. At the beginning or end of each lesson, groups meet to check their work in progress and try to make sense out of all their findings. Because their talk is not limited to the search for a single correct answer, students are less inhibited in their speech and more willing to express themselves than in whole-class discussions. As they discuss their findings, students clarify, expand, and modify new ideas and information and explore their affective and cognitive meaning. Explaining their findings to one another, as well as the reasoning behind their conclusions, facilitates the extension and refinement of the knowledge they acquire (Marzano, 1992).

Sometimes during these discussions students become aware of discrepancies between their respective ways of interpreting material or even between sources. At such times they will have to intensify the examination of their sources and seek ways of solving their dilemma. This might be an appropriate time for the teacher to help the group out by encouraging them to continue to explore their ideas and perhaps restructure their thinking (Sigel & Kelley, 1988; Thelen, 1981). Ongoing discussion and interpretation often lead to new questions that, in turn, call for investigating different resources, conducting new experiments, interviewing additional experts, or locating new information in other ways.

As investigators, students are constantly coordinating their efforts in order to reach their common goal. Each group member becomes the group's "expert" on a particular aspect of its subtopic and contributes his or her special knowledge to the group. Students interpret the findings individually as well as by discussing them with other members of their group. If the investigation lasts more than a week, the teacher should convene the class at least once a week to hear each group report its progress and discuss how all the investigations are related. At all times the investigation requires that students help one another and respect one another's interests.

As the investigation draws to a close, recorders note their groups' conclusions. Groups carrying out their first investigation, especially in the lower grades, may simply combine each member's answers to the questions he or she investigated. After some experience, students become more adept at integrating their findings into a summary statement. They weigh their respective findings in terms of the light they shed on the problem they set out to investigate. Together they formulate a statement that represents all the answers they discovered and the ideas they had about their topic of investigation.

The learning process and the teacher's role in stage 3 are summarized as follows:

Learning Process	Teacher's Role
Locating information from a variety of sources	Helping with study skills
	Helping to explore sources
Comparing and evaluating relevance of sources	Helping to find new connections between sources
Explaining, expanding, and refining knowledge and generalizing information	Helping to maintain norms of cooperative interaction
Formulating answers to questions	

Stage 4: Groups Plan Their Presentations

Group members have been telling one another all along about their work, what they did or did not understand, and what they find relevant to their common subtopic. Now they begin to plan how to teach their classmates the essence of what they have learned. In this stage, groups have to decide which of their findings to share with the class and how to present their findings to the class.

The main purpose of the presentation is to show the class what the group considers to be the main idea of its findings. In order to do so, the group members integrate all the parts of their investigation and plan a presentation that will be both instructive and appealing to the rest of the class. Now students ask themselves new questions: Of all the answers they found, which are the most significant? Which answers are most related to the subtopics investigated by other groups? The teacher, who has been constantly observing the groups at work, will know which groups need help in determining the main idea of their inquiry.

After they have decided what they will present to the class, groups decide how to present their ideas. Presentations can be made in one of many forms: a model, an exhibit, a dramatic skit, role play, a written report, a slide show, a quiz, or a learning station, just to name a few. In addition, groups prepare handouts that list their resources and present the most salient information they have gathered. This is an easy way of sharing basic facts and figures with the class. Since all groups' subtopics are related, there may be some overlapping in the list of resources or even in some of the basic data.

The following suggestions serve as helpful guidelines to groups when they plan their presentations:

• Emphasize the main ideas and conclusions of the inquiry.
• Make sure everyone in the group takes an active part in the presentation.
• Set and observe time limits for the duration of the presentation.

- Plan to involve classmates from the "audience" as much as possible by giving them roles to perform or otherwise having them be active during the presentation.
- Allow time for questions.
- Make sure all necessary equipment and materials are available.

When the teacher notes that most groups are nearing the end of their investigations, he or she convenes the steering committee, whose members were chosen in stage 2. The committee hears each group's plan for its report. With the teacher's guidance, committee members make sure that the ideas for presentations are varied and clear and can indeed be carried out. The teacher writes down each group's requests for special materials and coordinates the time schedule for presentations.

In this stage, the learning process and the teacher's role are as follows:

Learning Process	**Teacher's Role**
Identifying main idea of findings	Coordinating groups' plans
Explaining, comparing, evaluating findings	Meeting with steering committee
	Assisting in obtaining material
Connecting findings to the general problem	Making sure that all group members participate
Deciding how to present findings	

Stage 5: Groups Make Their Presentations

The teacher posts the schedule of presentations so that each group knows when its turn will come. During the presentations, which generally require two class periods to complete, the class is reconvened as "a group of groups," as each group sheds its specific light on the class's common concern.

While one group presents the essence of its findings, the rest are a receptive audience. Each group presents the one aspect of the general problem it knows best and simultaneously learns of other facets of the same problem.

Before the presentations begin, the teacher and students collaborate in preparing an evaluation sheet, which the class fills out as the presentations take place. The questions for evaluation help students reflect on the clarity, appeal, and relevance of the presentations. They refer to the content of the presentation as well as to the way it is organized. The following are a few suggestions:

Did you understand the main idea of the presentation?

Was each group member included?

Do you feel the group used its resources well?
What did you like best about the presentation?

The students' answers to these questions provide the presenters with instant reactions to their efforts.

Presenting before an audience may cause some students to be hesitant and self-conscious. They now have to take into account the interests of the larger group, which requires a more organized presentation of ideas than did small-group discussions. The teacher should make sure that presenters are comfortable with their role as "teachers" and that students in the audience do not become unduly critical. Rules for conducting the short discussion after each presentation should be established beforehand.

To sum up the presentations, the teacher should lead the class in a discussion that centers on how all subtopics combine to illuminate the general problem the class set out to investigate. Students' comments during this discussion will indicate the extent to which they connect what they heard and saw with their own subtopics. The students' reactions to the presentations and to the summing-up discussion are part of the evaluation process, which is the final stage of the Group Investigation project.

The learning process and the teacher's role in stage 5 are as follows:

Learning Process	Teacher's Role
Demonstrating meaningful use of knowledge	Coordinating groups' presentations
Evaluating the clarity, appeal, and relevance of other presentations	Leading discussions of students' comments
Making new connections between subtopics	Establishing rules for making comments
	Leading summing-up discussion
	Pointing out connections between subtopics

Stage 6: Teacher and Students Evaluate Their Projects

Evaluation of Group Investigation focuses on the knowledge acquired in the course of the project, as well as on the individual and group experience of investigating. Students and teachers can collaborate in the construction of a test that assesses students' understanding of the main ideas of their findings as well as of newly acquired factual knowledge. One way of doing this is to have each group submit two or three questions based on the main ideas of the outcome of its inquiry. In a class of six groups, for example, the test might consist of at least twelve questions. Each student answers ten questions, excluding those submitted by his or her group. The class is given a week or so to prepare, during which they read the various summaries and other sources groups recommend.

The teacher may wish to add questions that assess the recall and understanding of specific facts and terms germane to the general problem. The teacher should also evaluate how students integrate all the information they encountered in their search for answers. One way of assessing this is to pose questions that call for students to explain what causes a particular phenomenon or event.

Students should also be asked to demonstrate their ability to draw conclusions from their inquiry and to apply their newly acquired knowledge to related problems and situations. Although teachers can tap these abilities during the frequent meetings they have with students in the course of the investigation, there is room for more deliberate evaluation of these higher-level thinking skills. Specific questions that assess these skills may be part of the test that individuals take. They may also be less formally evaluated by a class assignment that integrates the various parts of the investigation project. For example, the class may publish a newspaper that includes all the group summaries as well as new material written specifically for the newspaper. An editorial board made up of a representative of each group, together with the teacher, evaluates the material. Another such assignment is an essay, which calls for individual students to demonstrate what they learned about the general problem and to reflect on the personal significance of their learning.

Throughout the investigation the teacher has many opportunities to observe students' academic performance, cooperative behaviors, and level of motivation. Students do not have to wait until after they have finished in order to find out how well they are doing or what problems they have. As the teacher circulates among the groups, he or she can form reliable judgments about the extent to which students understand and utilize the various sources, and about the way groups work together. The teacher is always there to answer questions, to acknowledge and encourage students' efforts, and to remind them of the norms of cooperative behavior.

The learning process in stage 6 sustains the skills students employed in all previous stages. They continue to make decisions about their learning; they compare, analyze, explain, and interpret ideas and information. Specifically, the learning process and the teacher's role in stage 6 are as follows:

Learning Process	Teacher's Role
Evaluating main ideas of outcome of inquiry	Evaluating understanding of main ideas
Evaluating factual knowledge	Evaluating knowledge of new facts and terms

Learning Process	Teacher's Role
Integrating all groups' findings	Evaluating integration of all groups' findings
Reflecting on performance as investigators and as group members	Facilitating students' reflection on process and content of investigation

PREPARING FOR A GROUP INVESTIGATION PROJECT

By and large, it is the teacher who initiates the Group Investigation project, determines its duration, and provides most of the resource materials. In the course of the investigation, the teacher coordinates and facilitates the learning process as well as the social process. He or she guides the students in carrying out all phases of their inquiry and, at the same time, weighs how much help each group needs in maintaining effective interaction among its members. Advance planning for this complex role includes the following (Miel, 1952):

* Assessing students' ability to plan and study together
* Choosing the problem for investigation
* Thinking through possible questions about the problem
* Locating resource material

Assessing Students' Ability to Plan and Study Together

Before undertaking a Group Investigation project, teachers should design short-term cooperative learning tasks that provide students with the necessary practice in participating in group discussions, in rotating group-management roles, in cooperative planning, and in processing their cognitive and affective experiences. Observing students as they carry out short-term learning tasks enables the teacher to assess their ability to plan and study together. The teacher will see how students conduct group discussions and how they help each other while studying together. He or she can also gauge how comfortable they might feel with the diversity of interests and attitudes brought out in the course of a Group Investigation project. These observations provide teachers with information that helps them determine how long the project should be and how much responsibility to give students for determining the content and process of their inquiry.

Choosing the Problem for Investigation

The teacher should choose a general problem that is both challenging and stimulating and invites genuine inquiry. A suitable problem is one that will lead to multifaceted inquiry by a variety of means, using a variety of sources that contribute different perspectives. The general problem is often part of the curriculum, or it may originate in a timely issue. Regardless of its origin, the general problem should have some implications for students' life in school and in society at large (Huhtala & Coughlin, 1991; Sharan & Sharan, 1993; Thelen, 1981).

Thinking Through Possible Questions for Inquiry

After the teacher has chosen the general problem, the next step is to think through the central issues it involves. As the teacher scans a wide range of sources and talks about the problem with experts or colleagues, he or she becomes aware of what is entailed in investigating the various facets of the problem. It is helpful to actually list the questions that come to mind. Time spent in this type of exploration will make it easier for the teacher to help the students see how their questions are connected to the key concepts of the general problem.

Locating Resource Material

While the teacher thinks through the possible questions that the general problem stimulates, he or she searches for appropriate resources in the class's textbooks, in the school and public libraries, and in various institutions and sites. Whenever possible, the teacher should visit one of the sites and discuss the problem with one or more experts. Before the project begins, the teacher brings a variety of materials to the class so as to arouse the students' interest in the topic and demonstrate its diversity.

Extensive preparation for a Group Investigation project obviously deepens the teacher's appreciation of the subject. It provides him or her with a broad base for facilitating the class's inquiry. As a result, the teacher may not be able to answer every question, and indeed that is not his or her responsibility. But the teacher will be equipped to encourage students to ask a wide range of questions, and to point out how the general problem is compatible with individual students' diverse interests. More important, he or she will be able to help students in their search for answers.

The teacher will also be able to focus on the relationship between the various parts of the project. In the course of the investigation, the teacher conducts frequent meetings with separate groups, during which the connection between individual group members' findings can be highlighted. In class discussions, the teacher can emphasize how the groups' various perspectives on the general problem are interrelated. Throughout the investigation, the collaboration among teachers and students combines the emotional involvement, the mental stimulation, and the personal significance of the investigation project to make it an authentic learning experience.

REFERENCES

Archambault, R. (Ed.). (1974). *John Dewey on education: Selected writings*. Chicago: University of Chicago Press.

Graves, N., & Graves, T. (1990). *What is cooperative learning? Tips for teachers and trainers* (2nd ed.). Santa Cruz: Cooperative College of California.

Huhtala, J., & Coughlin, E. (1991). Group Investigation, democracy, and the Middle East: Team teaching English and government. *English Journal, 80*(5), 47–52.

Joyce, B., & Weil, M. (1986). *Models of teaching* (3rd ed.). Englewood Cliffs, NJ: Prentice-Hall.

Kagan, S. (1992). *Cooperative learning: Resources for teachers*. San Juan Capistrano, CA: Resources for Teachers.

Marzano, R. (1992). The many faces of cooperation across the dimensions of learning. In N. Davidson & T. Worsham (Eds.), *Enhancing thinking through cooperative learning* (pp. 7–28). New York: Teachers College Press.

Miel, A. (1952). *Cooperative procedures in learning*. New York: Teachers College Press.

Olsen, R. W-B. (1992). Cooperative learning and social studies. In C. Kessler (Ed.), *Cooperative language learning* (pp. 85–116). Englewood Cliffs, NJ: Prentice Hall Regents.

Schmuck, R., & Schmuck, P. (1992). *Group processes in the classroom* (6th ed.). Dubuque, IA: Wm. C. Brown.

Sharan, S. (Ed.). (1990). *Cooperative learning: Theory and research*. New York: Praeger.

Sharan, S., & Hertz-Lazarowitz, R. (1980). A group investigation method of cooperative learning in the classroom. In S. Sharan, P. Hare, C. Webb, & R. Hertz-Lazarowitz (Eds.), *Cooperation in education* (pp. 14–46). Provo, UT: Brigham Young University Press.

Sharan, S., & Shaulov, A. (1990). Cooperative learning, motivation to learn, and academic achievement. In S. Sharan (Ed.), *Cooperative learning: Theory and research* (pp. 173–202). New York: Praeger.

Sharan, Y., & Sharan, S. (1992). *Expanding cooperative learning through group investigation*. New York: Teachers College Press.

Sharan, Y., & Sharan, S. (1993). What do we want to study? How should we go about it? Group investigation in the cooperative classroom. In R. Stahl (Ed.), *Cooperative learning in the social studies: A handbook*. Menlo Park, CA: Addison-Wesley.

Sigel, I., & Cocking, R. (1977). *Cognitive development from childhood to adolescence: A constructivist perspective*. New York: Holt, Rinehart, & Winston.

Sigel, I., & Kelley, T. (1988). A cognitive developmental approach to questioning.

In J. Dillon (Ed.), *Questioning and discussion: A multidisciplinary study* (pp. 105–134). Norwood, NJ: Ablex.

Tharp, R., & Gallimore, R. (1988). *Rousing minds to life: Teaching, learning, and schooling in social context*. New York: Cambridge University Press.

Thelen, H. (1981). *The classroom society*. London: Croom Helm.

8

The Structural Approach: Six Keys to Cooperative Learning

Spencer Kagan and Miguel Kagan

The six key components of the Structural Approach to Cooperative Learning are explored in this chapter. These six components are (1) structures and related constructs; (2) basic principles; (3) teambuilding and classbuilding; (4) teams; (5) management; and (6) social skills. The final section of the chapter examines the benefits of the structural approach for students, teachers, and the research community.

KEY 1: STRUCTURES AND RELATED CONSTRUCTS

The basic premise of the structural approach is that there is a strong relation between what students do and what they learn. That is, interactions in the classroom have a profound effect on the social, cognitive, and academic development of students. The construction and acquisition of knowledge, the development of language and cognition, and the development of social skills are largely a function of the situations in which students interact. For this reason, a major direction of the structural approach has been to quantify classroom interactions and to analyze them in terms of their effects on the students. In this way, teachers can be provided with the means to direct the interaction of students in ways that will result in a range of learning outcomes. It is relatively easy for teachers and students to learn various social interaction sequences, called "structures." Because these structures have different learning outcomes, the teacher who knows and uses a range of structures can efficiently produce specific academic, cognitive, and social outcomes among students. A full mastery in the use of structures includes an understanding and manipulation of the elements of structures, as well as an understanding of how to combine structures to create the sequences of activities we know as lessons. Understanding and use of structures complements other approaches to cooperative learning.

Elements of Structures

Elements are the most basic unit of classroom behavior. In a familiar classroom scenario, the teacher has given a writing assignment and the students are writing independently. This is an element. When we analyze this element, we find that there are actors (individual students) performing some kind of action (writing). The name of any element tells who the actors are and what they are doing. Thus the element in our scenario is called "Individuals Write."

In another scenario, the teacher asks a question, and students are asked to think about how they would answer. As the talking stops, the actors are individuals, and the action is thinking. This element is "Individuals Think." Of course, there is more to classroom behavior than just independent actors performing independent actions. The classroom is replete with interactions, especially the cooperative classroom. A typical classroom interaction occurs when a teacher instructs the class. Once again, there is an actor (teacher) and an action (instruction), but now there are also recipients (the class). Thus an element can have three components: actors, actions, and recipients. The name of the element in our last example reflects all three components: "Teacher Instructs Class."

An element is an actor involved in some type of action, sometimes with recipients (Kagan & Kagan, 1992). The teacher creates elements. That is, the teacher chooses a combination of actors, the action, and the recipients most effective to reach a given learning objective. For example, if a teacher's objective were for each student to find out what one other student in the class did over the summer, a single element might be the perfect tool. The teacher could simply ask each student in the class to pair up with another and interview his or her partner. "Individuals Interview Partners" works well to accomplish this objective.

In a cooperative learning classroom with eight teams, if the teacher wanted each student in each team to know what all of his or her fellow teammates did, a single "Individuals Interview Partners" would not work. A single element cannot accomplish the teacher's goal. Each element has its domain of usefulness, and elements are selected according to which would be most appropriate for a desired objective. In this case, where the desired result is beyond the domain of a single element, a combination of elements is used to accomplish the objective. Elements may be combined to form structures.

Table 8.1
Team Discussion versus Three-Step Interview

Structure	Elements	Characteristics
Team Discussion	1. *Teacher Instructs Class* 2. *Teams Discuss*	• Unequal participation • Not all participate • No individual accountability • 1/4 of class talking at a time • Off-task talk
Three-Step Interview	1. *Individuals Interview Partners* 2. *Individuals Interview Partners* (Students reverse roles.) 3. *Individuals Share with Teammates* (Each student in turn shares what their partner told them, a **Roundrobin**.)	• Equal participation • All participate • Individual accountability • 1/2 of class talking at a time

Structures

Elements in the classroom have certain qualities or characteristics of their own. Depending on how they are combined, classroom elements can complement each other and can take on an entirely new life. Single elements used alone are limited in their domain of usefulness. In conjunction with other elements, however, they can become powerful structures that may be used in a variety of classroom situations.

Returning now to the example of the teacher whose objective cannot be accomplished by a single element, we see the strength of structures. As you recall, the objective of the teacher was to make sure that everyone on each team knew what each team member did over summer vacation. The teacher simply could have the teammates in each team discuss what they did, that is, use the structure Team Discussion. But since this teacher is fluent in the structural approach, she knows that each structure has its domain of usefulness, and that Team Discussion is not the best structure for the job. She knows that there are many structures to choose from, and for her objective a Three-Step Interview would work better than a Team Discussion. Let us examine why this teacher chose a Three-Step Interview over a Team Discussion (Table 8.1).

A Three-Step Interview is a structure composed of three elements: (1) Individuals Interview Partners: students split into two pairs within the team of four, and in each pair there is one interviewer and one interviewee; (2) Individuals Interview Partners: the same as the first element, but the interviewee and interviewer in each pair switch roles; (3) a Roundrobin: each team member shares with teammates something he or she learned from his or her partner. In this case, the student would share what his or her partner did over summer vacation. Technically, a Roundrobin is a structure consisting of four elements: Individuals Share with Teammates, repeated four times—once for each teammate in turn.

The structure Team Discussion is composed of two simple elements: (1) Teacher Instructs Class: the teacher tells the class what they are to discuss in teams, and (2) Teams Discuss: teams discuss the topic. In the example, teams discuss what they did over the summer.

In Team Discussion, there is no individual accountability: Students do not have to share what they have heard. Because they know they will not be held accountable for what they have heard, students may not listen to each other and may get off the task. In some teams, all the individuals may be talking while none are listening. In Team Discussion, there may be very unequal participation: One student may do most or even all of the talking. Further, at any one moment, if one person at a time is speaking, only one-fourth of the class is involved in language production.

In contrast, in the Three-Step Interview, each person must produce and receive language about equally. Also, there is individual accountability for listening: in the Roundrobin, each student is held accountable for sharing what he or she has heard in the interview. Further, for the first two steps, students interact in pairs, so one-half rather than one-fourth of the class is involved in language production at any one time, doubling the amount of active participation.

If the objectives of the teacher in this case are developing language and listening skills as well as promoting equal participation, a Three-Step Interview is better suited than a Team Discussion. When the content of the activity is academic rather than social, the advantages of one structure over another can be magnified. However, it will not always be better to do a Three-Step Interview than a Team Discussion. If the scenario is different and the teacher's objective is to get the group to think together, brainstorm, or reach consensus, a Team Discussion is the better structure.

Thus the choice of one structure over another can have profoundly different outcomes, one being much more efficient than another for reaching a given set of learning outcomes. The appropriate structure is chosen according to the objective at hand. As teachers use structures, they learn their domains of usefulness. Becoming aware of the effects of different elements and structures, teachers can intelligently choose appropriate structures and design lessons that efficiently reach their objectives. The most important considerations when determining the domain of usefulness of a structure are the following:

1. What kind of cognitive development does it foster?
2. What kind of social development does it foster?
3. Where in a lesson plan does it best fit?
4. What kind of curriculum does it deliver?

Some structures have a very specific domain of usefulness, such as Talking Chips, which serves to regulate communication within a group. In contrast, other structures, like Three-Step Interview, can be used in many places in a lesson plan. Each structure has a different domain of usefulness. It is good for some steps, but not all steps, in a lesson plan, and for some, but not all, kinds of cognitive and social development. A teacher knowledgeable in a number of structures can choose the most efficient structure for a particular goal. For example, within the mastery structures, for acquiring a new skill a Pairs Check works well, but for memorization the Flashcard Game is superior. In contrast, Numbered Heads Together is a far better structure than either Pairs Check or the Flashcard Game if the goal is for the teacher to check for understanding. Part of the art of structuring successful cooperative learning lessons is analyzing the objective of a lesson and then knowing which structures to use.

A variety of structures is necessary because there are many objectives in a classroom and each structure is more efficient at reaching some objectives than others. In the structural approach, structures are categorized by their primary functions, such as classbuilding, teambuilding, communication building, information sharing, mastery, and higher-level thinking (Kagan, 1992). Many structures are multifunctional and can be used for a range of outcomes. A list of sample structures and their functions is provided in Table 8.2.

Modifying and Creating Structures

Structures can be tailor-made to meet desired social, cognitive, and academic objectives. Existing structures can be modified to fit the context in which they are being used. Modifying structures is based on understanding elements.

By the flexible combination of elements, we gain the ability to choose the most appropriate structures for desired objectives and the ability to create new structures for objectives that we may not envision at the moment. Kagan and Kagan (1992) showed how to modify existing structures and how to create new structures by playing with elements. They provided a deck of cards called the Element Deck and an Element Workboard. Teachers lay out the elements of a structure and then modify the structure by adding and subtracting elements, as well as resequencing existing elements. Later, teachers begin from scratch with objectives to create new structures.

Activities

An activity is merely a structure plus content, or sometimes just an element plus content. Returning to our example of the teacher who had

Table 8.2
Overview of Selected Structures

Structure	Brief Description	Functions Academic & *Social*
Roundrobin	**Teambuilding** Each student in turn shares something with his/her teammates.	Expressing ideas & opinions. Creation of stories. *Equal Participation: Getting acquainted with teammates.*
Three-Step Interview	Students interview each other in pairs, first one way, then the other. Students each share with the group information they learned in the interview.	Sharing personal information such as hypotheses, reactions to a poem, conclusions from a unit. *Participation. Listening.*
Corners	**Classbuilding** Each student moves to a corner of the room representing a teacher-determined alternative. Students discuss within corners, then listen to and paraphrase ideas from other corners.	Seeing alternative hypotheses, values, problem solving approaches. *Knowing and respecting different points of view; meeting classmates.*
Match Mine	**Communication Building** Students attempt to match the arrangement of objects on a grid of another student using oral communication only.	Vocabulary development. *Communication skills, Role-taking ability.*
Numbered Heads Together	**Mastery: Practice & Review** The teacher asks a question, students consult to make sure everyone knows the answer, then one student is called upon to answer.	Review. Checking for Comprehension. Knowledge. Comprehension. *Tutoring.*
Inside-Outside Circle	Students stand in pairs in two concentric circles. The inside circle faces out, the outside circle faces in. Students use flash cards or respond to teacher questions as they rotate to each new partner.	Checking for understanding. Review. Processing. Helping: *Tutoring, Sharing, Meeting Classmates.*
Pairs Check	Students work in pairs within groups of four. Within pairs, students alternate -- one solves a problem while the other coaches. After every two problems, the pair checks to see if they have the same answers as the other pair.	Practicing skills. *Helping, Praising.*
Think-Pair-Share	**Concept Development** Students think to themselves on a topic provided by the teacher; they pair up with another student to discuss it. They then share with the class their thoughts.	Generating and revising hypotheses; inductive reasoning, deductive reasoning, application. *Participation, involvement.*
Team Word-Webbing	Students write simultaneously on a piece of chart paper drawing main concepts, supporting elements and bridges representing the relation of ideas on a concept.	Analysis of concepts into components; understanding multiple relations among ideas: differentiating concepts. *Role-taking.*
Roundtable	**Info Exchange: Within Teams** Each student in turn writes one answer as a paper and pencil are passed around the group. With Simultaneous Roundtable, more than one paper is used at once.	Assessing prior knowledge, practicing skills, recalling information, creating cooperative art. *Teambuilding: Participation of all.*
Blackboard Share	**Info Exchange: Between Teams** A student from each team goes to the board and writes an opinion, solves a problem, or shares other information. Usually there is a predetermined place at the board for each team to record its answers.	Sharing information, contrasting divergent opinions or problem solving strategies. *Classbuilding: Participation of eight times as many as the traditional class.*

Figure 8.1
Element-based Activity

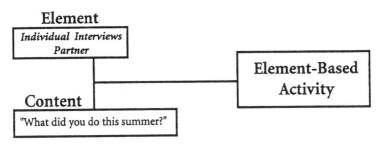

An element-based activity is an element combined with specific content.

each student interview one other student regarding what they did over the summer, we have an example of an element-based activity. The element was Individuals Interview Partners. The content was summer vacation. An activity is created when content is combined with an element. If the content or the element is changed, the activity changes. For example, if the students were asked to interview each other on their approach to a math problem, a very different activity would have resulted. Similarly, if we keep constant the content, say math problem solving, and change the element from Individuals Interview Partners to Individuals Write, a very different activity results. Each time we change either the element or the content, a new activity results, with a different learning potential (Figure 8.1).

A structure plus content is a structure-based activity. If the teacher chooses to use a Three-Step Interview on the content summer vacation, we have an example of a structure-based activity. As with element-based activities, when we change the content of a structure-based activity, we change the activity. A Three-Step Interview on the meaning of a poem is a very different activity than a Three-Step Interview on career aspirations (Figure 8.2).

Any one structure or element can be used to create an infinite number of activities. Elements and structures are the content-free "how" of instruction. They define the social organization of the classroom. Structures and elements can be used to deliver a wide range of academic content. The content is the "what" of instruction. The activity occurs when the content is delivered by either an element or a structure; at this point a learning experience occurs. An activity is a learning experience created by using an element or a structure to deliver content.

Activities are specific and content-bound; they cannot meaningfully be repeated many times. In contrast, structures are content-free ways of structuring group interaction. Structures may be used repeatedly with a variety

Figure 8.2
Structure-based Activity

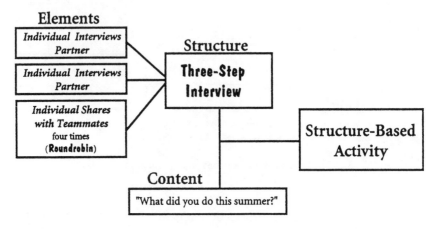

A structure-based activity is a structure combined with specific content.

of curriculum materials, at various places in the lesson plan, and with a wide range of grade levels. If a teacher new to cooperative learning learns five activities, he or she might well report back after a week, "Those worked well; what should I do next week?" If instead the teacher learns five structures, he or she can design meaningful cooperative learning in lessons all year to further the academic progress of students in any subject matter.

Lessons

Returning for the last time to the example of the students using the structure Three-Step Interview to find out what teammates did over summer vacation, let us examine the relationship of activities to lessons. The interview activity (structure = Three-Step Interview; content = summer vacation) was one part of a lesson. In fact, the activity was used to create an anticipatory set for a creative writing lesson "My Summer Vacation." The activity engaged the students in discussing summer vacation and aroused their interest. The activity (Three-Step Interview on summer vacation), though, is but one of a number of activities in the writing lesson.

A lesson is a set of activities sequenced to reach learning objectives. Activities are the building blocks of lessons. Cooperative learning lessons in the structural approach describe the structure and the content at each step of a lesson.

Lesson Designs

Activities in a lesson are often sequenced according to a lesson design. There is a strong analogy between structures and lesson designs. A structure consists of a series of structure elements. For example, Think-Pair-Square consists of three elements: Individual Thinks, Pair Discusses, and Team-mates Discuss. Similarly, a lesson design consists of a series of design elements. For example, Student Teams-Achievement Divisions (STAD) consists of five design elements: Direct Instruction, Teamwork, Individual Quiz, Improvement Scoring, and Team Recognition.

The difference between an element of a lesson design and an element of a structure, however, is profound. An element of a structure is an action or interaction in a classroom. Several structure elements are combined to form a structure, as in Think-Pair-Share. An element of a lesson design is a subobjective of the lesson design. Several of these design elements are combined to form a lesson design, as in STAD. Each design element or subobjective can be achieved through many possible means, often including a variety of cooperative learning structures. For example, many different structures could be used to implement the second design element of STAD, Teamwork.

Lesson designs, like structures, have their domain of usefulness. There are a number of prefabricated lesson designs; each is effective for reaching some lesson objectives. For example, there are lesson designs for mastery, like Color-Coded Co-op Cards, STAD, and Teams-Games-Tournaments (TGT); some are division-of-labor designs, like Telephone, Jigsaw II, and Partners; some designs are effective for projects, like Co-op Co-op, Co-op Jigsaw, Group Investigation, and Rotation Learning Centers; and some designs are multifunctional frameworks, like Effective Instruction, Johnson and Johnson, and the Big Four. A summary of a few sample lesson designs is presented in Table 8.3. The design elements of a number of lesson designs are presented in Table 8.4. These designs and frameworks were described in detail by Kagan (1992).

There is an analogy between learning to implement cooperative struc-tures and learning to implement co-op lesson designs. It is natural after using a structure many times to modify it by playing with its elements. For example, after becoming very familiar with a prefabricated structure like Think-Pair-Square, a teacher might modify the structure, inserting an ele-ment, to create a Think-Write-Pair-Square. Later yet, the teacher may begin to create original, freestyle structures like Think-Write-Roundrobin-Share. The same process occurs in learning to create original co-op lesson designs. First, a teacher learns well a prefabricated co-op lesson design, later begins to modify the design, and finally begins to play with design elements to create freestyle co-op lesson designs. For example, after using STAD many times, a teacher may modify it by inserting or subtracting design elements. One teacher may modify the design by inserting an an-ticipatory set and/or closure; another may take out improvement scoring and insert reflection time on social skills. At the highest stage of co-op lesson planning, teachers create freestyle lesson designs that do not resem-

Table 8.3
Overview of Selected Lesson Designs

Lesson Design	Brief Description	Functions Academic & *Social*
Color-Coded Co-op Cards	**Mastery** Students memorize facts using a flashcard game. The game is structured so that there is a maximum probability of success at each step, moving from short-term to long-term memory. Scoring is based on improvement.	Memorizing facts. *Helping, Praising.*
Co-op Co-op	**Project** Students work in groups to produce a unique group product to share with the whole class; each student has a unique contribution to the group.	Learning and sharing complex material, often with multiple sources. Evaluation. Application. Analysis. Synthesis. *Conflict Resolution. Presentation skills.*
Jigsaw	**Division of Labor** Each student on the team becomes an "expert" on one topic by working with members from other teams assigned the corresponding expert topic. Upon returning to their teams, each one in turn teaches the group and students are all assessed on all aspects of the topic.	Acquisition and presentation of new material. Review. Informed Debate. *Interdependence, Status equalization.*
Partners	Students work in pairs to create or master content. They consult with partners from other teams. They then share their products or understanding with the other partner pair in their team.	Mastery and presentation of new material; concept development. *Presentation and communication skills.*

ble any of the prefabricated designs. The freestyle designs are unique designs created to meet the requirements of specific curricula, student needs, and teacher objectives. The effectiveness of these innovations is a function of the teacher's understanding of the elements of lesson design. Knowledge of design elements is the basis for efficiently modifying and creating cooperative lesson designs.

Teaching is the art of efficiently reaching learning objectives. The structural approach to cooperative learning is aimed at providing teachers with tools to efficiently reach a range of learning objectives. Elements or structures are selected to deliver content. There are a number of established structures that may be used, and there is also the potential to play with elements to modify and create new structures. Structures and elements, when combined with content, are called activities. Activities are sequenced to form lessons. Lesson designs are sequenced sets of design elements or lesson objectives that serve to guide the direction of the lesson. There are a variety of prefabricated lesson designs, each designed to achieve different lesson objectives. Also, by playing with the elements of lesson design, a teacher may alter the lesson design to better reach specific lesson objectives.

Table 8.4
Design Elements of Selected Lesson Designs

Mastery Designs

Color-Coded Co-op
Cards
1. Pre-Test
2. Create Cards
3. Flashcard Game
4. Practice Test
5. Count Improvement Points
6. Flashcard Game
7. Final Test
8. Final Improvement Scoring
9. Individual, Team & Class
   Recognition
10. Reflection

STAD
1. Direct Instruction
2. Group Work for Practice
3. Individual Quiz
4. Improvement Scoring
5. Team Recognition

TGT
(Same as STAD except Tourna-
ment replaces Quiz, and points are
based on out scoring others.)

Division of Labor Designs

Telephone
1. A Student Exits Room
2. Remaining Students
   Instructed
3. Student Returns
4. Returnee Instructed by
   Teammates
5. Returnee Tested

Jigsaw II
1. Direct Instruction
2. Expert Topics Assigned
3. Expert Group Work
4. Experts Teach Teammates
5. Individual Quiz
6. Improvement Scoring
7. Team Recognition

Partners
1. Form Partners Within Teams
2. Class Division
3. Materials Distributed
4. Partners Work
5. Partners Consult
6. Partners Prepare to Present
7. Teams Reunite
8. Partners Present & Tutor
9. Reflection
10. Individual Assessment

Project Designs

Co-op Co-op
1. Class Discussion
2. Team Selection
3. Teambuilding/Social Skill
4. Team Topic Selection
5. Mini-Topic Selection
6. Mini-Topic Preparation
7. Mini-Topic Presentation
8. Prepare Team Presentation
9. Team Presentations
10. Evaluation
11. Reflection

Group Investigation
1. Identify Topic; Team Selection
2. Plan the Learning Task
3. Carry Out Investigation
4. Prepare Final Report

Multi-Functional Frameworks

Effective Instruction	*Johnson & Johnson*	*Big Four*
1. Anticipatory Set	1. Direct Instruction of Content	1. Classbuilding
2. Instructional Input	2. Teach Social Skills	2. Teambuilding
3. Check Understanding	3. Students Work in Groups	3. Mastery
4. Guided Practice	4. Teacher Observes for Social	4. Thinking Skills
5. Closure	Skills & Content	
6. Independent Practice	5. Process Social Skills & Content	

A visual summary of the theoretical constructs of the structural approach
is presented in Figure 8.3.

KEY 2: THE BASIC PRINCIPLES

There are four basic principles central to the structural approach of
cooperative learning: simultaneous interaction, equal participation, positive interdependence, and individual accountability. These principles are
discussed in detail (Kagan, 1992; Kagan & Kagan, 1992). We know that
cooperative learning is more effective when these basic principles are included. For that reason, almost all of the well-established structures in-

Figure 8.3
Overview of Theoretical Constructs

An element is the smallest unit of social interaction. A structure consists of one or more elements designed to produce a specific type of social interaction and learning; existing structures can be modified, and original structures can be created by playing with elements. When structures and elements are combined with content, we create a learning experience called an activity. A lesson is a logical sequence of activities. Sometimes lessons follow frameworks called lesson designs. Lesson designs, which are made up of design elements, provide the framework for the activities of the lesson just as structures are frameworks to hold content. There are a number of powerful lesson designs as well as the potential to combine structures to create numerous original designs.

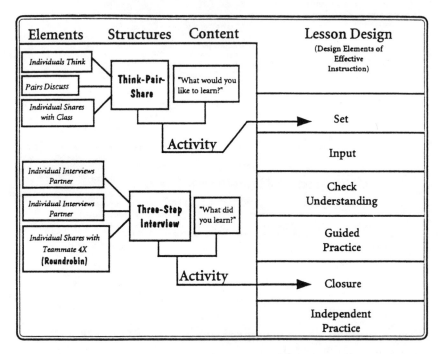

corporate these principles to some degree. That is, structures have the basic principles "built in."

Simultaneous Interaction

Interaction may occur simultaneously or sequentially. Sequential interaction occurs when students participate one at a time in a sequence, taking turns. If one person at a time is called upon to share an idea, the interaction is sequential. Sequential interaction is limiting and inefficient. To give each student in the class one minute to share ideas using a one-at-a-time structure takes about thirty minutes.

Simultaneous interaction occurs in a classroom when there is more than one active participant at a time. Simultaneous interaction is usually preferable to sequential interaction because it increases the number of students actively involved at any one moment and thus the amount of active participation time per student. To give each student one minute to share if students are taking turns talking in pairs takes only two minutes. Elements that include pair work are simultaneous elements because the action is taking place simultaneously in many places all at the same time.

Let us look at a discussion. When we have some issue to be discussed in the classroom, we have alternatives as to how it may be discussed. We can use the element Class Discusses, Teams Discuss, or Pairs Discuss. If active participation is our primary objective, applying the simultaneity principle, we would choose a Teams Discuss over a Class Discusses, and a Pairs Discuss over a Teams Discuss. In Class Discusses, there is one person speaking at a time; in Teams Discuss, on the average, one person in each team is talking at any one moment, so one-quarter of the class is talking at a time; and in Pairs Discuss, half the class is actively expressing ideas at any one moment.

What about presentations? If teams have prepared presentations, and it is time for them to share with the class, what element would we use? We could use Team Presents to the Class. If the presentation was five minutes long, and it took about a minute for transitions, eight team presentations to the class would take forty-eight minutes. Applying the simultaneity principle, we instead choose Teams Present to Teams. If every team makes its five-minute presentation to another team, a minute is taken for transition, and then the presenting team becomes the receiving team, in eleven minutes every team has given and received a presentation. This leaves time for teams to reflect, discuss their presentations, and fine-tune them. Then they can try them again with another team as a new audience. By applying the simultaneity principle, twice as much can be accomplished in less than half the time.

Equal Participation

Simultaneous interaction does quite well to get students actively involved. When we do Teams Discuss rather than Class Discusses, one in four students is speaking rather than one in about thirty-two. But if we look closely at what is happening in our team discussion, we may find that one outspoken student is doing all the talking while the teammates are doing all the listening. This is not equal participation. To make sure everyone has an equal chance to speak, we might choose to do a series of four Individuals Share with Teammates (a Roundrobin) rather than Teams Discuss. Now every student has an equal role in sharing information.

What would we do if we wanted to have our class read a short story? We know that when we have students read in teams, there will be more active reading and listening than if one individual or the teacher reads to the class. So we choose Individuals Read to Teammates. But if we just tell a team to read the short story, we will probably find that once again one student decides to do all the reading while teammates do all the listening. If we make it clear that after each minute teammates are to rotate the role of reader (a Roundrobin), every student will participate about equally.

Similarly, during a pair discussion focused on recalling the major events of a story, one student may do all the talking. To equalize participation, we may do a series of Individuals Share with Partner (a Rallyrobin), having students alternate, each in turn describing one event. As a general rule, we want to make sure that our students participate roughly equally, so when we are selecting, modifying, or creating structures, we must make sure to select elements in which all students are doing the same thing, or elements that ensure that each student gets his or her turn.

Positive Interdependence

Positive interdependence is the most basic principle in cooperative learning. Positive interdependence is created whenever a gain for one means a gain for another. Two individuals are mutually positively interdependent if the gains of either helps the other. Two powerful forces are released when we make students positively interdependent academically: If any student needs help, he or she finds among his teammates or classmates willing tutors (a gain for one is a gain for the other), and students are encouraged by their teammates and classmates to do their very best, raising motivation.

Positive interdependence is created within structures in various ways— usually not by the inclusion of one element, but rather by a sequence of elements. For example, let us look at a Three-Step Interview. In the first two steps, teammates are in pairs interviewing each other both ways. In the third step, students tell their teammates what they learned from their partner in the interview. The teammates have no other way of obtaining the information, so they are dependent on the interviewing, listening, and speaking skills of their teammate. Thus this third step creates positive interdependence; the better each student is at interviewing, listening, and sharing, the more each will learn. A gain for one is a gain for the others.

Let us take another example. In Numbered Heads Together, after the teacher asks a question, the students are given time to put their heads together to make sure their teammates all know the answer. At that stage, if any student knows, it increases the probability that the teammates will learn. Students know that following the team discussion, only one number is chosen. Thus each team member wants all of his or her teammates to do well. Again, the students are positively interdependent: A gain for one is a gain for the others.

Positive interdependence increases learning as well as closeness among teammates. They all feel that they are on the same side, tutoring and encouraging each other. Almost all well-established structures have built-in positive interdependence.

Individual Accountability

Individual accountability is making each member accountable for his or her own learning or contribution. For example, in Numbered Heads Together, each student is held accountable to the teacher and classmates for sharing an answer or idea. The element that holds students accountable here is the last step of Numbered Heads Together: Individual Shares with Class. When it is made clear to the students that they are being held accountable, it increases the likelihood that they will listen and participate. If, for instance, Numbered Heads Together was modified to exclude the element Individual Shares with Class, students would know that they were not accountable for sharing an answer, and some might decide to not pay attention at all.

Similarly, in Three-Step Interview, students are held accountable to the team for the information they receive from a teammate during an interview. This element, Individuals Share with Teammates, holds students accountable for what they heard. Because students know that they will be held accountable, they listen intently.

KEY 3: TEAMBUILDING AND CLASSBUILDING

What appears like time off-task can be viewed as a very important investment in creating the social context necessary for teams to maximize their potential. Again and again, we have observed greater long-run efficiency, learning, and liking of class, school, and subject matter if teachers take time for teambuilding and classbuilding. When there is a positive team identity, liking, respect, and trust among team members and classmates, there is a context within which maximum learning can occur.

When teambuilding and classbuilding are neglected, especially in classrooms in which there are preexisting tensions, teams experience serious difficulties. Kagan (1992) distinguished five aims of teambuilding and classbuilding and provided structures appropriate for each. The five aims of teambuilding are (1) getting acquainted, (2) team identity, (3) mutual support, (4) valuing differences, and (5) developing synergy. Hundreds of teambuilding and classbuilding activities and lessons were provided by Shaw (1992).

If the cooperative learning lesson is simple and fun, as with the Flashcard Game or Numbered Heads Together, usually little or no teambuilding is necessary. If, on the other hand, the lesson involves activities in which conflicts might arise (choosing a topic or format for a project), it is important that a strong positive team identity be developed prior to the lesson.

Classbuilding provides networking among all of the students in a class and creates a positive context within which teams can learn. Although students spend most of their time in teams, in the cooperative classroom, it is important that students see themselves as part of a larger supportive group—the class—not just as members of one small team.

KEY 4: TEAMS

What is a team? A cooperative learning team has a strong, positive team identity, ideally consists of four members, and endures over time. Teammates know and accept each other and provide mutual support. Ability to establish a variety of types of cooperative learning teams is a key competency of a cooperative learning teacher. "Teams" may be contrasted with "groups," which do not necessarily endure over time or have an identity. Kagan (1992) distinguished four major types of cooperative learning teams and assorted methods to produce them. The four most common cooperative arrangements are (1) heterogeneous teams, (2) random groups, (3) interest teams, and (4) homogeneous language teams. Each of these types of teams is useful for different purposes.

The most common cooperative learning-team-formation methods assign students to maximize heterogeneity. The heterogeneous team is a mirror of the classroom, including, to the extent possible, high, middle, and low achievers, boys and girls, and an ethnic and linguistic diversity. Heterogeneity of achievement levels maximizes positive peer tutoring and serves as an aid to classroom management.

If we always use heterogeneous teams, however, the high achievers would never interact (missing important academic stimulation), and the low achievers would never be on the same team (missing leadership opportunities). Thus there is a need for additional team-formation methods. Nonheterogenous teams can be formed in a variety of ways, including self-selection (allowing students to group themselves by friendships or interests) or random selection (students draw a number from one to eight for team assignments). Self-selection runs a strong risk of promoting or reinforcing status hierarchies in the classroom ("in-" and "out-groups"); random selection runs the risk of the creation of "loser" teams (the four lowest achievers in the classroom may end up on the same team if the choice is left to the luck of the draw). There are important benefits, however, derived from the occasional use of random, interest, or homogeneous language teams. In the structural approach, teachers are encouraged to learn the domain of usefulness of a range of team-formation methods and to choose the method most appropriate for the objectives at hand.

How long should teams last? If random team-formation methods are used, in most classrooms, teams must be changed frequently—every day or so—because the luck of the draw could result in "loser teams"—the four lowest achievers in the class could end up on the same team. If teams are carefully designed by the teacher, they can stay together for a long time and students can learn how to learn together. We suggest changing heterogeneous teams after five or six weeks, even if they are functioning well. This enables students to transfer their new social and academic skills to new situations.

How big should teams be? Teams of four are ideal. They allow pair work, which doubles participation and opens twice as many lines of communication compared to teams of three. Teams larger than four often do not lead to enough participation and are harder to manage. Much of the rationale for cooperative learning is based on the benefits of active participation. As the group size is made smaller, active participation increases. As students share in a group of eight, one-eighth of the class is an active participant at any one time. Groups of four allow one-fourth of the class to produce language at any one time—from the perspective of active participation, they are twice as good as groups of eight. Given this rationale, why not move to groups of three or even to pairs? There are three reasons why teams of four are most effective. (1) Pair work doubles the amount of participation. With groups of three, there is an odd person out with pair work. Pairs Check, Paired Reading, and the Flashcard Game are among the structures that maximize simultaneous interaction through pair work. (2) The social psychology of a group of three is often a pair and an outsider. Two people hit it off well and talk to each other often, leaving one left out. (3) Compared to a group of three, a group of four doubles the probability of an optimum cognitive and linguistic mismatch. The research on moral development and on linguistic development indicates that we learn well from someone only somewhat different from our own level of development—someone who will provide stimulation in our zone of proximal development. In a group of three, there are three possible pairs; in a group of four, there are six.

KEY 5: MANAGEMENT

Many teachers report that their management problems decrease dramatically once they switch to cooperative learning. The reason is that in the traditional classroom, there is a mismatch between the needs of the students and the structure of the classroom. The nature of a student is active and interactive: Students want to "do" and to talk. The traditional classroom demands that students be passive and isolated. Naturally, the students do not give up their basic needs without a struggle, so a great deal of energy is spent keeping the students in their seats, "not bothering their neighbors," and quiet. The cooperative classroom, in contrast, is better aligned with the needs of students. It is based on the assumption that learning occurs through doing and interacting. Students are encouraged to interact, move, create, and do. Feeling their basic needs met, students are no longer "management problems."

Nevertheless, there are a number of management skills necessary in the cooperative classroom that are not involved in managing a traditional classroom. Cooperative classroom management differs radically from classroom management in the traditional classroom. In the traditional classroom, managing student behavior means instituting a system to keep students from talking or interacting. In contrast, in the cooperative classroom, student-student interaction is encouraged, and so management involves different skills. Some of the management concerns introduced along with the introduction of teams include seating arrangement, noise level, giving directions, distribution and storage of team materials, and methods of shaping the behavior of groups.

The teacher establishes a quiet signal that at any time quickly focuses all attention away from peer interaction and toward the teacher. Extensive use of teacher and student modeling is an efficient cooperative management technique, as is extensive use of structuring. Efficient methods of distributing materials are established, for example, a materials monitor for each team. The room is arranged so that each student has equal and easy access to each teammate (ideally, each student on a team can easily put both hands on a common piece of paper), and all students are able to easily and comfortably orient forward toward the teacher and blackboard (Kagan, 1992).

KEY 6: SOCIAL SKILLS

Research reveals that with no social skills instruction at all, students in cooperative teams become more caring, helpful, and understanding of each other. Nevertheless, if we really wish to deliver a differentiated social skills curriculum and to have our teams and classrooms run as efficiently as possible, we cannot depend entirely on the natural acquisition of social skills. Teachers can structure learning so that students acquire social skills while they are doing math or science or social studies.

The Structured Natural Approach for social skills acquisition uses four tools: (1) roles and gambits, (2) modeling and reinforcement, (3) structures and structuring, and (4) reflection and planning time. Most important, these four tools are used in an integrated way to structure for the acquisition of one "skill-of-the-week." As the students interact in their cooperative groups, they become skillful in listening, paraphrasing, taking the role of the other, managing group processes, and dealing with the dominant, shy, hostile, and withdrawn group members. They acquire skills, not just learn about them.

REFERENCES

Kagan, Spencer. (1992). *Cooperative Learning*. San Juan Capistrano, CA: Kagan Cooperative Learning.
Kagan, S., & Kagan, M. (1992). *Advanced Cooperative Learning: Playing with Elements*. San Juan Capistrano, CA: Kagan Cooperative Learning.
Shaw, V. (1992). *Community Building in the Classroom*. San Juan Capistrano, CA: Kagan Cooperative Learning.

PART II

Applications

9

CDP Cooperative Learning: Working Together to Construct Social, Ethical, and Intellectual Understanding

Marilyn Watson, Daniel Solomon, Stefan Dasho, Peter Shwartz, and Sylvia Kendzior

The Child Development Project (CDP) is a classroom instructional program designed to promote children's social, ethical, and intellectual development. Cooperative learning is one major aspect of that program. The CDP approach to cooperative learning is based on "constructivist" learning assumptions and goals and assigns a central role to the intrinsic motivation of students. In these respects it is similar to the approaches of the Sharans (Sharan & Sharan, 1992) and to "collaborative" approaches to small-group learning (Barnes & Todd, 1976). CDP cooperative learning differs from these, however, in that it makes more direct and deliberate efforts to influence students' social and ethical development as well.[1]

THE IMPORTANCE OF FOSTERING ETHICAL AND INTELLECTUAL DEVELOPMENT: IMPLICATIONS FOR COOPERATIVE LEARNING

Our view asserts that it is essential for schools to focus on children's social and ethical development as well as their intellectual development. That position is not new, having been expressed more or less explicitly by Thomas Jefferson, Horace Mann, John Dewey, and many others, but it seems particularly pertinent now. It is more important than ever for our schools to teach children the skills, attitudes, and values necessary for full participation in the ethical and social functioning of our society, including the basic democratic values of fairness, respect for diversity, and personal responsibility. Such teaching is certainly as important as teaching the skills necessary for full participation in society's economic functioning. It can best be accomplished in school and classroom settings in which all children experience care, respect, and fairness, as well as intellectual stimulation.

A CDP COOPERATIVE ACTIVITY

An example of a specific activity will illustrate several aspects of our approach to cooperative learning as it has been shaped by our goals, our assumptions about how children learn, and our focus on the development of intrinsic motivation.

Following are three excerpts from a transcribed videotape of an activity done in a sixth-grade classroom in a small urban community. The students were producing magazines to inform others about what they had learned about urban ecology and recycling. Over the previous few weeks, they had performed experiments to see what kinds of materials are biodegradable, had conducted surveys to determine the kinds of waste products produced by their school and their families, and had done library research on composting and other forms of recycling. They worked in groups of four, and at the time of the taping the groups had begun writing about topics for their magazines. In the first excerpt, the teacher is helping the groups review what they have done and how they plan to proceed.

Excerpt 1

Teacher: Yesterday you spent time talking in your groups about what form you would like to use in writing this up for your magazine. I heard a lot of interesting possibilities. Is there any group that would like to tell us what you came up with as a way of writing up your experiment results? What did you come up with as a group?—Yes.

Julio: First we were going to like write a short paragraph and list all the things that will and won't biodegrade.

Teacher: And how did you divide that up in your group?

Julio: First we're just each going to pick something and write it on the list and then do it like that.

Teacher: Can you tell me a little more about that, Katie?

Katie: See, we're going to do it in our group, the list. We'll probably go around the class and see what did and what did not biodegrade, from every group.

Teacher: Okay. I'd like a little more information on your paragraph, too.

Katie: I think we're going to each write a paragraph and choose the one we'd like.

Teacher: Oh, so you'll each write one up and then share the information to come up with parts that you want?

Katie: Or probably we'll just pick a person to do it.

Teacher: Okay. So that still hasn't been decided, you still have some more talking to do?

Katie: Yeah.

Teacher: Any other questions? Does everybody already have a job to do? Okay, if your group hasn't had enough time to talk about the jobs, how you're dividing them up, please be sure that you are not being *assigned* something by somebody and you don't know what to do. Don't sit by quietly and wait for somebody to say, "Well, here, *you* do these procedures." *You* need to speak up and be part of the discussion. If you sit back, you get what's left. If you want to be a part of it, get in there, be a part of it. Otherwise you're going to be left out and maybe have something to do that you're not happy with.—Okay. I'm anxious to hear what you're talking about and anxious to see the writing as it gets accomplished. Good luck, and get to work.

Excerpt 2

The second excerpt shows a group at work. One of the group members, Maria, is a bilingual Spanish-speaking student who has just returned to the group after having been out of the classroom for extra instruction in English.

Denise: Maria, we were wondering if—since you speak Spanish and you can write in Spanish—if we write an article in English and then you could translate it and write it in Spanish so that all the other Spanish readers can read it.

Maria: All right.

Freddie: 'Cause, for like some of the Spanish readers—

Peter: Or we can help you write it—

Denise:—for some of the Spanish people that cannot read English so they have to read Spanish, so they could flip like the page and then there's the Spanish.

Peter: You could do that?

Maria: [Nods, with slight shrug, a bit dubious.]

Freddie: Since you're gone from the class a lot of the time . . .

Maria: What I—I'd have to do it in Spanish?

Freddie: We'll write the articles and we won't give you too many articles to do. We could each write one a day. And then we'll just hand it over to you until you finish it.

Maria: Okay. [Looking resigned.]

[Students pull out books and exchange articles.]

Denise: I need an ending for—

Freddie: Here, I'll rewrite this.

Maria: What is this? Do I have to translate all of these?

Denise: Oh, no. We shouldn't let Maria rewrite *all* the articles in Spanish because it's gonna be too much. Just like do it for some of the articles 'cause—

Freddie: Oh, I know—she could teach us to, how to write in Spanish.

[Maria smiles and laughs.]

Denise: Yeah.

Freddie: That way we could write it in Spanish too.

Denise: I think we should only let her write the—

Freddie: —do the important ones—

Denise: —yeah, in Spanish that we feel that we want everyone to know about.

Freddie: And then she can say what's the words and everything. And then if we want that word—

Denise: —we'll ask her to spell it—

Freddie: —the important ones. Yeah. And we could write it in Spanish. And then we could write it instead of having her write everything.

Maria: So, you guys could do the best articles and I could correct them for you guys.

Excerpt 3

The final excerpt shows part of a "wrap-up," in which the teacher is asking the groups to reflect on their work and to describe it to the class, including the problems they encountered and their remedies.

[Three students—two girls and one boy—are standing in front of the class, holding up their magazine. A fourth member of the group is out of the class.]

Teacher: Your group spent time dividing up the work, but I'm not sure the work actually was divided up evenly. How does your group feel about the amount of work that was done by each member? Can you tell me a little bit about your final product and how that came about?

Amy: Well, at first, everybody just thought it was time to go talk to people around you. We thought that it was like time to just go talk around the room. So that's what we were doing.

Teacher: So your group spent the time socializing and visiting and not doing the work?

Amy: The *first* half. Then Katie started making us—

Richard: Katie started getting on our case and making us work. So then we just started working and then we got it finished. No more stress.

[Laughter.]

Teacher: Okay. Katie, speak up for yourself. Tell us about it.

Katie: I think it was fair—I did the typing and the cover and the back. And they did some articles and we just divided it up.

Amy: But we didn't really make Katie write a lot because she was the one typing everything.

Teacher: Okay. Katie, they said you had to get on their case. Why did you think you needed to do that? How did it make you feel when you had to do that?

Katie: I didn't feel that good because they weren't really paying attention to me. Like when we started talking about it, they'd go off the subject and like go to clothes and music and stuff like that. So I just told them to listen and remind them that it's due soon. And so they started working on everything.

Amy: Since Julio's not here now, we wanted to say that he and Katie did the most because we were like laughing, walking around the room, talking. So we had to buckle down a lot.

Teacher: So you feel that most of the work in your group was done by Katie and Julio?

Amy: No, it was done by all of us. But I'm saying in the first half it was like that nobody was really paying attention to it.

Teacher: Okay.

Richard: It was boring at first.

Teacher: What—what changed it from boring to being something interesting that you wanted to work on?

Amy: When we started reading this stuff, thinking about what we were reading and the things we were writing, and it started making a lot of sense. So we realized this is really interesting.

These excerpts illustrate several of the CDP principles and goals, including a concern for the values guiding interpersonal interaction; emphases on intrinsic motivation, student autonomy, self-direction, and exploration—in the context of teacher guidance; and discussion and reflection about the group activity. From the initial scene, it is clear that the teacher is trying to get all students to participate in planning and that the activities provide substantial opportunity for student decision making, but with guidance provided by the teacher's questioning and input. In this excerpt, the teacher asks a group about its plans, and, although she has clearly given the members leeway in dividing the task, she is trying, through questioning, to make sure that they are attending to the collaborative nature of the task.

There is also a concern for equality and fairness in the group activity, both on the part of the teacher (in the first and third excerpts) and the students (in the second). In the first excerpt, the teacher reminds all students of the importance of active participation. In the second excerpt, the students on their own come to realize that it might not be fair to assign Maria the task of translating all their articles. In the third, the teacher questions the group members about the fairness of their distribution of the work. Through this, the students are learning something about interpersonal values and concern that we consider as important as the quality of their academic work or the depth of their knowledge about recycling. While there is no guarantee that students will arrive at such realizations, they also are not left up to chance. The introductions to CDP cooperative activities often focus on such issues, and it was clear in these episodes that the teacher was interested in having the students consider them.

In the second excerpt, students, without direct teacher intervention, exercised the judgment and reasoning necessary to conclude that they were being unfair. It was not until they discussed it with Maria that they saw that she did not really want to be relegated to doing all the translating and that the task would be too much for one person to do. The students eventually arrived at a redefinition of the task that involved a more equitable division of labor (involving Maria's teaching Spanish to the other group members, a collaborative approach to the translation task, and the decision to limit the translation to the "important" articles). They were not following a fairness "formula," but they were struggling to understand how fairness applied in this unique situation; in so doing, they further developed their understanding of fairness. The teacher tries to maximize the likelihood that such learning will occur.

It is this explicit focus on children's ethical and social development that distinguishes CDP's approach to cooperative learning. We assume that learning in the social and ethical domain requires the same kind of deliberate adult guidance as learning in the intellectual domain.

HOW CHILDREN LEARN: IMPLICATIONS FOR CDP COOPERATIVE LEARNING

Constructivism in CDP Cooperative Learning

The social constructivist view of learning (see Vygotsky, 1962; Rogoff, 1990) underlies the CDP approach to small-group instruction and can be seen in a number of its major elements. In the first place, all CDP cooperative lessons are designed to begin with the students' current knowledge and experience; to be open-ended enough to allow children to engage the activity differently, depending upon their unique experiences, skills, and levels of development; and to encourage them to exercise choice in the ways they approach each learning activity. Further, each activity is contextually rich, so that students will be able to understand its purpose or relevance to their lives and to their existing ideas and theories about the world. The goal of each activity is to develop student understanding, not simply to perfect student performance. Thus learning activities are designed so that performance follows from understanding and is not achieved on the basis of following a preset rule, procedure, or algorithm. Finally, these are collaborative, group activities; children develop their plans and understandings through joint effort and have the opportunity to come to new levels of understanding through the give-and-take of interaction, argument, and discussion.

In the sixth-grade classroom we observed earlier, the lesson was the conclusion of a unit that began with students expressing interest in recycling, pooling their knowledge, and then hypothesizing about which of a set of common objects (Styrofoam, broccoli, orange peel, tissue paper) would biodegrade. The lesson's writing activity was open-ended; students were free to write what and as much as they wanted. They were even free to increase the challenge by deciding that some of the "articles" would be translated into Spanish.

Similarly, the activity was not an isolated writing exercise, but part of a coherent whole. It gave meaning to, and derived meaning from, the experiments, surveys, and reading the students did to understand something of interest to them—recycling and the urban environment. The academic goal of the activity was not, for example, for students to come out with a list of ten things that do and ten that do not biodegrade, or to be able to give an acceptable definition of recycling, but was much more comprehensive and relevant to them. In addition to providing students with a motivating way to develop their reading, writing, and speaking skills, the activity also helped them understand the concepts of waste and recycling and how they might use this knowledge to influence their environments and their lives.

Constructivism and Prosocial Development

In addition to promoting academic goals, CDP cooperative learning activities are designed to foster students' ethical and social development. However, our social constructivist view of learning has led us to teach social skills and understanding in a way quite different from that used by most other approaches to cooperative learning. We emphasize increasing children's understanding of and commitment to broad underlying values, rather than the acquisition of specific behavioral skills, and help children to see what kinds of actions in the groups will relate to those values. When the teacher introduces an activity, he or she explicitly or implicitly refers to the values, such as fairness, consideration and respect, helpfulness, and personal responsibility, that should govern all classroom work and interaction. Then, through questions and discussion, the teacher helps the students think about how they can work together on the task in ways that are consistent with these values.

The teacher also tries to get the students to think both about the specific upcoming task and about the implications of previous tasks they have done that have had similar issues and problems. For example, the teacher might say, "In this activity you will all have lots of different ideas; how can you be sure that in your groups everyone's ideas are heard and treated with respect? Was this a problem the last time you did this task? What did you do about it?" Or the teacher might say, "I've heard some complaints that some people are feeling like they are being bossed around in their groups.

What can you do to avoid this bossiness? What can you do if you feel like you're being bossed? What have your groups done before when this came up? How can you be sure you aren't being bossy?" Similarly, at the conclusion of an activity, the teacher will lead the students to reflect on how their groups performed with respect to the relevant values by asking questions such as "Do you think everyone was treated fairly in your group today? What did you do to make sure that everyone got a chance to participate?"

To help promote both the academic and the social and ethical goals, the teacher encourages the students to reflect on their concrete experiences; this, in turn, helps them gradually to develop understanding that they can then build on in their future group work. The teacher's goal is to help children construct their understanding of complex social concepts in the same way they are helped to build understanding in the academic realm— through concrete experiences with meaningful, challenging activities at which they can succeed with effort. In other words, small-group learning activities help children to develop social and interpersonal skills in the framework of their growing understanding of the ethical principles of fairness, consideration, and responsibility.

Task Assignments

Some cooperative learning practitioners assign specific task roles to group members (for example, "recorder," "reporter," "materials manager") to ensure that every group member will have access to the activity, to prevent some students from freeloading on the work of their fellow group members and others from dominating the activity, to promote interdependence among the group members, and to provide an efficient way to divide responsibilities (Johnson & Johnson, 1984; Cohen, 1986). CDP initially used roles in much the same way (and still does in some circumstances), but gradually we have come to believe that such roles are not essential for cooperative learning and, in fact, may actually interfere with the accomplishment of its major goals. Teaching children to perform cooperative tasks by assigning each a unique role is analogous to breaking tasks down into component parts that may lose much of their meaning in isolation, or to teaching children to solve mathematical problems by getting them to memorize and apply appropriate algorithms. Furthermore, we feel that the kind of creative collaboration and negotiation we are trying to promote may be diminished by assigning predefined roles. It seems preferable to engage the students in thinking about what it means to divide a task fairly and to give each group member a meaningful chance to participate, and then to help them to develop and allocate roles with these goals explicitly in mind.

CDP teachers still sometimes assign specific task roles when their students first start working in cooperative groups as a way of introducing them to the process of working together and to the idea that group work can be divided. After this introductory phase, teachers gradually give the students more responsibility for deciding how to handle the task, whether there should be differentiated roles, what the roles should be, and how they should be filled. Once students have some experience with task analysis and division of labor, they are frequently left to analyze the tasks on their own and to devise their own ways to perform them, including the allocation of specific roles. (In the second excerpt reproduced earlier, for example, the other group members at first thought that they would assign Maria the role of sole translator, but then realized that such an assignment might be unfair to her.) In this way, students learn to deal with the issues of how best to perform the group task—and how to do the associated negotiation and decision making—rather than have this determined for them as part of the preset task structure.

DEVELOPING MOTIVATION IN THE CDP APPROACH

A major goal of CDP cooperative learning is to promote students' intrinsic motivation. Factors that are likely to undermine or thwart intrinsic motivation, such as the use of rewards or competition (see Lepper & Greene, 1978; Amabile, 1989; Nicholls, 1989) are minimized or avoided. Many academic learning tasks do, however, require more effort than many students appear inclined to make. How, then, is a teacher to increase student motivation without using extrinsic rewards or competition? A constructivist view of learning assumes that students will be intrinsically interested in learning if they see that the learning activity is relevant or important to their own lives and goals, and if they believe that they have a reasonable chance of being successful. Lack of motivation has become an increasing problem in our schools, and the breaking down of learning tasks into discrete parts has contributed to this lack of student motivation by making it more difficult for children to see how the individual learning tasks are relevant to personally meaningful goals.

What are the implications of these assumptions about motivation for CDP cooperative learning? First, as mentioned earlier, the learning tasks themselves need to be contextually rich and related to the lives and interests of the students. The tasks might contain discrete subtasks, such as looking up the spelling of words in a dictionary, but these subtasks must be seen as having a purpose within the context of the whole task. However, while such inviting learning activities will increase the likelihood that students will be intrinsically motivated, contextually rich learning activities alone are not enough. The activities also need to be introduced in ways that (1) help students see them as interesting or relevant; (2) let the students know that the activities will be challenging and that the challenge will add to their interest; (3) assure all students that, with effort, they can be successful; (4) provide ways for all students to engage the tasks with their existing sets of concepts and skills; and (5) reduce students' tendencies to compete with one another. As the students work on a task, it is important that the teacher carefully monitor the activity, intervening as needed to ensure that these conditions are provided for each group of students. Finally, at the end of each activity or unit, the teacher can enhance students' motivation for subsequent learning activities by helping them recognize and celebrate their genuine accomplishments.

In sum, CDP lessons have two basic elements in common, which are highlighted in separate sections of the lesson guides. One of these sections, titled "Motivation/Purpose," suggests ways to help students see the relevance, importance, or rewarding aspects of the activity. The other section, "Social Focus," suggests ways to help students understand how to be supportive, respectful, and fair to everyone while accomplishing the learning task. In addition, the tasks themselves are open-ended, allowing students to engage them at several levels, depending on their existing sets of skills and understandings; and they are usually multifaceted, allowing students to bring many different talents to the learning situation.

The excerpts presented at the beginning of this chapter were from the end of a unit on which students had been working for several weeks and thus did not show what the teacher did to enhance intrinsic motivation at the start of the unit. Nevertheless, the conditions necessary for enhancing intrinsic motivation were present. The task, creating a magazine, appeared to have prima facie meaning for most of the students. Although the task was complex and created difficulties for some of the students, they appeared capable of successful engagement at their various levels and with their various skills. The interpersonal environment was supportive and respectful, and there was no evidence of competition among the group members or between groups. The task allowed for the application of several different skills: interpersonal, organizational, English reading and writing, Spanish reading and writing, translation, drawing or illustration, and graphing. The students were also working quite hard, with no promise of stickers, no competition for the best magazine, and no grade to be received for the finished product—but they would have an opportunity to show their work to their classmates and to receive appreciation for it from the class members and the teacher, and the magazines would form part of a class library.

The task was not equally attractive for all students. The teacher's role in engaging the students' intrinsic motivation at the start of the task and in fostering it throughout was essential. Even when tasks do appear to be interesting to most students and have been introduced by the teacher in an engaging way, some students may still find them less interesting or valuable than socializing with their friends. When this happens, the teacher may look for ways to help the group to focus and to see the benefits of doing the task. In some cases, the group may perform this function for itself. The group appearing in the wrap-up excerpt had this problem with some of its members, but managed to solve it without teacher intervention.

Lack of interest is not the only problem teachers face as they strive to tap and promote students' intrinsic motivation. Sometimes groups are unable to find fair and meaningful ways for all members to engage the learning task. The group shown in the second excerpt had a version of this problem, but was able to solve it without teacher assistance.

Finally, when the learning task has been finished and the groups have an opportunity to discuss what they did and learned—their products, their problems, and their successful strategies—motivation is built for the next task. At this time, students receive meaningful recognition for their work, encouragement for future efforts, and ideas and strategies likely to be helpful in the future.

GOALS OF CDP COOPERATIVE LEARNING ACTIVITIES

Social and Ethical, as Well as Intellectual, Development

CDP cooperative learning activities are designed and orchestrated to foster social, ethical, and intellectual development simultaneously. These three general goals are seen as mutually consistent and of equal importance, with the intent that children not only progress in all three areas, but also develop internal commitments toward these goals.

Focus on Intrinsic Motivation

By focusing on the interpersonal values that are relevant to group members' behavior toward one another—values of caring, respect, fairness, and responsibility—CDP cooperative activities emphasize intrinsic reasons for social and ethical learning. Students think about and discuss the importance of these values and the ways in which they can realize and express them in their actions and behaviors within their groups. In the academic area, the teacher will emphasize intrinsic reasons for engaging in the tasks themselves (their inherent interest and importance, their relevance to long-range goals). At the same time, extrinsic reasons or incentives (rewards, grades, punishments, competition) are deemphasized, on the assumption that these divert attention away from the cooperative learning activity itself and onto the incentives, thus potentially undermining students' intrinsic motivation (Amabile, 1989; Lepper & Greene, 1978; Nicholls, 1989).

CHARACTERISTICS OF THE COOPERATIVE ACTIVITIES

Inherent Interest

For teachers to tap and help increase students' intrinsic motivation, the cooperative tasks must be worthy of such motivation. They must either be inherently interesting to students, or the interest, importance, or relevance to long-range goals must be made clear to them.

Developmental Appropriateness

CDP cooperative learning activities are designed to provide children with developmentally appropriate opportunities to work collaboratively. Explicitly designed to fit the intellectual and social skill levels of elementary school children, the activities are limited to those that children can perform with minimal assistance from their teacher. They involve hands-on exploration, allowing students trial-and-error experiences in concrete situations. They also have relatively simple interpersonal interaction requirements, particularly for students at the lower grades. Artificial social structures and rules are avoided (for example, giving each child a chip with the rule that "playing" a chip allows one to speak once, but not again until all the other chips have been "played"), because such structures allow elementary school children to mimic adult performance without really understanding the basis of that performance.

Open-endedness

Because each student's learning is based on personal experience and prior knowledge, each will need to deal with new learning in his or her own unique way within the group context. CDP cooperative learning tasks define broad goals and objectives, leaving room for the individuals and groups to set their own specific goals or to accomplish the task in ways that they find most suitable. When the different members of a group have different skills, interests, or styles, it becomes necessary for them to negotiate to find an approach to the task that will be maximally satisfying and useful for all members. The complementary role of the teacher requires that he or she provide encouragement, challenge, assistance, and feedback appropriate to each group and to each child as such issues are confronted.

Genuine Benefit from Collaboration

Not all learning tasks can be transformed into workable cooperative activities. Some tasks are better done by individuals and do not benefit from collaboration. Good cooperative activities are those in which students are likely to reap the benefits of multiple viewpoints, the security of shared responsibility, or the efficiency of many hands.

Benefit from Many Different Skills or Abilities

Cohen (1986) pointed out that it is important that all students be able to make meaningful contributions to group tasks if group work is to serve the goal of reducing status hierarchies in the classroom. CDP cooperative tasks usually require combinations of different skills, so that different group members will be "good" at different aspects of the task.

HOW GROUPS ARE ORGANIZED

Group Size

Some CDP activities are designed to be done in pairs, and some in larger groups (usually of three to five members). Paired activities are used especially often with younger children and are also very useful for older children who are first being introduced to cooperative learning activities. Larger groups are more appropriate when children have mastered the more complex cognitive and social skills that they require.

Group Membership

CDP cooperative activities are generally designed to be performed by groups that are heterogeneous with respect to ability, knowledge, skill, gender, and any other background characteristics. This provides students at different levels of skill or knowledge the opportunity to help one another, thereby promoting both learning and social competence for the various group members.

Because children naturally gravitate toward others who are like them, we do not have students select their own groups, as this would not be likely to produce heterogeneity. However, there is also evidence that when teachers choose group members for heterogeneity, and the basis of selection is too obvious (e.g., a class has seven Hispanic students, and one is placed in each group), the effect can be to increase the salience of the student background or "status" characteristics and thus to undermine the very understanding and support among the students that is desired (Miller & Brewer, 1986). Group composition is primarily on a random basis, but teachers make adjustments to increase the likelihood that the group members will be able to work well together (for example, by not placing one shy child in a group with three highly assertive ones).

Group Duration

We recommend that teachers use many short-duration partner activities at the start of the year, assigning new partners every day or for every activity. During the first three or four weeks, while the children are getting to know one another and are building their collaborative skills, the teacher works to understand the children, with their particular personalities, talents, and interests. Once the students have developed some collaborative skills and the teacher has learned enough about the students to create groups that are likely to be successful, we recommend forming longer-lasting groups. These groups need to stay together long enough for stable relationships to develop and for students to learn to understand and accommodate to the other members of their group. At the same time, it is important for each student to experience working closely with as many others as possible. This helps students to broaden their interpersonal skills and to develop a sense of community in the classroom as a whole. They also begin to learn that interpersonal values extend widely and should apply to all others, not just to those with whom they are most closely associated.

We recommend that teachers have students change groups often enough so that each student will have worked with all of his or her classmates by the end of the school year. This can be accomplished in various ways: Some teachers organize students into different groups for different subjects, with each group staying together for a month or more before being changed; others have one set of groups at a time, with each group working in all subject areas (with this arrangement, it is necessary to change groups every two or three weeks, in order to give each child experiences with all classmates during the school year).

LESSON STRUCTURE

CDP cooperative lessons are divided into three phases: set-up (or introduction), monitoring (or group activity), and wrap-up (or processing). The set-up phase is designed to orient students to the activity—giving them a clear idea of its academic and social goals and demands—and to elicit their intrinsic motivation by pointing out the task's importance, inherent interest, and/or relevance to long-range goals. During this phase, the teacher describes the various aspects of the activity and engages students in a discussion of how the activity is to be done, how it relates to other activities or experiences, what interpersonal values will be involved, and how these will be expressed in their behavior.

In the monitoring phase, students are engaged in the activity in groups, and the teacher is attentive but not overdirecting. The teacher's role is to assist students' thinking as they perform the task by asking a question or by making a comment or suggestion without undermining the students' responsibility for their own learning. Within a general framework that has been set by the teacher, students are given substantial leeway to come up with their own approaches to tasks. The teacher is available to redirect students when they seem unable to solve a problem, but is careful not to do so too soon or too readily; a certain amount of trial and error and struggle is seen as a valuable part of learning. Student autonomy and self-direction increase as they become more familiar with a particular type of task and with cooperative activity in general.

In the wrap-up phase, the teacher helps students reach a broader understanding of what they have done, both socially and academically. Students are encouraged to think about the activity and their performance as a group, to celebrate their successes, to try to understand their problems, and to come up with their own ideas, generalizations, and plans for future approaches to similar tasks. They are encouraged specifically to think about the implications for their next group activities.

THE TEACHER'S ROLE IN FOSTERING LEARNING DURING CDP COOPERATIVE ACTIVITIES

Foster Intrinsic Motivation

The teacher creates a supportive, noncompetitive environment, avoids the use of extrinsic rewards, and helps students see the intrinsic reasons for learning and for treating one another with care, respect, and fairness.

Relate New Learning to Students' Prior Knowledge and Experience

The teacher presents new information or skills in ways that relate to students' experiences, previous activities, or existing ideas and skills, thereby facilitating their efforts to assimilate new information into their existing knowledge bases.

Challenge Students to Reach beyond Their Existing Knowledge and Skills

The teacher provides students with experiences that create productive confusion or that foster productive mistakes and encourages students' efforts to understand or succeed. For example, the teacher may expose students to different and conflicting points of view or create physical or logical situations that students find surprising (because they are inconsistent with their current concepts and beliefs), thereby facilitating the students' efforts to modify their existing knowledge to incorporate and be consistent with the new information.

Help Students Think More Clearly or Perform at a Higher Level

The teacher gently guides or assists students to reach higher levels of understanding or performance than they would if unassisted. For example, the teacher may design the learning environment to increase the likelihood that students will see certain relationships or regularities, may ask questions or make suggestions that help students focus their efforts, or may engage students in "instructional conversations" (Tharp & Gallimore, 1988) that help them to elaborate on and see the implications of their own thinking.

Help Students Reflect on and Evaluate Their Own Learning

The teacher helps students think about what they learned and how they worked together, not only so that they will better understand what they know, but also so that they will become more aware of attitudes and behaviors that help or hinder their learning or their abilities to work collaboratively.

Intervene Appropriately

When students are working on cooperative tasks in their groups, the teacher takes a monitoring role. The aim is to promote the students' autonomy and self-direction—to give them a chance to solve their social and academic problems in collaboration with their peers, with as little adult guidance as possible. Here the teacher must walk a fine line—giving the students every opportunity to work out their own solutions to social or academic problems, but stepping in when students are floundering unproductively and are unlikely to be able to solve the problems on their own.

THE CLASSROOM SETTING

To operate effectively, the CDP approach requires a total classroom (and, preferably, school) context in which students experience these same values every day. Cooperative learning not only depends on a consistent setting with respect to these values, it also helps to promote their continued development among students and helps to further the climate of caring in the classroom as a whole. Extensive use of CDP cooperative learning helps students and teachers to feel that they are participating in a caring community.

LEARNING CDP COOPERATIVE LEARNING

Students

Students are introduced to cooperative learning gradually, beginning with partner work (groups of two). Depending upon their age and experience, they are presented with tasks that vary not only in their intellectual complexity, but also in their interpersonal complexity (Watson, Hildebrandt, & Solomon, 1988).

Begin with Simple Forms of Collaboration

CDP lessons for younger students (grades K–2) begin with simple open-ended activities that allow, but do not require, joint decision making. Such relatively easy activities are useful for teaching the basic principles of collaborative work because they allow children to focus on fair and considerate ways of working together. Initial lessons allow children to work independently and then see the benefits of combining their work. Young students typically work in pairs at the beginning of the year and progress to larger groups of three or four as their collaborative skills and comfort levels increase.

Older students will have more developed academic and interpersonal skills, but they also may have learned to view their classmates as competitors. When teachers start cooperative learning with such students, they often need to be more explicit in pointing out the benefits of cooperation. In such cases, whole-class projects and other unity builders can be used to help set a friendly, cooperative tone. Class meetings or discussions about what it means to work together cooperatively, and why this is a good thing to do, can help them overcome a competitive or individualistic mindset. It is also usually helpful to begin with partner work when first introducing older students to cooperative learning. Once students are able to work smoothly and effectively as partners, cooperative activities involving larger groups and more complex tasks can then be introduced.

Provide Repeated Opportunities to Do the Same Type of Cooperative Task

When students work cooperatively, they are learning many things at once: interpersonal interaction skills, such as listening and trying to understand another's point of view or explaining and arguing for one's own point of view; ethical understanding, for example, how values such as fairness and respect apply in many different interpersonal situations; academic skills, such as reading, writing, computing, inferring, and synthesizing; and understanding the processes and concepts of the academic disciplines (science, literature, art, mathematics, social science, and so on). Such learning requires repeated trial-and-error opportunities—ideally, using the same or similar cooperative tasks with varying academic contents. With repetition of tasks, students become less uncertain about the task requirements and more adept at the procedures, thereby improving the quality of collaboration.

CDP has developed a large number of cooperative lessons, grouped together by the kind of cooperative process or format they employ. For example, in the "Group Collage" format, students first work jointly to define the overall structure of a collage, each student then creates his or her own individual section, and the students finally work together to combine the individual pieces.

Give Students Opportunities to Reflect on Their Cooperative Learning Experiences

A basic assumption held by proponents of most approaches to cooperative learning is that reflection improves learning (Yager, Johnson, Johnson, & Snider, 1986). Quite simply, this means helping students think back on each learning activity to identify what they did that benefitted their learning and collaborative work, to recognize what was counterproductive, and to review and think about the content of their learning—academic, social, and/or ethical. This process, done primarily during the lesson wrap-up, is an essential element of CDP cooperative learning.

Teachers

Teachers who are learning CDP's approach to cooperative learning need many of the same supports students do: beginning with partner work, repeating the same type of cooperative lesson until familiarity is reached, and having opportunities to reflect on successes and failures. Teachers have also found the CDP cooperative lessons and formats we provide to be helpful to their learning. The lesson guides give examples of all the major aspects of CDP's approach to cooperative learning.

NOTES

We want to thank the teachers of the San Ramon and Hayward, California, school districts who helped and inspired us.

1. Descriptions of this project's origins, development, and evaluation findings appear in many publications (Brown & Solomon, 1983; Solomon et al., 1985; Solomon, Watson, Delucchi, Schaps, & Battistich, 1988; Battistich, Solomon, Watson, Solomon, & Schaps, 1989; Watson, Solomon, Battistich, Schaps, & Solomon, 1989; Solomon, Watson, Schaps, Battistich, & Solomon, 1990; Battistich, Watson, Solomon, Schaps, & Solomon, 1991; and Solomon, Watson, Battistich, Schaps, & Delucchi, 1992).

REFERENCES

Amabile, T. M. (1989). *Growing up creative: Nurturing a lifetime of creativity*. New York: Crown.

Barnes, D., & Todd, F. (1976). *Communication and learning in small groups*. London: Routledge & Kegan Paul.

Battistich, V., Solomon, D., Watson, M., Solomon, J., & Schaps, E. (1989). Effects of an elementary school program to enhance prosocial behavior on children's social problem-solving skills and strategies. *Journal of Applied Developmental Psychology*, *10*, 147–169.

Battistich, V., Watson, M., Solomon, D., Schaps, E., & Solomon, J. (1991). The Child Development Project: A comprehensive program for the development of prosocial character. In W. M. Kurtines & J. L. Gewirtz (Eds.), *Handbook of moral behavior and development* (Vol. 3). Hillsdale, NJ: Lawrence Erlbaum Associates.

Brown, D., & Solomon, D. (1983). A model for prosocial learning: An in-progress field study. In D. L. Bridgeman (Ed.), *The nature of prosocial development: Interdisciplinary theories and strategies*. New York: Academic Press.

Cohen, E. G. (1986). *Designing groupwork: Strategies for the heterogeneous classroom*. New York: Teachers College Press.

Johnson, D. W., & Johnson, R. T. (1984). *Cooperation in the classroom*. New Brighton, MN: Interaction Book Company.

Lepper, M. R., & Greene, D. (1978). *The hidden costs of reward*. Hillsdale, NJ: Lawrence Erlbaum Associates.

Miller, N., & Brewer, M. B. (1986). *When do the benefits of cooperation and contact generalize?* Paper presented at the meeting of the American Educational Research Association, San Francisco.

Nicholls, J. G. (1989). *The competitive ethos and democratic education*. Cambridge, MA: Harvard University Press.

Rogoff, B. (1990). *Apprenticeship in thinking: Cognitive development in social context*. New York: Oxford University Press.

Sharan, Y., & Sharan, S. (1992). *Expanding cooperative learning through group investigation*. New York: Teachers College Press.

Solomon, D., Watson, M., Battistich, V., Schaps, E., & Delucchi, K. (1992). Creating a caring community: A school-based program to promote children's sociomoral development. In F. Oser, A. Dick, & J. L. Patry (Eds.), *Effective and responsible teaching: A new synthesis*. San Francisco: Jossey-Bass.

Solomon, D., Watson, M., Battistich, V., Schaps, E., Tuck, P., Solomon, J., Cooper, C., & Ritchey, W. (1985). A program to promote interpersonal consideration and cooperation in children. In R. Slavin, S. Sharan, S. Kagan, R. Hertz-Lazarowitz, C. Webb, & R. Schmuck (Eds.), *Learning to cooperate, cooperating to learn*. New York: Plenum Press.

Solomon, D., Watson, M., Delucchi, K., Schaps, E., & Battistich, V. (1988). Enhancing children's prosocial behavior in the classroom. *American Educational Research Journal*, *25*, 527–554.

Solomon, D., Watson, M., Schaps, E., Battistich, V., & Solomon, J. (1990). Cooperative learning as part of a comprehensive program designed to promote prosocial development. In S. Sharan (Ed.), *Cooperative learning: Theory and research*. New York: Praeger.

Tharp, R. G., & Gallimore, R. (1988). *Rousing minds to life: Teaching, learning, and schooling in social context*. New York: Cambridge University Press.

Vygotsky, L. (1962). *Thought and language*. Cambridge, MA: MIT Press.

Watson, M., Hildebrandt, C., & Solomon, D. (1988). Cooperative learning as a means of promoting prosocial development among kindergarten and early primary grade children. *International Journal of Social Education, 3*, 34–47.

Watson, M., Solomon, D., Battistich, V., Schaps, E., & Solomon, J. (1989). The Child Development Project: Combining traditional and developmental approaches to values education. In L. Nucci (Ed.), *Moral development and character education: A dialogue*. Berkeley, CA: McCutchan.

Yager, S., Johnson, R. T., Johnson, D. W., & Snider, B. (1986). The impact of group processing on achievement in cooperative learning. *Journal of Social Psychology, 126*, 389–397.

10

Creating "Thought-Full" Classrooms: Fostering Cognitive Literacy via Cooperative Learning and Integrated Strategies Instruction

Edwin S. Ellis and R. Kevin Feldman

> In times of change learners inherit the earth, while the learned find themselves beautifully prepared for a world that no longer exists.
> Eric Hoffer

The instructional model described here, called Integrated Strategies Instruction, is intended to promote "cognitive literacy." It draws on key contributions from both the cooperative learning and the thinking improvement schools of instruction. Cognitive literacy refers to the notion that all students need to become "literate" in the strategies and processes of "how to learn" as they develop the "habits of mind" consistent with effective information processing and problem solving. The rationale for the integration of cooperative learning and cognitively based instruction is presented in the first part of this chapter. Later we describe how the two approaches can be integrated into content-area (subject-matter) instruction to promote "thought-full" classrooms.

WHY THINK TOGETHER?

Presseisen (1992) viewed the nexus of cooperative learning and thinking improvement programs as a natural outgrowth of cognitive-developmental psychology. Marzano (1992) noted that cooperative learning fosters cognitive development by (1) generating rich and varied alternatives to traditional teacher-directed instruction and (2) providing opportunities for students to check for accuracy and explore options by comparing their ideas to those of other group members. Resnick (1987a) reviewed a variety of thinking improvement programs and found that the more effective methods had some kind of cooperative/collaborative components and advocated cooperative thinking to enhance learning. Working in cooperative groups gives students a window into the thought processes of their team members, thus mediating and shaping their own thinking. This is especially true in heterogeneous groups where achievement levels, sociocultural backgrounds, divergent perspectives, and other characteristics are intentionally mixed when students engage in structured cooperative group work. The students' diversity is a potential asset that can enhance the breadth and quality of peer and teacher-student communication in the classroom, rather than simply being seen as a problem to be remedied. Students who effectively collaborate in cooperative group work have access to a vastly increased range of options, topics to investigate, strategies to apply, and reactions to ponder, thus fostering a much richer context in which to solve problems (Sharan & Sharan, 1992). Exchanging and discussing ideas in cooperative groups also provides a safe and "risk-encouraging" environment when the teacher creates a user-friendly approach to conceptual development (Presseisen, 1992).

HOW DOES COOPERATIVE LEARNING ENHANCE THINKING?

Numerous studies have noted the positive effects of cooperative learning on general student achievement (Slavin, 1990; Johnson & Johnson, 1989). A review of the literature (Johnson & Johnson, 1992) found equally impressive support for the relationship between cooperative learning and increases in various measures of higher-order thinking skills, cognition, and metacognition. These include improved quality of reasoning strategies, increased transfer of learning to novel situations, more frequent use of metacognitive strategies, and higher levels of cognitive and moral reasoning on Piagetian and Kohlbergian tasks. The Johnsons concluded that "the superiority of cooperative over competitive and individualistic learning increases as the task is more conceptual, requires more problem solving, necessitates more higher level reasoning and critical thinking, needs more creative answers, seeks long term retention and requires more application of what is learned" (1992, p. 122).

If thinking is fundamentally a personal process, how do we account for the findings that collaboration and cooperation appear to be so beneficial to this individual activity? There are any number of appealing explanations based on social-cognitive learning theory and the basic tenets of cooperative learning that help us to understand how it promotes the kind of cognitive activities so critical to successful learning and achievement. A brief accounting of this phenomenon states the following:

1. The creation of a positive "mental climate" (Marzano, Pickering, & Brandt, 1990) encourages risk taking, speaking up/out, and viewing the classroom as a "community of learners" (Brown & Campione, in press).

2. The expectation that one will have to summarize, explain, and perhaps teach what one is learning requires higher levels of cognitive organization and elaboration than simply learning the material for one's own use.

3. Discussion in cooperative learning groups promotes more frequent oral summarizing, explaining, and elaborating of what one knows (these cognitive activities are associated with memory and retention). "Meaning is formulated via the process of conveying it" (Johnson & Johnson, 1992).

4. Heterogeneous grouping combined with multiple-ability tasks fosters divergent thinking, creative responses, use of the diverse talents each member contributes, mixed expectations for competence, perspective taking, and respect for individual differences such that diversity becomes an asset to be valued, not a problem to be gotten rid of (Cohen, Lotan, & Catanzarite 1990).

5. Peers mediate each other's learning by modeling different levels of thinking, explaining how they solved a problem, and giving each other feedback and encouragement (Maheady, Mallette, & Harper, 1991).

6. Conflicting opinions, interpretations, and explanations must be resolved, causing more sophisticated dialogue among group members. Johnson and Johnson (1992) found that structured controversy is superior to debate in terms of learning outcomes.

7. Many cooperative learning approaches (e.g., Complex Instruction; Cohen, 1986) explicitly prompt students to focus on the cognitive and metacognitive aspects of their task by asking how the group arrived at the answer, not simply on trying to find the "correct answer."

The integration of cooperative learning and cognitive strategy instruction can provide educators with the tools they need to create schools and classrooms where students construct their own understanding of knowledge.

INTEGRATED STRATEGIES INSTRUCTION

The Integrated Strategies Instruction model focuses on how teachers can facilitate cognitive literacy in the context of specific subject matter. Integrated Strategies Instruction is a multidimensional model involving a wide variety of specific instructional procedures that facilitate use of cognitive strategies during instruction. It is specifically designed for use in heterogeneous classes whose students require in-depth and intensive instruction to ensure success (Ellis, 1992). These students include those with learning disabilities and other mild learning handicaps. Through teacher-guided heuristic applications, students learn how to use information-processing and problem-solving skills when mediating learning and performing. In short, the goal is to assist students to become cognitively literate.

To assist students with learning difficulties to become cognitively literate, the model involves (*a*) teaching subject matter strategically in a manner that promotes rapid understanding, assimilation, and retention via teacher mediation of student information-processing skills; (*b*) teaching a cognitive literacy strategy to promote subsequent student mediation of information-processing skills; and (*c*) integrating these two instructional orientations so that strategy instruction takes place as part of subject-matter instruction. The instructional model integrates components of teacher-directed instruction, collaborative problem solving, and cooperative learning. Before proceeding with the instructional aspects of this model, some comments are necessary on the theoretical basis underlying the design of the cognitive literacy strategy.

THE COGNITIVE LITERACY STRATEGY

A generic cognitive literacy strategy called PASS was developed to facilitate students' understanding of how metacognition and cognitive strategies can be used strategically. The purpose of teaching PASS is to connect students and teachers to the essence of cognitive theory, which is learning. At the heart of the PASS strategy is learning how to think strategically, to curb impulsiveness, to encourage reflection, and to develop students' "habits of the mind" conducive to effective information processing and problem solving.

PASS is composed of a set of steps corresponding to three critical phases of thinking: activation processing, on-line processing, and consolidating and extending processing. The terms "think ahead" (activation processes), "think during" (on-line processes), and "think back" (consolidation processes) are used when communicating with students about effective thinking. The strategy steps are designed to make key cognitive processes more concrete for novice learners (see Figure 10.1).

THREE PHASES OF THE PASS COGNITIVE LITERACY STRATEGY

Recent research on cognition has provided a wealth of information regarding cognition and learning. These findings support a model of the mind that recursively engages in activating on-line processing or schema building, and consolidating or extending processes (Jones, Palinscar, Ogle, & Carr, 1987). To activate thinking, the learner becomes cognizant of new information and then does something to activate prior knowledge. During this activation process, the learner focuses attention on the new information and its features and on appropriate strategies for understanding it as well as establishing a purpose for learning it, performing a task related to it, or solving a problem that involves it. Comparing the new information to

Figure 10.1
Cognitive Processing and Corresponding Cognitive Literacy Strategy Steps

type of cognitive processing	steps of PASS cognitive literacy strategy
activating processes(*THINK AHEAD*)	**P**review, review & predict

* understanding task demands and establishing goals
* activating background knowledge
* forming hypotheses & predictions about nature of task & topic

on-line processing *(THINK DURING)*   **A**sk & answer questions

* questioning to confirm or revise predictions
* questioning to utilize background knowledge
* questioning to monitor comprehension & progress toward goals
* questioning to solve problems & direct thinking
* questioning to relate & integrate new knowledge with old
* questioning to look back or anticipate future

consolidating processes *(THINK BACK)*   **S**ummarize
* summarizing / paraphrasing   **S**ynthesize
* relating parts to a larger context or whole
* extending new knowledge by relating it to other areas
* extending new skills to new problem domains

prior knowledge results in forming hypotheses, predictions, and/or questions about the new data or the nature of the task before the learner. As the hypotheses are formed, the mind then shifts into on-line processing or schema building. In essence, previewing new information, reviewing related prior knowledge, and predicting what the new information is about are key activation processes. These processes are manifested in the "P" step of the PASS strategy: "Preview, review, and predict."

During on-line processes, the mind engages in two important operations. The first is interacting with the information using self-questioning strategies, visualizing the information, forecasting, looking back to verify, looking ahead to anticipate, and so on. The second operation is the testing of hypotheses or predictions against prior knowledge and the monitoring of comprehension. Some hypotheses are confirmed and assimilated into an overall schema of understanding about a topic, while others are held in abeyance and new hypotheses, predictions, and/or questions are formed in order to "recycle" the "making sense" of the new information. The "A" step in the PASS cognitive literacy strategy, "Ask and answer questions," is designed to cue students to engage in these thoughtful behaviors.

During consolidating or extending processes, the mind is consolidating what was learned and understanding the information as a whole. Some of these processes involve efforts to extend what was learned, some involve synthesizing or connecting various new ideas as they stream in, and some involve efforts to summarize and/or express what has been learned. These

Figure 10.2
Writing Version of the Cognitive Literacy Strategy

Preview, review & predict

Preview your knowledge, audience & goals
Review main ideas / details to tell
Predict best order

Ask & answer questions

How can I link the reader's background knowledge with my topic in the first sentence?
Does this make sense? How can I rephrase this so it will be clearer?
Have I left anything out?
Should I explain this idea more? What else can I say about this?
What is an example of this idea? Another example?
What background knowledge will the reader have that I can link this idea to?

Summarize

Think about who will read this.
Think about the main thing you want them to remember about it.
Write a sentence that tells what the whole message was about.

Search for errors & correct

Search for sentences that don't make sense.
Search for "left-out" words.
Search for punctuation, capitalization, and spelling errors.

key processes are represented by the last steps of the PASS strategy, "Summarize" and "Synthesize."

In this chapter we focus on the use of the Integrated Strategies Instruction model as a writing strategy. The next section explains how the strategy is used to facilitate expository writing, and in the section that follows, we discuss the role of cooperative learning in integrating instruction in the writing version of the cognitive strategy with instruction in traditional content areas.

THE WRITING VERSION OF THE PASS COGNITIVE
LITERACY STRATEGY

The purpose of the PASS cognitive literacy strategy is to teach students to use an efficient and effective approach to expository writing, and to facilitate students' use of self-regulation behaviors related to self-motivation, self-reinforcement, and goal-directed self-speech during prewriting (think-ahead), production (think-during), and revision (think-back) processes. Figure 10.2 illustrates the steps to the writing strategy.

Since writing is thinking on paper, the student must manipulate and impose order on data according to logical methods or organization. The ultimate aim of writing should be to have students actively consider their

Figure 10.3
A Graphic Organizer

What? *What is this whole thing about?*

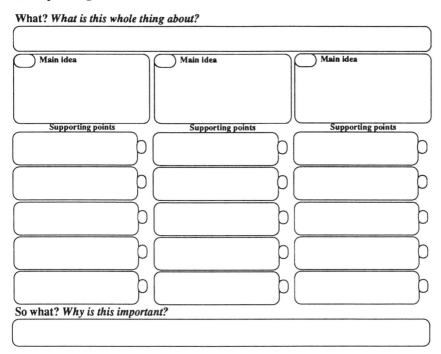

So what? *Why is this important?*

reading audience and to choose the ways in which they impose order on the information they are dealing with so that the information will make sense to others. Use of graphic organizers has been found very beneficial in helping students organize their ideas for writing. Figure 10.3 illustrates a "general-to-specific" graphic organizer that we have found very beneficial. The steps of the writing strategy and the planning forms provide a framework that encourages students to look at specific situations, perceive key elements about which to write, and organize the major attributes.

The Think-Ahead Process

The initial steps of the strategy facilitate prewriting activities. Students learn that effective writing requires about as much time for thinking and organizing as for the actual act of writing. Prewriting by analysis is a three-stage process:

1. Preview. Before putting pencil to paper, students are taught to preview their knowledge about a topic and focus on those aspects of the topic they know the most about. They also think in terms of who their reading audience will be and consider what the readers will know about their topic and want to know about

it. In addition, the writers consider the intrinsic goals of their task (e.g., to entertain, to inform, to create suspense, to make someone feel empathetic, liked, appreciated, and so on) and their extrinsic goals (relative importance of the writing product, to get a high grade, to finish within a certain time, and so on).

2. Review main ideas and details. Writers use their background knowledge of the topic in conjunction with ongoing information gathering to identify and list the main ideas they plan to write later. These are indicated on a graphic organizer (Figure 10.4). Once main ideas have been identified, students then list specific details that will be used to explain or elaborate upon each of the main ideas. During this phase, main ideas and supporting points are identified without concern for the order in which they will be written.

3. Predict best order. Once students have brainstormed their ideas and listed them on the graphic organizer, they then consider the needs of their reading audience and predict the best order for expressing these ideas in a manner that will make sense to the reader. First they determine the order of the main ideas that will be expressed by indicating their order in the appropriate boxes on the graphic organizer. Then they prioritize the specific supporting points in a similar fashion for each main idea (see Figure 10.4).

The Think-During Process

Having completed the prewriting activities, students are now ready to begin the production process. Students use the ordered main ideas and supporting points to guide the organization of their draft. However, they need to realize that they are not limited to writing only those ideas noted on their graphic organizer. Students use self-questioning strategies that focus on two closely related areas of production: (1) questions related to monitoring the needs of the anticipated audience in relation to what they have written, and (2) questions related to fluency and elaboration. During the production stage, writers ask these questions repeatedly to ensure a quality product.

1. Ask and answer questions related to monitoring audience needs. These types of questions are designed to help writers keep their audience in mind as they write. For example, students use self-questioning to produce an opening sentence that cues the reader's background knowledge related to the topic of the essay (e.g., "You probably know that the Bald Eagle is our National Bird, but you may not know that it is in danger"). Other questions focus on the clarity of their message to ascertain if it will make sense to readers (e.g., finding jumbled sentences or needing to explain an idea more fully).

2. Ask and answer questions related to fluency and elaboration. Young writers often say as little as possible. Therefore, students are taught to ask questions to promote fluency in writing (e.g., "What else can I say about this?" "What is an example of this idea? What is another example?" "What background knowledge will the reader have that I can link this idea to?").

Figure 10.4
Main Ideas and Supporting Points on a Graphic Organizer

What? *What is this whole thing about?*

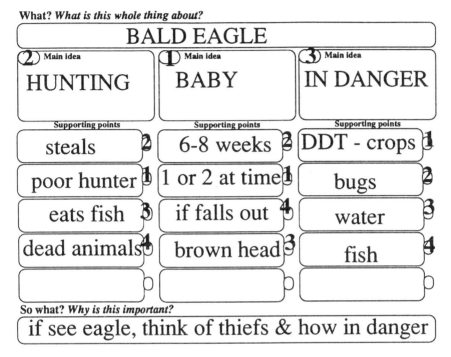

So what? *Why is this important?*

if see eagle, think of thiefs & how in danger

The Think-Back Process

In the writing domain, thinking back focuses primarily on (1) processes related to reviewing the ideas communicated and summarizing them in a closing paragraph or sentence, and (2) thinking back about the goals for the written product and determining what else needs to be done to attain these goals. Specifically, it involves reviewing what was written and editing and revising.

1. Summarize the message. Writers reflect again on their potential reading audience and their overall message. To help young writers generate a summary statement, they are encouraged to ask themselves questions such as, "If the reader only remembers one idea from your writing, what would you hope it would be?" "When somebody reads your writing, what would they say the whole thing was about?"

2. Search for errors and correct. Although writers are encouraged to think of the needs of their reading audience throughout the prewriting and production process, this last step is the final opportunity for them to think back and check for

Figure 10.5
Sample of Writing about Bald Eagles

You probably know that the bald eagle is our national bird, and you have seen it on U.S. symbols and money. There are many interesting things about bald eagles. They usually lay only one or two eggs at a time. The eggs are white with blue spots. It takes about 6-8 weeks for them to hatch. Baby bald eagles have brown heads. If the baby falls out of its nest, it dies.

Most people think bald eagles are great hunters. Actually, they are terrible hunters. They usually get their food by stealing from other birds. They eat fish and dead animals. Not many people know that our national bird is really a thief!

Bald eagles are in danger of becoming extinct because of what is happening to the environment. Farmers put poison called DDT on their crops. Bugs eat the DDT. Fish eat the bugs. When the bald eagle eats the fish, DDT gets in them. The DDT causes egg shells to be too thin, so they break. Babies cannot hatch. If the babies cannot hatch, then there will be fewer bald eagles. Ever since farmers found out about this, they have been more careful about using DDT and other chemicals, but it is still a problem. The next time you see a picture of a bald eagle, remember that although it is a thief, it is in danger.

clarity, word omissions, or errors in conventions of print (e.g., spelling, capitalization, and punctuation).

Figure 10.5 illustrates a writing sample based on the ideas outlined on the general-to-specific graphic organizer described here.

THE ROLE OF COOPERATIVE LEARNING IN INTEGRATING STRATEGY AND CONTENT INSTRUCTION

Different types of cooperative learning activities for different learning tasks are employed during Integrated Strategies Instruction. Some focus on facilitating understanding of a complex idea or concept. Other applications focus primarily on cultivating skills in applying information-processing strategies. Thus the type of cooperative learning activity employed at any point in a lesson must fit the learning demands of the task. Teachers must skillfully choose the appropriate cooperative learning strategies for a given lesson or unit (see chapter 20 in this volume).

Four instructional stages, their general focus, and a brief description of teaching the writing version of the cognitive strategy using cooperative learning are noted in Figure 10.6. The four instructional stages are (1) orienting, (2) framing, (3) applying, and (4) extending. These processes generally occur in phases, but they have considerable overlap. These teaching processes provide a loose framework for integrating teacher-directed instruction with dialytic or constructive learning. We have found that with less capable learners, initial instruction should be primarily explicit and

Figure 10.6
Summary of ISI Instructional Stages, General Purpose, and Examples

STAGE	Instructional Emphasis	What Happens in the Context of Teaching a Writing Strategy	Sample Cooperative Learning Activities
ORIENTING	Orienting students to ways of processing information. Teaching content strategically; providing an experiential base for key information processes strategies, but not explicitly teaching these processes.	Teacher uses general-to-specific graphic organizer when addressing to-be-learned content information; students learn how information can be structured in general-to-specific format and how to construct these types of graphic organizers.	**Think-Pair-Share:** Students dialogue to summarize key content information, prioritize in terms of relevance or importance. **Modified 'Jigsaw':** Students given partially completed graphic organizer (main ideas listed); students conduct research & fill in details; teams then teach other members their findings.
FRAMING	Framing student's background knowledge of related information = processing tactics into a specific cognitive strategy.	Teacher describes the writing strategy steps, discusses rationale for its use & situations and settings in which it can be used. Teacher models the strategy steps using think-aloud techniques.	**Thin-Pair-Share:** Identify different situations and settings where using the strategy would be beneficial; identify how the writing strategy ties in with their knowledge of the graphic organizer used to learn content. **Modified group investigation:** Students dialogue to identify components of the strategy that are similar and different from what they usually do when writing.
APPLYING	Applying the strategy to meet task-demands of content course; Integrating use of the strategy with ongoing content instruction.	Teacher collaborates with students in the writing tasks related to the content of the course; designs learning activities that integrate use of graphic organizers and the writing strategy with acquiring an understanding of the content; integrates cues to use the writing strategy with writing tasks; e.g., *"Draw a graphic organizer that illustrates three reasons why Columbus went home in chairs on his last voyage. Include related facts. Explain these reasons using PASS."*	**Team writing about content taught:** C-L teams use completed organizers to write about content previously mediated by teacher. **Group investigation with writing assignment:** Teams investigate information related to specific topic; collaborate to create graphic organizer, use graphic organizer to share findings with class and plan and write report.
EXTENDING	Use what was learned about the cognitive strategy as a basis for understanding new applications; creating & using new strategies.	*Extending writing strategy & graphic organizer to use with other information formats:* compare / contrast, cause / effect, etc. *Extending writing strategy to other problem domains:* Teacher collaborates with students to create a new version of the cognitive literacy strategy; in this case, they work together to create an editing version of PASS.	**Group investigation: Research and evaluation:** C-L teams engage in writing projects related to content of the class and experiment with editing version of the cognitive literacy strategy; engage in team editing of writing assignments; teams share results, make refinements in strategy as needed.

directive in nature. This should gradually give way to more constructive types of learning experiences. This pattern is illustrated in the following sequence by Vickie, a middle school social studies teacher.

Orienting

Orienting instructional processes are used to provide a basis for subsequent instruction in the cognitive literacy strategy. The teacher uses instructional devices to evoke the cognitive processes relevant to the subject matter. In other words, teachers prompt the use of cognitive strategies that facilitate content mastery. During the next phase of instruction, students will learn a strategy for self-mediating similar cognitive processes. For example, if the teacher is planning on teaching a writing strategy that uses specific graphic organizers, these are employed to teach subject matter during orienting instruction. The intent is to provide students with a set of experiences showing the benefits of performing the strategic processes.

Orienting instruction occurs throughout the course of instruction. Thus the mediation of subject-matter learning via strategy-based instructional procedures and devices continues throughout the framing, applying, and extending stages. A variety of strategy-based instructional routines are applied, including (1) the mediation of think-ahead, think-during, and think-back processes for text perusal, interpreting visual aids, and reading comprehension; (2) the use of graphic organizers depicting various information-organization formats (e.g., hierarchial, compare/contrast, cause/effect, and sequential process); and (3) use of various mnemonic memory devices (e.g., key-word mnemonics, peg-word mnemonics, first-letter mnemonics, paired associates, and analogical anchors).

Initially during the orienting phase of instruction, Vickie integrated instructive techniques with specific cooperative learning activities to help students understand the content. First, she analyzed her social studies curriculum and reflected on her own knowledge of the subject. Then she constructed graphic organizers depicting the overall topic, the main ideas of the lesson, and the various specific details associated with each. She provided students with blank graphic organizers on which to take notes during the class discussion, and she presented the information while mediating students' discussions and questions. After the main ideas and supporting information had been discussed and noted on the graphic organizers, Vickie then initiated a "Think-Pair-Share" cooperative learning format (Kagan, 1990). Students were asked to evaluate each of the main ideas and supporting details and to rank-order them in terms of their group's perception of the ideas' relative importance. Students were then asked to share their rankings with other groups and explain why specific ideas attained the rankings assigned to them.

Vickie used similar versions of this lesson structure for several class meetings. As students became familiar with the graphic organizer and its advantages, her lessons began to take on a more constructive orientation. Students were given partially completed graphic organizers where the main ideas had been listed. Each group was assigned a main-idea topic and was then responsible for identifying the various supporting details that should be listed in association with the main idea. After Vickie had introduced the main ideas, cooperative groups of students were given opportunities to use information source materials such as textbooks, encyclopedias, and interviews to identify additional important related information. Groups later shared their findings with the other groups. At the end of the activity, each student had developed an extensive graphic organizer depicting the main ideas of a topic and a host of related details. Vickie then had the groups rank the main ideas in terms of their importance.

As students became more competent and confident in the use of the general-to-specific graphic organizer, Vickie's class became more constructive in its orientation. In the tradition of the Jigsaw II format (Kagan, 1990), groups selected topics that they researched and created general-to-specific graphic organizers. For example, using the Jigsaw II strategy, Vickie placed her class in heterogeneous teams or home groups of four students each and introduced a new unit on the Crusades. She guided the class in identifying four key themes or questions to research (e.g., What role did propaganda play in recruiting men to fight?). The teams met and discussed who would become the expert on each of the four topics. The students met in expert groups with three students from other teams that had chosen the same topic. In the expert groups, team members discussed ideas, examined source materials, and explored how to best complete a general-to-specific graphic organizer that explained their topic. (Vickie might have chosen to give each team a resource card describing what kinds of reference materials they had available and listing additional subquestions to help them zero in on essential information.)

Students then returned to their home groups with a completed graphic to contribute to their team's overall understanding of the unit. Vickie monitored the expert groups' progress to ensure that they were able to accurately cover the key ideas in their graph and that each student could adequately convey the findings to his or her home group. During the process, Vickie took on the role of the "expert learner" as she collaborated with the students during their research. At this point she modeled through her dialogue with students the thinking processes she used as she weighed information and made decisions about it.

Framing

Framing instructional processes are used to show students how the set of strategic processes previously modeled and prompted during the orienting instruction can be "framed" into a strategy. The purpose of this stage is to have students acquire their own personalized understanding of these processes and how they are used. Students need to understand that performing the various cognitive strategies is a circuitous, nonalgorithmic process and that the steps of the cognitive strategy provide a general framework for using various information processes systematically and circuitously.

When framing is used, the strategy instruction involves describing the strategy to students, modeling how it is performed, and promoting student elaboration on the strategic processes. During the explanation of the learning strategy, the teacher draws upon students' experiences associated with the information processes provided during the orientation stage. To do this, analogies are drawn between the instructional routines used by the teacher to teach the content lessons and the cognitive strategy that students can use to mediate their own learning. Thus "informed training" procedures (Brown, 1978) and "direct explanation" (Roehler & Duffy, 1984) are used when communicating the critical features of a set of problem-solving processes. Teacher-student dialogue focuses on the critical overt or covert behaviors associated with each step in the strategy. It also focuses on why these behaviors are essential to the overall problem-solving process (Roehler & Duffy, 1984). When the teacher is modeling the strategy, he or she uses "think-aloud" techniques to show students how self-instruction is used to analyze problems or tasks, activate prior knowledge of potential strategies and tactics, hypothesize about which strategy will best address the task at hand.

Initially, the framing stage may appear to be primarily expository, but it entails considerable dialogue with students. The teacher describes and models the strategy while at the same time engaging students in dialogue about the strategy and related experiences of their own. Short cooperative learning activities can be embedded into the framing stage.

Once Vickie's students were familiar with the graphic organizer and its relative benefits for organizing information, Vickie facilitated Think-Pair-Share. Students were asked to identify as many uses of the hierarchial graphic organizer as possible (to take notes in class, to organize information when studying for a test, to organize plans for a trip, and so on). As students presented their findings to the class, she channeled the discussion onto using the graphic organizer when planning to write. She then began to describe the writing version of the cognitive strategy and to tell and model for students how the organizer is used in conjunction with the strategy. To facilitate personal investment and motivation to learn the strategy, she had the cooperative groups identify settings in which the strategy could be applied to make writing tasks easier and to improve the quality of their products. The groups were asked to share the strategy and graphic organizer with other students and adults, and to find out in what ways the strategy was similar to writing processes they used and valued and in what ways it was different.

Applying

Applying instructional processes is designed to teach students to use the learning strategy independently. Nevertheless, at this point in the instructional sequence, content and strategy instruction become integrated. During this type of instruction, information-processing skills are applied in multiple contexts. For example, students practice using the cognitive literacy strategy with various kinds of subject matter, and the teacher continues using the instructional routines to teach the content that is loosely matched with the strategy.

To teach students to use the task-specific strategy, various forms of coaching are provided by the teacher. Cooperative learning activities are used extensively during this stage of instruction. Teachers provide students with a variety of stimulus materials from their curriculum to practice applying the strategy. These multiple practice opportunities should be accompanied by extensive use of teacher-student dialogues to ensure that students are learning to perform the strategy effectively.

The steps of the cognitive literacy strategy serve only as a general guide for one approach to performing a specific academic task. Students need to recognize that (*a*) the approach is not necessarily a strictly linear process and thus can be modified if it increases student effectiveness, and (*b*) other approaches may also be effective in solving the problem. The strategy should be viewed as a routine that can be flexibly applied and modified, and students can be encouraged to adapt or extend the strategy for other academic problems.

Once Vickie had thoroughly described, modeled, and discussed the writing application of the cognitive literacy strategy, she began coaching students in its application to the social studies curriculum. Initially, Vickie used fairly explicit coaching techniques commonly associated with "guided practice" forms of direct instruction. The first writing task was essentially a classwide activity. Vickie taught the social studies lesson using traditional presentation/question/discussion techniques. Then she directed the class to form cooperative groups and to write a brief essay about the topic previously taught. She collaborated with students to identify main ideas and supporting details on a graphic organizer. Together, via brief minidebates with the class at large and, at times, within the cooperative groups, decisions were made with regard to prioritizing main ideas and details for writing. For example, the prioritization of the details for the first main idea was undertaken primarily by Vickie. Students observed her thinking aloud as she weighed the information. The prioritization of the details for the second main idea was undertaken by the class at large as Vickie facilitated a minidebate. The prioritization of the details for the third main idea was undertaken by cooperative groups.

She then wrote the brief essay on the board as students collaborated with her to phrase sentences, decide what to say next, and so forth. A similar format was used in the construction of the sentences for the essay. For the first main idea and detail sentences, Vickie modeled the thinking processes involved in constructing the sentences and wrote them on the board. For the second main idea and subsequent detail sentences, Vickie collaborated with the class at large to construct them. Students worked in their cooperative groups to construct the third main idea and related sentences. As this process progressed, each group completed its own graphic organizer, constructed sentences for the essay, and structured the essay.

Throughout this process, Vickie referred to the strategy, cueing students to tell her what to do next. Subsequent writing activities and tasks gradually became more student directed as students demonstrated competence in using the strategy. Eventually, groups were assigned group projects that required them to create graphic organizers and a written product using the writing version of the PASS strategy. The teams selected the prewriting graphic organizer that best fit their topic and completed it as a group, drawing on the combined resources of the members. For example, the team might choose a compare/contrast graphic organizer to help it develop a prewriting map to discuss the lives of Frederick Douglass and Abraham Lincoln. The students would explore in detail how to best fill out their graphic organizer using the dialogue format Vickie had previously modeled for the class. The last step required each student to use the completed graphic as a guide to help structure the writing of an individual essay on the Douglass/Lincoln topic.

Vickie also integrated cues to use the writing strategy throughout her curriculum, requiring its use on essay test questions, when answering study-guide questions, and in other areas. She also continued to use the graphic organizers as a means for facilitating comprehension.

While Vickie provided ample opportunities for students to capitalize on the benefits of cooperative learning when practicing the writing strategy, she realized that she had to ensure that students were also able to perform the strategy independently as well as cooperatively with others. She was then able to monitor each individual student's progress in mastering the strategy and take actions to ensure that students who lagged received extra instruction from her or from peer tutors.

Extending

Many students are relatively ineffective at conducting a rational analysis that reveals underlying structures involved in strategies that they are attempting to learn (Derry, 1990). Nor do many appear to activate appropriate prior knowledge that can be used strategically (Short & Weissberg-Benchell, 1989). They do not use what they know about strategic functioning to extend this knowledge into new problem-solving domains. The focus of extending instruction, therefore, is on teaching students to (a) adapt the previously learned version of the strategy as well as create versions for different academic problems, and (b) experiment with these adaptations and creations. Thus the primary purpose of extending instructional processes is to help students extend their knowledge of how information processes associated with a recently learned version of the strategy can be used in other ways and on other problems.

The instructional processes during the extending phase focus on enabling students to use the PASS cognitive literacy strategy to create new strategies for use in other problem domains (Ellis, Deshler, & Schumaker, 1989; Harris & Pressley, 1991). Once these student-designed strategies have been developed, then teachers design opportunities for students to experiment, evaluate, and refine them. Although new strategies may be "framed" during this stage of instruction, the teacher's role differs somewhat from that which occurred during the framing stage. During this earlier stage, the teacher provided a considerable degree of direct explanation and explicit instruction in the information processes, that is, exogenous constructivism (Moshman, 1982). Here, experts' understandings of these different kinds of knowledge were explicitly communicated to students. Declarative knowledge was addressed by telling students what the strategies are; procedural knowledge was addressed by telling and modeling for students how to use the strategies; conditional knowledge was addressed by discussing with students when and where the strategies can be applied to help them reach their goals. On the other hand, the teacher's role when using extending processes is more consistent with the notion of dialectical constructivism (Moshman, 1982). A degree of prompting and guidance is provided by teachers, but they avoid explicitly telling students what to do and how to do it. The intent here is for students to construct their own understandings of declarative, procedural, and conditional knowledge as a result of interacting with others. Dialogue is designed to provide the learner with just enough support and guidance to accomplish a goal that would not be possible without the mediation (Vygotsky, 1978; Wood, Bruner, & Ross, 1976). During this stage, the teacher acts more like a facilitator or collaborator in the learning process than a deliverer of knowledge. This is not to imply, however, that teachers do not provide input or share their knowledge and expertise with students during this process.

Once Vickie was confident that her students were performing the writing strategy and understood its operations thoroughly, she began to extend students' knowledge of the strategy and general-to-specific graphic organizer in two ways. First, Vickie wanted to extend students' understanding of general-to-specific information formats and of graphic organizers to other formats. To do this, she taught a modified version of orienting, framing, and applying, focusing on the use of compare/contrast formats and graphic organizers to facilitate understanding of the content and in conjunction with the writing strategy.

Second, while she continued to provide activities that required integration of the writing strategy with the learning of the social studies material, she facilitated student construction of new applications of the cognitive literacy strategy. Vickie had noticed that although the organizational aspects of her students' writing had improved considerably, the editing aspects left much to be desired in many of her students. She decided to facilitate students' use of general knowledge of think-ahead, think-during, and think-back processes in order to create a more specific strategy for editing. She began the activity by reviewing students' writing skills and noting the manner in which they had improved, but also noting the problems with editing. Although Vickie had a fairly clear idea of the elements of an effective editing strategy, she wanted her students to struggle with the process of constructing the new strategy. With this goal in mind, she mediated a discussion that first focused on the critical elements of the editing process (e.g., checking sentences to see if they make sense and are complete, checking spelling) and then focused on critical elements of the cognitive literacy strategy (e.g., think-ahead processes for editing, think-during processes for editing). Finally, she worked with her students to create a new version of the cognitive strategy that focused specifically on editing.

Vickie initiated a group project that focused on conducting research to determine the impact of the strategy on written products generated by the class. Each group selected a specific aspect of the editing dimension (spelling, incomplete sentences, and so on) of writing. They checked the class's written products to learn which aspects of writing were improving (e.g., number of misspelled words). The groups were also charged with investigating the effectiveness of the new strategy by using it and making recommendations for change.

In this vignette, Vickie channeled students' attention toward the cognitive literacy strategy that would be used for editing. It is important to understand, however, that teachers will differ in their eventual applications of the strategy. For example, with another class, Vickie might have channeled students' attention toward using their knowledge to create a self-advocacy strategy, or a reading comprehension strategy, or for whatever problem-solving domain a strategy is needed. Likewise, some students may not need channeling by the teacher. Our experience suggests that students often indicate the direction they wish to go with strategy extensions (e.g., "Ms. Steele, could we make up one of these for test taking?").

Whatever direction teachers take during the extending stage, the new strategy versions need to be practiced with ample feedback. Teaching too many strategies at once results in confusion, little actual competence developed, and subsequent abandonment of the whole idea. The cooperative group setting is ideal for providing feedback to all of the students in the class, as well as for achieving the main goals of Integrated Strategies Instruction.

REFERENCES

Brown, A. L. (1978). Knowing when, where, and how to remember: A problem of metacognition. In R. Glaser (Ed.), *Advances in instructional psychology*, (Vol. 7, 55–111). Hillsdale, NJ: Erlbaum.

Brown, A. L., & Campione, J. C. (in press). Communities of learning and thinking: Or a context by any other name. *Human Development*.

Cohen, E. G. (1986). *Designing groupwork: Strategies for the heterogeneous classroom*. New York: Teachers College Press.

Cohen, E. G., Lotan, R., & Catanzarite, L. (1990). Treating status problems in the cooperative classroom. In S. Sharan (Ed.), *Cooperative learning: Theory and research*. New York: Praeger, 203–229.

Derry, S. J. (1990). Remediating academic difficulties through strategy training: The acquisition of useful knowledge. *Remedial and Special Education, 11*, 19–31.

Ellis, E. S. (1992). *Integrated Strategies Instruction: A guide for facilitating content subject matter learning and writing skills*. Tuscaloosa: University of Alabama.

Ellis, E. S., Deshler, D. D., & Schumaker, J. B. (1989). Teaching learning disabled adolescents to generate and use task-specific strategies. *Journal of Learning Disabilities, 22* (2), 108–119.

Harris, K., & Pressley, M. (1991). The nature of cognitive strategy instruction: Interactive strategy construction. *Exceptional Children, 57*, 392–404.

Johnson, D. W., & Johnson, R. (1989). *Cooperation and competition: Theory and research*. Edina, MN: Interaction Book Company.

Johnson, D. W., & Johnson, R. (1992) Encouraging thinking through constructive controversy. In N. Davidson & T. Worsham (Eds.), *Enhancing thinking through cooperative learning* (pp. 120–137). New York: Teachers College Press.

Jones, B. F., Palinscar, A. S., Ogle, D. S., & Carr, E. G. (1987). *Strategic teaching and learning: Cognitive instruction in the content areas*. Alexandria, VA: Association for Supervision and Curriculum Development.

Kagan, S. (1990). *Cooperative learning: Resources for teachers*. San Juan Capistrano, CA: Resources for Teachers.

Maheady, L., Mallette, B., & Harper, G. F. (1991). Accommodating cultural, linguistic, and academic diversity within integrated school settings: Some peer mediated options. *Preventing School Failure, 36*, 28–31.

Marzano, R. J. (1992). The many faces of cooperation across the dimensions of learning. In N. Davidson & T. Worsham (Eds.), *Enhancing thinking through cooperative learning* (pp. 7–28). New York: Teachers College Press.

Marzano, R. J., Pickering, D. J., & Brandt, R. S. (1990). Integrating instructional programs through dimensions of learning. *Educational Leadership, 47,* 17–24.

Moshman, D. (1982). Exogenous, endogenous, and dialectical constructivism. *Developmental Review, 2,* 371–384.

Presseisen, B. Z. (1992). A perspective on the evolution of cooperative thinking. In N. Davidson & T. Worsham (Eds.), *Enhancing thinking through cooperative learning* (pp. 1–6). New York: Teachers College Press.

Resnick, L. B. (1987a). Constructing knowledge in school. In L. S. Liben (Ed.), *Development and learning: Conflict or congruence?* (pp. 19–50). Hillsdale, NJ: Lawrence Erlbaum Associates.

Resnick, L. B. (1987b). *Education and learning to think.* Washington, DC: National Academy Press.

Roehler, L. R., & Duffy, G. G. (1984). Direct explanation of comprehension processes. In G. G. Duffy, L. R. Roehler, & J. Mason (Eds.), *Comprehension instruction: Perspectives and suggestions* (pp. 265–280). New York: Longman.

Sharan, Y., & Sharan, S. (1992). *Expanding cooperative learning through group investigation.* New York: Teachers College Press.

Short, E. J., & Weissberg-Benchell, J. A. (1989). The triple alliance for learning: Cognition, metacognition, and motivation. In C. B. McCormick, G. Miller, & M. Pressley (Eds.), *Cognitive strategy research: From basic research to educational applications* (pp. 33–63). New York: Springer-Verlag.

Slavin, R. (1990). *Cooperative learning: Theory, research, and practice.* Englewood Cliffs, NJ: Prentice Hall.

Vygotsky, L. S. (1978). *Mind in society.* Cambridge, MA: Harvard University Press.

Wood, P., Bruner, J., & Ross, G. (1976). The role of tutoring in problem-solving. *Journal of Child Psychology and Psychiatry and Allied Disciplines, 17,* 89–100.

11

Teaching and Learning the Language Arts with Cooperative Learning Methods

Aryeh Wohl and Esther Klein-Wohl

Educators, who have been given the herculean task of teaching communication skills, constantly seek more efficient ways of bringing learning and literacy to their pupils. Applying the philosophy and methods of cooperative learning to the instruction of the language arts is one suitable means for meeting that need.

Our intention is to suggest practical and useful ways of integrating literacy learning with cooperative methods. Our focus is on the employment of the collaborative approach as a valuable instructional procedure to promote literacy learning. It is hoped that teachers will not only grasp the specific techniques mentioned but will also adapt the suggestions to other language activities as well as to other subject areas, where applicable.

LITERACY AND COMMUNICATION

One of the most important areas of study, which crosses all boundaries of subject matter, is the acquisition and use of language arts skills and strategies, in other words, becoming literate. These skills and strategies involve the "ownership" of communication processes such as reading, writing, listening, and speaking abilities, which are necessary for success in academic achievement as well as in everyday, real-life situations. Thus helping children to emerge, develop, and become literate is, and should be, one of the major goals of all school systems. "Our schools must mold and direct learners to use printed and written information to function in society, to achieve one's goals, and to develop one's knowledge and potential" (National Assessment of Educational Progress [NAEP], 1985).

COOPERATIVE METHODS AND LITERACY

A review of the research in cooperative learning pedagogy reflects the following positive elements: an on-task approach, shown to produce higher pupil achievement; greater use of higher-level reasoning; increased intrinsic motivation; and increased content retention by learners. Students learn with higher motivation and develop better attitudes toward themselves, their teachers, their peers, and the school. Thus cooperative learning generates better development as well as stronger and healthier relationships. These findings have motivated greater use and implementation of collaborative methods in the classroom. Slavin (1990) noted that "the uses of cooperative learning methods have mushroomed in recent years at all levels of schooling."

We would like to suggest that instructional environments for developing literacy should be built around cooperative and collaborative activities since these activities best approximate real-life communicative situations. By introducing cooperative methods, we are likely to better prepare our learners for literate functioning inside and outside school. To optimize success in learning language arts, it would be judicious to combine all of the elements of the language arts with collaborative learning.

METHODS AND APPROACHES: NATURAL TRENDS

Literacy educators are becoming aware of newer trends in pedagogy where natural, relevant, and functional learning is required. These "natural" trends, such as Whole Language, call for a different teaching/learning approach. In Whole Language, the teacher must not only prepare the classroom with real-life, authentic, learning materials and offer a variety of reading and writing activities that give the student a wealth of literacy learning possibilities, he or she must also introduce cooperative learning modes. Goodman and Goodman (1982) felt that the "natural" learning setting gives the learner meaningful, integrated reading and writing experiences.

In contrast, the traditional basal-reader approach, with a highly structured scope and sequence of skills, does not reflect the objectives of real-life communication. In the "natural" context, children have to form their own rules about language as they use language. Instead of talking about reading and writing, the children actually read and write.

Learning is made more authentic and efficient through the use of various group structures. The flexibility and social interactions of the cooperative learning/teaching mode offer the Whole Language teacher more opportunities for natural and successful learning situations. They also give the pupils more time to read and write, to share that work, and to build and expand their literacy knowledge base. Philosophically, Whole Language offers the closest literacy methodology to cooperative work. Learning in the classroom mirrors learning outside the class. It becomes functional, relevant, and, most important, meaningful, and the children learn how to "mean." Watson and Crowley (1988) noted that in "whole language... students become aware by discussing and reflecting on the strategies involved in real reading instead of drilling on skills."

Good reading behavior includes elements of risk taking: educated predicting, speculating, developing hypotheses, and guessing the meaning. In a traditional reading program, the children do not take many "natural" risks, since time and frontal presentations do not encourage risk taking. Yet risk taking is an essential element in literacy growth and is possible and more conceivable in a cooperative mode. The atmosphere, the wide range of possible activities, the flexibility, the sense of satisfaction, the social interaction, the openness and peer acceptance, all the elements of cooperative learning, offer strong scaffolding for risk taking.

In a cooperative class, learning is built on the literacy base pupils bring with them to the learning situation. The opportunity for asking questions and for finding answers is greater; students work and learn from each other as well as from the teachers; and students use many resources, communicate with each other, and think most of the learning day. What better and more interesting learning can there be than when the student is challenged and motivated to be an active learner?

COOPERATIVE LEARNING AND DIFFERENT LITERACY PHILOSOPHIES

A major philosophical debate is now raging among literacy educators. As mentioned earlier, the proponents of direct instruction call for the teacher to be in command and ask that he or she guide the students through the scope and sequence of skills and strategies in the language arts (Adams, 1990; Chall, 1967). Based on behavioral psychology, they subscribe to teaching specific, well-directed skills for most of their program. On the other hand, other literacy specialists feel the need for an open, authentic, holistic learning environment and oppose any type of direct instruction. Goodman (1992b) and others (Goodman & Goodman, 1982; Harste, Burke, & Woodward, 1984; Smith, 1988) subscribed to current cognitive psychology and called for active student involvement in the learning process. They could not accept a passive learner guided by a preset of skills and strategies since they found such learning counterfeit and nonproductive. They preferred real-life, functional material and sought to encourage the curiosity and natural desires of the student to learn.

There is a middle-of-the-road group (Spiegel, 1992; Heymsfeld, 1989; Mosenthal, 1989; Stevens, Madden, Slavin, & Farnish, 1987) who adopted a combined approach. They felt that the best way to initiate learning is to start the student, regardless of level, by using authentic materials, as in a Whole Language class. However, if at any point the teacher assesses a functional problem, it is then suggested to use the necessary skills-approach material to assist in correcting and remedying the difficulties. Thus, when the need arises, basal materials can and should be used by the teacher to intervene and assist the learner. Here direct instruction complements Whole Language. These "eclectic" educators believe that when needed, the "hole" in Whole Language should be filled with direct instruction (see chapter 2 in this volume).

THE TEACHER AS MEDIATOR

If we accept the middle-of-the road approach to literacy learning and plan to use cooperative learning methods, we must remember not to place all of the responsibility of learning in the hands of the children. Teachers do not abdicate language instruction in a dynamic, cooperative class. Instead, the teacher's role expands since he or she has to plan carefully, moderate wisely, record constantly for assessment purposes, and model and demonstrate intricate thinking/learning patterns within the subject area. In this context, teachers mediate and use their instructional skills in focusing, directing, and guiding their pupils through the rough edges of understanding and of strategy construction while pupils are actively discovering the world of literacy. When things go wrong for learners, the teacher as mediator deals with the necessary strategies (the planning and monitoring elements in literacy) and skills (the knowledge and ability to perform isolated elements automatically) in literacy to remedy the problem. Skills are performed automatically, but strategies are a series of skills that are planned and organized based on a particular purpose. For example, the skill of noting important details is used for understanding a story or for writing a summary, newspaper article, or other essay. It is an important skill, and no reader/writer or communicator can be without it. But knowing how to find the details is not enough. Knowing how, when, where, and why to use a skill in concert with other skills in order to achieve successful communication is necessary.

Teachers must consciously train their pupils in these operations and not assume that they will automatically be discovered. Children must be given the opportunity of learning "how to mean" and how to express themselves, not only with the teacher's help, but also by themselves and with their peers. Some elements of language learning do not come easily to all students, and hence they have to be given models and explanations that tell them how to proceed with the learning. In many instances nothing is automatic. In the natural learning mode, students try to solve the problem by themselves or with the assistance of their peers; but that does not work all of the time. Students may require scaffolding while learning a new skill, and they may also need the teacher's guidance. Teaching metacomprehension monitoring strategies, along with a variety of remedial strategies to solve "misses" in information processing, is also a necessity.

Getting Ready

Collaborative group work is an ideal setting for peer scaffolding in literacy, but only when the group has been enlightened and taught how, when, where, and why to operate with various communication strategies. Students need literacy learning models and demonstrations. They also need instruction in the procedures of cooperative group operations.

Learning Environment

Teachers should consider the importance of a conducive learning environment. There is a need for planning and creating "activity centers" that offer interactions with the world of print, interactions with interesting and exciting reading materials, creative writing corners, and space to think, discuss, and listen. These learning stations provide pupils with a dynamic and exciting environment where they can talk and share together. For example, the provision of a small library of books, magazines, newspapers, and other authentic materials and the availability of a writing corner with trigger idea cards, lively bulletin boards, and other resources encourage and motivate appropriate behavior in reading, writing, speaking, and listening. Working in a literate environment surely assists in giving students the literacy they need not only for daily, real-life situations, but also for academic learning.

VOCABULARY: ONE SECRET INGREDIENT IN LITERACY

Vocabulary is one of the main underpinnings in reading comprehension and in written production. A reader/writer devoid of vocabulary knowledge has severely handicapped receptive and expressive skills. Authentic real-life interactions build experiences, concepts, and vocabulary. Small learning groups provide the opportunity for vocabulary usage through the communicative exchanges facilitated by a group. When teachers are dealing with lexical items in the classroom, they should be aware of three major categories of basic vocabulary that require attention (Johnson & Pearson, 1984):

1. High-frequency sight words, a small group of words that occur in printed materials very frequently and are thought of as essential for early reading development

2. Selection-critical core words necessary for the comprehension of a specific reading selection

3. Known words with new meanings, multiple-meaning words, very common lexical items that have various meanings depending upon contextual surroundings

The vocabulary-building activities suggested here are concrete applications for teaching literacy in a cooperative mode. The activities have been divided into categories of behaviors good readers are likely to use. They should not be seen as a hierarchy of skills but rather as a classified cluster of ideas to assist in guiding, reinforcing, and remedying. Each suggestion should be applied to cooperative learning structures in which the optimum of communication and social sharing can take place.

- Organize small groups by any number of methods and give each group a funny story with nonsense words placed properly. For example:

A long time ago there was a glippe. He was a sort of happy fellow who smiled and zllode with everyone. He would girk and fernal all of his dems. In fact he wiz so junvate at it that all of the sibnons said that he was really a harn at it.

Ask the children to discuss, in their cooperative groups, the meanings of the nonsense words. Tell them to rework the story by substituting real words for the nonsense words. The discussion that will take place will offer students a good opportunity to think out syntactical messages as well as semantic possibilities in the sentences.

As a follow-up activity, questions may be composed by the teacher or the children regarding the content of the story, both on a literal and an interpretive level. Examples might be: Who was . . . ? What was he or she doing? What did . . . think about him? Children can answer orally or in writing. They may also write their own stories, include nonsense words, and ask that the group "decode" the story.

- Have the pupils rewrite headlines, advertisements, poems, nursery rhymes, or make-believe television interviews. Tell children to replace real words with invented nonsense words. Ask other members of the group to guess the meaning and replace the nonsense words with real words. The children can then compare their words with the authentic text. The objective of this activity is to develop the awareness of vocabulary selection and to learn new words as well as new meanings for known words. It also provides the opportunity for context-clue drill.

- Students can discuss the various ways they use context clues. To assist them in their discussions, the teacher can prepare a "guide card" that notes some of the possible types of context clues:

a. Is there a definition in the same sentence or before or after?

b. What do you know about the topic?

c. Can you think of a word that sounds like this word?

d. Can you find a synonym for this word in the sentence or paragraph?

e. Is this word part of a familiar expression?

f. Has the word in question been used by the author as a summary of what was said before?

- Have students write two sentences using the same word but with a different meaning each time. The pupils may then share these sentences with the group and discuss the different meanings and usages of the words. For example: "I like to run." "She had a run in her stocking." "He will run for office."

- Use analogies as another technique for building vocabulary. Two pairs of students can challenge each other to find the most analogies within a specified time frame. Give the students examples of analogy thinking before they begin. Some examples:

Red is to fire engine as blue is to . . .

Funny is to clown as serious is to . . .

- Have the pupils, in pairs, work with antonyms and synonyms. Ask one student to build a list of words in one column and have the other find the antonym(s) and synonym(s) for each word. Prepare card-matching games by making card pairs, a word and its synonym or antonym. Groups of students can then play any number of card-matching games. Also ask the pupils to take written material from various magazines and newspapers and lyrics from popular songs and replace some of the words with their antonyms and/or synonyms.

- Focus on ambiguous meanings as they may appear in the children's reading or writing material. See how many ambiguous words and phrases the students can find. Prepare a "two-faced box" where students can place new words found to be ambiguous. Have the groups discuss and use these words to write sentences or short stories. Some examples are:

Held in a lock (wrestling); locked in jail.

Grown; grown wild; developed.

He was out; he was knocked out; he left; he never came in.

average, mediocre, plain, regular, standard.

- Help the pupils become aware of precise language and find the specific meaning in relation to an expressed idea. Ask them to polish each other's work by using more precise words, for example, refuse, garbage, waste. Have them discuss how a sentence changes its meaning when they use precise words. They may also select sentences from any reading material and share their feelings as to why the author specifically used a word or phrase.

- Have the pupils enrich their writing by including figurative language using similes and metaphors. For example:

The mouse ran like a frightened cat.

He was as large as a house.

The ice cream was as cold as a block of ice.

She is as strong as an ox.

- Have children explain how strong an ox is or how a deer runs. What is so cute about a little baby girl? Ask the students to compose metaphors and similes and to explain their logic and figurative meaning. Have groups search for examples of figurative language in their reading material and then introduce a contest to see which group can find the most metaphors and/or similes within a week. Winners become "Metaphor/Simile Wizards."

- Have children work in pairs to create semantic, hot/cold word lists. In the beginning you may give the students lists of words that almost say the same thing and ask them to arrange them in progression from extreme to extreme, for example, boiling, very hot, hot, warm, lukewarm, cool, cold, freezing.

Although most of the suggested activities have an elementary school flavor, they can be used in a junior and even senior high school setting.

SELECTED LITERACY BEHAVIORS

Literacy educators recognize the need to build a classroom setting that encourages, stimulates, motivates, teaches, and advances development in reading comprehension. They also understand and accept the need for instructors to teach strategies and skills that will also aid the student in developing good behaviors and expertise using the expressive and receptive language arts (Pearson, Roehler, Dole, & Duffy, 1992).

From the work of cognitive psychologists and reading comprehension researchers, a profile of the reading "expert," a model of the thoughtful, expert reader, has been developed (Dole, Duffy, Roehler, & Pearson, 1991). By studying the behavior of good readers, the researchers found that good readers

- search and use what they know to build a bridge to the new information in the text;
- synthesize and generalize the text information and their prior knowledge;
- predict outcomes and draw inferences before, during, and after they have read;
- distinguish relevant from irrelevant information in the text;
- monitor and control the successes and failures of their reading;
- ask questions consciously and unconsciously regarding the material they read; and
- repair and remedy poor comprehension when they discover that they have erred.

It is these traits in particular that we would like to foster and encourage in our quest for literacy, and it is precisely the cooperative classroom that provides the necessary setting for their development.

Synthesizing and Generalizing

The identification and comprehension of textually important information, ideas that the author deems central to the text (Winograd & Bridge,

1986), are significant and important abilities that good readers exhibit. Cunningham and Moore (1986) noted the confusion in understanding the concept of main idea and suggested that teachers clearly explain what they mean by it and what kind of answer they expect from a main-idea or generalization question. Is it the gist, interpretation, key word, selective summary, theme, title, topic, topic issue, or topic sentence they are looking for? All these elements can be relevant to a main idea and might require synthesizing or generalizing. Teachers must be explicit as to what kind of "main idea" they want the children to look for. The following are activities that deal with synthesizing and generalizing tasks:

• Have pairs of children match paragraphs with photographs, pictures, drawings, and sketches. Ask them to explain to each other how and why they matched a picture with a paragraph. Their rational and logical connections should also be explained. Students may differ in their answers or in their logic, but as long as there is credence to their thinking, you must encourage and accept their suggestions.

• Have one or more groups read the same passage and write down what they think the generalization or main idea is. The groups then compare and discuss their choices.

• Ask the children to prepare headlines for a newspaper using radio and television news broadcasts or events that have taken place at home, in school, or elsewhere. They can then expand the headlines and write subheadlines with additional information.

• Have the children in one group separate articles and headlines. Ask a different group to then match the articles with the headlines and/or subheadlines.

• Students may gloss a text or story with content generalizations next to each paragraph or group, of paragraphs. They prepare short marginal notes with information on vocabulary and background for the text. In this way other students with less background or those who function on a lower level may be able to read the original text with the assistance of the glossed notes.

Summarizing

Summarizing skills take into account the abilities that readers and writers have in determining relevant information, deleting redundant information, locating appropriate topic sentences, condensing that information, and presenting it in general terms. Summarizing is an excellent activity to help the learner focus on his or her learning, review the information, and assess general comprehension, as well as remember the material.

• Direct a pair or group to select various ideas or concepts and try to describe them in the fewest words. Other pairs or groups read or listen to the "product" and try to name the idea or concept.

• Ask students who draw well to summarize what has been read through pictures.

Others who enjoy photography may capture the summary in photographs. Some can create collages or other visual art forms to represent summaries.

- Have the group play classification games. Provide them with lists of items from all of their areas of interest. They can even prepare their own lists and exchange them with other groups. For each group classified, pupils may suggest a broad title. Prepare or ask them to prepare a variety of sentences on one topic and then guide them in writing generalizations. The pupils can now work with their own content reading material. Allow them to work on their own only after you are satisfied that they have understood what has to be done. Have members of each group check the products and the thinking behind them.
- Have groups prepare signs for stores, offices, and outdoor advertisements. Have them shorten the signs using fewer words, for example,
  We Sell Fresh Fish; We Sell Fish; Fresh Fish; Fish; Or, Offices of Doctor John E. Healthy; John E. Healthy, Doctor's Office; Dr. Healthy.
- Ask the children to write and send letters to their classmates. Later have them send telegrams with the same content.
- Small groups can read the same book or short story and prepare a "book-jacket" summary of the story. Prepare the children by having sample book jackets available for examples.
- Ask pupils to summarize the story line of simple fairy tales, such as Little Red Riding Hood, Hansel and Gretel, Robin Hood, and the Ugly Duckling. These stories may also be used for many activities suggested in practicing for generalization, main idea, and relevant details.

Drawing Conclusions and Predicting Outcomes

Drawing conclusions and predicting outcomes are tasks that can be practiced with almost every suggestion made until now. Asking riddles, playing detective, and finding the answer based on clues given that are explicit and/or implicit are all appropriate small-group activities.

- Suggest that children watch various television shows and ask them to prepare critiques that they will share with their group. Remind them that they have to try and justify their opinions.
- Have the pupils study pictures, drawings, and other visuals and, based on the contents, predict what will happen next and why. Additional activities can deal with what happened to the people before the picture was drawn or photographed. These questions can also be asked about films and television programs.
- Using any historical event or part of history, have the students discuss what would have happened if something else had happened differently. Suggest a small change and ask students to discuss, write, or draw their answers.

Relevant and Irrelevant Details

Determining the relevance of details in texts is one of the most important elements of good reading behavior. Knowing what is and is not important in a text helps in grasping the purpose of reading and in processing all aspects of comprehension. Learning how to discriminate between relevant and irrelevant details is a most important literacy behavior. The following are some suggested activities:

- Hand out pictures, photographs, drawings, and other visuals to the group. Have the groups determine criteria for what is and is not relevant for each item, such as color, content, or interpretation. Have the children justify why they have selected these details. It is important to stress the need for understanding the purpose of the activity done, since different purposes give us different relevant and irrelevant details. For example, if we want to study a building in the photograph, information about the street may not be relevant. If we want to discuss color schemes, the type of concrete or the people on the street may not be relevant. This activity can also be done with various types and lengths of printed materials such as newspapers, advertisements, magazine material, and textbooks. Have children ask one another questions about the various details selected. The same group or another can try to find the answers from the pictures and/or written materials.
- Relevant details can also be reinforced while the children write creatively. Diaries, personal journals, and group-work journals, where the children record what has happened to them at home, in school, during a project, or during interaction in a group, are all good writing activities for this purpose. Discuss with them what should or should not go into a personal diary or journal. What is the purpose of writing a diary, and who is it addressed to?
- Letter writing is another way of dealing with decisions regarding relevant details. Groups decide to write to someone, but each student states a different purpose for writing. Establish with the children that style depends on the target reader. For example, a letter written to the president will require a different style than a letter to a close friend or a complete stranger. Children find out that different receivers of different written messages require different information and different details. They learn that relevancy is dependent on purpose.
- Determine relevance of details through lists of key words. Select or have the children, in pairs or small groups, select the concepts and vocabulary in a text that are essential for its content. Request the children to predict from the list what the text might be about (good for previewing). Then have them read the text and go back to the list to determine which of the words might help them in remembering relevant details.
- Have members of a small group select a story that they all liked. Have each member make a list of relevant events they think can be illustrated. Have them share and compare selected details. Perhaps some of the children would like to draw some of these details.
- Create "character lists" for describing story heroes. Do the same with background, descriptions of places, and descriptions of things. Suggest making extended lists of possible adjectives and adverbs that can add "color" to the characters, places, and things in a story.
- Have the group analyze the main character of a story and prepare a list of

important details about him or her. Have the group members discuss his or her personality and then select music that fits this character. There may be some students who can compose a melody of their own for this task. Encourage your pupils to learn about the variety of music available. You may even reverse the process and have the children listen to music and then respond in any written way.

• Develop flowcharts, networks, and maps of character development, highlighting a story's important events and details.

• Role-play story personalities. Make a list of important details you wish to highlight and have students role-play the character as placed in different situations. How would he or she react if placed in another setting? What would happen if ... ?

Following Directions

Learning how to follow directions is a most important reading and study behavior, especially because many instructions for cooperative learning are often in writing. It sharpens focus and exactness and allows for better test results. Following instructions, of course, also gives the student a better product. Many students have the tendency to skim or never read the directions given and end up with incomplete work. Here are some suggestions on how to develop the ability to follow directions through collaboration.

• Have the children play board games that require careful attention to instructions. Have them build a model plane or ship that requires following instructions carefully.

• Have each child develop and write instructions for a game he or she would like to teach other children and then have them play the game based on these instructions.

• Have one of the children describe how to bake a cake or cookies. Ask the group to carry out these instructions.

• Ask student A to write down directions how to reach a part of the neighborhood unfamiliar to student B. After school A and B go out to find the place, with B doing all of the looking. A learns if he or she explained all of the directions correctly, and B learns if he or she followed the instructions properly.

The following activities are necessary to help learners function in a cooperative setting:

• Hand out a sample set of instructions and ask the children to read and then explain what was asked of them in the instructions to check their understanding. Stress the need to read carefully all instructions before they begin and then to recheck at the end of the work if all of the instructions have been followed. Encourage them to underline and number each "instruction verb" in the activity so that they learn exactly what has to be done. Expose the children to the many possible types of instructions they will have to deal with.

- Ask students to bring small machines, toys, and tools to class and have them explain how to work with the tool, toy, or machine. Other pupils should then attempt to use the tool or machine to show that they have grasped the instructions given.

- Have the pupils, working in pairs, prepare maps of the school grounds, neighborhood, or even places from the stories or content textbooks they are reading. Various map keys for the legend can be planned and drawn to help the students discover and learn them.

- One of the nicest ways to help develop confidence, self-image, and poise, as well as to train in following directions, is to have children learn how to do some magic tricks and then perform for the class and/or school. Have the children select some magic books from the library and set up a "magic club" where they can read, practice, and later perform what they have learned.

- Many families have home video equipment. Teachers can put it to use with the help of parents by inviting parents to help on the planning, writing, and producing of short video programs. Using the world of photography and video in the cooperative class gives the students multiple ways of learning how to follow directions as well as real-life literacy experiences. Teachers can turn to photographic and video equipment companies for guidelines and suggestions.

Evaluating Fact or Opinion

- Ask small groups to contribute questions regarding an important class or school issue. Make sure that the questionnaire includes both fact and opinion (What do you think about this?) questions. Have each student answer the questionnaire and then discuss the various opinions revealed. In small groups, discuss the difference between fact and opinion.

- Using different characters in a story, a historical event, or a television show, ask groups to analyze what these characters thought, what they did, and the opinions they had.

- Have the students in a cooperative group record a news program from the radio and/or television. Have them discuss what is presented as fact and what may be opinion.

- Compare a historical event to its fictionalized version in books, films, and/or television.

METACOGNITIVE BEHAVIOR—THINK-ALOUDS

Until recently think-alouds have been used as a method for discovering how one develops meaning. Today many language specialists agree that they may also be used for teaching readers and writers how to understand their world. Davey's work (1983) suggested that poor readers can improve their comprehension by learning how to make predictions, to draw on their prior knowledge, to visualize, to monitor their reading, and to self-correct errors. She noted that when teachers, while reading or writing, share and articulate their own thoughts with students, the students become aware of models and concrete examples they may use while reading or writing.

Tierney, Readence, and Dishner (1990) elaborated on Davey's think-aloud model. They suggested the following instructional steps for teacher modeling toward student empowerment:

1. Show students how to develop hypotheses:

   From this title I predict that . . .

   In the next part I think that we will find out . . .

   This will happen next because . . .

2. Use analogies to pull out prior knowledge and show its application:

   It's almost like the time . . .

   I once had a pain in my leg like . . .

3. Describe your own visual images:

   In my mind he looks like . . .

   I can see the fire roar.

   That hat looked like the one I bought for my wife.

   He reminded me of that clown . . .

4. Monitor your understanding out loud. Modify it as you construct meaning and direct it toward total meaning.

   Is that what he meant?

   A ship? No, a small boat. No, a rowboat.

   I thought that it would be a . . . , but it was a . . . instead.

5. Modeling remedial strategies:

   That word is not understood. I think I will read on.

   I better look it up in the dictionary.

   I missed his point; I better reread the paragraph.

These are some examples of think-alouds the teacher should share with the class before asking the students to use think-alouds themselves.

Working in small groups, the students can select from the modeling already done by the teacher and work toward grasping the technique. Students can read the same paragraph and think aloud, record on tape, write notes, and then compare their thinking with that of others. One student can read and think aloud, with the others reacting to and expanding his or her thoughts. This work can be done with any kind of text and is useful for building comprehension. One can and should expand the skill toward independent pupil practice.

Davey (1983) suggested using a checklist with a value system to allow the student to benefit from this independent work. Tierney et al. (1990)

mentioned the use of an index card or sheet of paper where the student lists the five steps noted in the think-aloud model—predictions, use of prior knowledge, visualizing, monitoring understanding, and modeling remedies—and evaluates the procedures with four grades: (1) all of the time, (2) much of the time, (3) a little, and (4) not very much. We highly recommend this procedure for reinforcement and review. The metacognitive behavior of think-alouds gives us the opportunity of looking into the window on our minds and allows those who look, talk, and listen to understand how to solve and construct good comprehension.

Group-work literacy activities can and should be introduced in almost every facet of schoolwork since we are always communicating while learning. This then gives credence and justification to the concept that every teacher and every student is a teacher/learner/participator in literacy growth. We learn and help others learn when we work together.

We have emphasized the need for students to become effective and efficient group participants. To this end, teachers have to demonstrate, model, and discuss all the activities in class. For enjoyable and productive interactions in all types of cooperative groups, pupils must first be shown how to do it to ensure successful collaborative work and good literacy behavior. It now remains the turn of the reader to implement and expand these suggestions.

REFERENCES

Adams, M. (1990). *Beginning to read: Thinking and learning about print.* Cambridge, MA: MIT Press.

Chall, J. (1967). *Learning to read: The great debate.* New York: McGraw-Hill.

Cunningham, J. W., & Moore, D. W. (1986). The confused world of main idea. In J. Baumann (Ed.), *Teaching main idea comprehension.* Newark, DE: IRA.

Davey, B. (1983). Think-aloud-modeling the cognitive processes of reading comprehension. *Journal of Reading, 27,* 44–47.

Dole, J. A., Duffy, G., Roehler, L., & Pearson, P. D. (1991). Moving from the old to the new: Reasearch on reading comprehension instruction. *Review of Educational Research, 61,* 239–264.

Goodman, K. S. (1984). Unity in reading. In A. Purves & O. Niles (Eds.), *Becoming readers in a complex society,* 83rd yearbook of NSSE, 79–114. Chicago: University of Chicago Press.

Goodman, K. S. (1992a). I didn't found whole language. *The Reading Teacher, 46,* 188–198.

Goodman, K. S. (1992b). Whole language research: Foundations and development. In S. J. Samuels & A. Farstrup (Eds.), *What research has to say about reading instruction,* 2nd ed. Newark, DE: IRA.

Goodman, K. S., & Goodman, Y. (1982). A whole language comprehension centered view of reading development. In L. Reed & S. Ward (Eds.), *Basic skills: Issues and choices, 2.* St. Louis, MO: CEMREL.

Harste, J., Burke, C., & Woodward, V. (1984). *Language stories and literacy lessons*. Portsmouth, NH: Heinemann.

Heymsfeld, C. (1989). Filling the hole in whole language. *Educational Leadership, 46,* 65–68.

Johnson, D. D., & Pearson, P. D. (1984). *Teaching reading vocabulary.* New York: Holt, Rinehart, & Winston.

Mosenthal, P. D. (1989). The whole language approach: Teachers between a rock and a hard place. *The Reading Teacher, 42,* 628–629.

National Assessment of Educational Progress (1985). The reading report card, progress towards excellence in our schools. Princeton, NJ: Educational Testing Service.

Pearson, P. D., Roehler, L. R., Dole, J. A., & Duffy, G. (1992). Developing expertise in reading comprehension. In S. J. Samuels & A. Farstrup (Eds.), *What research has to say about reading instruction,* 2nd ed. Newark, DE: IRA.

Slavin, R. E. (1990). *Cooperative learning: Theory, research and practice.* Englewood Cliffs, NJ: Prentice-Hall.

Smith, F. (1988). *Joining the literacy club.* Portsmouth, NH: Heinemann.

Spiegel, D. L. (1992). Blending whole language and systematic direct instruction. *The Reading Teacher, 46,* 8–44.

Stevens, R. J., Madden, N. A., Slavin, R. E., & Farnish, A. M. (1987). Cooperative integrated reading and composition: Two field experiments. *Reading Research Quarterly, 22,* 433–454.

Tierney, R. J., Readence, J. E., & Dishner, E. K. (1990). *Reading strategies and practices: A compendium.* Boston: Allyn & Bacon.

Watson, D., & Crowley, P. (1988). How can we implement a whole language approach? In C. Weaver (Ed.), *Reading process and practice.* Portsmouth, NH: Heinemann.

Winograd, P. N., & Bridge, C. A. (1986). The comprehension of important information in written prose. In J. Baumann (Ed.), *Teaching main idea comprehension.* Newark, DE: IRA.

12

An Integrated Groupwork Model for the Second-Language Classroom

Yael Bejarano

This chapter describes the conceptual framework of a second-language teaching model. The model proposed here draws upon theories of second-language learning and instruction as well as on theories and methods of cooperative learning. Each of the two major parts of the model, content and process, is then treated separately, and the model is applied to the design of a teaching unit.

THE INTEGRATED GROUPWORK MODEL: THEORETICAL FRAMEWORK

The purpose of a second-language teaching model is to take into consideration the interplay between the content of the curriculum and the process by which it is realized. Such a model must be flexible enough to accommodate differences between individual learners and the expected linguistic outcomes. It should also allow for the planning of future teaching objectives and teaching processes on the basis of feedback received in past and present teaching procedures (Spolsky, 1989).

The Integrated Groupwork Model (IGM) presented here is based on the interaction between Spolsky's (1989) general theory of second-language learning and theories of cooperative learning and teaching. It takes into account the reciprocal influences of the content and process of learning in the second-language classroom (see Figure 12.1) and provides the framework for a teaching unit in English as a second language (ESL).

Moreover, the Integrated Groupwork Model provides guidelines for moving from one lesson to the next within the plan of the teaching unit as

Figure 12.1
An Integrated Groupwork Model for the Second-Language Classroom

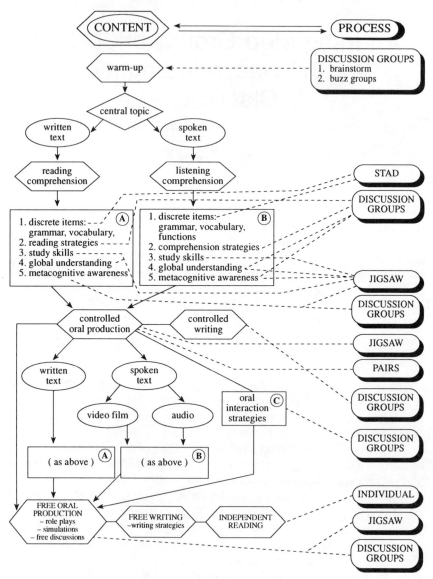

a whole. It guides teachers in the design of the teaching tasks and in the selection of those methods that serve teaching objectives.

CONTENT

The content of the ESL teaching unit is based on the analysis of what it means to "know" a language and on the interactive and integrative nature of language learning, which takes place in a social context. The linguistic outcome in Spolsky's model of second-language learning is affected by four groups of factors: previous knowledge; ability factors; various affective factors such as personality, attitudes, motivation, and anxiety; and opportunity for learning. The last factor consists of "time multiplied by kind, the latter covering the range of formal and informal situations in which the learner is exposed to language" (1989, p. 15). Since the model is interactive in nature, if any of the parts is absent, learning could be distinctly impeded; and the greater any one part is, the greater the amount of learning.

Each component in Spolsky's model involves the interaction of several clusters of interrelated conditions, based on current research in second-language learning. "Some of these are necessary conditions without which learning is impossible and others are [less essential]. . . . The model shows that there are in fact multiple paths to a complex set of outcomes . . . and that there is a relation between the extent to which the various conditions are met and the outcomes" (1989, p. 14). The direct implication of this for language teaching and learning is that there are many ways of teaching and learning. Good language teachers are therefore flexible enough to respond to the individual needs of their students and the goals of their course.

The IGM integrates Spolsky's factors in its "content" and "process" components. The content of the language-teaching curriculum (Figure 12.2) includes the following two components:

1. Linguistic knowledge, which according to Spolsky's Linguistic Outcome Condition (Spolsky, 1989, p. 80) encompasses the following:

   a. Knowledge of discrete items (individual structural items) and productive and receptive skills (language skills)

   b. Functional knowledge for specific purposes such as academic studies or communication

   c. A combination of (*a*) and (*b*) with a specified degree of accuracy and fluency

2. Sources of language input, which provide language chunks that serve as models of varieties of language use for teaching and learning purposes.

Figure 12.2
The Content Component in the IGM

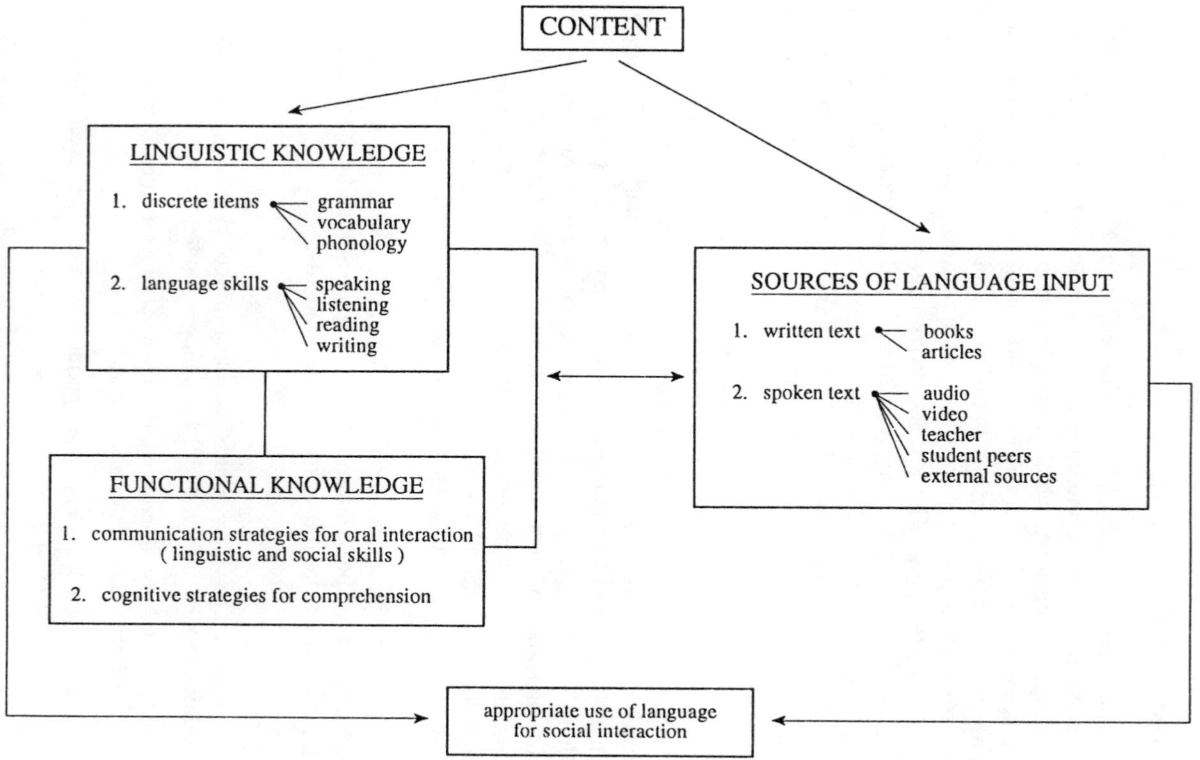

CONTENT

SOURCES OF LANGUAGE INPUT

1. written text — books, articles

2. spoken text — audio, video, teacher, student peers, external sources

LINGUISTIC KNOWLEDGE

1. discrete items — grammar, vocabulary, phonology

2. language skills — speaking, listening, reading, writing

FUNCTIONAL KNOWLEDGE

1. communication strategies for oral interaction (linguistic and social skills)

2. cognitive strategies for comprehension

appropriate use of language for social interaction

Linguistic Knowledge

"Knowing a language" is a complex combination of linguistic knowledge and functional or pragmatic knowledge, together with the appropriate use of language as an instrument for social interaction. Linguistic knowledge consists of individual language items (grammar, vocabulary, phonology, and so on) and language skills (reading, writing, speaking, and listening). Functional or pragmatic knowledge consists of communicative functions for oral production (apologizing, agreeing, asking, and so on) and strategic knowledge for receptive purposes (reading and listening). The appropriate use of language as an instrument for social interaction consists of general interaction skills, background knowledge of the topic at hand, and familiarity with the situation. All of these factors function interactively and facilitate appropriate communication.

A general theory of second language learning must . . . be able to define all these possible outcomes, [and] show how various combinations of conditions will be most likely to lead to each of them. . . . [It] must allow for all the complexity of what it means to know and use a language . . . to combine the macro level of developing various kinds of functional proficiency with the micro level of learning specific items and structures. (Spolsky, 1989, p. 12)

The content of the language-teaching model proposed here includes components of linguistic knowledge (discrete items) at the micro level (indicated by rectangles in Figure 12.1); productive and receptive skills (indicated by hexagons in Figure 12.1); and components of functional knowledge for specified purposes and communication strategies for oral interaction and cognitive strategies at the macro level (in rectangles in Figure 12.1). The combination of these components in the curriculum will lead to the expected outcome of knowing and using a foreign language (see Figure 12.2). All of these components of linguistic knowledge are organized under "content" in the model (Figure 12.1), while the frequency and quantity of occurrences of each of the elements are left unprescribed. Thus a teacher might introduce one reading text in the unit and deal with one grammatical point in one situation, or choose to use two or three texts and deal with four or even more grammatical issues in another; it might be necessary to train the students in a specific communication strategy (e.g., asking for information or checking for comprehension [Tarone, 1980]) in one case, and, in another instance, to practice cognitive strategies (e.g., finding the main idea, listening for a specific detail, or using logical connections for comprehension) for purposes of reading or listening comprehension (Grabe, 1991). This flexibility in the model takes into account variability in students' learning styles and needs, which is a necessary condition for language learning in the classroom (Spolsky, 1989, p. 110, condition 31).

Sources of Language Input

Meaningful language instruction must present a context that consists of comprehensible and authentic units of the language, both written and spoken. Language chunks of this kind may appear in a variety of forms:

- Spoken texts such as video excerpts (films, news clips, or videotaped interviews), audiotexts (taped lectures, interviews, or selected radio programs), or teacher talk
- Written texts such as stories, newspapers, or journal entries (advertisements or articles), textbook entries (description of a theory or a process), or selected written texts
- Student-student interactions, teacher-led class discussions, student-teacher interactions for purposes of formal learning, or student interactions with native speakers outside the classroom for purposes of informal learning (Spolsky, 1989)

The content component in the model (Figure 12.1) presents several typical sources of language input (in ovals). The flexibility of the model allows for the inclusion of different sources of input dictated by individual factors relating to both students and teachers and their specific needs.

PROCESS

According to the communicative language-teaching approach, knowledge of a language is not to be viewed as including merely grammatical and lexical abilities. Rather, it demands that the student integrate all language, communication, and social skills necessary for communication with others in different social contexts.

Communicative language-teaching theory has raised many questions concerning the connection between classroom organization and language learning. Stern (1983) distinguished between learning a language through use in the environment and learning through processes of language study and practice. Allen (1981) relates to experiential activities and analytic activities. The former are based on the principle that the learner must become a participant in a real-life context of language use as a condition for effective language learning, while the latter are structure or grammar based. Allen proposed a combination of experiential and analytic activities in the second-language classroom. Breen (1984) and Nunan (1991) observed that in task-based language teaching, syllabus content and instructional processes are selected with reference to the communicative tasks in which learners will need to engage both within and outside the classroom.

However, none of the studies available thus far specifies how to organize the classroom and the lesson on the basis of empirical assessment of cause and effect in which motivation and opportunity are critical variables accounting for success in language learning and language use (Spolsky, 1989). In the model presented here, cooperative learning methods provide a match between teaching goals and processes.

COOPERATIVE LEARNING AND THE LANGUAGE CLASSROOM

The use of small groups in the ESL classroom has been supported by pedagogical and psycholinguistic arguments (Pica & Doughty, 1985; Doughty & Pica, 1986; Long & Porter, 1985; Bejarano, 1987). Learning in small groups has been shown to increase opportunities for meaningful practice and fairly realistic language use, to improve the quality of student talk (namely, the range of language functions, such as asking questions or requiring additional information), to create a positive affective climate in the classroom, and to increase student motivation (Long & Porter, 1985; Sharan & Shachar, 1988; Sharan & Shaulov, 1990). DiPietro (1987) also found that groupwork in the second-language classroom fulfills many of the goals of learner-centered instruction. It lowers the psychological barrier that might arise among some students vis-à-vis the target language, facilitates the pooling of resources by the students, and enables them to become generators of knowledge for others.

The psycholinguistic arguments for groupwork emerge from research on the important role of comprehensible input and output of the students (Long, 1980; Long & Porter, 1985; Swain, 1985). According to Seliger (1983), learners receive more comprehensible input as a result of conversing with their peers. This is facilitated by the small group, which provides the social setting for comprehensible output as well. Pica and Doughty (1985) reported that students' output is at the same level of grammatical accuracy in small groups of nonnative peers as it is in a whole-class setting led by the teacher or in conversation with a native speaker. However, research to date has not explained what is meant by groupwork in the language classroom and how such work should be implemented. Affirmations of its effective use in second-language teaching have remained largely at the level of "desired states" rather than treating specific methods for classroom instruction.

Slavin (1990) noted that cooperative learning in small groups is "the application of social psychology to education. Not surprisingly, the emphasis of cooperative learning methods was on interpersonal processes, incentives, task structures and so on" (p. 261). It is an educational approach based on positive interdependence among group members who share leadership as well as responsibility for each other's learning. Cooperative learning encourages individual accountability in groups that are heterogeneous in ability and personal characteristics, recognizes that students need to be taught social skills, lets the teacher observe group interaction and intervene only when necessary, and incorporates opportunities for groups to process their effectiveness (Johnson & Johnson, 1987).

Different groupwork methods presented in other chapters in this volume are applicable to a broad range of subjects and levels. The IGM was designed by adapting several cooperative learning methods to the needs of the second-language classroom, with different groupwork methods adapted to fulfill different purposes and to provide diverse opportunities for second-language learning and practice (Figure 12.3). Following are the theoretical bases and practical applications of the different cooperative learning methods to language learning.

STAD AND KNOWLEDGE OF INDIVIDUAL STRUCTURAL ITEMS

One of Spolsky's (1989) conditions for second-language learning is the discrete-item condition, according to which "knowing a language involves knowing a number of the discrete structural items (sounds, words, structures, etc.) that make it up." Canale and Swain (1980) emphasized the divisible nature of linguistic ability rather than its unitary nature and maintained that successful communication results from the interaction of separate components, and not from the operation of a single language faculty. It is by isolating and focusing on specific language features such as grammar, lexis, or specific sociolinguistic strategies that learners come to grips with them; they isolate, practice, and internalize them and thus master them in order to be able to apply them in free communication. Canale (1983) noted that the question of how these separate competencies are acquired and how they interact with one another requires a model of second-language pedagogy. The Integrated Groupwork Model seeks to fulfill this requirement.

Research on cooperative learning methods has indicated that STAD (Student Teams-Achievement Divisions) is an appropriate method for teaching and learning basic skills with clearly defined objectives and single correct answers (Bejarano, 1987). STAD is a team learning method based on three central concepts: individual accountability, equal opportunities for success, and team rewards, which are essential for basic skills achievement. Simply telling students to work together will not suffice; they must have a reason to take one another's achievements seriously (Slavin, 1990). Bejarano (1987) adapted the STAD technique and the Discussion Group (or Group Investigation) cooperative learning methods (Sharan & Sharan, 1976, 1992) for ESL purposes and compared the effects of these two techniques and the whole-class method on academic achievement. Results from an extensive experiment conducted in thirty classrooms indicated that both groupwork methods produced better results than the whole-class method. The study also showed that the change that occurred on the discrete-point

Figure 12.3
The Process Component in the IGM

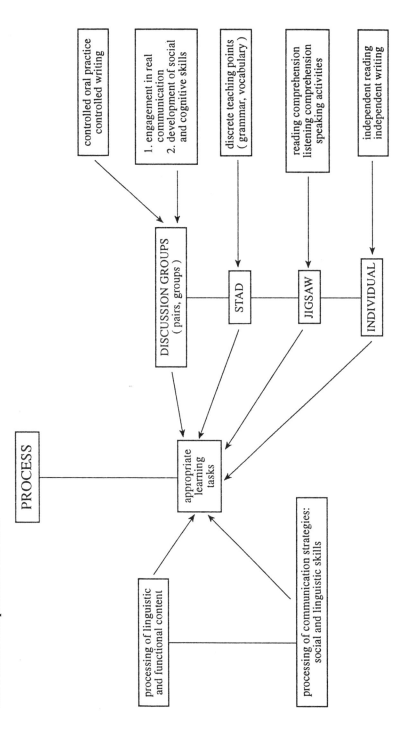

test was greater in the STAD classes than in the Discussion Group classes (Sharan et al., 1984). Based on these findings, the model proposed here indicates use of the STAD method for teaching and learning individual structural items such as grammar, vocabulary, and language functions in appropriate learning tasks (see Figure 12.2).

The original STAD consists of five components: class presentation, learning in teams, individual quizzes, individual improvement scores, and team recognition (Slavin, 1986; chapter 1 in this volume). For ESL purposes this method was slightly reorganized in light of six stages: setting up heterogeneous teams of four students, class presentation, learning in pairs, practice in pairs and then in teams, quizzes, and team recognition. A STAD activity can be easily designed using a selected grammar, vocabulary, or discrete-item exercise from any textbook by simply dividing the exercise into two parts and using the first part for learning in pairs and the second for practice. An example of a STAD activity is presented later in this chapter in the model unit.

JIGSAW AND KNOWLEDGE OF LANGUAGE SKILLS

The Jigsaw peer-tutoring technique (Aronson, Blaney, Stephan, Sikes, & Snapp, 1978; chapter 3 in this volume) can be implemented in several variations. The variation selected is determined by the particular teaching goal. Students work primarily in their "home groups," but reassemble into "expert groups," each of which masters a different learning assignment. All of the assignments are essential parts of the same unit of work. When the expert groups have mastered their part of the unit, the students return to their home groups and teach each other the new knowledge they have acquired. The activity ends with a stage in which every student must utilize knowledge of the entire unit. This can be accomplished by administering an individual test or by a whole-class discussion or role play in which students are called upon individually to contribute their "expertise." Jigsaw may be used for reading and listening comprehension and conversation activities, using appropriate learning tasks (see Figure 12.3).

Jigsaw and Reading Comprehension: Theoretical Framework

Research has established that skillful use of reading strategies enhances reading comprehension (Grabe, 1991). Much emphasis has been placed on the important role that metacognition plays in learning how to read and understand a text (Brown, Armbruster, & Baker, 1986). Metacognition refers to faculties of planning, monitoring, and regulating one's cognitive processes during learning. Research has shown that students can be successfully trained in metacognitive skills. When they are explicitly taught and made aware of the reasoning involved in the process of reading, they are better able to regulate and apply that reasoning to future reading situations (Carrell, 1989).

Cooperative learning has been found to be efficient for the teaching of reading comprehension (Stevens, Slavin, & Farnish, 1991). This author and colleagues found improvement in students' metacognitive awareness in reading comprehension when they were taught with cooperative learning methods, and where they were instructed to verbalize the reading strategies they were using. Reading performance improved to a greater degree than that of students in traditional reading classes. This is probably due to the fact that cooperative learning in small groups provides a platform for multifaceted analysis, discussion, and synthesis of ideas that can lead to a higher level of thinking and understanding (Sharan et al., 1984). In addition, interaction in small groups helps students clarify in their own minds what they have already learned and what they still have to learn (Sharan, 1990). During cooperative practice, "students evaluate, explain, and elaborate the strategies to one another . . . and thus they successfully internalize and master the complex cognitive process" (Stevens et al., 1991, p. 15).

Features of the Jigsaw method make it suitable for enhancing two essential and related teaching goals that contribute to reading comprehension: developing students' metacognitive awareness, and learning the content while teaching it to peers in the small group. These goals are essentially achieved in the two phases of the Jigsaw method. In the first phase, the students articulate the processes they go through as they try to become "experts" in their portion of the text. In the second phase (in their home groups), they teach both the content of the text and the process of comprehension to their peers. By teaching, the students further internalize both the content and the process of their own reading. The social and learning processes students go through in the first phase are parallel to those of the Discussion Group interactive processes (described in the next section).

Jigsaw can be used in different ways for reading comprehension:

1. A selected text can be divided into four or five parts, and each student in the home group becomes expert in one of the parts (possible only if the text can be divided into reasonably independent content units).

2. A selected text is used as a whole, and each student in the home group becomes expert in a different aspect of that text.

3. Four or five related texts are used, and each student in the home group becomes expert in one text.

Appropriate tasks should be designed to serve specific teaching purposes. Examples of Jigsaw tasks appear in the sample unit presented later.

Jigsaw and Listening Comprehension

Although written and spoken texts constitute quite different forms of presentation, Danks and End (1987) argued that they impose similar cognitive demands on the learner. Townsend, Carrithers, and Bever (1987) reported that learners' comprehension in reading and listening are highly related. Based on these findings, the IGM includes Jigsaw for teaching listening and reading comprehension, although the specific differences between them must be borne in mind while planning a listening activity.

Jigsaw and Speaking Activities

Jigsaw can be used with any speaking activity, such as role play and simulation, that is divisible and in which each element can stand on its own. In both role play and simulation, the roles are initially prepared in expert groups, following which the different roles interact together in home groups. Appropriate tasks for each stage, with very clear instructions to the students, should be designed.

DISCUSSION GROUP TECHNIQUE AND LANGUAGE TEACHING

Discussion Group and Oral-Aural Interaction

The Discussion Group (DG) approach emphasizes discussion of abstract ideas and the synthesis of different ideas or dimensions of a topic into a complex study unit. Bejarano (1987) reported that small-group cooperative teaching promoted higher language achievement than frontal teacher-led instruction because of the active communication approach used. This study also indicated that the Discussion Group method is more efficient for practicing global language skills, such as speaking or listening, than the STAD technique, which is more effective for learning and practicing basic skills. These two techniques activate different kinds of group processes and consequently affect students' behavior differently, despite their common features of small-group interaction and mutual assistance among members.

Effective interaction in DG requires social skills such as attentive listening, inclusion of peers' ideas, cooperation and sharing of information, mutual help, talking in turn, and serving as group leader (Sharan & Sharan, 1976). Effective communication in discussion groups is also conducive to second-language learning since it generates increased language practice and negotiation work and allows many more students to be personally involved in learning. It is therefore crucial that students be trained in interaction strategies.

This author and colleagues have found that students who have been trained in using interaction strategies skillfully use more interaction strategies than students who have not been trained to do so, and that their rate of participation in a group discussion is significantly higher than that of students who did not receive the training (Bejarano, Levine, Olshtain, & Steiner, in progress). Included in the training were modified interaction strategies and social interaction strategies. The modified interaction strategies are foreign-language specific: they include comprehension checks, appealing for assistance, self-correction, and giving assistance. The social interaction strategies are important for any social communication; they include elaborating, facilitating flow of conversation, responding, seeking information, and paraphrasing. Special learning tasks were designed specifically for the purpose of training the students; each task tapped an interaction strategy and at the same time practiced a language-teaching issue. The study indicated that students can be trained in effective interaction. Skilled use of interaction strategies also appears to have a positive effect on the quality of oral interaction; students trained in interaction strategies use language structures of the kind that keep a coherent conversation going and prevent conversational deadlocks.

Learning tasks suitable for the DG technique are usually based on topics that require bilateral or multilateral communication, negotiation, and interaction. A variety of resources can be used, such as personal interviews, books, articles, and recorded radio and television programs.

HOMOGENEOUS AND HETEROGENEOUS GROUPS

One of the major concerns of second-language teachers utilizing cooperative learning in heterogeneous classes is whether the small groups should be homogeneous or heterogeneous. Students can differ in several respects, such as prior knowledge, cognitive abilities, learning rates, or learning styles, which may be of great concern to the teacher. The greatest advantage of small-group teaching is its flexibility, which allows for different group structures within the class, thus accommodating instruction to individual differences. This can be done in several ways:

1. Assigning students to homogeneous groups and designing different language tasks suited to the needs of the different groups
2. Directing students to study centers that focus on different teaching points for learning or practice
3. Varying classroom activities so that students with different learning styles are accommodated
4. Assigning different language tasks to the students in a heterogeneous group, taking into account their differences and levels of ability
5. Assigning different social roles such as teaching, monitoring, or recording in-

formation to students in heterogeneous groups on the basis of personal qualities and abilities

Homogeneous grouping facilitates remedial instruction for slower students and enrichment activities for further and more rapid progress for more able students. Heterogeneous grouping provides the social and academic opportunities for peer tutoring and mutual assistance.

INTEGRATION OF COOPERATIVE LEARNING TECHNIQUES, TEACHER-LED INSTRUCTION, AND INDIVIDUAL LEARNING

Adequate communication requires the integrated utilization of all the elements of "knowing" and "using" a language (Spolsky, 1989) or of "communicative competence" (Canale & Swain, 1980). Groupwork provides appropriate settings for such communication.

An integrated combination of all these techniques, each of which serves a different purpose in a well-structured language teaching unit, is the basis for the Integrated Groupwork Model and makes the methodological connection between content and process, as presented in Figure 12.1. Teachers who are trained to use the IGM are equipped with the principles of the methods and are therefore able not only to plan the content of the teaching, but also to design the teaching tasks and activities according to the principles of the instructional methods and to implement the activities in the classroom along the lines of these principles. Thus all tasks and activities have a specific teaching/learning function in the overall teaching unit.

This approach addresses some of the issues raised by proponents of "process syllabi," "procedural syllabi," and "task-based language teaching," such as "how tasks are selected and sequenced and what kind of methodological options are to be used [to carry out the tasks], such as groupwork and the focus on form, that they prescribe and proscribe" (Long & Crookes, 1992, p. 47; Nunan, 1991). The model is innovative in several ways:

1. It provides the framework for clear sets of goal statements and thus indicates the explicit links between the task and the broader curriculum it is designed to serve (in this case a teaching unit).
2. It lays out a set of theoretically based and empirically tested teaching techniques, each catering to a different need in the language classroom (additional research is still necessary).
3. The interaction between content and process elements is clearly demonstrated and can be referred to for practical use.
4. The model is flexible enough to account for individual differences and individual needs.

A SAMPLE ESL UNIT UTILIZING THE INTEGRATED GROUP-WORK MODEL

Teaching ESL units according to the IGM syllabus revolves around a central topic. This allows teachers to build up students' schemata, both content and social, and to present new vocabulary items and grammatical structures.

The following unit plan demonstrates the interplay between the content and the process of the unit.[1] It exemplifies the integration of the various content elements and the groupwork methods selected to serve the teaching objectives set for each element. It also shows how each step in the unit ties in with the preceding step and leads on to the next. In this model unit, teaching objectives are set up independently of a specific class level or a particular student population and should therefore be considered as a basic model on which teachers can pattern self-created units. (Of course, one unit cannot contain every one of the elements appearing in Figure 12.1.) The topic of the unit is the model school, and the following are its objectives:

1. Teach and use vocabulary pertaining to the topic.
2. Review the past simple (active and passive forms).
3. Teach and practice functional expressions that facilitate the flow of conversation (agreeing, disagreeing, suggesting).
4. Practice reading for specific information.
5. Provide opportunities for oral communication.

The unit begins with a warm-up in which the teacher asks the students to individually brainstorm the word *school* and then, in groups of four to five students, to create a comprehensive group list to be reported to the whole class. These lists are used for vocabulary elicitation and introduction of new items. The vocabulary items are then formally presented to the whole class.

The second activity is related to vocabulary study and begins with a competition between groups. The groups are given two pictures of a classroom in which a teacher is talking to a couple with a young child; the students are requested to find the differences between the two pictures. Once the differences have been found, students move on to the next stage of the activity: learning the new vocabulary. The STAD technique is used for this purpose, since it is particularly suitable for the teaching of discrete items.

Students now begin the learning stage of STAD. A worksheet containing a set of questions for discussion related to the pictures used earlier provides contextualized examples of the new vocabulary. For practice, on the same worksheet, students complete a cloze passage (fill-in exercise) related to the topic of the picture. Within the small heterogeneous STAD groups, students are assigned roles according to their abilities and personality traits; for example, a verbally expressive student is appointed leader, and a less expressive student serves as dictionary monitor. An assessment of student learning could consist of another cloze passage related to school, for which a word bank is provided. Groups exchange papers, mark and correct the quizzes, and calculate group scores.

The new vocabulary items thus learned appear in the reading passage "Summerhill, the Open School," which is the focus of the next activity. The activity has several purposes: to practice reading for specific information, to see the new vocabulary items in context, and to gain general knowledge regarding open schools. As indicated by Figure 12.1, the Jigsaw method serves these purposes best, and in this lesson a modified version is used: The expert groups all read the same passage but have different tasks focusing on different facts. The activity ends with an individual quiz consisting of questions assessing students' understanding of the whole text. Alternatively, the activity may be summed up by a group report or a whole-class discussion.

One of the objectives defined for this unit is to review the past simple. Since this is a review, and students are expected to know the basics of the past simple, students are assigned a pair activity for controlled oral production, not STAD, which is recommended for teaching basic skills. Their task is to compare their own school to Summerhill. If the teacher notices many errors during this pair work, a STAD activity can be added for remedial work.

The next step is development of interaction skills as well as training for peer correction. A modified Discussion Group technique, the "fishbowl," is used for this discussion. The class is divided into three groups of eight students each. Students of Group 1, seated in the middle of the room, are each given five cards with different functional expressions and are asked to hold a discussion on the subjects that should be taught in school. They are instructed to use the expressions as they participate in the discussion. Each card used appropriately is placed in the center of the table; the first student to use all five cards is the winner. The eight students of Group 2 sit around Group 1 and monitor their use of the expressions and their language in general. Their task is to alert the erring student and jot down the linguistic problems encountered. The eight students of Group 3 also serve as observers and note any breakdown in the flow of conversation and its causes. When the discussion ends, all the groups are given three to five minutes to prepare reports on it. Groups 2 and 3 report their findings. The teacher then sums up the activity by drawing students' attention to the use and importance of functional expressions, as well as the importance of peer correction and the use of strategies necessary for keeping the conversation flowing. At this stage, students possess sufficient general information, vocabulary, and functional language for the final activity of the unit, the simulation. The Jigsaw technique is used for this activity. The model-school simulation consists of a committee (the "home group") of five members (a government official as chairperson, a teacher, a parent, a school principal, and a pupil) who must submit recommendations for a model school. The situation is described to them and their roles designated. Now students prepare their roles together in "expert groups." It is possible for there to be more than one group preparing the principal's, or any other, role. When the preparation time has elapsed, students return to their committees—the "home groups"—and enact the simulation. They are encouraged to use DG processes in their home groups. The simulation ends with a whole-class discussion and, if necessary, is followed by the teaching of problem points uncovered by the teacher during the simulation.

IMPLICATIONS FOR LANGUAGE TEACHERS

To prepare an ESL unit according to the Integrated Groupwork Model, teachers must have a clear grasp of the teaching content; teaching objectives must be defined considering the learners' previous knowledge, individual characteristics, and needs. Once these have been ascertained, teachers can select the topic and the materials. The objectives and the learners' needs will dictate what is to be taught, and understanding of the IGM will facilitate the selection of the appropriate technique for each activity. Teachers should create connections between old and new knowledge to provide adequate scaffolding.

Teachers who adopt the IGM are advised to plan their teaching in teams and experience the process themselves. Effective adoption of the IGM model requires intensive teacher training in both the content and the process, and in their integration.

NOTE

1. This teaching unit was developed in collaboration with Lily Vered of the Open University of Israel.

REFERENCES

Allen, J. P. B. (1981). *A three-level curriculum model for second language education.* Keynote address at the Annual Conference of the Ontario Modern Language Teachers Association, Toronto, April 1981.

Aronson, E., Blaney, N., Stephan, C., Sikes, J., & Snapp, M. (1978). *The Jigsaw classroom.* Beverly Hills, CA: Sage Publications.

Bejarano, Y. (1987). A cooperative small-group methodology in the language classroom. *TESOL Quarterly, 21,* 483–504.

Bejarano, Y., Levine, T., Olshtain, E., & Steiner, J. (In progress). Can skilled use of interaction strategies facilitate interaction in small groups in the EFL classroom?

Breen, M. (1984). Processes in syllabus design. In C. Brumfit (Ed.), *General English syllabus design.* Oxford: Pergamon Press.

Brown, A., Ambruster, B., & Baker, L. (1986). The role of metacognition in reading and studying. In J. Orasanu (Ed.), *Reading comprehension: From research to practice.* Hillsdale, NJ: Lawrence Erlbaum.

Canale, M. (1983). On some dimensions of language proficiency. In J. Oller (Ed.), *Issues in language testing research.* Rowley, MA: Newbury House.

Canale, M., & Swain, M. (1980). Theoretical basis of communicative approaches to second language teaching and testing. *Applied Linguistics, 1,* 1–47.

Carrell, P. L. (1989). Metacognitive awareness and second language reading. *Modern Language Journal, 73,* 121–134.

Danks, J. H., & End, L. J. (1987). Processing strategies for reading and listening. In R. Horowitz & S. J. Samuels (Eds.), *Comprehending oral and written language.* New York: Academic Press.

Di Pietro, R. (1987). *Strategic interaction.* Cambridge: Cambridge University Press.

Doughty, C., & Pica, T. (1986). "Information gap" tasks: Do they facilitate second language acquisition? *TESOL Quarterly, 20,* 305–325.

Grabe, W. (1991). Current developments in second language reading research. *TESOL Quarterly, 25,* 375–406.

Johnson, D. W., & Johnson, R. T. (1989). *Cooperation and competition: Theory and research* Hillsdale, NJ: Lawrence Erlbaum Associates.

Long, M. H. (1980). *Input, interaction, and second language acquisition.* Unpublished doctoral dissertation, UCLA.

Long, M. H., & Crookes, G. (1992). Three approaches to task-based syllabus design. *TESOL Quarterly, 26,* 27–56.

Long, M. H., & Porter, P. A. (1985). Group work, inter-language talk, and second language acquisition. *TESOL Quarterly, 19,* 207–228.

Nunan, D. (1991). Communicative tasks and the language curriculum. *TESOL Quarterly, 25,* 279–296.

Pica, T., & Doughty, C. (1985). The role of group work in classroom second language acquisition. *Studies in Second Language Acquisition, 7,* 233–248.

Schmuck, R. A., & Schmuck, P. A. (1992). *Group processes in the classroom* (6th ed.). Dubuque, IA: Wm. C. Brown.

Seliger, H. W. (1983). Learner interaction in the classroom and its effects on language acquisition. In H. W. Seliger & M. H. Long (Eds.), *Classroom oriented research in second language acquisition.* Rowley, MA: Newbury House.

Sharan, S. (Ed.). (1990). *Cooperative learning: Theory and research.* New York: Praeger.

Sharan, S., Kussell, P., Hertz-Lazarowitz, R., Bejarano, Y., Raviv, S., & Sharan, Y. (1984). *Cooperative learning in the classroom: Research in desegregated schools.* Hillsdale, NJ: Lawrence Erlbaum Associates.

Sharan, S., & Shachar, H. (1988). *Language and learning in the cooperative classroom.* New York: Springer.

Sharan, S., & Sharan, Y. (1976). *Small-group teaching.* Englewood Cliffs, NJ: Educational Technology Publications.

Sharan, S., & Shaulov, A. (1990). Cooperative learning, motivation to learn, and academic achievement. In S. Sharan (Ed.), *Cooperative learning: Theory and research.* New York: Praeger, 173–202.

Sharan, Y., & Sharan, S. (1992). *Expanding cooperative learning through group investigation.* New York: Teachers College Press.

Slavin, R. E. (1986). *Using student team learning* (3rd ed.). Baltimore, MD: Johns Hopkins University, Center for Research on Elementary and Middle Schools.

Slavin, R. E. (1990). *Cooperative learning: Theory, research, and practice.* Englewood Cliffs, NJ: Prentice Hall.

Spolsky, B. (1988). Bridging the gap: A general theory of second language learning. *TESOL Quarterly, 22,* 377–396.

Spolsky, B. (1989). *Conditions for second language learning.* Oxford: Oxford University Press.

Stern, H. H. (1983). *Fundamental concepts of language teaching.* Oxford: Oxford University Press.

Stevens, R. J., Slavin, R. E., & Farnish, A. M. (1991). The effects of cooperative learning and direct instruction in reading comprehension strategies and main idea identification. *Journal of Educational Psychology, 83,* 8–16.

Swain, M. (1985). Communicative competence: Some roles of comprehensible output in its development. In S. Gass & C. Madden (Eds.), *Input in second language acquisition.* Rowley, MA: Newbury House.

Tarone, E. (1980). Communication strategies, foreign talk, and repair in interlanguage. *Language Learning, 30,* 417–432.

Townsend, D. J., Carrithers, C., & Bever, T. G. (1987). Listening and reading processes in college and middle school age readers. In R. Horowitz & S. J. Samuels (Eds.), *Comprehending oral and written language.* New York: Academic Press.

13

Cooperative Learning and Postmodern Approaches to Teaching Literature

Mark Brubacher and Ryder Payne

In this postmodern information age, we are still grappling with the concept that "modern" is no longer synonymous with "contemporary." Cooperative and collaborative learning have played an important role in the gradual evolution toward new perspectives on what defines our underlying values and attitudes. Trying to identify the elements of postmodernism as they apply to the classroom experience is still a somewhat nebulous task, but we decided to focus on six aspects that appear to describe some major trends relevant to school and society in general.

In keeping with the postmodern propensity for playful manipulation of old forms and new purposes, or, as John Willensky (1982) described, "its style of appropriation and its appropriation of style," we will create new word forms as the need arises. The following six elements of postmodernism are implicit in, or compatible with, the five approaches to learning we will describe further on:

1. *Multiplicity*: There is an acceptance of the fragmentation of point of view: that there is a plurality of voices, of eyes, of experiences that allows for nothing to be universal or value-free.

2. *Authority*: In the foreword to *Likely Stories: A Postmodern Sampler* (1992) Linda Hutcheon spoke of the eroding distinction between original and copy, and as John Willensky (1990) explained, since all "text comes out of previous text . . . we must question authority."

3. *Eclecticity*: Postmodernism delights in mixing and matching in new ways (note the old motifs of cathedrals and coliseums infused into new forms and materials in contemporary architecture). It delights in breathing new life into traditional

forms and playing with what Linda Hutcheon referred to as the "interzones" of conventional genres.

4. *Textuality*: We make and remake text, and text makes and remakes us. We live within the weave (*texere*, to weave) or texture of the world. Electronic media are based on the written word. Not only do we record with text, but we re-create ourselves through writing.

5. *Contextuality*: Nothing has meaning in isolation—not even a word. Learning has meaning only in the context of community. We cannot avoid the social concerns of racism, classism, and sexism, much less escape the issue of global environmentalism. Everything is interconnected. Reality is constantly appearing and reappearing, frame within frame.

6. *Reflectivity*: There is a self-consciousness about the creative act and an accompanying sense of irony and sometimes parody. One is aware of being in shifting/changing paradigms within a context of increasingly sophisticated levels of metacognition.

DISCUSSION AND DIALOGUE

In writing about literacy, John Willensky (1990) described two changes in classroom structuring. The first restructures the classroom around the students' rather than the teacher's pursuit of meaning. The second is taken up with literacy that would transform the student from supplicant to advocate in search of what has not been expressed or found before, a literacy that engages the student and that would encourage a greater engagement with the world.

The challenge that faces English teachers is how to implement these changes in the classroom. How might English classrooms be restructured so that students can extend their control over language and its empowering facility? How can the English classroom be identified with the democratic imperative of education, which Dewey described as "a mode of associated living of conjoint communicated experience"?

To begin with, we might look at aspects of communication. David Bohm (1990) made an important distinction between "dialogue" and "discussion." Dialogue, Bohm asserted, means that the object of talking in a group is to have different views presented as a means of discovering a new view. Dialogue, then, is characterized by divergent thinking. Discussion, on the other hand, is group talk that has as its objective the presenting and defending of different views in order to find the best one. Its thinking, then, is convergent.

In dialogue, all participants must deliberately reveal their assumptions so that the whole group may be aware of them. All members of the group must relate to each other as equals, and whoever is facilitating the group must influence the flow of participation by reminding participants that "the opposite might also be true." By contrast, in discussion, assumptions, hierarchy, and the negation of antitheses characterize the discourse. This distinction has important significance for the kind of discourse that is appropriate when students in small groups negotiate their curriculum.

Keeping this important distinction between dialogue and discussion clearly in mind, we will now attempt to answer the questions raised by Willensky and others by synthesizing the ideas and applications of five approaches to learning that have influenced us most in our English classroom practice. Brian Johnston and Steven Dowdy (1988) outlined a number of strategies for developing a negotiated curriculum. Alan Howe (1988) demonstrated the need for a continual interplay between small-group discussion and whole-class talk. Patrick Dias (1987) developed a very effective collaborative approach to response to literature that respects the learner's ability to make meaning. Peter Forrestal, Christine Cook, and John Dainutis (1991) have created a sequence of classroom activities that adapt a postmodern approach to literature for the English curriculum. Yael and Shlomo Sharan (1992) presented the rationale, planning, sequence of stages, and a variety of applications for Group Investigation.

THE NEGOTIATED CURRICULUM

Johnston and Dowdy's ideas on negotiating curriculum echo the "new literacy" approach to teaching. They observed that "negotiation in education is at the heart of preparation for active life in a democratic society." When they described the rationale for the program, they emphasized a restructuring of the classroom so that it "becomes more like a workshop and less like a literature theatre. The teacher spends more time helping students individually and in small groups, and less time talking to the whole class."

To make this new emphasis and transformation happen, a written contract is drawn up between teacher and student. This may involve negotiations among students, or teacher-student conferences. What is negotiated is a formative evaluation process based on the assumption that if one approaches "the test of teaching from the powerful end—the answering end," everything else will fall into place. We have adapted a negotiated contract from Johnston and Dowdy (1988) to look like this:

Process	Work to Be Done
Capture attention.	Take part in small-group planning session.
Maintain interest.	
Inform.	

Process	Work to Be Done
Develop an audiovisual component.	Prepare slide show, video, overhead, or equipment demonstration.
Present to group of peers and teacher.	Give a twenty-minute presentation on a significant procedure learned at your co-op placement.

The information under "Process" refers to the nonnegotiable part of the curriculum. In this case, it was the given part of a unit on public speaking set up for students who spent 80% of their school time in a work placement, attending school one day each week. The contract was negotiated in a combination of small-group sessions and teacher conferences. The twenty-minute presentation evaluation criteria, for example, were negotiated in small groups whose members brainstormed possible criteria and marks distribution. The brainstorming was very much a "dialogue" session in which the range of possibilities was explored with the goal of establishing an evaluation sheet that could be used by peers and teachers to evaluate the presentation. Each group displayed its list of criteria and marks distribution and orally provided a rationale. Then followed a whole-class "discussion" as each group made its case. The whole class eventually decided on a single format that was acceptable to all participants.

This kind of negotiation exposes students to the experience of planning their own work within practical constraints. They must use both "dialogue" and "discussion" to communicate their plans. They have to identify a purpose or rationale for how they will mark and prioritize criteria for evaluation. They appreciate the opportunity to reflect on both the content and the process of learning and accept responsibility when things do not work out exactly as planned. This makes them more willing to renegotiate better approaches next time.

The result is a general improvement in the quality of presentation. This is to some extent accounted for by the sense of healthy competition. But more is due to the pride of ownership and the understanding of purpose and rationale built into the negotiation process. As one student commented, "When you take on the job, it's like the real world. You make a commitment to do something in your own job placement, you do it or the supervisor gets mad. Same thing with this. You talked through it. You know what to expect."

The elements of postmodernism in the "Work to Be Done" approach are readily apparent: the plurality of voices, the genuine and respectful questioning of authority through continuous negotiation, the re-creating of self through the text of talk, the reflection on the process and content, and the connection to larger contexts outside the school.

MAKING MEANING: RESPONSE TO POETRY

Now we turn our attention to Patrick Dias's *Making Sense of Poetry*. The contribution that Dias has made to the study of literature is his insistence that students be encouraged and allowed to take ownership of the meaning they make when reading and discussing texts. Students in no way are to be channeled into predetermined ways of interpretation, either through teacher-set questions or Socratic dialogue. Still, the process takes place within a definite and repeated structure:

1. The teacher selects and reads a text, a poem, for example, to the whole class.

2. Each small group of four or five has two more people read the poem in the small-group setting.

3. The groups then have about twenty minutes to discuss what the poem could mean. Before they begin, difficult words and allusions are defined or explained by the teacher.

4. Near the end of the small-group discussion, one student takes the role of spokesperson for the group with the responsibility of explaining the group's interpretations to the class. After the first report, each person must begin by agreeing with, disagreeing with, or extending something said by the previous group. Each day a different person assumes the role of spokesperson.

5. During the class discussion, the teacher assumes a role of total neutrality, responding with interest and enthusiasm, but withholding all judgment about the value of the answers. After every group has been heard, a general class discussion follows until all the ideas and responses to ideas have been aired.

6. Now is the first time any writing takes place, as students make their entries in response journals.

7. The response journals are collected by the teacher periodically and commented on as a fellow reader, not an evaluator or judge.

8. Only at the end of the process, after about ten sessions, does the teacher take on the role of evaluator when students are given a sight passage to respond to individually. As they continue to grow in confidence, students eventually become partners in the evaluation process.

What is essential during the whole process is that the teacher does not intervene with meaning interpretation, either directly through leading questions or indirectly through subtle evaluation of answers during the class discussion. It is difficult to refrain from "correcting wrong answers," but it is necessary if students are to grow in self-confidence. What happens is that students challenge and refine each others's ideas and eventually achieve the ability to interpret text independently, confidently, and insightfully to a degree beyond that achieved through teacher-fed methodology.

How would this translate into an actual classroom situation? Here is a short fable to illustrate how it might fall into place.

A Postmodern Fable

Once upon a time there was a classroom, and in that room sat five and twenty students in five neat rows of five desks each. Before the class, with his own desk, which was much larger and more imposing than the students', stood the teacher. He looked old and wise, and all twenty-five students thought that there was nothing he did not know. So they waited eagerly for him to share his knowledge with them since they wanted nothing more than to be as wise as he. Equipped with his wisdom, so they thought, the world would be their oyster and every day would be as calm and serene as his appeared to be, in contrast to the chaotic turmoil that appeared to characterize their own lives. Each day he filled their minds with his knowledge, then followed this up with carefully worded questions and regular assignments to make sure everything had been learned according to his words. This went on for years. Then one day, he failed to show up. In his place stood a young woman, not much older than they were, and they panicked.

Ms. Poetica tried to calm them as best she could, but her hesitancy and obvious diffidence only increased their anxiety. Nevertheless, they decided to give her a chance. The subject of the day's class was poetry. The particular poem to be taught was "The Red Wheelbarrow" by William Carlos Williams, and when she gave it to the class it looked like this:

"So much depends upon the red wheelbarrow glazed with rainwater beside the white chickens."

"Class," she said in a matter-of-fact way as if she were talking about a normal, everyday occurrence, "Organize yourselves into groups of four. Choose for your group students you think you can work with and vice versa." Pandemonium broke out. Once things had quieted down, the teacher asked what the problem was. At first, the response was silence, not exactly a sullen silence, but more like an anxious silence. Nobody wanted to answer such a dangerous question in case the answer was wrong and the teacher singled her out for special attention. The teacher, too, kept silent until the tension became too great for one student, who blurted out, "What are we going to do once we've formed these groups?"

"Talk about the poem. More specifically, discuss how you think the poet might have presented this sentence as a four- or five-line poem. Once your group has decided, share your answer with the rest of the class. After each group has presented an answer by writing it on the chalkboard and given explanations for its choices, we'll try to produce a composite answer for the class, if that's possible."

"But what would be the point of that, Miss?" the student quickly replied. "Couldn't we just look at the original poem?"

"Yes, Jennifer, we could. But which would be more interesting, trying to explain why the poet organized the poem's form the way he did, or each of you trying to decide on the best form for the sentence? In the first case, you would simply be trying to second-guess the poet. The assignment I have given you requires you to re-create the poem according to the meaning you perceive it to have."

Jennifer, now fully aroused by such a ridiculous answer, replied hotly, "What's that got to do with anything? You know what the poem means. You tell us. That way we understand the poem and when you give us a test, we'll know the answers. That's the way Mr. Centex used to do it!" Loud murmurs of approval came from Jennifer's classmates.

"Well, that's certainly not Ms. Poetica's way!" said the teacher with a disarming smile. "Now, get into your groups quickly, and let's see what happens. Trust me, class. Everything will be fine, I assure you." And so, reluctantly, the class formed into groups of four and began to speculate on how the words of the poem might be divided into a four- or five-line poem.

Talk in the groups grew lively as students began to appreciate the variety of choices available and the effect each arrangement of lines had on the meaning of the poem. Eventually, the groups came up with arrangements such as these:

A. So much depends upon
   the red wheelbarrow
   glazed with rainwater
       beside the white chickens.

B. So much
   depends
   upon the red wheelbarrow
   glazed with rainwater
   beside the white chickens.

Each group was invited to write out its choice of lines and explain to the class the particular meaning the arrangement of lines seemed to suggest. The importance of form as a factor contributing to meaning became immediately obvious to the students.

Then the activity was repeated, this time concentrating on the word "glazed." Each group was asked to consider alternative words, trying them out in the poem and reflecting on the effect the new word had, if any, on the meaning. The following alternatives were suggested: shiny, glistening, shimmering, glossy, cleansed, washed, splashed, sparkling, viscous, coated, gilded, and mucussed. The excitement as each possibility was discussed and its contribution to meaning debated generated a whole new approach to meaning in poetry. As one student said, "It's only when you start to move things around and try out alternatives that you begin to realize how carefully the poem has been put together." Which led another to observe that such a discovery would not have been made had they not had an opportunity to fool around with the poem in the first place. And all agreed except Jennifer, who interjected rather harshly, "But what did the poet actually write? Let's have a look at the original poem."

"Ah, the poem," said the teacher wistfully. "Do you really want to look at that? Look at the many beautiful alternatives you have created."

But she showed it to them anyway, and again Jennifer burst out, "So, what does it mean then? Aren't you going to tell us?"

This time, another student beat the teacher to the answer. "I'll answer. It means

all the things the poet has put into it to give it meaning. Didn't you follow what happened when we started to change things around?"
"And what are those things?" said Ms. Poetica, jumping in with perfect timing. "Would you like to get back to your groups and discuss that now?"
"Yes!" the class chorused in unison. "Let's do that." And they did, discovering all kinds of interesting things about the poem and the way it was written, and how these might contribute to the meaning: the imagery, the diction, the tone, figurative language, the structure, the experimental language, the sounds and rhythms.

One week later, Ms. Poetica was basking in papers. Yes, she was reading student responses to last week's poetry classes and was confirming that her students actually enjoyed discussing difficult poetry. She found herself most pleased by the students' reactions. One student commented, "When you announced we were going to study poetry I sort of said to myself, 'Oh no, not again.' In the past, I hated analyzing a poem. Now the poetry workshops helped me to look at poetry in such a different way that I started to enjoy it. People had different thoughts and views, and that helped me to explore other meanings of poetry."

Another explained, "Actually, I do not find poetry all that enjoyable. The group discussion helped a lot to make it enjoyable. As I got to know my classmates better, I was able to express my interpretation of a particular poem. The whole group got into the enthusiasm of being able to interpret the poem in their own ways. They began to enjoy the pleasure of poetry along with the fun of conversing with each other."

So the process worked. Ms. Poetica structured the activities and let the students find the meaning. And this applied to their understanding of the process of understanding themselves as a member of a group as well as understanding the poetry they were exploring.

After the initiation into the unit with "The Red Wheelbarrow," she used the "fishbowl." Pairs of groups worked together so that an inner circle debated a current issue while the outer circle observed each participant's various roles during the discussion using a "roles in groups" checklist. At the end of the session, an observer in the outer circle shared perceptions with a participant in the inner circle and gave the sheet to that student for future reference. Groups then exchanged places for a second observation and feedback session.

Students were now introduced to the idea of poetry workshops. They were placed in random groups and given a poem to discuss for half an hour before returning to the whole-class discussion forum. Once the students were comfortable, they were ready to tape discussions with careful instructions on how to speak into the mike, introduce themselves and the topic, and conclude the taping. After three tapings, Ms. Poetica asked the students to select one or two minutes of tape that they found particularly interesting and that included all participants and to write a transcript recording every detail in one column and analyzing the roles of the speakers in a second column. Then she asked them to write a commentary on the strengths and weaknesses of the taped discussion followed by an individual self-assessment by each group member. The insights of the students into their own participation were reassuring. One commented: "I feel that I made suggestions when I had something to contribute and that I was accepting of other people's ideas. However, I need to improve in the area of summarizing how the work has been going on and looking for things that block group progress."

Another simply gave his own impressions of the process: "I thought the idea of getting into assigned groups was a good idea. I got the chance to work with other classmates I haven't worked with before. This was fun because we helped each other bring out more ideas and thoughts on the poem." And these were items she had not even thought of putting on the "roles in groups" sheet.

But what really made Ms. Poetica happy was the very next week when Mr. Centex celebrated his return by giving a surprise sight poem to the class to respond to as individuals. Not one student failed.

WHOLE-CLASS AND SMALL-GROUP DISCUSSION

Let us look more closely at the balancing of whole-class and small-group activities. Alan Howe (1988) saw whole-class discussion as "but part of a process in the classroom which is designed to lead pupils towards fuller understanding." At the start of a sequence of work, whole-class discussion is "a way of raising issues and setting an agenda." In the middle of a sequence of work, it becomes a way of reshaping and clarifying an idea, while at the end of a sequence, it can become "a way of presenting and considering committed viewpoints." Thus whole-class discussion is effective largely to the extent that it is built upon and integrated with small-group discussion and emerges out of the interests and concerns of the students.

Howe used a swimming analogy to explain the dangers of plunging too quickly into large-group discussions:

Moving too quickly towards expecting pupils to talk openly in a large group is rather like throwing a whole class into the deep end of a swimming pool. As well as the few non-swimmers who might drown (never to be heard from again?!), there will be others who are unhappy out of their depth. Whilst a few strong, natural swimmers splash about happily, the nervous ones are so anxious about drowning, or so conscious and embarrassed about their lack of finesse as swimmers, that they lose all confidence and cling silently on to the side of the pool. They need to be brought gradually up to the deep end. (Howe, 1988, p. 34)

Consequently, he perceived a symbiotic relationship between small-group and whole-class discussions. Neither can flourish without the other. The small group gives energy, while the whole class brings discipline of thought and further creative insights, plus a wider perspective on the subject matter being explored. The end result is greater individual confidence, competence, and knowledge.

ADAPTING COOPERATIVE LEARNING TO POSTMODERNISM

A fourth approach reflecting postmodernism came from Australia. Peter Forrestal (1992) looked at learning from the perspective of how postmodernism is influencing critical theories about reading. Instead of being asked to uncover the author's elusive purpose or the meaning of a poem, short story, or novel, students ought to be asked to consider possible "meanings" of a poem or any other text. They may be encouraged to comment on how different readings are constructed, what values or beliefs are suggested by each reading, and in whose interests different readings are made.

Thus students become owners of the many influences on their own readings or constructed meanings. They become aware of ironic or frivolous readings, values and belief systems behind interpretations that emphasize and suppress parts of a text, dominant and resistant readings, and so on. All these considerations will influence how a reader will respond to a text.

Using Dias's approach with an eleventh-grade class reading George Orwell's essay "Shooting an Elephant" produced an illustration of Forrestal's multiple responses to reading a text:

1. The narrator was justified in killing the elephant because he was part of the British Empire controlling Burma, so he had to show his courage and authority.

2. The narrator was not justified in killing the elephant. He was merely swept away by the demands of the crowd and afraid they would laugh at him if he didn't shoot.

3. The crowd of Burmese were just as bad as the British since they used the incident to strip the elephant's body, just as the British took advantage of them as part of the Empire.

The integration of small-group and large-group processes described and advocated by Dias, Howe, and Forrestal has as its central thesis that students can and do construct meaning from text most effectively when their values, beliefs, and backgrounds are respected. Not only do students enjoy learning more, but they actually do learn more.

INTERDEPENDENCE IN THE CLASSROOM ENVIRONMENT

As we look at the increasingly complex patterns of learning relationships, it might be useful to examine more closely various dimensions of interdependence that are at the center of a healthy classroom environment. Cooperative learning, seen from this perspective, fosters three continua, each with interdependence at its center.

SOCIETAL NEEDS	SOCIAL NEEDS	INDIVIDUAL NEEDS
external curriculum	interdependent small groups	personal goals and interests
STUDENT ROLE	CO-LEARNER ROLE	MENTOR ROLE
neophyte	interdependent small group	sharer of expertise
DEPENDENT SITUATION	INTERDEPENDENT SITUATION	INDEPENDENT SITUATION
learning is a whole class context	interdependent small groups	acquiring information, creating and reflecting in solitude

At the core of each of these three continua is the interdependent small group, giving energy and meaning to the learning. The roles of dependence and independence, student and mentor, and the individual and society can have meaning ultimately only when they are synthesized through the dialogue and discussion of a small group where information is shaped, honed, and given meaning through human discourse.

In this context, Group Investigation (Sharan & Sharan, 1992) provides the most complete approach for a balanced and healthy learning environment. If we look at the three continua more closely, we find that they all can flourish in Group Investigation:

1. The curriculum is designated by the teacher as the representative of society; the small group investigates purpose and method and is empowered by asking questions about why and how; the individual pursues personal interests, talents, and needs.

2. All the while, students grow by going through the continuous cycles of receiving knowledge (student), giving knowledge (mentor), and negotiating meaning through colearner activities such as planning investigations and coming to common understandings about new information.

3. The student will also take increasing ownership of decisions of when to be dependent on others or other sources (teacher, peer, print, electronic media, and so on), when to interact as an equal in negotiating understanding in small-

group situations, and when to assimilate knowledge, reflect on it, or create privately for a period of time before testing the results on a wider audience of peers or mentors.

Group Investigation thus provides a context for every mode of learning, a framework for the reader-response approaches of Dias and Forrestal, and an environment in which oracy and negotiation are natural elements of learning. It provides a structure where postmodern attitudes can flourish, and it is in itself a postmodern process because of the values it is built upon. We will examine briefly an eleventh-grade class investigating novels that focus on social issues.

Stage 1: Class Determines Subtopics and Organizes into Research Groups

Right from the start, Group Investigation invites and encourages the concept of multiplicity. In this class, students eventually selected six novels and agreed to work together in groups around six subthemes: *The Color Purple*, personal emancipation; *The Diary of Anne Frank*, racism; *Lost Horizon*, utopia; *Brave New World*, dystopia; *Dreamspeaker*, cultural intolerance; *Kramer versus Kramer*, marital breakdown.

Stage 2: Groups Plan Their Investigation

Students were then asked to find another novel or biography of their own choice on a similar theme with the purpose of discovering similarities and differences in values, attitudes, and approaches. At this point, they discussed what they thought they might find and how they would keep track of their readings and the premises or backgrounds of the author.

Stage 3: Groups Carry Out Their Investigations

Now students became involved in reading their novels, keeping a response journal for each novel to record their impressions, interpretations, questions, and comparisons to other similar stories in other genres. These journals were shared with others in the group and with the teacher. At the end of the reading, each student wrote a short essay focusing on any significant comparisons found. A student who read *The Diary of Anne Frank* also read *Obasan*, the story of Japanese internment in Canadian work camps during World War II, and had insights about the universality of prejudice.

Stage 4: Groups Plan Their Presentations

Planning presentations is the crucial learning stage where students both make new text and are made by the text they have explored. The group who read *Dreamspeaker* created a play with a moving scene in which the still-living characters tried to communicate with the young boy, Peter, and his mentor, an old Indian, the Dreamspeaker.

Stage 5: Groups Make Their Presentations

The presentations often offer the greatest opportunities for awareness of contextuality. The group investigating *The Color Purple* decided to imitate (parody) an Oprah Winfrey talk show. The class became a lively forum for a wide range of views on male-female relationships and oppressed minority groups. The frames of reality ranged from the courageous heroine (Celine) of the novel, the author (Alice Walker), the critics, the persona of Oprah Winfrey, and the student assuming her role to the mixture of genuine and "in-role" responses of the classroom audience. All were evident to the students. Lost on none were the interweaving ironies of oppressive attitudes emerging at every level: in the novel, within the talk show, and in the multiracial classroom.

Stage 6: Teacher and Students Evaluate Their Projects

Learning about how we learn permeates all stages of Group Investigation, but during the final stage, self-reflexivity assumes a greater prominence in the context of peer and teacher evaluation of the projects. Students discover that literature really does influence their attitudes about life, their ability to see life in wider and new contexts, and their own ability to create text and be re-created by it. Group Investigation makes it possible for students to see the interrelated contexts of Anne Frank, Obasan, the Dreamspeaker, John Foster, and Celine as all part of the same human condition.

CONCLUSION

The term *postmodern* may turn out to be ephemeral, but its elements do describe values, attitudes, and approaches that are in harmony with cooperative learning. We may still be confounded by the daily tyranny of the "either/or" belief systems of the modern age, but we also have hope that by fostering negotiation and response in our classrooms, our world will become increasingly hospitable to the postmodern text-ture of "both/ and."

REFERENCES

Bohm, D. (1989). *The special theory of relativity*. New York: Addison-Wesley.

Bowering, G., & Hutcheon, L. (Eds.). (1992). *Likely stories: A postmodern sampler*. Toronto: Coach House Press.

Dias, P. (1987). *Making sense of poetry: Patterns in the process*. Ottawa: Canadian Council of Teachers of English.

Forrestal, P. (1992). Rereading, Reading. *English Journal, 81*, 25–29.

Forrestal, P., Cook, C., & Dainutis, J. (1991). *Making meaning*. Melbourne: Chalkface Press.

Howe, A. (1988). *Expanding horizons: Teaching through whole class discussion*. Sheffield, England: National Association for Teachers of English.

Johnston, B., & Dowdy, S. (1988). *Work required: Teaching and assessing in a negotiated curriculum*. Victoria, Australia: Robert Anderson & Associates.

Sharan, Y., & Sharan, S. (1992). *Expanding cooperative learning through group investigation*. New York: Teachers College Press.

Willensky, J. (1982). Postmodern literacy: a primer. *Our Schools/Ourselves, 3*, 31–51.

Willensky, J. (1990). *The new literacy*. New York: Routledge.

14

Cooperative Learning and Science

Sharon J. Sherman

DISCOVERING SCIENCE

Science is filled with excitement. It carries the challenge of the unknown and the unexpected. It demands curiosity, imagination, emotional invest-ment, and passion, as well as logic and reason. To understand science, students must experience science as scientists do. Only then will they see science as blending reason and logic with "wrong turns taken, hunches that didn't pan out, downright errors and mistakes, and the sometimes hostile behavior of equipment" (Cross, 1990).

The marriage of cooperative learning and science is seen as a natural union for many experienced science teachers who have worked extensively with small groups. When cooperative learning is properly implemented, it provides a vehicle for student teams to share materials and equipment, as well as ideas. The utilization of teamwork allows the science educator to achieve a variety of academic and social goals in the classroom setting so that students can discover the adventure of science.

WHAT RESEARCH SAYS

Research findings show that using cooperative learning with science in-struction offers much promise. A program developed and studied at Rut-gers University, called SCIENCE TEAMS, implemented cooperative learning to study environmental science in thirty-two New Jersey elemen-tary school classrooms over a two-year period. Results showed that students using cooperative learning with environmental science had significantly more positive attitudes toward science and saw science as more exciting than did students in the control group. The SCIENCE TEAMS students were more comfortable doing science and taking science tests than the control group. In addition, the students who experienced cooperative learning not only did more hands-on science than the control group, but reported liking it more. Teachers reported including more environmental science topics in the curriculum than those in the control group (Mastny, Kahn, & Sherman, 1992). Attitudes toward science are enhanced when students engage in hands-on science, and both thinking skills and use of science process skills are improved when students experience science in this way (Kyle, 1984; Lazarowitz & Karsenty, 1990).

GETTING STARTED

Team Formation

Team formation is most effective when four students work together in a specific academic mix (Johnson, Johnson, & Holubec, 1987, 1989; Kagan, 1992). Combining one high achiever, two average achievers, and one low achiever maximizes peer teaching and fosters the individual learning of each team member. The team should be balanced by gender and by race to promote equity. Such a group is called a home team or base group.

Each team member must have a role, so duties are shared in a predetermined way. Students usually prefer to choose their roles, rotating roles each time the group meets. In a science class, the roles can include principal investigator, materials manager, recorder, and spokesperson. The *principal investigator* is in charge of the group, and he or she coordinates the activity or experiment. Specific directions for the activity may be given to the principal investigator. This person also assumes the responsibility of overseeing the rotation of roles before the next activity begins. The *materials manager* is responsible for collecting the materials the group needs. This person may be supplied with a list of materials to gather from a general supply area, or he or she may collect preassembled materials packets for the activity. In some instances, two materials managers may be needed for a complicated activity. The materials manager returns the items after the activity is completed. The *recorder* is responsible for writing down the observations of the group. The recorder may create tables or charts for the group. On occasion, the *spokesperson* reports the group's findings to the class. He or she works closely with other members to be sure that each one understands the material and can explain what has been done.

The *timekeeper* keeps the group working within the assigned time period, while the *gatekeeper* tries to have each member participate equally. Quiet students are encouraged to speak, while more talkative students are reminded to wait for a turn. The gatekeeper role is especially good for a student who has difficulty working in the group. This particular role keeps the student very busy, and it tends to occupy the student who has extra energy. The *checker* makes sure that each group member understands the task and agrees with how the group arrived at its conclusions. The *encourager/praiser* looks for individual contributions that deserve praise and rewards those contributions with positive comments. After examining the activity, the teacher decides which roles will be needed.

Teams can be kept together for varying lengths of time. If they are kept together for about a month to a month and a half, students will be able to bond with each other and the team will be able to grow and develop. Some teachers prefer to keep teams together for shorter periods of time. This fosters more frequent formation of new teams and enables students to mix at a faster rate. It is best for each teacher to try both methods and go by individual preference.

Teambuilding Activities

The science teacher must bring the class from a group of students who sit side by side to a class filled with teams enjoying cooperative team spirit. This is accomplished by the process of teambuilding. Teambuilding activities emphasize the analysis of work procedures to improve productivity, relationships among team members, and the social skills of members. It also focuses on the ability of the team to adapt to environmental demands (Johnson & Johnson, 1991). Teambuilding is especially important where significant tensions exist in the class. Teams balanced by gender and by race often include students who are not likely to have chosen each other as teammates. Such teams may need extra time to get acquainted. Content-related teambuilding activities both unite the team and create a starting point for the lesson.

A good teambuilding activity for students of any age is the Team Name–Team Logo–Team Cheer. Members work together to devise a team name with a scientific theme. Each member must have a say in the name. It is important that no decision be reached unless each member agrees with the decision. If a member objects seriously, he or she should not go along with the decision. After the team is named, a team logo is created. If time allows, have students come up with a short rhyme of about four lines. They can use the rhyme when introducing their team to the whole class. Sometimes teams devise a team handshake or a team cheer or create a team banner. When all teams have completed the task, have teams take turns presenting their work to the whole class. When debriefing the activity, ask teams to name one thing the team did well. They might also consider one way in which they could improve. Refer to the teams by name.

Roundtable and Roundrobin are two cooperative techniques that can be used to foster teambuilding, active listening, thinking, and participation.

In both cases, students take turns contributing to the group. In Roundrobin, participation is oral, while in Roundtable, it is written.

Before beginning a nutrition activity, have students take turns reciting (for Roundrobin) or writing (for Roundtable) the names of as many fruits and vegetables as possible (in alphabetical order). As a lead-in to an astronomy unit, they can take turns naming as many constellations as they can. Students can be given the name of a planet, such as Jupiter or Saturn, and asked to form as many words as possible from each word. To process, have students discuss the personal skills or competencies they brought to the team to help carry out the activity. These activities should be enjoyable, helping to build good relationships between team members, while allowing them to see how the group functions.

FITTING SCIENCE PROCESS SKILLS INTO THE COOPERATIVE FRAMEWORK

The Process Skills

Scientific theories explain phenomena by presenting a systematic view of them. The process of science involves a number of skills that scientists utilize to build theories. Scientists start by formulating *research questions* about a particular phenomenon. They identify and observe the *variables* that will be examined and formulate conjectural statements or tentative propositions called *hypotheses*. Hypotheses state relationships between variables and are based on the theoretical framework that has been developed. The scientific process is the testing of these hypotheses.

Scientists make *observations* to describe the phenomenon under investigation. *Classification* involves the grouping of observations into categories. Measuring devices are used to make quantitative observations of the phenomenon in the *measurement* process. *Communication* is essential to science, as graphs, tables, charts, reports, and oral discussions are used to build models that describe the phenomenon under investigation. Scientists aim to explain phenomena, and they use their models to make *predictions*. They search for *patterns* or *regularities* when interpreting the data that have been collected. Based on what they have observed, scientists draw *tentative conclusions* or make *inferences*. *Experimentation* involves manipulating variables in order to see what results. Based on the results of the experiments, the theoretical framework may be modified, and new hypotheses can be formulated.

Cooperative learning provides a framework for promoting scientific investigation in the classroom. Discussion, which is so essential for understanding in science, as well as in other subjects, is fostered in the cooperative classroom. Hands-on science activities are wonderful vehicles for use and practice of the process skills. Not every process skill is used in every lesson, but every science lesson should focus on one or more of the skills.

Cooperative Learning Lesson Plans That Incorporate Science Process Skills

A science lesson begins with an *overview of the lesson*. What material will be covered? How does the lesson fit into the unit? What type of activity will be used? Will it be a hands-on activity? Will it be a reading? Will it be a team discussion? Once these questions are answered, decide on the *team roles* that will be used. Be sure that the students change roles for every new activity. Cooperative learning activities often require more than just one forty-five-minute period. Estimate how much time will be needed. It may be necessary to continue the activity for more than one day. If the school has flexible scheduling, the activity should be continued as needed. Next, the appropriate *cooperative learning strategy* should be chosen. Among the possibilities are Group Investigation, Student Teams-Achievement Divisions (STAD), Teams-Games-Tournaments (TGT), Four Corners, Team Word Webbing, Jigsaw, or any other cooperative learning technique that fits the lesson.

Identify the *science process skills* that will be used in the lesson. It is possible to choose the process skills that will be addressed and build them into the lesson. If there is a particular activity in mind, it should be examined to see which process skills are highlighted in the activity. It is uncommon to focus on just one process skill at a time. For example, communication occurs in all activities. Where there is observation, there is usually classification. Where there is data collection, there is usually measurement, observation, classification, communication, inference, and experimentation.

In most cooperative learning activities, *materials* are required. It is important to prepare the materials in advance and decide how the materials will be distributed. The materials manager role makes distribution and clean-up go smoothly. Sharing materials structures positive interdependence within the team.

Science activities often specify *procedures*. The procedures can be supplied by the teacher, or teams can brainstorm ways in which to carry out the investigation on their own. No matter which way the procedure is carried out, it is important for teams to take time to review them. Students must be sure that all team members understand what will be done. The principal investigator or the gatekeeper can be chosen to question all of the team members. If a lesson has a particularly difficult procedure to understand, appoint a *clarifier*, who makes sure that all members understand what is to be done. If the team still has questions, the clarifier asks the teacher for help and brings the information back to the team.

Once the lesson is complete, it must be brought to *closure*. The teacher devises questions for closure that bring all of the elements of the lesson together. They help students understand what has been accomplished in the activity. Questions for closure are generally given to the whole team to discuss at the end of the activity. To ensure individual accountability, it is a good idea for each student to answer the questions for closure in his or her own words, either in written or oral form.

Processing the group's effectiveness is the next part of the lesson. Some questions that can be asked are: What did your group do well? What could your group have done better? Did working in a team allow you to work more efficiently? Did working in a team help you understand the material better? Did all members of the group do a fair share of the work? Were any group members too bossy? What cooperative skills did your group practice? Was there any conflict in your group? If so, how did you resolve the conflict?

Individual team members can process their own participation in the group. Did I assist other students when asked? Did I ask for assistance when I needed it? Was the help I received useful? Did I praise and encourage my fellow teammates? Did I receive praise and encouragement during the activity? How did I feel when I received praise? Choose one or two questions for processing at the end of each lesson.

Using Cooperative Learning and Science for Process and Product

When students engage in hands-on science in a creative way, they experience the process of science. Ideally, they will learn the basic skills and the simple facts in this way. Through the scientific process, they achieve a product.

There are times when the science teacher aims toward review and mastery of the subject matter. This is usually accompanied by a product orientation, where there is a great deal of emphasis on assessment and evaluation. On most other occasions, emphasis should be on experimentation, collaboration, discussion, and exchange of information. This is characteristic of a process orientation, where developing thinking skills and experiencing science are the goals. Cooperative learning provides a way to address both process and product in the science classroom, as there are strategies that help with mastery of basic skills and memory of facts, and those that help develop thinking skills in an experiential fashion.

COOPERATIVE LEARNING STRATEGIES FOR THE SCIENCE CLASSROOM

Four Corners

Four Corners is a strategy that fosters thinking at all grade levels. This example is appropriate at the middle school level and can be used in grade nine. The activity takes about twenty minutes. The materials required are index cards and pencils.

Students start out in their home teams. The teacher introduces the topic of safety and gives a brief overview. This may also be accompanied by a reading on safety. The teacher asks: "If you were designing a science room, think about your priorities for ordering safety equipment. Would you first order (a) a fire extinguisher, (b) safety goggles, (c) an eyewash station, or (d) a safety shower?" Students think about why they should choose one device over the others and write their responses on an index card. The teacher then designates each corner of the room as one of the four choices. Individual students walk to the corner they have chosen and discuss the reasons for the particular choice. A spokesperson for each corner is chosen and reports to the class. A second round then follows, as students are asked if they would then order (a) a fire blanket, (b) a heat-resistant mat, (c) a fume hood, or (d) a phone. Once again, students report to their respective corners and discuss their choices. Spokespersons report to the whole class.

Students then return to their home teams, where they brainstorm a list of safety precautions. This sets the stage for further discussion of safety procedures. As the lesson is brought to closure, safety regulations are discussed and specific questions are asked of each group.

Numbered Heads Together is an example of a cooperative learning technique that can be used for lesson closure (Kagan, 1992). First, all students work together to answer all questions. Then each student within the team is given a different number, either one, two, three, or four. A number is called, and that student explains the group's answers to the whole class. This technique brings equity to the group, as all students must be equally prepared to answer all of the questions. Students teach each other so that all team members understand the material. As an assignment, students individually research local safety regulations and put together a team report. As a processing activity, students debrief the group's effectiveness. They might discuss how they felt as individuals in the four corners, and how they felt when working with the home team.

Paired Partners: Think Aloud

A strategy called Paired Partners: Think Aloud (Whimbey & Whimbey, 1975) focuses on problem solving and thinking. This method has students think aloud and talk their way through problems, thereby fostering *metacognition*, which means thinking about one's own thinking and learning. This particular application of Paired Partners: Think Aloud is appropriate for students of grade four and beyond. It takes thirty to forty minutes. As the activity begins, teams of four break up into two dyads as students pair off. One student is the *problem solver* and the other is the *monitor*. The teacher tells the story of the cricket thermometer.

To measure temperature, physicists use the Kelvin scale, and we use the Fahrenheit and Celsius scales. In both cases, a thermometer is used. Did you know that crickets can be used as thermometers? Like grasshoppers, crickets have long hind legs. Their wings are folded on their backs. Crickets produce high-pitched sounds by rubbing their wings together. The underside of the wing has an area of ridges. The upper side of the wing has a scraper. When the ridges of one wing are rubbed against the scraper of the other wing, a chirping sound is produced. Male crickets chirp to attract female crickets and to keep other male crickets from their territory.

People who study crickets have discovered that as the air temperature rises, the number of chirps increases. The next time you hear a cricket chirp, listen carefully to it. Count the number of chirps per minute. Add thirty to this number. Divide your answer by seven. The result will be a number that is close to the air temperature in degrees Celsius (Continuous Electron Beam Accelerator Facility Manual, 1992). For example, if a cricket chirps 75 times per minute, 75 + 30 = 105, and 105 divided by 7 = 15°C.

The teacher poses the following problems: Find the temperature in C° for each of the following:

a. 96 chirps per minute

b. 117 chirps per minute

c. 61 chirps per minute

d. 40 chirps per minute

The monitor asks questions while the problem solver thinks aloud and solves problem (*a*). The monitor attempts to bring out his or her reasoning. The problem solver continues to elaborate while thinking through the problem. The students switch roles as problem (*b*) is answered.

To process the activity, students are asked to describe their own thinking. The teacher might ask, "Did thinking about how you think and learn help you to understand and solve the problem?" Pairs share their responses with other members of the home team. If time allows, home teams could share their responses with the whole class.

As paired partners, students practice listening skills as they hear a story or listen to directions. They engage in problem solving and analyze their own thinking, receiving feedback and direction from a partner. Communication skills are practiced as the activity proceeds. The roles are reversed and the other student practices these skills.

This technique structures the discussion that is needed to help students understand scientific concepts. Instead of sitting quietly and answering the questions alone, each student has a chance to examine his or her own thinking and learning. If questions arise that cannot be answered, the teacher can be summoned to help. Students should not leave the classroom without having clarified the subject matter.

Think-Pair-Share

Another technique that helps clarify thinking is called Think-Pair-Share (Lyman & McTighe, 1988). Home teams are broken into two pairs. Partners are given a problem, and they think about it. Wait time (at least three to ten seconds) is given for thinking. Students pair up and share their thoughts. Pairs then share their answers with the whole class.

Think-Pair-Share is appropriate for a chemistry class. About ten minutes are needed for the whole activity. It can be used during a lecture to stimulate thinking and break from the lecture format for a brief time. An example is the nitrocellulose story, or starting things off with a bang. This is the story of an accidental discovery made by the German-Swiss chemist Christian Schönbein (1799–1868). In 1845, Schönbein was working in his home with a mixture of nitric and sulfuric acids when he accidentally spilled some of the mixture. He used his wife's cotton apron to mop up the mixture. (Keep in mind that cotton is composed of cellulose, a natural polymer). Schönbein hung the apron up to dry over a stove. But as the moisture evaporated from the apron, the entire apron went "poof." You might say it went off with a bang (Sherman & Sherman, 1992, p. 329). What had Schönbein done?

Students are given time to *think* about the problem on an individual basis. They then *pair* up with their partners and share ideas. Finally, pairs *share* answers with the class. (Schönbein turned the cellulose into nitrocellulose, which is a powerful explosive.)

Think-Pair-Share gives students time to think. The wait time used during the thinking phase is important. If the story were told during a lecture, many students would not have time to stop and think about what happened. Thought and articulation are used to help students understand.

Three-Step Interview

Three-Step Interview is a cooperative learning method that works best with a team of four. It consists of a number of steps. At the start, each student chooses a letter, A, B, C, or D. In the first step, students pair off,

A with B and C with D. A interviews B, while C interviews D. In the second step, roles are reversed. B interviews A, while D interviews C. The third step involves a Roundrobin. A reports what he or she learned from B, then B reports what he or she learned from A, and so on. The report can be addressed to either the group or the whole class.

The Three-Step Interview for the science classroom involves students choosing a famous scientist to study. Each student reads about the scientist and "becomes" that scientist during the lesson. A can be Marie Curie, B can be Barbara McClintock, C can be Rosalyn Sussman Yalow, and D can be Rita Levi-Montalcini. Students take turns interviewing each other and reporting their findings to the team and then to the class.

The Three-Step Interview also can involve experimentation in science. The question for the lesson is this: If the amount of water in a one-liter jar is changed, will the sound change? Four one-liter glass jars are needed for the activity. Jar 1 is filled (with water) one-eighth of the way to the top, jar 2 is one-quarter filled, jar 3 is half filled, and jar 4 is three-quarters filled. Students pair off. One student in each team uses a spoon to strike the outside of jars 1, 2, and 3. Jar 4 is not tapped. Students consider this question: Based on the sounds you heard when the first three jars were tapped, do you think the sound produced by the fourth jar will be higher or lower than that of the third jar? Explain your reasoning.

The interview proceeds as A interviews B and C interviews D. Roles are reversed as B interviews A and D interviews C. Students share answers in a Roundrobin. The fourth jar is tapped as predictions are tested. In the final part of the activity, teams work together to apply what they learned. They adjust the amount of water in each jar so that they can play a musical scale.

Three-Step Interview is also an excellent strategy for closure. Students can interview each other and find out what they learned from the lesson. They can highlight what they learned best and what they still need to have clarified. They can summarize the main points of the lesson. Ways in which the principles learned in the lesson can be applied are also good questions for closure.

Graphic Organizers

Ideas can be generated using *graphic organizers*, which provide a visual way to represent facts and concepts in an organized manner. They are useful for generating new ideas, elaborating on the ideas, and illustrating relationships between concepts. Graphic organizers also help relate new knowledge to prior knowledge. Team word webs, sequence chains, and attribute wheels are especially useful in science instruction.

Team word webs begin with a central idea placed in the center of the

Figure 14.1
Team Word Web

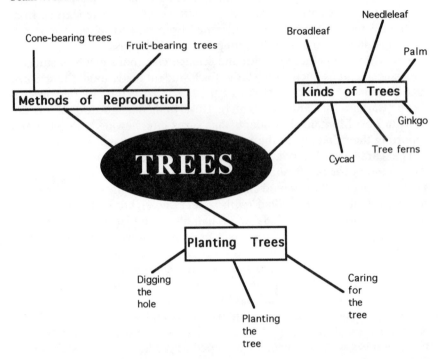

web (see Figure 14.1). The branches of the web contain related categories and specific details. Word webs can be used at the beginning of a lesson as a way to assess prior knowledge, or at the end of a lesson to summarize what has been learned.

Sequence chains map the flow of knowledge in a sequential fashion (see Figure 14.2). They track the steps of a process, such as the path of blood through the circulatory system or the steps in a chemical reaction. This is a good tool for organizing knowledge and is helpful in summarizing what has been covered.

Attribute wheels represent what has been analyzed. The main category or concept is placed in the center of the wheel, and its attributes are located on the ends of the spokes (see Figure 14.3). Students can be presented with a topic or concept, and they brainstorm its attributes, recording the data on the wheel.

Using Cooperative Learning for Review and Practice

Several cooperative group structures are especially useful for reviewing material, including Numbered Heads Together, Roundtable, Roundrobin, and Pairs Check.

Figure 14.2
Sequence Chain

How cone bearing plants reproduce

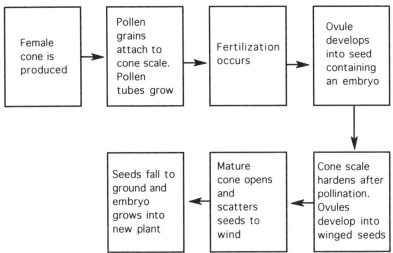

With Pairs Check, teams of four are broken into dyads. One person in each pair is the problem solver, and the other is the coach. The problem solver finishes the problem, and the coach checks it over. If it appears that the problem has been done correctly, praise is given and partners switch roles. When two problems have been answered, both pairs check answers. If there is agreement on the answers, partners switch roles, and two more problems are done. If there is disagreement, the problems are discussed. The teacher is summoned if extra help is needed.

Roundtable and Roundrobin are useful when reviewing for a test or quiz. Students review the facts they learned by taking turns writing or reciting the answers. In Numbered Heads Together, students number off, one, two, three, or four. If they are reviewing the parts of a plant, each person is responsible for naming one part of the plant. The teacher might pose a question to the team, and each member would be responsible for coming up with a different solution strategy.

PUTTING THE STRATEGIES TOGETHER: SAMPLE SCIENCE LESSONS

Experimenting with Oobleck

Lesson Overview

The object of this activity is to develop skills in scientific observation. Science and literature are integrated, as the lesson begins with the reading of *Bartholomew and the Oobleck* by Dr. Seuss.

Figure 14.3
Energy Forms Attribute Wheel

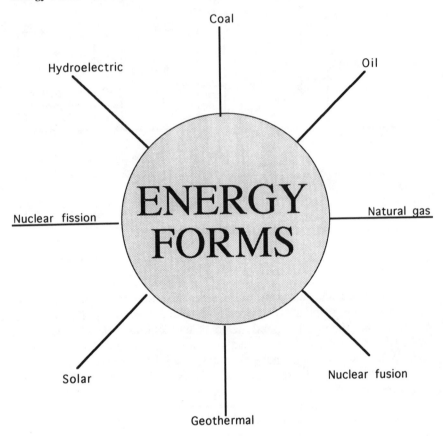

Team Roles

The roles needed for this activity are materials manager, principal investigator, recorder, and spokesperson.

Cooperative Learning Strategies

The Roundtable strategy is used to construct an attribute wheel. Three-Step Interview is used for closure.

Process Skills

Communication, observation, classification, and searching for patterns and regularities will be practiced in this activity.

Materials

Newspapers to cover each table, one 6″ × 12″ piece of aluminum foil per group, and one Popsicle stick per group are needed. To make the Oobleck, the teacher needs one sixteen-ounce box of corn starch, one cup of water, five drops of green food coloring, and ten drops of peppermint flavoring. Mix the green food coloring and the peppermint flavoring in the water. Slowly add the box of corn starch and stir with a spoon. You will have Oobleck. Do not breathe in the corn starch powder as you make the Oobleck. Keep it in a covered bowl. (Oobleck begins to dry out within thirty minutes when dropped by spoonful onto the aluminum foil.)

Procedure

1. Begin the lesson by reading *Bartholomew and the Oobleck*. In the book, Bartholomew Cubbins watches as King Derwin orders his wizards to make something new come down from "his" sky. The wizards succeed, and Oobleck is born. In a short time, the kingdom is covered with Oobleck. Tell students that you know how to make Oobleck and have prepared some for them to observe.

2. Have each group's materials manager get newspaper to cover the desk. A piece of foil containing a spoonful of Oobleck is also needed. Use a Popsicle stick to manipulate the Oobleck.

3. Teams work together to construct an attribute wheel. The word Oobleck is at the center. They use Roundtable to name the properties they observe. They may use all of their senses except taste. Advise them to look at color, size, shape, texture, weight, hardness, odor, and sound.

4. Whole-class discussion follows as spokespersons discuss each group's attribute wheel. The similarities and differences in each group's attributes are examined.

5. Teams of four break up into two pairs. Three-Step Interview is used as the lesson is brought to closure. The question for closure is, "What are the general properties of Oobleck?" Team members interview each other to answer this question. A general class discussion follows.

6. The lesson ends with another look at the book. The kingdom is covered with Oobleck, and it must be stopped. Ask teams to write their own endings to the story. How can the king get the Oobleck to stop coming down from the sky?

Application

Students are asked to think of other substances that they encounter in life that have properties similar to those of Oobleck (possible answers: Pepto-Bismol, liquid antibiotics, milk of magnesia).

Processing

Do you think that working in a group helped you come up with more observations than you would have come up with on your own? How did you feel as a member of the team? Do you think that all members participated equally?

Finding Science in Bubbles: Using Group Investigation

Group Investigation is easy to use in the science classroom and gives students a flavor of true scientific investigation. When students are given support from the teacher, they are limited only by their creativity (Sharan & Sharan, 1992).

Introducing the Project

The object of this project is to investigate bubbles. It has been used with students as young as second graders and has also been successfully received by high school students. The investigation becomes more sophisticated as the grade level increases. In this particular example, a teacher worked with students of the upper elementary grades.

Students were introduced to a variety of geometric shapes in the mathematics classroom. They then used bubble solution to blow bubbles and look for geometric shapes in the bubbles. The teacher introduced the bubble investigation by asking this question: "What more would you like to know about bubbles?" The teacher and the class then engaged in the investigation.

Choosing Subtopics and Research Groups

Students looked around the room for materials. They found index cards, two large bottles of bubble solution, pipe cleaners, plastic cups, a small bottle of glycerin, paper towels, and several books about bubbles. The teacher asked each student to take an index card and write what more he or she wanted to learn about bubbles. Several minutes later, students paired up and compared and combined their lists of questions. Ten minutes later, pairs joined to form quartets, and they repeated the procedure.

Each quartet chose a spokesperson, and the whole class worked together to form one large list of questions to investigate. The class compiled a large list of topics of interest. The questions were sorted into subtopics, and each student was asked to choose a subtopic of interest. The next day, groups were formed based on a subtopic of interest.

Planning the Investigation

The teacher organized the room by forming clusters of desks. Each cluster was marked with the name of the subtopic. The subtopics included making long-lasting bubbles, measuring bubbles, making durable bubbles, and making bubbles with different-shaped bubble wands.

Groups spent thirty minutes discussing their ideas. Each group member talked about what he or she wanted to learn from the investigation and about how the investigation would be carried out. They looked at the large list of questions compiled by the whole class and decided upon which questions they would address. Group roles were chosen, including principal investigator, spokesperson, recorder, and materials manager. One person was chosen to join a steering committee comprised of representatives from all groups to coordinate final presentations.

The teacher circulated among the groups and offered help to resolve problems. The group that was interested in making durable bubbles needed help with finding out how to vary the composition of bubble solutions. At the end of the session, all groups posted their plans. Individual questions were formulated by each group to address the question "What more would you like to know about bubbles?"

Carrying Out the Investigation

During this two-week phase, students located resource materials, organized information, and conducted experiments to answer their questions. Members of one group learned that if they dipped a ruler in a bubble solution, they could insert the ruler in the bubble and measure its diameter. Another group found that adding glycerin to the bubble solution would make durable bubbles. The third group made square, rectangular, and triangular bubble wands. They all formed spherical bubbles. Groups also did library research. At the end of each session, groups reviewed what they had done. They continued to focus on their questions and on the particular subtopics they were studying.

Planning Presentations

Groups gathered to discuss what they believed to be their most significant findings. They planned ways to present these findings to the whole class. The teacher helped those groups that were having difficulty accomplishing this task.

One member of each group met as a steering committee. Its task was to coordinate the groups' presentations, ensuring that appropriate materials were available. A presentation schedule was devised.

Group Presentations

The groups decided to have hands-on presentations. Each group devised a ten-minute presentation that the other class members could enjoy. One group made bubbles that could bounce. Another group showed how to measure bubbles without having them burst. A third group showed how to tell when a bubble will burst by looking at the colors reflected on the surface. The fourth group had its classmates experiment with making bubbles that lasted a long time.

Evaluation

Each group summarized the five most important concepts learned from its investigation. Questions were then written by the group to address these concepts. The teacher took all groups' questions and made a class test for individual evaluation.

The Effects of Solutions of Varying pH: A Group Investigation

Teacher's Introduction of the Project

The pH of a substance reflects the degree to which it is acidic or basic, and you are going to measure the pH of various substances. The pH scale is numbered from 0 to 14. A solution with a pH between 0 and 2 is considered very acidic, one with a pH between 2 and 5 is moderately acidic, and one with a pH between 5 and 7 is slightly acidic. A solution with a pH equal to 7 is neutral. If a solution has a pH above 7, it is basic. A solution with a pH between 7 and 9 is slightly basic, one with a pH between 9 and 11 is moderately basic, and one with a pH between 11 and 14 is very basic (Sherman, Sherman, & Russikoff, 1992).

To determine the pH of a solution involves placing a few drops of a chemical dye (also called a chemical indicator) into the solution to be tested. The dye turns a specific color, depending on the pH of the solution. We will begin the lesson by determining the pH of various substances, and then we will form subgroups to investigate the effects of solutions of varying pH.

Subtopics and Research Groups

The class brainstorms topics of interest. Students express a great deal of interest in studying the effects of pH on plants, animals, rocks, minerals, fabrics, building products, and rivers, lakes, and streams. Students decide which topics are of interest to them. Four interest groups can be formed. These groups will study (1) the effect of pH on plant life; (2) the effect of varying pH on fabrics; (3) the effect of pH on rocks and minerals; fabrics; and (4) the formation of acid rain and its effects on rivers, lakes, and streams. Groups brainstorm questions to address each topic.

Planning the Investigation

Groups discuss the subtopic they would like to study. The teacher helps the students decide what they will study. In the group that will study the effects of pH on plant life, two students decide to learn about solutions of different pH. They decide to test the pH of familiar substances such as lemons, vinegar, soft drinks, oranges, tomatoes, rainwater, milk, pure water, sea water, and ammonia water. The three other students in the group study plant life to learn about optimum conditions for growth. They also learn about what causes plant disease. Another group wants to study different fabrics and plans to expose them to acids and bases of different strengths. The third group plans to treat different rocks and minerals with acids and bases of different strengths. The fourth group wants to know how rivers, lakes, and streams are affected by acid rain.

Carrying Out the Investigation

In the first group, two students prepare solutions of moderate and slight acidity. After doing research into pH, they decide to use vinegar (pH 2.8), orange juice (pH 3.5), and milk (pH 6.5). Three students plant grass seeds in three different cups. They research different types of grass seeds and decide to use the quick-growing type. The seeds are planted. Once they sprout, the grass is treated with the different solutions. Students observe the results. The teacher encourages them to consider solutions that are basic. The students use sea water (pH 8.5) and ammonia water (pH 11.1). More grass seeds are planted for this part of the investigation. In the second group, different fabrics are treated with a variety of acids and bases. Students examine the results. In the third group, five sets of beakers are filled with different acids and bases. Five different minerals are tested to see how they are affected. In the last group, a great deal of research is done. Students visit the library, and they view films to see the effects of acid rain on rivers, lakes, and streams throughout the world.

Planning the Presentations

During this process, group members discuss their research and identify the most important points. They talk about how they will present their findings. One group plans a television commercial, and another makes a short film. The third group presents its information using poster board. The last group makes a board game called "The Acid Rain Game."

Group Presentations

Groups gather to present their information. The presentations shed light on each topic. Students learn from each other, and in the end, the general topic is addressed.

Evaluation

The class collaborates on a group project. Using written reports, charts, figures, and graphs, it produces a newsletter on acids and bases. Each group contributes equally, and the class produces a product that creatively addresses the general topic.

After each group reports, the teacher gives written copies of each group's report to each student. The class is given one week to study the contents of each report. A test is then given that includes recall of facts as well as open-ended essay questions.

REFERENCES

Continuous Electron Beam Accelerator Facility Manual. (1992). *BEAMS Handbook*. Newport News, VA.: U.S. Department of Energy.

Cross, B. (1990). A passion within reason: The human side of process. *Science and Children, 27,* 16–21.

Johnson, D., & Johnson, R. (1989). *Cooperation and competition: Theory and research*. Edina, MN: Interaction Book Company.

Johnson, D., & Johnson, R. (1991). *Joining together: Group theory and group skills* (4th ed.). Englewood Cliffs, NJ: Prentice Hall.

Johnson, D., Johnson, R., & Holubec, E. (1987). *Structuring cooperative learning: Lesson plans for teachers*. Edina, MN: Interaction Book Company.

Kagan, S. (1992). *Cooperative learning*. San Juan Capistrano, CA: Resources for Teachers.

Kyle, W. (1984). Curriculum development projects of the 1960s. In D. Holdzkom & P. Lutz (Eds.), *Research within reach*. Charleston, WV: Appalachia Educational Laboratory.

Lazarowitz, R., & Karsenty, G. (1990). Cooperative learning and students' academic achievement, process skills, learning environment, and self esteem in tenth grade biology classrooms. In S. Sharan (Ed.), *Cooperative learning: Theory and research* (pp. 123–149). New York: Praeger.

Lyman, F., & McTighe, J. (1988). Cueing thinking in the classroom: The promise of theory-embedded tools. *Educational Leadership, 45*:7, 18–24.

Mastny, A., Kahn, S., & Sherman, S. (1992). *SCIENCE TEAMS: Lessons in environmental science and cooperative learning*. New Brunswick, NJ: Rutgers University Consortium for Educational Equity.

Sharan, Y., & Sharan, S. (1992). *Expanding cooperative learning through group investigation*. New York: Teacher's College Press.

Sherman, A., & Sherman, S. (1992). *Chemistry and our changing world* (3rd ed.). Englewood Cliffs, NJ: Prentice Hall.

Sherman, A., Sherman, S., & Russikoff, L. (1992). *Laboratory experiments for basic chemistry* (5th ed.). Boston: Houghton Mifflin.

Slavin, R. (1990). *Cooperative learning: Theory, research, and practice*. Englewood Cliffs, NJ: Prentice Hall.

Whimbey, A., & Whimbey, L. (1975). *Intelligence can be taught*. New York: Innovative Science.

15

Cooperative Learning to Support Thinking, Reasoning, and Communicating in Mathematics

Laurel Robertson, Neil Davidson, and
Roberta L. Dees

A NEW DIRECTION

In considering how best to prepare students for the challenges of the next century, educators are changing the content of the mathematics curriculum and the ways we teach it. We are moving from a focus on arithmetic and computational skills toward a curriculum that develops students' abilities to think, reason, and communicate mathematically. The goal is to help students construct their conceptual understanding of mathematics, not just memorize facts and rules.

The teaching of mathematics is likewise changing in order to meet these new goals. Instead of teaching by telling or by demonstration, a blend of instructional methodologies is recommended that includes individual and group work and direct instruction. The focus is to provide frequent opportunities for students to explore and solve problems, individually and with others; and to develop their mathematical skills in the context of this exploration. The teacher is a facilitator of learning, guiding students' explorations, asking questions that extend their thinking, and encouraging students to communicate their thinking. Direct instruction is provided as the need emerges during this process.

The mathematics curriculum outlined by the National Council of Teachers of Mathematics (1989) suggests standards for kindergarten through grade twelve and lists content and strategies that should receive increased or decreased attention, such as the following:

Increased Attention	Decreased Attention
Number sense and meaning of operations	Complex paper and pencil computation
Students create own algorithms and develop own problem-solving strategies	One answer, one method, and rote memorization of rules
Writing and talking about mathematical thinking and strategies	Focus on *the* answer
Student use of manipulative materials	Worksheets
Use of a variety of instructional methods, such as small groups, individual explorations, peer instruction, whole-class discussions, project work	Teaching by telling; teacher and text as exclusive sources of knowledge
Assessing learning as part of instruction	Testing for sole purpose of assigning grades
Mathematics for all students	Mathematics for only some students

RATIONALE

Why does cooperative learning deserve a central place in mathematics instruction? The study of mathematics is often viewed as an isolated, individualistic, or competitive matter. One works alone and struggles to understand the material or solve the assigned problems. Perhaps it is not surprising that many students and adults are afraid of mathematics and develop math avoidance or math anxiety. They often believe that only a few talented individuals can function successfully in the mathematical realm. Small-group cooperative learning addresses these problems in several ways.

- Small groups provide a social support mechanism for the learning of mathematics. "Small groups provide a forum in which students ask questions, discuss ideas, make mistakes, learn to listen to others' ideas, offer constructive criticism, and summarize their discoveries in writing" (National Council of Teachers of Mathematics [NCTM], 1989, p. 79). Students learn by talking, listening, explaining, and thinking with others.

- Small-group cooperative learning offers opportunities for success for all students in mathematics (and in general). The group interaction is designed to help all members learn the concepts and problem-solving strategies.

- Mathematics problems are ideally suited for cooperative group discussion because they have solutions that can be objectively demonstrated. Students can persuade one another by the logic of their arguments. Mathematics problems can often be solved by several different approaches, and students in groups can discuss the merits of different proposed solutions.

- The field of mathematics is filled with exciting and challenging ideas that invite discussion. Mathematics offers many opportunities for creative thinking, for exploring open-ended situations, for making conjectures and testing them with data, for posing intriguing problems, and for solving nonroutine problems. Students in groups can often handle challenging situations that are well beyond the capabilities of individuals at that developmental stage.

RESEARCH OUTCOMES

Reviews by Davidson (1985, 1990b) and Webb (1985) focused specially on mathematics learning, addressing achievement and group interaction and dynamics, respectively. Davidson (1990b) reviewed about eighty studies in mathematics comparing student achievement in cooperative learning versus whole-class traditional instruction. In over 40% of these studies, students in the small-group approaches significantly outscored the control students on individual mathematical performance measures. In only two studies did the control students perform better, and both of these studies had design irregularities. In support of these findings, Webb found a high correlation between students who gave directions in mixed-ability mathematics groups and their own achievement.

Davidson also found that the effects of cooperative learning of mathematical skills were consistently positive when there was a combination of individual accountability and some form of team goal or team recognition for commendable achievement. The effects of small-group learning were not significantly different from traditional instruction if the teacher had no prior experience in small-group learning, was not aware of well-established methods, and did little to foster group cooperation or interdependence.

For many mathematics teachers, the social benefits of cooperative learning are at least as important as the academic effects. In his review, Davidson concluded that cooperative learning is a powerful tool for increasing self-confidence as a learner and problem solver and for fostering true integration among diverse student populations.

A recent volume of the *Journal for Research in Mathematics Education* was devoted to cooperative learning in mathematics and included reports by several investigators (Davidson & Kroll, 1991; Dees, 1991; Yackel, Cobb, & Wood, 1991; Webb, 1991).

THE TEACHER'S ROLE

A cooperative mathematics lesson might begin with a meeting of the entire class to provide an overall perspective. This may include a teacher presentation of new material, class discussion, posing problems or questions for investigation, and clarifying directions for the group activities.

The class then works in small groups, often in pairs in the elementary grades and groups of four in upper grades. Each group has its own working space, which in the upper grades might include a flip chart or section of the chalkboard. In their groups, students might work together to discuss mathematical ideas, solve problems, look for patterns and relationships in sets of data, and make and test conjectures. Students actively exchange ideas with one another and help each other understand their work. The teacher circulates from group to group, providing assistance and encouragement and asking thought-provoking questions.

Planning

As the teacher plans, several questions specific to cooperative mathematics lessons need to be addressed, including the following:

- What are the important mathematical concepts of this lesson? How will I help students link these goals with previous work and with long-term goals?
- Does the problem or exploration allow for multiple strategies, perspectives, and solutions?
- What opportunities for direct instruction or class discussion of a mathematics concept or skill might arise from students' exploration?
- What are some possible opportunities for supporting social, as well as mathematical, learning?
- How can I make this lesson interesting, accessible, and challenging for students at all levels of mathematical understanding and proficiency?
- How will this lesson provide opportunities for students to make decisions about such things as questions to explore and strategies and tools to use for problem solving?
- What open-ended questions might extend students' thinking? What questions might be asked to introduce the lesson? What questions might help students during group work? What questions might help students reflect on their experience?
- How can I link assessment with instruction?
- What are appropriate extension activities for groups that finish early or for the next day?

Introducing a Lesson

Cooperative mathematics lessons might begin with a problem statement or a question for exploration. Setting a context for the mathematical investigation serves as a motivator and helps students link the exploration to their own lives. It is also important to help students understand the mathematical goals of the lesson and how these goals connect to prior lessons and learning; what is expected of them; and how they will be held accountable. In addition, the teacher might facilitate a discussion about the group work by asking questions, such as "What do you want to find out?" "What are some possible strategies you might try?" "What has helped your group work well in the past?" "How will you share the work?" and "How will you agree on decisions?"

Facilitating Group Work

During group work, the teacher's role is to encourage students to define the problems they are investigating, to solve interpersonal problems, and to take responsibility for their learning and behavior. The teacher may intervene to refocus a group, to help its members see a problem from another perspective, to ask questions that extend mathematical and social learning, or to assess understanding. The teacher should try not to interrupt the flow of the group work and, instead, should wait for a natural pause in the action. The teacher might ask open-ended questions that require progressively more thought or understanding and avoid giving the impression that there is a "right" answer. It is important to allow groups time to solve a problem themselves before intervention. Asking key questions to help them resolve the difficulty is more beneficial than solving the problem for them or giving lengthy explanations.

Helping Students Reflect

Reflection on the mathematical and social aspects of group work helps students develop their conceptual understanding as they discuss their experience and hear about the strategies, problems, and successes of others. Asking open-ended questions helps students consider such important issues as the following:

- What strategies did you try? Were they effective? Why?
- What solution do you think is reasonable? Why do you think that? Is there another solution that might work?
- What problems did you have? How did they affect the group? Were you able to solve them? If so, how?
- What are some ways to work that you would recommend to other groups?
- What was something someone in your group did that was particularly helpful to you or the group?

The reflection time should be kept relatively short and include use of a variety of methods such as group reflection, whole-class reflection, and reflection through writing or drawing pictures. If appropriate, the teacher might wish to give feedback regarding both successes and problems he or she observed as groups worked.

Figure 15.1
Example of a Class Chart

What is the most important quality in a friend?

Honesty	/ / / /
Loyalty	\
Cheerfulness	/ /
Good Listener	/ / / /
Intelligence	
Dependability	////-

Make a tally mark

COOPERATIVE LEARNING FOR ELEMENTARY MATHEMATICS INSTRUCTION

Cooperative learning strategies can be easily integrated into the elementary mathematics classroom. The choice of strategy and group size will depend on the time of year, the sophistication of students with cooperative problem solving, and the mathematical activity itself.

Individual Activities That Lead to Cooperative Discussion

Graphing

After students have individually responded to a class graph, chart, or table such as Figure 15.1 (Freeman, 1986), several simple cooperative strategies can encourage students to analyze and discuss the data.

Simple Cooperative Strategies

Turn to Your Partner: Students turn to a person sitting next to them to discuss an issue or question, such as "What do you notice about the data?"

Heads Together: Similar to Turn to Your Partner, but for groups of four. Students might put their heads together, discuss the data, and agree on at least two factual mathematical statements, such as "More than half the students chose honesty and dependability," or "The same number of students chose honesty as good listener." These statements can then be discussed as a class.

Think-Pair-Share: Students individually take a short period of time to think about a question such as "What inferences can you make from the data?" and discuss their thoughts with a partner. (An example of an inference statement might be "Intelligence is not an important quality in a friend.") Pairs then share their thinking with another pair (*Think-Pair-Square*) or report their thinking to the class.

Think-Pair-Write: This structure is like Think-Pair-Share, except that pairs write about their thinking after they have discussed their thoughts with each other. Pairs can exchange their written statements and decide whether or not they agree with the other pair's statement. The teacher might also collect the statements and place them near the graph for students to read, discuss, and decide whether or not they agree with the statement (see Kagan, 1992).

Mental Math

One way to encourage student discussion of mental strategies is to ask them to individually think for a short time about a question, such as "How many ways can you double 38 mentally?" Groups of four can then discuss and list as many strategies as they can and make sure each member can explain one of the strategies. The teacher then asks the class to stand and has one student explain a strategy. After checking with the class for understanding and agreement, the teacher asks all students with a similar strategy to sit down. The activity continues until all students are sitting.

Paired Activities

Pairs are an important group size for elementary mathematics lessons. In a pair, both students can easily manipulate materials and have frequent opportunities to share their thinking.

Games

Many mathematical games can be turned from a competitive experience to a cooperative one. The game of POISON! (Burns 1991b) is a good example. The rules for two players are as follows:

• You need thirteen objects.
• Take turns. On your turn, take away one or two of the objects.
• The last object to be taken is POISON! Whoever gets stuck with it loses.

To make this a cooperative activity, you might add these directions:

• Your job as a pair is to discover a winning strategy for this game.
• Play several games. Discuss what you notice about the game.

- When you think that your pair has a winning strategy, play with another pair or with the teacher.
- As a pair, discuss what you learned.

For an extension activity, students can develop strategies for playing this game with a number of objects other than thirteen.

Paired Practice

It is now recognized that mathematical skills are most effectively developed in the context of their use. Some practice, however, is appropriate and can be a paired activity. Guidelines for pairs completing a practice page in their textbook might be as follows:

- Work together to solve problems.
- Be sure you both agree to the solution before you go on to the next problem.
- Be sure you can both explain how to get your solutions.
- Both sign your record sheet to show you have checked and agree to the solutions.

An extension of this activity might be for pairs to exchange and check each others' record sheets:

- Exchange your record sheet with another pair.
- Check the solutions. If you both agree, sign the record sheet.
- If you disagree with a solution, write about why you disagree or discuss the problem with the other pair.

Partner Interview

One way to conduct a partner interview is for one partner to interview the other, then switch roles. Pairs can then discuss points of agreement and disagreement, write about their thinking, and/or share their thinking with other pairs or the class. Examples of interview questions might include the following:

- The weather person said that there is a 100% chance of rain for tomorrow. Is this a good prediction for this month? Why?
- Tanika loaned Jamal a dollar. She said that the interest would be 75% a day. Is this a good deal for Jamal? Why?

Partner Problem Solving

Students benefit from solving mathematics problems individually and with others. Some guidelines that might help pairs or groups solve problems include the following:

• Tell each other the problem and discuss anything you don't understand.

• Talk about different ways you could solve the problem.

• Decide on a strategy or strategies to try.

• Try your strategy or strategies. Discuss the results. Try other strategies if you wish. Decide on a way to show what you did and to share your results.

Partner problem solving is particularly appropriate for open-ended problems that provide opportunities for students to have many interpretations, strategies, and solutions. For example: "Your class of thirty-two students is going on a picnic. How many packages of hot dogs and how many packages of buns will we need?" Problems such as this one can lead to exciting discussions not only about strategies and solutions, but also about assumptions students made in order to solve the problem, such as the number of hot dogs and number of buns in a package, how many hot dogs each student would eat, whether some students would not eat any hot dogs, how many people would be going on the picnic, and many others.

Menus

Menu activities are a set of activities or problems that provide numerous opportunities for students to explore a set of mathematical concepts. The teacher introduces approximately four to eight related activities that may be the work for several days, a week, or several weeks. Students, in pairs or groups, are responsible for choosing and completing a specified number of the activities during the time period. This provides opportunities for students to make decisions and learn to manage their time. During or at the end of the time period, each activity is discussed in terms of students' approaches to the problem and solutions. (For an in-depth discussion of how to use menus and examples of menus for elementary grades, see Burns, [1991b].)

The following three activities might be part of a menu focusing on multiplication and division.

Hit the Target

You need: A partner, a calculator, your journal.

The game: Starting at 36, hit the target range of 2,000–2,100, using as few guesses as possible.

How to play:

1. One partner enters 36 into the calculator and presses ×.

2. The other partner estimates a number that when multiplied by 36 will produce a product in the target range.

3. If this estimate misses, the first partner must estimate a number to multiply with

the number now showing on the calculator window to produce a product in the target range.

4. Keep playing, taking turns and keeping track of guesses, until you hit the target range (NCTM, 1991).

Mystery Equation

You need: A partner, your journal.
To do: Copy the following in your journal:

Choose any five digits, discuss each of these questions, then write about your thinking.

1. How would you arrange the digits in the problem to produce the largest product possible?
2. How would you arrange the digits in the problem to produce the smallest product possible?
3. How many different products are possible using the five digits you have selected?

Choose another five digits and answer the questions again. Suggest a method for arranging any five digits as a three-by-two-digit multiplication problem to form the largest and smallest possible product (NCTM, 1991).

What Happens When?

You need: A partner, your journal.
To do: Find out what happens when you multiply a number less than 1.

Copy the table below into your journal and complete it. Discuss the following questions and write about your thinking.

Pick a whole number	Multiply by 0.05	Multiply by 0.48	Multiply by 0.9

1. In general, what happens when you multiply a whole number by 0.05?
2. In general, what happens when you multiply a whole number by 0.48?
3. In general, what happens when you multiply a whole number by 0.9? (NCTM, 1991)

Group Activities

Many cooperative elementary mathematics activities are appropriate for groups of three or four students.

Many Pieces Problems

Many Pieces problems are a good introduction to group problem solving, as each student has specific information to contribute to the group. Each group receives clue cards that are then dealt one to a group member. Students share their clues verbally, without showing each other their clue cards, and work together to solve the problem. (Some forms of these problems have two extra clues that are put face down and turned over when the group needs another clue or wants to check to see if its solution fits with all the clues.)

Many Pieces problems can be developed from problems found in a text-book. A typical problem might be the following: Maria is learning to swim. She swam one lap on the first day, three laps on the second day, six laps on the third day, and ten laps on the fourth day. If this pattern continues, how many laps will she swim on the fifth day? This problem can be written as four clues:

• Maria is learning to swim. She swam one lap on the first day.
• Maria swam three laps on the second day.
• Maria swam six laps on the third day.
• Maria swam ten laps on the fourth day. How many laps will she swim on the fifth day?

(See EQUALS, 1989, and GEMS, 1992, for Many Pieces problems with a focus on logical thinking.)

Group Problem Solving

Short- and long-term group explorations, investigations, and problem-solving activities provide opportunities for students to cooperatively tackle problems that are not easily solved, to define questions to be studied, to determine the information required, to decide on methods for obtaining this information, and to determine the limits of acceptable solutions. These experiences might include real-world investigations that involve students in solving actual problems that relate to their lives, for example, studying food waste at lunchtime and making recommendations to the principal based on their research. These experiences might be projects that engage students in mathematical exploration and thinking as they develop a product, such as designing and making a quilt. These experiences might also involve students in investigating mathematical ideas and relationships, such as generating their own algorithms and developing ways to compare the capacity of several containers or the areas of various shapes. (See Robertson, Regan, Freeman, & Contestable, 1993, as a source for group problem-solving curriculum materials.)

Whole-Class Activities

Whole-class activities provide opportunities for classbuilding as well as for mathematical development. The following are just two of many possibilities:

Line-up Activities

Students line up based on a specific characteristic, such as their birthdates. Many options for mathematical activities can follow. For example, the class can form a human birthday graph with all students born in January standing in a line, all born in February forming a second line, and so on. This produces a bar graph that can be transferred to paper. Students can also find the median birthdate and the percentage or fraction of the students born in each month.

Four Corners

Students with a common characteristic meet in a corner of a room. In a primary classroom, for example, corners might be labeled with numbers such as 0, 10, 20, and 30. Students go to the corner with the number closest to the day of the month they were born. The teacher asks questions that help students explore the relative magnitude of numbers. The numbers might then be changed to 5, 15, 25, and 35. Students move to the corner now labeled with the number closest to the day of the month they were born. Students discuss how their position and the groups have changed, as well as issues of relative magnitude.

COOPERATIVE LEARNING FOR SECONDARY MATHEMATICS INSTRUCTION

To get started using cooperative learning in the secondary mathematics classroom, the teacher might begin with some simple cooperative structures that encourage student interaction. The following describes several useful structures and sample applications for use in general mathematics, algebra I, and geometry classes.

Simple Cooperative Structures

The Three-Step Interview

The Three-Step Interview is conducted in a group that consists of four members subdivided into pairs: A and B, C and D.

Step one: A interviews B while C interviews D. The interviewer listens, asks questions, and paraphrases, but does not elaborate or share personal data.

Step two: Reverse roles: B interviews A, while D interviews C.

Step three: Share-around: Each person shares information about his or her partner in the group of four.

Math Class	Applications of Three-Step Interview
General math	How can you use fractions? What examples of fractions did you find in the newspaper?
Algebra I	What are some variable attributes of people in our class or of our classroom (for example, height or age)?
Geometry	Give examples of geometric shapes that occur in your home.

Thoughtful responses to interview questions are more likely to occur with advance preparation by the students. It is useful to give these interview questions to the students a day or two in advance.

Roundtable

The teacher poses a question having multiple answers or gives each group a worksheet. The group has only one piece of paper or worksheet and perhaps only one pencil. One student in the group writes down one response, says it aloud, and then passes the paper or worksheet to the person on his or her left. The process continues in this way. A student may choose to pass on one round and give an answer the next time.

Math Class	Applications of Roundtable
General math	Find combinations of three numbers whose sum is 60.
Algebra I	Give specific examples of the rule $(a^m)^n = a^{mn}$.
Geometry	State a variety of terms in geometry (for example, "point").

Roundtable can be used for creative brainstorming, simple applications, or review. It fosters cooperative skills such as taking turns and listening without interrupting.

Numbered Heads Together

Each student in the group is given a number from one to four. The teacher poses a question, issue, or problem. Students talk this over within the group and prepare to respond. The teacher then calls upon students by number to represent the group.

Math Class	Applications of Numbered Heads Together
General math	Find all factor pairs for a given whole number.
Algebra I	State examples of perfect square trinomials.
Geometry	State possible values for the base and height of a set of rectangles that all have the same given area.

Because Numbered Heads Together allows discussion and interaction, it is more appropriate than Roundtable for more difficult mathematical questions. Numbered Heads Together gives all students equal opportunities to respond successfully in the whole class after small-group discussion.

Think-Pair-Share

As mentioned earlier in this chapter, this strategy allows the teacher to pose questions to the students sitting in pairs. Students silently think of a response individually for a given period of time, then pair with their partners to discuss the question and reach consensus. The teacher then asks students to share their agreed-upon answers with the rest of the class.

Math Class	Applications of Think-Pair-Share
General math	Describe the meaning of the terms area and perimeter and show how to compute them for a rectangle.
Algebra I	Is the slope computed for a given line always the same, no matter which two points on that line are used to calculate that slope? Illustrate with examples.
Geometry	Clarify the relationships among these figures: rectangle, square, rhombus, parallelogram.

Think-Pair-Share can be used for discussion of concepts or procedures, for problem solving, or for practice. It can also be used spontaneously to clear up ideas given during a presentation. The teacher asks the students to think about what has been presented, and then, in discussion with a partner, students either clarify it or pose a question. Clarifications or questions are then stated to the whole class.

Here is an example of a guess-my-rule task well suited for Think-Pair-Share. The teacher asks students working first individually and then with a partner to find possible rules for the following function tables:

x	f(x)		x	g(x)
0	2		0	1
1	5		1	2
2	8		2	5
3	11		3	10
4	14		4	17

x	h(x)		x	k(x)
0	2		0	2
1	3		1	4
2	10		2	8
3	29		3	16
4	66		4	32

Pairs Check

The Pairs Check procedure is used for practice and mastery of skills or procedures. Within groups of four, each pair takes two roles: performer (or solver) and coach.

1. One partner performs the task or solves the problem. The second partner functions as coach by observing carefully, giving hints or pointing out errors as needed, and giving positive feedback to the first partner. (Exaggerated praise can be used here for fun.)
2. Partners switch roles for the second performance or problem in the set.
3. The two pairs check their responses to the first two problems to see if they agree. When both pairs agree, they give a team handshake or cheer.

Math Class	Applications of Pairs Check
General math	Find the greatest common factor of two whole numbers.
Algebra I	Complete the square for a quadratic expression.
Geometry	Construct the perpendicular bisector of a line segment.

Group Problem Solving

Once students have become skillful in working in pairs or groups with simple structures, they may be ready to solve some challenging problems in pairs or groups of four. The teacher then states guidelines, such as the following, to foster cooperative group problem solving:

1. Cooperate with other group members.
2. Achieve a group solution for each problem.
3. Make sure that everyone understands the solution before the group goes on.
4. Listen carefully to others and try, whenever possible, to build upon their ideas.
5. Share the leadership of the group.
6. Make sure that everyone participates and no one dominates.
7. Take turns writing problem solutions on the board.
8. Proceed at a pace that is comfortable for your own group.

The following is an appropriate problem for pairs in algebra or geometry. The teacher asks the students to work together to solve the problems and to make sure both partners understand their strategies and solutions.

1.   a. Find the area of the rectangle with vertices at $(-4,5)$, $(3,-1)$, and $(-4,-1)$.
     b. Find the coordinates of the fourth vertex.
2. Refer to problem 1. In each case, first predict how the area of the rectangle will change. Then graph and check your prediction.
   a. The x- and y-coordinates of each vertex are multiplied by 2.
   b. The x- and y-coordinates of each vertex are decreased by 1.
   c. The x- and y-coordinates of each vertex are replaced by the opposites of the original vertex.

Group problem solving can be used in the discovery and/or proof of mathematical generalizations. For example, in algebra I, students in groups can readily discover laws of exponents such as $b^m \cdot b^n = b^{m+n}$. They do so by choosing a value for b and systematically selecting values for m and n, recording results, and looking for a pattern.

b	m	n	b^m	b^n	$b^m \cdot b^n$	$=$	b^-
7	2	3	7·7	7·7·7	7·7·7·7·7	$=$	7^5
7	3	4	____ ____		____ ____		____

Groups can also pose problems for other groups to solve. This is sometimes known as "send a problem" or "pass a problem." For example, each group might pose a coin problem such as the one that follows. Such problems can lead to lively discussions between groups, because there is often more than one correct solution that fits the stated conditions. (Incidentally, educated "guess and test" procedures are more manageable than algebra for these coin problems.)

A person has nineteen coins, which may include nickels, dimes, and quarters. The total value of the coins is $2.95. Find the possible number of coins of each type. Is there a unique answer? It may help you to use a data table.

Q	D	N	# of Coins	Total Value

Many Pieces

The Many Pieces problem described earlier in this chapter is also a useful structure for group problem solving in secondary mathematics. Consider the following problem one might find in a textbook:

The Simpsons are converting a section of a warehouse into an apartment. They are decorating an open 20' × 30' area that will serve as both living room and dining room. They have bought a new 9' × 12' carpet for the living room area. Mrs. Simpson's mother gave them an antique braided circular rug, 10' in diameter, that they plan to use in the dining area. The Simpsons will paint only the floor area not covered by the carpets. How much floor area needs to be painted?

After some editing, this case, converted to the Many Pieces format, gives us five clues:

- The Simpsons are converting a section of a warehouse into an apartment.
- Mrs. Simpson's mother gave her an antique braided circular rug, 10' in diameter, that she plans to use in the dining area.
- The Simpsons have bought a new 9' × 12' carpet for the living room area.
- The Simpsons will paint only the floor area not covered by the carpets.
- They are decorating an open 20' × 30' area that will serve as both living room and dining room.

You might wish to make a scale drawing of a possible layout on graph paper.

Jigsaw

Jigsaw is another useful structure for cooperative problem solving. The following are guidelines for group problem solving using Jigsaw.

1. *Task division:* A task or passage of text material or a problem set is divided into several component parts (or topics).

2. *Home groups:* Each group member is given a topic on which to become an expert.

3. *Expert groups:* Students who have the same topics meet in expert groups to discuss the topics, master them, and plan how to teach them.

4. *Home groups:* Students return to their original groups and teach what they have learned to their group members.

Math Class	Applications of Jigsaw
General math	Compute the area and perimeter for various triangles.
Algebra I	Explore slopes of lines.
Geometry	Prove congruence of pairs of triangles, using SSS, SAS, ASA, or base and adjacent angle in an isosceles triangle.

The procedure for exploring slopes of lines is as follows:

In your expert group, make a table of values and carefully draw the graph of each assigned line. Put all your graphs on the same axes. Be prepared to explain your graphs to others.

1. $y = x, y = 2x, y = 3x.$
2. $y = 1/2x, y = 1/3x, y = 1/4x.$
3. $y = -x, y = -2x, y = -3x.$
4. $y = -1/2x, y = -1/3x, y = -1/4x.$

Discuss the effect on the graph of changing the coefficient of x in the equation $y = mx$. (The number m, the coefficient of x, is called the *slope* of the line. The terminology can be introduced after the activity demonstrating the need for it.)

A similar Jigsaw activity varies the y-intercept while keeping the slope constant. In other words, for the equation $y = mx + b$, we fix m, vary b, and notice the effect on the graphs.

Group Projects and Investigations

Group projects and investigations often require several days to several weeks and may require groups to work outside of class. Groups gather and analyze data as steps toward problem solving and decision making, then prepare a report for presentation to the class. Many projects can be conducted using the Group Investigation model (see chapter 7 in this volume).

A textbook problem is the genesis of a small-group investigation for general math students. This problem concerns a rate and a range for a particular car and reads: A particular car is advertised as getting 25 to 32 miles per gallon. If the gas tank holds 11.4 gallons, what is the range for the number of miles the car can travel on one tank of gasoline?

After class discussion of this problem, ask groups to discuss the following question, which also incorporates the mathematical concepts of maximum and minimum, and ways they might gather data: Of the cars sold today, which have the shortest and which have the longest range?

As a class, discuss the question and ideas groups have for collecting data. Have groups decide how to divide the data collection. (To make the task manageable, groups may decide to research representative cars in several categories.) Be sure groups know how much class time they will have and the due date for their presentation of their findings. Provide time for groups to meet to plan their work.

When groups are ready, have them present their data to the class. First in groups, then as a class, compare the data from all the groups and see if consensus can be reached regarding the cars with the longest and shortest ranges.

Another example of a group project for secondary students is to investigate the variables that impact how high a ball bounces. For this project, each group will need two meter sticks, taped one on top of the other, and one tennis ball or superball per group. Begin by posing the question and asking groups to discuss the variables they think can affect how high a ball bounces. (Groups may brainstorm such variables as type of ball, surface, initial velocity, and so on.)

Begin by asking groups to test the effect of dropping balls from different heights. You might wish to suggest that groups assign members these roles: someone to drop the ball, two observers, someone to record the original height H and bounce height B, and someone to compute. Assign different heights H from which to drop the ball: 200 cm, 190 cm, and so on. Ask each group to drop the ball five times from its own height H. Have each group compute the average B of its five bounce heights and the ratio B/H.

Record the data from all groups on the board and ask groups to look for patterns. Students are astonished to find that the ratio B/H is a constant for a given type of ball and surface. (Students in more advanced courses note that the ratios for consecutive bounces—first, second, third, and soon—are terms in a geometric progression, for example .6, $(.6)^2$, $(.6)^3$, and so on.) Ask groups to propose various modifications of the experiment to further test this finding as well as to test other variables; then have them experiment.

The following are examples of other group projects:

1. Design a city park including a playground within a specified cost range (Johnson & Johnson, 1991).

2. Plan a talent show, using a computer simulation to keep track of the effects of variables such as the ticket price, costs of publicity, costs of refreshments, and other expenses (Sheets & Heid, 1990).

3. Design a theater according to specifications about the shape, number of seats, and other variables (Serra, 1989).

4. Construct geometric solids such as prisms, pyramids, or dodecahedra.
5. Conduct survey research, for example, about political preferences or consumer choices.
6. Observe and record traffic flow at a busy intersection (with carefully regulated safety precautions).
7. Gather and analyze environmental data, for example, relating to the proportion of certain substances in different water samples.

Cooperative learning is a viable and effective instructional methodology for teaching and learning mathematics and helps make mathematics exciting and enjoyable for both students and teachers. Cooperative strategies can be integrated at any grade level and for any mathematical topic. Davidson (1990a) reported that many positive effects are noted by teachers and students. Students "learn to cooperate with others and to communicate in the language of mathematics. The classroom atmosphere tends to be relaxed and informal, help is readily available, questions are freely asked and answered, and even the shy student finds it easy to be involved. Students tend to become friends with their group members, and the teacher-student relationship tends to be more relaxed." In addition, "Many students maintain a high level of interest in the mathematical activities" and "have an opportunity to pursue the more challenging and creative aspects of mathematics while they achieve at least as much information and skill as in more traditional approaches."

REFERENCES

AIMS Education Foundation. (1988). *Project AIMS*. Fresno, CA: AIMS Resource Books.

Andrini, B., with Kagan, S. (1990). *Cooperative learning and math: A multi-structural approach*. San Juan Capistrano, CA: Resources for Teachers.

Artzt, A., & Newman, C. M. (1990). *How to use cooperative learning in the mathematics class*. Reston, VA: National Council of Teachers of Mathematics.

Burns, M. (1987). *A collection of math lessons, grades 4 through 6*. New Rochelle, NY: Cuisenaire Company of America.

Burns, M. (1991a). *About teaching mathematics*. New Rochelle, NY: Cuisenaire Company of America.

Burns, M. (1991b). *Math by all means*. New Rochelle, NY: Cuisenaire Company of America.

California State Board of Education. (1987). *Mathematics: Model curriculum guide, kindergarten through grade eight*. Sacramento: California Department of Education.

California State Board of Education. (1992). *Mathematics framework for california schools*. Sacramento: California Department of Education.

Chakerian, G. D., Crabill, C. D., & Stein, S. K. (1986). *Geometry: A guided inquiry*. Pleasantville, NY: Sunburst.

Corwin, R., & Russell, S. (1990). *Used numbers: Real data in the classroom— Measuring from paces to feet*. Palo Alto, CA: Dale Seymour Publications. A series of six books for grades K through 6.

Davidson, N. (1985). Small group learning and teaching in mathematics: A selective review of the research. In R. Slavin, S. Sharon, S. Kagan, R. Hertz-Lazarowitz, C. Webb, & R. Schmuck (Eds.), *Learning to cooperate, cooperating to learn*. New York: Plenum Press.

Davidson, N. (Ed.) (1990a). *Cooperative learning in mathematics: A handbook for teachers*. Menlo Park, CA: Addison-Wesley.

Davidson, N. (1990b). Cooperative learning research in mathematics. Paper presented at the International Convention on Cooperation in Education. Baltimore, MD.

Davidson, N., & Gulick, F. (1976). *Abstract algebra: An active learning approach*. Boston: Houghton Mifflin.

Davidson, N., & Kroll, D. L. (1991). An overview of research on cooperative learning related to mathematics. *Journal for Research in Mathematics Education, 22,* 362–365.

DeAvila, E. A., Duncan, S. E., & Navarette, C. J. (1986). *Finding out Descubrimiento*. Northvale, NJ: Santillana.

Dees, R. L. (1991). The role of cooperative learning in increasing problem-solving ability in a college remedial course. *Journal for Research in Mathematics Education 22,* 409–421.

Duncan, L., & King, J. *Graphing primer*. Palo Alto, CA: Dale Seymour Publications.

EQUALS. (1989). *Get it together: Math problems for groups grades 4 through 12*. Berkeley: University of California, Lawrence Hall of Science.

Freeman, M. (1986). *Creative graphing*. New Rochelle, NY: Cuisenaire Company of America.

GEMS. *Group solutions: Cooperative logic activities for grades K-4*. (1992). Berkeley: University of California, Lawrence Hall of Science.

Graves, T., Graves, N., & Davidson, N. (1989) Cooperative learning in mathematics [Special issue]. *Cooperative Learning, 10*.

Johnson, D., & Johnson, R. (Eds). (1991). *Learning mathematics and cooperative learning: Lesson plans for teachers*. Edina, MN: Interaction Book Co.

Kagan, S. (1992). *Cooperative Learning* (4th ed.). San Juan Capistrano, CA: Resources for Teachers.

Lappan, G., Fitzgerald, W., et al. (1986). *Middle grades mathematics project*. Menlo Park, CA: Addison-Wesley. Five volumes.

National Council of Teachers of Mathematics. (1989). *Curriculum and evaluation standards for school mathematics*. Roston, VA: National Council of Teachers of Mathematics.

Robertson, L., Regan, S., Freeman, M., & Contestable, J. (1993). *Number power: A cooperative approach to mathematics and social development*. Menlo Park, CA: Addison-Wesley. (1989). Five books for grades 2 through 6.

Serra, M. (1989). *Discovery geometry*. Berkeley, CA: Key Curriculum Press.

Sheets, C., & Heid, M. K. (1990). Integrating computers as tools in mathematics curricula (grades 9-13): Portraits of group interactions. In N. Davidson

(Ed.), *Cooperative learning in mathematics: A handbook for teachers*. Menlo Park, CA: Addison Wesley, 265–294.

Stein, S., & Crabill, C. (1986). *Elementary algebra: A guided inquiry*. Pleasantville, NY: Sunburst.

Stein, S. K., Crabill, C. D., & Chakerian, G. D. (1986). *Algebra II/ trigonometry: A guided inquiry*. Pleasantville, NY: Sunburst.

Stenmark, J. K., Thompson, V., & Cossey, R. (1986). *Family math*. Palo Alto, CA: Dale Seymour Publications.

Webb, N. (1985). Verbal interaction and learning in peer directed groups. *Theory into Practice, 24,* 32–39.

Webb, N. (1991). Task-related verbal interaction and mathematics learning in small groups. *Journal for Research in Mathematics Education, 22,* 366–389.

Weissglass, J. (1990). *Mathematics for elementary teaching: A small-group approach for teaching*. Dubuque, IA: Kendall-Hunt.

Yackel, E., Cobb, P., & Wood, T. (1991). Small group interactions as a source of learning opportunities in second grade mathematics. *Journal for Research in Mathematics Education, 22,* 390-408.

FOR FURTHER READING

Chakerian, G., Crabill, C. & Stein, S. (1986). *Geometry: A guided inquiry*. Pleasantville, NY: Sunburst.

Davidson, N. & Gulick, F. (1976). *Abstract algebra: An active learning approach*. Boston: Houghton-Mifflin.

Lappan, G., & Fitzgerald, W. (1986). *Middle grades mathematics project*. Menlo Park, CA: Addison-Wesley.

Stein, S., & Crabill, C. (1986). *Algebra II–Trigonometry: A guided inquiry* Pleasantville, NY: Sunburst.

Stein, S., & Crabill, C. (1986). *Elementary algebra: A guided inquiry*. Pleasantville, NY: Sunburst.

Stenmark, J., Thompson, V., & Cossey, R. (1986). *Family math*. Palo Alto, CA: Dale Seymour.

16

Cooperative Learning and Computers

Mary Male

Many teachers, either because of shortages of equipment or beliefs in the value of students working together, are seeking cooperative learning strategies that lend themselves to computer learning activities or particular types of software. This chapter is designed for teachers who are interested in trying cooperative learning for the first time or who are struggling with the appropriate balance of "high tech" with "high touch" and is intended to provide (1) software recommendations for maximizing the benefits of cooperative learning; (2) the essential ingredients of cooperative learning at the computer; and (3) scenarios and sample lesson plans for cooperative learning at the computer.

LEARNER-CENTERED SOFTWARE

Most surveys of school uses of computers document a continuing reliance on drill and practice activities, in which students build fluency in existing skills. While cooperative activities can be built around such software, the real power of the computer, as well as the power of cooperative learning is best devoted to software emphasizing problem-centered or "learner-centered" software (Russell, 1989; Male, 1988, 1993). In learner-centered software, the goal of the task is for students to take intellectual risks and to communicate about the task with each other. Learner-centered software means that the learner (1) is in charge of the goal or the means to reach the goal; (2) receives informational rather than judgmental (positive or negative) feedback; and (3) is encouraged to make approximations as a part of solving the problem.

With a team or cooperative learning approach, many possible solutions are generated. A diversity of skills may contribute to solving a problem, and students experience the importance of being able to complete the task. For those teachers unfamiliar with cooperative learning principles but familiar with software, learner-centered favorites might include the following:

American Discoveries (Great Wave)

AppleWorks (Claris Corporation)

Bank Street Writer (Broderbund)

Children's Writing and Publishing Center (The Learning Co.)

Decisions, Decisions (Tom Snyder)

The Factory (Sunburst)

Geology Search (Tom Snyder)

Geometric Supposer (Sunburst)

Logo (and LogoWriter and LegoLogo)[1] (Logo Computer Systems, Inc.)

Math Blaster Plus (Davidson)

Odell Lake (MECC)

Safari Search (Sunburst)

States and Traits (Designware)

Story Tailor (Humanities)

Ten Clues (Sunburst)

Whale Search (from Voyage of the Mimi) (Sunburst)

Where in the World Is Carmen Sandiego? (Broderbund)

In addition to practical and logistical considerations, cooperative learning has substantial research support. Investigators found that "cooperative learning with computers promoted greater quantity and quality of daily achievement and more successful problem-solving. Cooperative learning resulted in higher performance on factual recognition, application, and problem solving test items than did competitive learning or individualized learning with computers" (Johnson, Johnson, & Stanne, 1986).

ESSENTIAL INGREDIENTS OF COOPERATIVE COMPUTER LESSONS

Heterogeneous Team Assignment

The purpose of team assignment is to assure a good heterogeneous mix of students, taking into account sex, race, cultural and language differences, problematic behaviors, and past performance (academic achievement in the subject area to be addressed). In the past, schools have made every effort to group students homogeneously by chronological age, ability, or other factors, with limited success. Cooperative learning offers teachers an opportunity to capitalize on the benefits of heterogeneity and to abandon the near-impossible task of finding homogeneous groups.

Some teachers prefer to use random assignment of students to teams in order to keep team assignment simple and to demonstrate to students that they are expected to work together in groups, no matter where they are assigned. Assignment to teams can be as simple as having students count off or deal a deck of cards. Other teachers prefer a more structured approach to take personality variables into account. Some teachers allow students to request one or two people to work with as team assignments are made, so that students have some choice and so does the teacher.

Teambuilding

"Again and again, I have seen greater long run efficiency, learning, and liking of school in classrooms if teachers take time for team-building and class-building. When there is a positive team identity, liking, respect, and trust among team members and classmates, there is a context within which maximum learning can occur" (Kagan, 1990). When computer activities are introduced in a cooperative classroom context, not only are students working in an unfamiliar goal structure with students they may not know well, but they are also using equipment and software that may add stress (as well as excitement) to the situation.

In her work with a variety of students in small groups at the computer, Anderson (1989) found that "putting children together to work at the computer is not enough. They need to feel a commitment and concern for others in their group. When responsible for their own and each other's learning, they learn to understand each other as well as master academic content. Working together with the emphasis on teamwork makes the experience a positive one."

A getting-acquainted activity, such as having students complete a crossword puzzle designed by the teacher with clues about each person on the team, a team brainstorming of a list of shared interests, characteristics, or possessions, or selecting a team name and designing a team poster or team motto, models the teacher's philosophy that how well students work together is as important as how much they learn. Many teachers, particularly in the upper grades, feel that teambuilding activities are awkward or take up too much time. These same teachers, however, later wish they had taken time in the beginning to establish a good basis for group work, rather than having to back up and solve problems.

Establishing Positive Interdependence

Positive interdependence is the feeling among team members that no one is successful unless everyone is successful. Some examples of types of interdependence include the following:

- *Goal interdependence:* "You're not finished until everyone in the group can explain how to teach the turtle to polygon.

- *Task interdependence:* "Each of you will be an expert on a different aspect of the story—one on the setting, one on the characters, one on the plot. You must agree on how to put your story together."

- *Resource interdependence:* "I will give only one worksheet to the group. You must record your group's predictions of what the turtle will do on the worksheet."

- *Role interdependence:* "Each of you will have a job; one of you will be a checker, for example, to make sure that everyone can explain how they came up with that answer. I will be giving your group credit for how well each of you does your job."

- *Reward interdependence:* "If everyone on the team scores at least x, then you can earn y bonus points for your own grade."

Because students have had so much practice with the competitive and individualistic structures, this positive interdependence must be communicated clearly, concretely, and in advance of the group work. Otherwise, students may use their usual ways of working to get the job done, and this will result in problems for the group. For example, before you start the groups, establish why it is important to work in the groups: What is the payoff? "You will want to work closely with each other, so that your group grade will go up." "You will receive bonus points for your grade for every student who makes 100% in your group." "If your group does all of its work correctly, you can earn up to fifteen minutes of free computer time."

Direct Teaching of Social Skills

Teachers who use cooperative learning make no assumptions about the social skills of their students; they teach these skills just as they teach any other area of the curriculum or just as they teach students how to use a computer. The direct teaching of social skills involves selecting the skills to be practiced in a cooperative computer lesson, defining the skills, discussing with students why the target skill is important, providing practice in using the skill by role playing or brainstorming words or phrases that could be used, and monitoring to make sure that students continue to use the skill.

Individual Accountability

Most teachers who have experienced learning in traditional groups or who have tried using traditional learning groups in their classrooms find that the addition of individual accountability ensures that each student contributes to the group and that the teacher can monitor exactly how much each student has contributed or the level of mastery of each student of the target skills. In a cooperative computer activity, for example, each student must be able to explain, or produce a printout, or score at a certain level on a quiz on his or her own. Each student must know, in advance, that he or she will be responsible individually for demonstrating mastery.

Processing

The teacher's role in observing and assisting not only with the curriculum content questions but also with issues about how well groups are functioning emphasizes the importance the teacher places on group skills. The time for students and the teacher to process what they observed, what they learned, and how they want to improve is essential if the teacher wants students to behave as though, in the classroom, "We are all in this together, sink or swim." Along with teambuilding and preparation for teamwork, processing frequently gets shortchanged, which results in taking extra time as problems come up for the groups that they are unable to solve for themselves. Giving the class an opportunity to generate solutions for problems and to become aware of the behaviors and social skills that make the group work frees the teacher from dealing with problems group by group.

COOPERATIVE CLASSROOM DESIGNS FOR COMPUTER USE

The Center for Special Education Technology (1991) described four illustrative scenarios of classrooms where cooperative computer use promotes social as well as academic development.

Scenario 1: Word Processing

Students are clustered around a computer using word processing. They are in the prewriting stage and are making a vocabulary list about a topic. Each student gives an idea that is added to the list on the screen. If someone doesn't know what to say, others give suggestions. When the list is complete, it may be printed out, and students can go to their desks to write their story, or the group may continue working together to create a group story. A model for cooperative writing at the computer is presented here, followed by a literature-based lesson plan from the children's book *Wilfrid Gordon McDonald Partridge* by Mem Fox.

Cooperative Writing
(adapted from Cooperative Integrated Reading and Composition)

1. Team assignment and teambuilding.

2. The teacher reads a story or selection of writing aloud, setting the stage for the writing assignment.

3. The teacher discusses the story in the large group, culminating in the specific writing assignment.

4. The brainstorm/prewriting stage is begun in the large group, then continued individually, using "mind maps," clusters, or skeleton plans.

5. Students share their individual mind maps in pairs within teams.

6. Students do individual drafts of stories at the computer (emphasis is on content, not mechanics).

7. Students read a draft of their story to a new partner on their team. The partner gives feedback: What did you hear? What did you like? Is there anything that is unclear? Where could more details or information be added?

8. Students incorporate changes into their next draft of their story.

9. Students volunteer to read their story from the "author's chair"; teacher and students give feedback as team partners did.

10. Students edit each other's work for mechanics according to specific guidelines provided by the teacher.

11. The teacher reviews/evaluates the papers and provides recognition to teams and individuals for their work.

12. The teacher debriefs the writing process with the class, getting and giving feedback on how effectively the groups helped with the individual compositions.

13. The stories are published.

14. Ground rule for the teacher: Never assign a piece of writing that you don't plan to do yourself. Share your mind maps, drafts of stories, and final product with the class to model that "we're in this together, sink or swim!"

The following lesson plan applies these principles to a specific topic, memories, and a specific piece of children's literature, *Wilfrid Gordon McDonald Partridge*.

Grade Level: 3–12.
Subject: Writing your memoirs.
Length: Two to three class periods.

Step 1: Select a Lesson

In this lesson, students discuss memories and the role of sights, smells, and sounds in re-creating memories.

Step 2: Make Decisions

Group size: Four.
Group assignment: Random or teacher assigned to assure heterogeneity.
Room arrangement: Clusters of desks or three chairs at the computer.
Materials needed: One copy of Memories II software (optional); one copy per student of mind map/clustering worksheet; editing checklist; peer-review guide.
Assigning roles: no roles are used in this lesson.

Step 3: Set the Lesson

Task: Teacher reads the book aloud to the class and discusses.

The teacher models the brainstorming/mind-mapping/clustering process by recalling a memorable experience and completing a clustering form on the blackboard or with the overhead projector. Students individually think about their own memorable experiences and begin their mind mapping.

In teams, students take turns sharing their mind map of their memorable experience with a partner. After sharing, the partner gives feedback by asking questions about any part of the mind map that was not clear. The partner also makes at least one positive comment about the mind map or memory shared.

Students then work individually on their drafts, using their mind maps to help structure the writing and to suggest specific words or images to be used. Each team is assigned to one or two computers and makes decisions about how computer time is divided up equitably. Students may do their drafts at the computer or on paper. Make sure that students double-space work on paper or at the computer for ease of editing.

Students then read their drafts aloud to a new partner on the team. After listening to the draft, the partner gives feedback as follows:

• What did you hear?
• What did you like about the story?
• What are three things that would make this story even better?

When both partners have shared their drafts and given feedback, they make the revisions at the computer or on paper.

The teacher models the "author's chair" process by sitting in the designated chair and reading his or her composition and asking the class to respond to the feedback questions, making notes on needed revisions. The teacher then calls at random on a student from each team to sit in the "author's chair" to share with the class the edited version of the story, as time permits. Every student who sits in the author's chair receives special recognition points for his or her team.

Students complete final revisions and print out a copy to contribute to a class book of memories, which can be checked out by class members to read, donated to a local rest home or doctor's office, or used as stories to read to younger children in a nearby school.

Positive interdependence: Each group in which every student turns in mind maps and completed drafts earns points for team bonus.

Individual accountability: Individual compositions; sitting in author's chair.

Criteria for success: Completed compositions.

Specific behaviors expected: Sharing ideas; complimenting each other on their ideas; giving supportive and helpful feedback.

Step 4: Monitor and Process

Evidence of expected behaviors: All group members listening, giving supportive and helpful feedback.

Plans for processing: Teacher circulates among the groups and notes instances of supportive and helpful feedback. After stories have been shared, the teacher asks for examples of how well the groups worked together. The teacher then shares examples of good group work from the observations.

Scenario 2: Problem Solving

A group around the computer is using problem-solving software. Each group member is performing a different role. One member is designated as the keyboarder, one as the manager to identify group consensus, one as the reference person to consult additional materials that are available, and one as the recorder to keep notes on information the group gets from the computer. They work together, talking over the information on the computer screen and the options available to solve the problem. When it is finally solved, they share their success. For the next episode, they change roles until everyone has a chance to do each of them. At the end of the lesson, they discuss successful strategies with the class and reflect on how the group process worked in their group.

An example of such a lesson using the software Where in the World Is Carmen Sandiego? follows. Students are detectives using clues to catch a thief who is hiding in one of thirty cities. The *World Almanac and Book of Facts* helps in exploring cities and countries.

Subject areas: Problem solving and logical thinking, geography.
Grade level: Fifth grade and up.

I. Objectives

    A. Students will be able to use problem solving and logical thinking skills while working with clues to solve a mystery.

    B. Students will be able to use the dictionary and *World Almanac* as reference tools.

    C. Students will gain information to enlarge their understanding of geography.

    D. Students will be able to ask team members why they are advocating an action and will be able to listen for the response.

II. Materials needed: Where in the World Is Carmen Sandiego? software and manual, *World Almanac,* dictionary, police dossiers in software booklet, paper and pencil, marbles, jar, job cards, evaluation forms.

III. Time required: One class period per activity.

IV. Procedures

    A. Preparation

        1. Assemble needed materials.

        2. Practice using Where in the World Is Carmen Sandiego? to solve several cases.

    B. Assignment

        1. Ask students what mystery programs they have seen on television. Ask what the role of the detective is.

        2. James Bond always started with an assignment. Today you have an assignment to catch a thief. You will use clues about Carmen Sandiego's gang and clues about cities and countries to solve the mystery. Your team will work together in the investigation.

    C. Input

        1. As a total class, use the program Where in the World Is Carmen Sandiego? to solve a case. Ask three random students to decide on a menu option. Then use another three students for the next option.

        2. Ask three students what to do next, ask each for their reason for their decision, and listen to the response. Get agreement on their next action for the case. Repeat with additional decisions and additional ideas from three students.

        3. Assign students to heterogeneous teams.

        4. Set the group goal. "Your team will work together on a case assignment today to catch a thief. You may use the *World Almanac,* the dictionary, the police dossiers in the manual, and the hints that you get as you run the program. As you decide what to do next, you are to ask each member for his or her idea and then listen carefully to the response. Then you are to agree on your course of action."

        5. "To help you accomplish your task, there are job cards at each computer. Please distribute these among team members. You may make

suggestions to the reference people and the recorder. All of you are to use the social skill of asking for a reason and listening to the response."

    6. "Every group that catches a thief will be permitted to put a marble in the jar. When the jar is filled, we will have a class party. In the meantime, every group that puts a marble in will have a day when they are first in the lunch line."

D. Guided practice

    1. Students work in their teams to catch a thief.

    2. Teacher observes and records instances of team members' asking others for the reason behind their ideas. Teacher also records students listening for the responses of others.

E. Closure

    1. Each individual fills out an evaluation form.

    2. With the total class together, the teacher calls on students to give comments on work in their group. Afterwards the teacher gives comments with examples of what asking for a reason sounded like and what the behavior of listening to a response looked like.

F. Independent practice

    1. Teams work on additional cases in succeeding days, adding marbles to the class jar as they are solved.

    2. Teams can gather together their members and work on cases before or after school or during unscheduled times.

Note-Taking Guide
Where in the World Is Carmen Sandiego?

Country	Capitol	Population	Geography	Flag	Money

Scenario 3: Database Use

Students read different reference books as they focus on one aspect of the topic being studied. Then they gather at the computer to use a database. Together they have the information to complete each of the fields for the database entries. Later they may merge this information with what the whole class has collected and analyze all of the information. An example of such a lesson follows.

No matter what kind of information you are working with, PFS: File lets you record it faster and organize it more efficiently. It allows you to select for viewing any category you need. It works like a paper-filing system where you can enter new information or update old.

Subject area: Language, critical thinking, study skills.
Grade level: 4–12.

I. Objectives

    A. Students will be able to brainstorm categories (fields) for their database.

    B. Students will be able to enter data into their database, sort, and print out their database.

    C. Students will be able to identify other information that could be useful on a database.

II. Materials needed: A database-management program, such as PFS, a data disk for each team, a reference card with commands for the program, pencils, paper.

III. Time required: One to three hours.

IV. Procedure

    A. Preparation

        1. Assemble needed materials.

        2. Make sure you know how to use the database-management program.

    B. Assignment

        1. Ask students if they have ever used a file box or a file cabinet, and if they know what it is used for.

        2. Open the file box and ask how you would find what you are looking for (labels on box, folders, and so on).

        3. Ask students if they would like to teach the computer to be an electronic file cabinet, and to see who can find information best—an electronic file cabinet or a person with a file box.

        4. Brainstorm with the class the kinds of information that might fit into a box labeled "Our Class." List these on the blackboard.

        5. Explain to the class that it is going to be developing a database on "Our Class" in teams.

    C. Input

        1. Ask the class to select from the brainstormed list two or three categories (birthdays, hobbies, and the like).

        2. Ask the students to list these categories on their paper and to fill in the information (for example: Suzie Smith—Birthday: June 23, 1985; Hobbies: fishing).

        3. Load the database program into the computer, insert the file disk, and design a form to collect the data while students watch.

        4. Ask for a volunteer to sit at the computer to enter his or her data. If time permits, allow two or three other students to enter their own data. Finish the data entry yourself.

        5. Give each student a file folder and a label. Ask each student to put his or her name on the folder and to put his or her papers in it. Put the folders in the file box.

6. Ask students if they think that the computer remembers what was entered. Flash through the files on the computer to make sure.

7. Ask for a volunteer to race the computer to see how many students were born in 1983. Set up the program to sort for year of birth, and give the file box to the volunteer.

8. Read out the data as it is sorted by the computer.

9. Ask the students which way is faster, more fun, easier, and more useful.

10. Assign students to teams. (See Chapter 3).

11. Set the group goal. "Your team will be designing a database for 'Our Class.' It will be important for you to work together, because your database will work only if each person does his or her job. Each team that completes the database will get to have a copy of it to keep."

12. Assign task roles in the group: form designer, data-entry manager, sorter, and printer. The form designer decides how the data should be laid out on the form and enters the fields on the form. The data-entry manager enters the data that team members have collected from the expert groups into the database. The sorter decides what characteristics to look for (for example, students whose favorite food is ice cream; students who have more than one pet). The printer decides what the final report should contain and enters the information the computer needs to print out the report.

D. Guided practice

1. Teams meet first to select the fields (categories) for their "Our Class" database.

2. Teams meet in expert groups to interview and gather data for the database from other teams.

3. Team members return to their teams with the data they have collected.

4. Teams move to the computer to design their form, enter the data, and sort to see what characteristics the students in the class have in common.

5. When a printer is available, teams print out their database.

E. Closure

1. The teacher calls on each team to share the most interesting aspect of its database and what its members learned by designing it.

2. The teacher asks what other ways the class might use its "electronic file cabinet," and students may brainstorm ideas such as book reports, social studies projects, and school databases.

3. The teacher leads a discussion of the job roles and students' feelings about how well the groups worked. Questions such as "What helped you to get the job done? What could your group do differently next time? What job would you like to have next time?" may stimulate student thinking and problem solving of group process issues.

F. Independent practice

1. Students may practice creating their own individual databases in other subject areas.

2. Students may design teambuilding activities based on the data gathered from the database (a class crossword puzzle or autograph hunt).

Scenario 4: Review

Group members review class material, checking to make sure each member understands the material. Then each member is assigned to a different game table where he or she meets with members from other groups. At each table, a computer presents an educational game using the material studied. As the game progresses, the computer tallies the points earned by each player. At the end of the class, students bring their points back to their original group. These points are added together for a team score, and winners are acknowledged.

Research evidence documents the effectiveness of classroom activities such as those described here. In one study (Mevarech, Stern, & Levita, 1987), students were given an achievement test and then assigned at random to an individualistic setting or a paired-learning setting, with each pair being approximately equivalent in scores on the achievement test. After two months, students were asked to complete questionnaires on their attitudes toward classmates, computer learning, and cooperative learning. The results showed that students became more altruistic toward their partners in the cooperative setting and preferred cooperative to individualistic learning.

NOTE

1. Additional software suggestions and lesson ideas are also available in Male, Johnson, Johnson, & Anderson, 1986.

REFERENCES

Anderson, M. (1989). *Partnerships; Teambuilding at the computer*. Arlington, VA: Ma-Jo Press.

Center for Special Education Technology. (1991). *Computers and cooperative learning*. Reston, VA: Council for Exceptional Children.

Johnson, D., Johnson, R., & Stanne, M. (1986). Comparison of computer-assisted cooperative, competitive, and individualistic learning. *American Educational Research Journal, 23*(3), 382–392.

Kagan, S. (1990). *Cooperative learning: Resources for teachers*. San Juan Capistrano, CA: Resources for Teachers.

Male, M. (1988). *Special magic: Computers, classroom strategies, and exceptional students*. Mountain View, CA: Mayfield.

Male, M. (1993). *Creating exceptional classrooms: Technology options for all.* Boston: Allyn & Bacon.

Male, M., Johnson, D., Johnson, R., & Anderson, M. (1986). *Cooperative learning and computers: An activity guide for Teachers.* Santa Cruz, CA: Educational Apple-cations.

Mevarech, Z., Stern, D., & Levita, I. (1987). To cooperate or not to cooperate in CAI: That is the question. *Journal of Educational Research.*

Russell, S. (1989). *Beyond drill and practice: Expanding the computer mainstream.* Reston, VA: Council for Exceptional Children.

PART III
Implementation

17

Creating a Community Context for Cooperative Learning

Liana Nan Graves

WHY DO WE NEED TO BUILD COMMUNITY?

Societal Factors

In many schools today, competition is rampant among a few, while others feel imprisoned and wait for the parting bell of the day. Yet others, who are sincere in wanting to teach or learn for intrinsic reasons, find their efforts frustrated by endless requirements and distractions that seem to have little to do with either human relations or intellectual development. Lacking a sense of belonging to a group with whose members they share goals and values, many students and teachers alike pare their aspirations down to hoping for survival without further loss of self-esteem.

Schools foster competition and the diminution of cooperation even among students whose ethnic groups come from traditionally cooperative societies. Placing cooperative learning groups into the competitive and fragmented climate of the average school seems like setting out tropical flower seeds in Alaskan tundra during the winter. As great as the potential of cooperative methods might be for improving student learning and self-esteem, the approach could easily die without a beneficent environment (Graves & Graves, 1978a, 1978b, 1983).

If we could simulate in the classroom and school the sense of community that can gave rise to and support cooperative behavior, it should be easier for children to work together effectively and help each other in small learning groups (Graves & Graves 1983, 1985). Moreover, numerous studies emphasize society's need for cooperative, group-oriented skills, since 70% to 80% of today's jobs require a complex coordination of efforts and ideas (Naisbitt, 1982).

Schools may be our major hope for rejuvenating a sense of community since there often is precious little of it to be found in the neighborhoods, towns, or cities surrounding them. Schools are often the hubs of their neighborhoods. If schools were true "communities of learners," they possibly could become seeds for the spread of community in alienated urban areas.

Educational Factors

Several outstanding educators (Gibbs, 1978; Schmuck & Schmuck, 1974; Stanford, 1977) took into consideration what had been learned about the stages of group development when they suggested how to create a caring classroom community. Yet many teachers consider the idea of taking time for "community building" a diversion from the real purpose of the school. Others assume that community feelings will develop automatically as students study together in small groups. But many teachers have discovered that just applying cooperative procedures in small groups does not work well without first preparing the class for collaboration. Children often do not want to work together and have no skills to do so. Other teachers resent having to structure the interaction of small groups for effective collaborative learning. There are content-oriented educators, whose approach to cooperative learning is based on academic outcome, and there are holistic, affectively oriented educators, who want to "play it by ear" and tune into individual learners. Teachers can learn to build a community context in their classrooms and schools and help students gain the skills to become members of effective working subgroups.

Numerous programs in the last two decades have specifically focused on fostering a "climate of cooperation" or "building classroom community" (Costa, 1992). There is also a growing interest in more holistic learning that includes the context of the learners, the background experiences they bring to the classroom, and relevant social situations that inhibit or facilitate learning. Small-group learning without considering these factors is as inappropriate as learning to read without whole-language approaches, studying mathematics without real-life problem solving, or, most recently, evaluating learning without authentic assessment techniques. In fact, the brain learns better by including contextual social and emotional factors (Caine & Caine, 1990). One of the three environmental conditions considered essential for intellectual growth by some leading educators is that schools and classrooms are interdependent, cooperative communities (Costa, 1992).

Whole-school cooperative communities have tremendous long-term advantages despite requiring additional efforts in the short term. Cooperative learning methods are significantly more effective if they are spread through the entire school. Since results from this new method of learning can sometimes be delayed when there is much remedial work to be done with students from disruptive home environments, teachers are better able to assess the effectiveness of their interventions by seeing the cumulative effects on students of cooperative methods in every classroom. Colleagues teaching at higher grade levels can also give one feedback on how one's former students are improving over time. The school as a whole has a unified concept of each student as a growing, developing individual within a supportive, caring community.

A cooperative learning community means a more comfortable and in-spiring work environment for teachers as well as students. Teachers can expect peers to support and assist them in implementing new instructional strategies, they can collaborate to develop both methods and curricula, and they are empowered to run faculty meetings more actively and effi-ciently. In one school, a fragmented and isolated faculty was unified with cooperative methods first in faculty meetings, several years before coop-erative learning methods for students were introduced. Then teachers helped to plan and implement the use of cooperative learning in the class-room, integrated with other innovations they felt important, and at a pace they found comfortable. Through close collaboration with the principal, ways were found to release teachers and provide substitutes so that the faculty had time to work together to develop curriculum and observe and coach one another.

We also need to face what happens when we do not make the effort to build a community context for cooperative learning within a school. In many schools, extensive staff development in cooperative learning has failed to result in an increased use of cooperative methods among most of the staff. Teachers are isolated among their colleagues, and cooperative learning does not "catch on" with much of the staff. The specific reasons are many: feelings of being coerced from above or, conversely, lack of administrative support, introduction of methods mechanistically with little regard for specific school populations or situations, competing demands, no release time for planning and collaborating with colleagues or dem-onstrating the methods in other classrooms, and teachers accustomed to focusing on content rather than process (Staff Development, *Cooperative Learning*, Winter 1991/92).

At root, however, these reasons boil down to factors related to lack of community. Teachers in these schools generally do not feel that they belong to a common community within which they have a sense of ownership, efficacy, and power leading to real commitment and responsibility. The quality of teacher action depends on these factors, and without them, most efforts at reform and innovation will ultimately fail. No matter how good a job a teacher does at creating a cooperative community within his or her classroom, much of this work can be undone when students move to classes with competitive or alienating environments. In upper-level classes where students have many teachers in a school day, the cooperative classroom may become an oasis for some students, generating jealousy and suspicion from other teachers. Implementers of cooperative methods face a great deal of negativity from colleagues in some schools, complete indifference and lack of support in others. For many teachers, a school community where they feel included and empowered is the necessary first step to adopting cooperative learning methods in the classroom.

Concrete examples of schools where cooperative learning programs treat community building as a major concern, both in the classroom and throughout the school, are still relatively rare (Schmuck & Schmuck, 1990), and schools with cooperative learning groups that are part of their daily instructional repertoire are unfortunately a minority in every country. If we are to place learning in an environment that promotes growth, we need to assure that we understand the components of cooperative community and what steps we must take to develop these components. Costa reminded us that "recent efforts to bring intellectual, cooperative, and empowered focus to our schools will prove futile unless we create a school environment that signals the staff, students and [wider] community that the development of the intellect, cooperative decision making and the enhancement of individual diversity are of basic importance as the school's core values" (1992, p. 93).

What we are considering here is a complete revision of what most learning environments are today. If certain groups or individuals within a school or classroom do not feel included and do not see how they can contribute to and influence the group, they will never actually commit themselves to group goals. There are no real shortcuts to building community thoroughly from the ground up and maintaining it vigilantly over time. In this chapter I present some major themes defining the cooperative learning community in schools and common stages in the development of these communities.

A DEFINITION OF COMMUNITY

"Community" as used here in respect to the classroom and the school will be defined as "an inherently cooperative, cohesive, and self-reflective group entity where everyone feels that he or she belongs, and whose members work on a regular, face-to-face basis toward common goals while respecting a variety of perspectives, values, and life styles." Let us examine the specific elements of this definition further.

Community Is Where Everyone Feels That He or She Belongs and Is Respected

In their work on managing classroom learning communities, Putnam and Burke (1992) offered a definition similar in part to ours: "A group of

people who are associated by common status, pursuits, or relationships."
However, without the added emphasis on the honoring of heterogeneity,
these groupings could result in the creation of homogeneous clubs or vol-
untary associations united by a single issue. We need to examine further
what elements are necessary to a truly cooperative, democratic, and in-
clusive community in the school and classroom. The same authors note
that "a community is not so much a collection of like-minded believers as
a commitment to shared differences. . . . A learning community gathers up
differences and celebrates them, because differences are rich resources
which improve the quality of group interaction" (Putnam and Burke, 1992,
p. 40).

Everyone is equally eligible for inclusion in a truly cooperative classroom
community, and no one is excluded because of race, religion, differences
of perspective, or nonconventional attitudes or interests. In addition, if I
feel I belong, I know I have a place in that group that only I can fill; that
I contribute something that is necessary to the group and is valued by the
other members. I also know other members well enough to value and
respect their unique contributions. Together we define who we are as a
group. This definition may change, evolve, and grow, but we construct its
meaning together out of what we all have to give. This means that we must
find out what resources each of us brings and communicate this positively
to the group as a whole, not only at the beginning of building the group,
but before (and often during) every group project so that the group always
knows what resources it has to do the task at hand. If this process is
thorough, members of a school or classroom community are seen as colleagues, rather than as competitors.

M. Scott Peck (1987) called this aspect of community "integrative." He
suggested that true community does not try to obliterate the diversity in
the group, but rather works toward an integrity of the whole by seeking
to balance and reconcile the tension between conflicting interests, needs,
and demands instead of isolating and compartmentalizing them or reducing
them to an average.

Community Is Where Interaction Is Ongoing, Face-to-Face, and Regular

If we are trying to build a classroom or school community, we need
sustained transactions between people that are developed around common
goals, joint tasks, important sharings, and meeting one another's needs on
a daily, weekly, or regular basis. More intermittent contacts can comprise
a network or a fellowship, but only when people meet, work, and play
together regularly does deeper community arise. This kind of regularity
combined with inclusion fosters a sense of trust in others' dependability
and a feeling of responsibility to the group in oneself. It cultivates the kind
of respect that is needed to risk being vulnerable in front of others, and

the skills to coordinate efforts with balance, compromise, and gain-gain solutions.

Classroom communities struggle with the fact that students are constantly being taken out of the class for special activities, with competing activities in which not all its members engage, and sometimes with a lack of commitment to regular cooperative class meetings and unifying events. The fifty-minute classroom hour is especially hampering. School restructuring that considers longer periods, teacher teams that seek to integrate concepts or methods across subject-matter areas, and those programs that teach the same group of students over several years can help to build true community for students as well as for teachers.

Two problems need to be addressed. First, integration of several aims can reduce the feeling that cooperative learning is "one more thing." For example, a school district found that combining cooperative learning methods with integrated and outcome-based curriculum design and authentic assessment improved all these school initiatives (Hibbard 1990, 1992). Second, most schools do not provide release time for cooperative support groups that would provide teachers with the community backing they need to master difficult innovations in the classroom. These problems are not insurmountable, but we need to recognize that it takes time and continuity to develop ties of community and the skills needed to work together well. Structural obstacles and administrative habits are major barriers to solving these problems in many schools.

Community Is a Cohesive Yet Self-reflective Group

Even if schools attempting to build a community are able to include diversity without prejudice and their members meet regularly to work together, they will fall short of their goal if they do not seek to balance a sense of solidarity and unity with an ability for self-examination and reflection on the functioning of the group. The coexistence of these two traits presents something of a paradox, since the more we see ourselves as interdependent, stand up for one another, and express solidarity, the less willing we might be to consider how such a splendid group as we are could improve. We finally included everyone, didn't we? What if someone should take offense at someone else's suggestion for better functioning? Wouldn't this tear our hard-won unity apart?

This fear of discovering or exposing disunity or a lack of information about how to give suggestions or feedback with caring may be one reason that the "reflection," "processing," or "debriefing" segment of cooperative lessons is so superficial in many classrooms, and teachers find the regular holding of effective class meetings so difficult to implement. It may account for why faculties exhibit a great deal of "pseudo-community" that has little substance when put to the test of making major reforms.

In some classrooms, social skills are assigned grades like academic skills. No wonder students are either artificial in or resistive to learning them. We need models of self-awareness that are neutral, nonjudgmental, and supportive, yet are aimed at gradual improvement. Putnam and Burke (1992) suggested that "a classroom learning community is characterized by public reflection on what has happened. . . . Group reflection on events influences students powerfully to view events as external circumstances to be examined for understanding, and not as internal character flaws to be evaluated and blamed."

DEVELOPING COMMUNITY

Educators concerned with a school or classroom community realize that intention to include the three elements is essential but not sufficient. Building community is a slow process that develops in stages. The suggestions for each of the following stages are intended to be used for all participants in the school community: faculty, administrators, other school staff, and parents as well as students.

Forming the Community: Who Are We?

In the early stages of building a community, whether classroom, school, faculty group, or administrative team, people are concerned with finding a place for themselves within the group. This involves (1) becoming acquainted with other group members on a friendly basis (Who are you?) and (2) presenting oneself to the group and being accepted as a valuable member (Who am I?).

Remember that classrooms, schools, or educator support groups are not natural communities. That is, there is no built-in reason such as kinship or generational village ties to bring these people together. We need to encourage strong standards of equality and honoring of diversity, so that each member will come to find her or his place physically, emotionally, and mentally within the growing community. This can be done in two ways. The first is by offering opportunities to get to know one another under circumstances that maximize enjoyable interaction while fostering information exchange and problem solving. This might include such activities as the following:

• Whole-group mixers, icebreakers, and get-acquainted activities that introduce members to one another in a light-hearted context when community is first being built or when new members enter. Care should be taken to make these relevant and authentic experiences, not silly games. They should involve persons learning information they would really like to know about one another, such as names, interests, skills, and experiences.

- Whole-group challenges that help community members feel that they can accomplish something together as a unit. For faculties, these may arise around social or fund-raising events that may also include parents.
- Using graphs for discovering and plotting the characteristics of classroom or school members along a wider variety of dimensions.

For example, the first time that a classroom convenes or a faculty meets, the convener (teacher, a group of teachers, or principal) might let everyone know that one goal will be for everyone to get to know everyone else on a more personal basis. The goal is that everyone realizes that he or she can work with anyone in the group on joint projects. Then a general mixer such as a human treasure hunt or "minding our Ts and Qs" can be held so that students or teachers learn something about others' talents, qualities, interests, and experiences while introducing themselves (Graves & Graves, 1990, 3.3–3.45). The activity can end with pairs interviewing one another in more depth and each person then introducing his or her partner to another pair, perhaps about some of the categories covered, or about the origin and meaning of the partner's names. The next time the group meets, a group challenge may be given to gather certain information from one another within a given time limit or to be sure every category is covered by every person. This unifies the group in its first common goal because the members realize that "none of us is finished until all of us are finished." Graphs may be used by the small groups formed after the challenge to record the information (Graves & Graves, 1988, 8.1). These are then posted in the faculty lounge or classroom, and a sense of group identity through exploring our diversity begins to emerge.

A second way to build community is through the use of assessment and planning activities that further help the community to learn the resources and needs of its members. Putnam and Burke suggested that "students talk and write about things to accomplish, things to change, and things they would like others to support them in doing" (1992, pp. 194–195). They provided an example of a worksheet that would help students identify what they are satisfied with in the environment and themselves, what they want to do differently, and what kinds of support they would need to make such changes. A similar exercise would be useful for faculty groups at the beginning of a school year or semester.

Once acquainted, the participants can further refine the process of defining who they are as a group. The following are some ways of finding commonalties and establishing symbols of group identity (Graves & Graves, 1988, 4.1–4.5):

- Choosing a name, a motto, or logo, and displaying this on a banner, crest, or T-shirts. Many schools have days where "school spirit" is displayed in this way.
- Creating events to celebrate group unity, such as celebrations for holidays, community achievements, or accomplishments of members.

A sense of whole-group identity needs continuous and ongoing affirmation throughout the life of the community, not merely at the beginning. We can reaffirm our whole-group identity by

* using unifying daily classroom or school rituals;
* collaborating on periodic events such as field trips, parties, cooperative adventures, or trips to other schools;
* keeping an ongoing record of our community life in the form of a scrapbook, a group history, or a photograph album;
* building in bonding experiences at least yearly, such as a retreat, a campout, a schoolwide carnival with cooperative games in which parents participate, or family math nights; and
* fostering ownership of the community physical environment by involving members in exploring, organizing, and improving or decorating the campus and classroom.

This focus on whole-group identity is balanced by recognizing and incorporating subgroupings within the larger group. It is seldom possible for the entire school or classroom community to interact at the same time, although even congregating in assemblies or class meetings is beneficial. Small learning or task groups will need to be formed, but these must not become more important than the class or school community as a whole, or rivalries and factionalism can develop, making it difficult to switch teams and work with someone else.

Teachers can increase their chances of preventing cliques in the classroom by building a firm community identity within the class as a whole. This is done by establishing norms such as "We can work with anyone in our class," "Everyone knows something, nobody knows everything," or "We each have a piece of the puzzle." Using short activities such as the Bavelas 5-Squares or Broken Circles (Graves & Graves, 1990, 4.21–4.22) introduces students to these norms empirically, bringing the consequences of noncooperation to consciousness to be discussed afterwards. During this formative period, spending more time with random groupings and short activities where students change groups often helps community members realize the possibility of these norms. Giving students a "home" or "family group" with whom they sit to begin and end each day, share personal experiences, or write in their journals can alleviate the "group fatigue" of moving between different groupings throughout the week. Throughout this period, the teacher can encourage reflection and listening skills on a spontaneous and informal basis.

Once a feeling of belonging is established, students can work with one cooperative team for a longer period (up to six weeks). At that time it is a good idea to introduce more whole-class cooperative activities, such as whole-group challenges, to reestablish the sense of community cohesion before changing teams.

At the faculty level, departments or grade-level groupings can siphon off loyalty and leave little for the entire school community. While practicality and face-to-face–interaction needs dictate that teachers collaborate more frequently in small groups, the composition of these can change, and teachers can meet with different task forces for different purposes. In addition, structural organization in a school that encourages cross-disciplinary and cross-grade-level collaboration for purposes of developing integrated curricula or authentic assessment techniques can build community. Tutoring programs where older students help younger ones can cultivate commitment to the school as a whole as well as creating more responsible learners. Reemphasizing the need for wider community with bonding experiences and schoolwide events points up common goals.

Exploring Community: What Can We Do Together?

As members of the group feel accepted and begin to value one another, the work they collaborate on together becomes more important to them. Now they are more ready to explore their purpose as a group. What do we want to accomplish together? What are our group goals?

It is important to realize that these group goals are both person oriented and task oriented. On the one hand, group members are now ready to form deeper connections, to learn to communicate in ways that convey empathy for one another's feelings and respect for each other's opinions. Members need to learn how to own their particular point of view, and after doing that, to step out of their own shoes and into someone else's. This is the time for the following:

- More teambuilding activities for small groups to build rapport and practice communication skills

- Empathy-building and perspective-taking activities, role plays, and role reversals with their colleagues or classmates

- Explicit teaching of group-formation procedures and cooperative skills that are necessary for collaborative tasks

Those facilitating the teambuilding may note differences arising between participants in small groups as well as differing problems among the groups. Members of one group may simply have difficulty listening to one another without constant interruptions. They can be given a topic to discuss while holding an object (such as a make-believe microphone made out of a broomstick handle and a tennis ball or even a pencil with a lump of eraser), with the added rule that only the person with the "mike" can speak. Be sure to include time after the exercise to discuss what it felt like to "sit on" what one had to say until it was one's turn, and whether this stimulated participants to listen and remember more (Graves & Graves, 1990, 4.42). Another group may be dominated by only one or two speakers. It will be more appropriate for its members to learn their interaction patterns by passing a ball of string from person to person as they take turns, each person retaining a loop of string around the wrist each time he or she speaks. Afterwards they can analyze the patterns that emerge and compare them to what was happening before they created their visual web (Graves & Graves, 1990, 4.41).

Many resources are now available for these cooperative activities (Bellanca, 1991; Graves & Graves, 1988, 1990; Johnson, Johnson, Bartlett, & Johnson, 1988; McCabe & Rhoades, 1992; Moorman & Dishon, 1983). Recent books on general cooperative learning methods include sections on "climate building," "classbuilding," and "teambuilding" (Bennett, Bennett, & Stevahn, 1991; Kagan, 1992). Time spent on these preliminary activities always pays off in more efficient and smooth teamwork later on.

Members are now also concerned as to how they will accomplish the tasks they set out to do together. Who will be responsible for what? How much time do we need? How will we know when we are finished? What will be the expected outcome? Facilitators, whether classroom teachers or faculty leaders, should reserve time for groups to explore these questions rather than simply predetermining these factors. If groups are floundering, facilitators can add their suggestions to the list of solutions and remind participants that each group member needs a job, role, or piece of the task.

During this period, the group needs to explore possible goals, standards, procedures, and expected outcomes. The community can jointly establish class and school standards, rules, or a "bill of rights"; group responsibilities for regular chores of the community and rotation of leadership; regular community meetings for raising issues and solving problems; and regular and frequent celebrations of accomplishments (Schwab, 1976, p. 246, suggested that celebrations help a community develop a historical memory).

The community becomes more self-aware through regular practice of reflection. Community members need to pose and answer questions such as "Are we following the goals we earlier set?" "Do group members remember what the community expects of them?" "How well did we organize and carry out our community work, our events and routines?" and "What are the consequences and celebrations we want to implement now?" Although the content of these goals and work differs among the different units of the community (faculty, classrooms, the PTA), the process is basically the same.

In the classroom, every small-group activity and weekly whole-class meetings should include some time for addressing such questions. Faculty meetings, as well as other cooperative small groups functioning as task groups, should be conducted collaboratively, and time needs to be set aside for reflection on these issues of group process. While these questions need to be answered by a developing consensus within the whole community, the actual questioning and planning can be done in small groups and reported back to the larger whole, whether the participants are students or faculty. Integrating individual and small-group opinions to form decisions for the larger community of the classroom, faculty, or whole school is an excellent use of cooperative structures and promotes thinking skills as well.

In one classroom, children individually consider questions that must be settled in a "community meeting," talk them over with parents as homework, then discuss the ideas with their classroom "family group" of four. Finally, they add the ideas from their small group to a whole-class list, which is discussed with one partner or several (using a concentric-circle structure), and the ideas are eventually voted upon. Similar structures could be used with faculty or administrative groups.

Functioning Productively: How Can We Do Our Best?

Through these exploratory activities, community members come to know one another well, determine their standards of conduct, and begin to work together on practical, tangible tasks. One would think that there were no more hurdles to jump. However, once the group tackles more symbolic, abstract, or complex academic or professional tasks, the community may encounter many internal resistances and obstacles. Applying cooperative skills in the context of dealing with complex and challenging content, with topics where there may be strong differences between members, or when it becomes clear that the outcome of group work seriously and significantly affects each individual becomes much more difficult. This is where positive interdependence may seem less of a privilege than a pain.

Groups at this stage often lapse into nonconstructive fighting and struggle, combined with misguided attempts of members to convert one another to their point of view. Other reactions to this difficult stage may be flight (avoiding troublesome issues through artificial niceness, scapegoating, or ignoring others' feelings), alliances between some members that exclude others, or dependency (expecting some authority figure, such as the teacher or principal, to solve the problems instead of taking on the challenge of shared leadership). The community may yearn to go back to earlier stages where everything seemed more fun and friendly and less hard work.

The only way out of this dilemma is through learning to solve conflicts, listening to the other's point of view, and taking on the responsibility of finding an adequate balance between the individual and the group. Groups can use the help of a number of the cooperative structures they have gradually been learning in the context of practical tasks:

- More regular use of roles within the small group and whole group
- Task structures such as Roundrobin or Think-Pair-Share that build in cooperative skills (Graves & Graves, 1990; Kagan, 1992; Lyman, 1992)
- Interpersonal structures that ensure equal participation and rapport, such as Talking Chips or "give two positive comments for every negative feedback" (Graves & Graves, 1990)
- Constructive Controversy techniques that structure disagreement and discussion (Johnson & Johnson, 1992)
- Conflict-management and resolution strategies (Kriedler, 1984, 1990; Creating a Cooperative Learning Community, *Cooperative Learning* December 1990).

In one classroom, a teacher was having difficulty because of the disruptive behavior of two boys who considered themselves class cutups. Before, their "clowning around" had drawn favorable attention from other students, but now that students were working in interdependent teams and feeling a sense of accomplishment for their group work, they no longer appreciated these boys' off-task behavior. Not wishing to scapegoat these students directly, the teacher set the whole class the task of brainstorming in groups how to deal with a member who might "goof around" and not want to help the group get its work done. To his surprise, a wide range of very useful suggestions was generated, including "find out what that person really wants from the group," "what would make him or her feel included," and "give them a task they are really good at." The class also generated consequences to be invoked if these suggestions did not work, such as time out from group work for a specified period and contracts with learning buddies to catch the person doing positive acts and give him or her recognition for these. Students felt empowered by being allowed to generate their own solutions to the problem, and the two renegades soon joined the class because they found alternative ways to get attention and acknowledgment for more suitable behavior.

In the classroom, work in cooperative small groups is most effective when a teacher includes the cooperative skills students will need in the goals of the lesson and builds in enough time for reflection at the end to assess how well they were able to use them. Care must be taken that the members do not become overly dependent on the structures and unable to operate without them. The ultimate goal is interpersonal sensitivity and the ability to coordinate efforts without losing individual contributions. To aid with this, it is wise to incorporate into cooperative lessons some content that helps students reflect on issues of fairness, equity, and social problem solving (Schniedewind, 1992).

Adult groups are as prone to fall into chaos and recrimination as are student groups. We have a harder job, however, since we must all be leaders to suggest structures, initiate reflection, or volunteer reminders of successes at the darkest times, while students can rely on the teacher to fill this role. Faculty and administrative groups can use some of these structures as well.

Many structural and personal roadblocks to working together will become apparent at this stage, and community members will need to grapple with them. The complex logistics of scheduling group meetings, classroom demonstrations, or teacher study groups for curriculum change may seem daunting. It is helpful to turn to examples from other schools and districts going through such restructuring efforts (Costa, Bellanca, & Fogarty, 1992; Hibbard, 1991, 1992).

During this difficult time, the community needs frequent reminders of its unity and its good times to achieve a broad perspective on its current struggles. The whole group can be used to help small groups brainstorm gain-gain solutions to difficulties in cooperating, taking care not to scapegoat individuals. Cooperative challenge games or trust initiatives (Orlick, 1978, 1981) and group singing (Graves & Graves, 1988; Creating a Cooperative Learning Community *Cooperative Learning*, December 1990) can lighten the atmosphere. Groups can share successes they are having as well as difficulties. A running record of improvements for the community as a whole reduces negative comparisons. Recognition of tasks completed and conflicts resolved is essential. Also, every cooperative community will need to recycle the stages of community building, reviving cohesion by applying the principles of honoring diversity and taking responsibility again and again.

This is also, however, the stage where, if conflict is handled creatively, groups learn to address challenging and relevant content and produce interesting and useful results. Adapting Stanford's (1977) stages of group development, Putnam and Burke placed the stage of "supporting and expanding production" after a stage of "identifying and resolving conflicts" (1992, p. 90). In practice, we find these stages intertwining. The conflicts that arise will be of a different nature depending on the degree to which the community has jelled and the complexity of the material with which the group is working. Conquering roadblocks creates stronger community bonds at each challenge, but although conflict changes, it can never be considered a stage the community will forever leave behind. The key is to view conflict as a harbinger of further growth, requiring the group to develop a higher synthesis that takes account of differing needs and views.

Providing Outreach: How Can We Help Others?

As a community masters the skills of working together, one of the ways its members can choose to celebrate their increasing success in cooperating is to provide services to other groups or communities. This is a normal stage of community development, comparable to publishing written work or displaying visual art, and should be encouraged when the time is appropriate. It also functions as an intrinsic form of reward for the accomplishment of good group work.

The well-functioning community is capable of providing a cooperative model to others. Teachers and students may be willing to serve as demonstration sites for others new to cooperative learning. Support groups of teachers may find it possible to share resources within their wider school or district communities. Cooperative structures found to be useful in the classroom may be transferred to faculty meetings. Students may wish to present one of their cooperative ventures, such as a cooperative game, radio show, or participatory art project, to the class next door or in neighborhood homes for the elderly, city community centers, or civic groups. Interdisciplinary projects with a social-issue emphasis can tie the school to the wider society in which it is embedded and provide positive, authentic outcomes in the form of neighborhood improvement. For instance, cooperative classrooms and schools at this stage may want to develop units in social studies, science, history, or literature to learn about the wider communities in which they are nested. Some may develop projects that produce an interactive link with these wider groups.

When Community Must End: How Do We Say Good-bye?

For many groups such as a cooperative classroom, there is a definite life expectancy, and we need to plan ahead for this. The greater the group's success, the harder it will be to part. It may be easier to move on if the students know that they will be in other cooperative classroom communities throughout the school, and that the school as a whole is a supportive community.

One method for ensuring continuity throughout a student's tenure in the school is to create vertical groupings across grade levels. All students belong to a vertical group throughout the grades and can identify with it by name, color, and other symbols. This also helps students who are in and out of school with the seasons. They will at least come back into their vertical group, be assisted to readjust by older "sisters" and "brothers," and, in turn, assist younger "family members."

When a classroom community is ending, it is a good time to acknowledge the grief of leave taking, to remember special shared moments, to celebrate successes, and to make a formal ritual of farewell. Students can write letters to one another thanking each person for specific characteristics or acts that were appreciated by the writer. There may also be plans for a final party or a reunion of the class sometime during the coming year. Finally, students need activities to help them recall all they have gained by the risks they took to form community, and to realize that now they have the skills to do it again and again.

REFERENCES

Bellanca, J. (1991). *Building a caring, cooperative classroom: A social skills primer.* Palatine, IL: Skylight.

Bennett, B., Bennett, C., & Stevahn, L. (1991). *Cooperative learning: Where heart meets mind.* Toronto, Ontario: Educational Connections.

Caine, R., & Caine, G. (1990). Understanding a brain-based approach to learning and teaching. *Educational Leadership, 48,* 66–70.

Costa, A. (1992). The learning community. In A. Costa, J. Bellanca, & R. Fogarty (Eds.), *If mind matters: A foreword to the future.* (Vol. I, pp. 93–101). Palatine, IL: Skylight.

Costa, A., Bellanca, J., & Fogarty, R. (Eds.). (1992). *If mind matters: A foreword to the future.* Palatine, IL: Skylight.

Creating a cooperative learning community. (1990). [Special issue]. *Cooperative Learning, the magazine for cooperation in education, 11*(2).

Gibbs, J. (1987). *Tribes, a process for social development and cooperative learning.* Santa Rosa, CA: Center Source Publications (revised edition).

Graves, N., & Graves, T. (1978a). Growing up Polynesian: Implications for Western education. In C. Macpherson, B. Shore, & R. W. Franco (Eds.), *New neighbors—Islanders in adaptation* (pp. 161–177). Santa Cruz: University of California at Santa Cruz, Center for South Pacific Studies.

Graves, N. & Graves, T. (1978b). The impact of modernization on the personality of a Polynesian people. *Human Organization, 37,* 115–135.

Graves, N., & Graves, T. (1983). The cultural context of prosocial development: An ecological model. In D. Bridgeman (Ed.), *The nature of prosocial development* (pp. 243–264). New York: Academic Press.

Graves, N., & Graves, T. (1985). Creating a cooperative learning environment: An ecological approach. In R. Slavin, S. Sharan, S. Kagan, R. Hertz-Lazarowitz, C. Webb, & R. Schmuck (Eds.), *Learning to cooperate, cooperating to learn* (pp. 403–436). New York: Plenum Press.

Graves, N., & Graves, T. (1988). *Getting there together: A source book and guide for creating a cooperative classroom.* Santa Cruz: Cooperative College of California.

Graves, N., & Graves, T. (1990). *What is cooperative learning? Tips for teachers and trainers* (2nd ed.). Santa Cruz: Cooperative College of California.

Hibbard, K. (1991). Beyond the first kiss. *Cooperative Learning, the magazine for cooperation in education,* 12(2), Winter 1991/92, pp. 29–31.

Hibbard, K. (1992). Interdisciplinary instruction: Shining star or black hole? *Cooperative Learning, the magazine for cooperation in education,* 12(3), pp. 28–30.

Johnson, D., & Johnson, R. (1992). *Creative controversy: Intellectual challenge in the classroom.* Edina, MN: Interaction Book Company.

Johnson, D., Johnson, R., Bartlett, J., & Johnson, L. (1988). *Our cooperative classroom.* Edina, MN: Interaction Book Company.

Kagan, S. (1992). *Cooperative learning: Resources for teachers.* San Juan Capistrano, CA: Resources for Teachers.

Kreidler, W. (1984). *Creative conflict resolution.* Glenview, IL: Goodyear Books, Scott, Foresman.

Kreidler, W. (1990). *Elementary perspectives: Teaching concepts of peace and conflict.* Cambridge, MA: Educators for Social Responsibility.

Lickona, T. (1990). Cooperative learning and moral development. *Cooperative Learning, the magazine for cooperation in education, 10*(3), pp. 2–5.

Lyman, Jr., F. (1992). Think-pair-share, thinktrix, thinklinks, and weird facts: An interactive system for cooperative thinking. In N. Davidson & T. Worsham (Eds.), *Enhancing thinking through cooperative learning* (pp. 169–181). New York: Teachers College Press.

McCabe, M., & Rhoades, J. (1992). *The cooperative classroom: Social and academic activities.* Bloomington, IN: National Education Service.

Moorman, C., & Dishon, D. (1983). *Our classroom: We can learn together.* Bay City, MI: Personal Power Press.

Naisbitt, J. (1982). *Megatrends: Ten new directions transforming our lives.* New York: Warner.

Orlick, T. (1978). *The cooperative sports and games book.* New York: Pantheon Books.

Orlick, T. (1981). *The second cooperative sports and games book.* New York: Pantheon Books.

Peck, M. (1987). *The different drum: Community making and peace.* New York: Simon & Schuster.

Putnam, J., & Burke, J. (1992). *Organizing and managing classroom learning communities.* New York: McGraw-Hill.

Schmuck, R., & Schmuck, P. (1974). *A humanistic psychology of education.* Palo Alto, CA: Mayfield.

Schmuck, R., & Schmuck, P. (1990). Democratic participation in small town schools. *Educational Researcher, 19.*

Schniedewind, N. (1992). Appreciating diversity, promoting equality: The promise of integrating cooperative learning and the social studies. *Cooperative Learning, the magazine for cooperation in education, 12*(3), pp. 4–7.

Schwab, J. (1976). Education and the state: Learning community. In *The Great Ideas Today* (*Encyclopedia Britannica*), p. 240.

Staff development: Building communities of learners. (1991/1992). [Special issue]. *Cooperative Learning, the magazine for cooperation in education, 12*(2).

Stanford, G. (1977). *Developing effective classroom groups.* New York: A. & W. Visual Library.

18

Facilitating Teachers' Power through Collaboration: Implementing Cooperative Learning in Elementary Schools

Rachel Hertz-Lazarowitz and
Margarita Calderón

A spiral-stage model for implementing cooperative learning in elementary schools is presented in this chapter. The implementation model includes stages that can be presented sequentially on eight dimensions. It also consists of spiral structures that refer to the interaction among students, teachers, and the school's organization. This model is presented in Figure 18.1.

Components A–C in Figure 18.1 deal with the content, and components D–F refer to the process of implementation. We first identify key considerations for assessing a school's potential for quality implementation of cooperative learning (components G–H). Then we present the content of training and implementation, followed by the process. Without a thorough knowledge of cooperative learning methods and curriculum development, teachers and principals will experience great difficulty with implementation.

ASSESSING THE POTENTIAL FOR IMPLEMENTATION

The first step in the process of negotiation between a change agent and a school is to identify the existing potential for effective implementation. The following characteristics are critical for the maintenance and institutionalization of cooperative learning (CL).

The Principal

The principal's role and commitments are to:

• have some knowledge about CL and appreciate its benefits;
• know or learn about instruction and attend in-service training sessions with teachers;

Figure 18.1
Professional Development Model

A. Cooperative Climate
1. Team building
2. Discipline management
3. Discourse of cooperation
4. Academic and Social scaffolding
5. Orchestrating the mirrors of the classroom

B. Cooperative Learning Methods
1. Team building
2. Simple structures
3. Methods and models
4. Investigation and creativity models
5. Creative teacher models

C. Teachers as Curriculum Developers
1. Packaged curricula
2. Develop tasks and activities
3. Develop a lesson or unit
4. Adapt CL to school curricula
5. Write new integrated curricula

D. Teachers as Learning Community
1. Peer observation
2. Peer coaching
3. Analysis of own video tapes
4. Problem solving and reflection
5. Teachers as professional developers

E. Stages of Professional Development
1. Knowledge and enthusiasm
2. Building a safety net
3. Basic competencies
4. Taking charge of own prof. dev.
5. Creative and constructive stage

F. Teachers as Researchers
1. Analyze instruction
2. Analyze own teaching
3. Analyze students' learning
4. Analyze student assessment
5. Become partners in CL research

G. The Cooperative School
1. Isolated teachers use CL
2. Grade level cohorts only
3. Majority of teachers
4. School-wide use
5. School/community use

H. The Cooperative District
1. CL is marginal
2. Principals trained on CL
3. District supports model schools
4. District-wide training on CL
5. District commitment to CL schools

© Margarita Calderón, Ph. D. and Rachel Hertz-Lazarowitz, Ph. D.

- be a facilitator for teachers (of resources, peer coaching, mentoring, fiscal allocations, and other means of support);
- allow time for teacher growth and experimentation;
- avoid fast and simple solutions;
- understand teachers' needs for support; and
- have a focused vision and mission for the school.

The Teachers

The teachers' role and commitments are to be willing to:

- experiment, be flexible, and be open to innovations;
- participate in collegial activities such as grade-level coordination, curriculum or site-based management committees, and Teachers Learning Communities;

- build on their prior learning about teaching and learning; and
- study their own classroom cultures.

The Change Agent

The change agent's role and commitments are to

- demonstrate knowledge and a strong background in the specific innovation;
- demonstrate competence in staff development and teacher development;
- demonstrate knowledge of classroom research and observational techniques;
- demonstrate genuine respect for teachers and children;
- demonstrate genuine respect for the cultural diversity of teachers and students;
- demonstrate interest in the whole school;
- conduct a study of school culture, climate, and goals;
- maintain confidentiality and loyalty to the school and its individual parties;
- become a "learner" along with the teachers; and
- enable teachers to become researchers and trainers of other teachers.

School Factors

The school factors to consider as crucial for success are as follows:

- A school whose staff numbers 25–35 teachers is of ideal size.
- Formal and informal communication structures already exist among teachers, between teachers and students, among the students, between parents and students, and between parents and teachers.
- The school professes a child-centered philosophy.
- The school has a history of experimenting with innovations, but does not experiment with fads every year and then drop them.
- The school has organizational routines to maintain channels for down-up influence and decision making.
- The school has a secure environment for teachers and students.
- The school seeks academic as well as social and emotional gains for students.
- The school is realistic in setting goals.

The Central-Office Administrative/Support Personnel

The role and commitments of central-office administrators are

- demonstration of knowledge of CL and of the process of implementing instructional innovations beyond surface changes by one or two key people;

• willingness to structure or restructure teacher support systems, such as peer coaching, release time or stipends for in-service training, and time for Teachers Learning Communities;

• provision of in-depth in-service training in CL for their resource teachers and supervisors to provide follow-up support to classroom teachers;

• allowance of time for learning, reflection, and experimentation (they do not expect perfection the first year and adjust teacher evaluations accordingly);

• willingness to integrate CL with other changes that are going on in the district or are being planned;

• willingness to assist and provide means for data collection and research; and

• allocation of funds, key resources, and/or assistance in proposal writing for additional funds.

The list of important characteristics appears to be very demanding. Nevertheless, many districts and schools have a number of these elements already in operation. The elements are often diffused and need restructuring and focusing, which is one of the tasks of the change agent (Johnson & Johnson, 1989). The change agent can help develop or restructure those elements that will lead to comprehensive long-term implementation and positive outcomes.

When in-service training is isolated from the other organizational factors, implementation will not take hold. Teachers will try CL, experience failure, and conclude that CL does not work. Because CL is such a comprehensive innovation, its successful implementation requires the participation of, and coordination among, the various elements listed in this section.

THE CONTENT OF TRAINING AND IMPLEMENTATION

The beginning phase for implementing CL in elementary schools typically takes about six months, usually from the August in-service training sessions to January. It is usually launched by five to ten days of workshop experience, with eight or more days of training during the year. The most desired approach is to have the whole school participate in the training, including part-time teachers, special-education teachers, resource and physical education teachers, long-term substitutes, the principal, the assistant principal, and parent representatives. Another option is to start with a cadre of interested teachers from one or more schools, letting these teachers be the pioneers and enthusiasts, preparing the ground for others to come in the following years.

In this chapter, we distinguish between content and process even though it is the integration of content and process that is crucial for the success of the implementation. This model is based on a theoretical background rooted in staff development (Joyce & Showers, 1988; Little, 1982), teachers' professional development (Barth, 1990), psychology of change (Fullan & Stiegelbauer, 1991; Hall & Hord, 1987), organizational development (Schmuck & Runkel, 1988), and cooperative learning (Sharan & Sharan, 1992; Slavin, 1990).

The content of a comprehensive professional program consists of those components necessary for effective CL instruction at the classroom level and also for those intangible elements that enable the teacher to implement instruction effectively and consistently. Teacher training for the competent implementation of cooperative learning includes three areas: (1) creating a cooperative climate through teambuilding and debriefing for teachers' bonding, and classroom-management skills at various levels; (2) becoming competent with simple, complex, and creative structures of CL; (3) curriculum development for CL at various levels of complexity.

The model emphasizes the potential of the school for working together with change agents to construct a cooperative school. The change agent facilitates teachers' development in terms of their understanding of and competence in the implementation of cooperative learning.

Cooperative Climate

Teambuilding and Debriefing

The initial content of CL includes teambuilding activities and debriefing skills to build cohesiveness, sensitivity, and reflection within the school faculty. Teambuilding products are a permanent part of every workshop, and each time a different teambuilding activity is introduced. Teambuilding activities are found in various sources (Dishon & O'Leary, 1984; Gibbs, 1987; Hertz-Lazarowitz & Fuchs, 1987; and Johnson & Johnson, 1991). However, many activities can be developed for specific groups of teachers (Calderón, 1991a). These activities model for teachers the importance of teambuilding and debriefing. Teachers are encouraged to implement these activities in their classroom as first steps in adopting CL.

After each teambuilding activity, debriefing is modeled and discussed. Debriefing is presented as the main tool for developing metacognitive skills and for enabling teachers to reflect upon their thinking and learning patterns. In the workshop setting, depending on the group of teachers in the workshop, debriefing activities or questions are employed that address contextual issues such as the following: What did you learn from this activity? What did you discover about yourself? What kind of cognitive, linguistic, and affective skills do these simple teambuilding activities develop for language-minority students? How would you conduct this activity in a bilingual classroom? In a special-education classroom? With gifted students? How can you use this in the classroom? What are the specific elements you have to design for this particular group of students? After debriefing with teachers, questions for debriefing with students are suggested, such as the following: What did we learn? What did we do? How? Why? What did you observe? How can our team improve for the next activity?

Throughout the cycle of in-service training sessions, debriefing is conducted after each demonstration or activity in order to anchor further knowledge, discuss basic principles of CL, and learn how to apply it in a classroom setting. The workshop presenter ends the session by reflecting on the process in order to model the specific process strategies.

Classroom Management/Orchestration

The term *management* in our model refers to a wide range of skills and knowledge about managing, orchestrating, and understanding learning in a cooperative classroom. From the beginning of the training sessions, lectures, discussion, and role-play activities are used to teach strategies for effective cooperative classroom management. The implementation of classroom-management techniques is monitored through classroom observations.

We distinguish between three developmental stages of classroom management. First is managing work routines within a disciplined context through teambuilding and debriefing, as discussed earlier. This initial stage requires establishing (1) social rules, (2) signals, and (3) group roles. The second stage requires teaching students the discourse of helping and cooperation (Hertz-Lazarowitz, 1989; Farivar & Webb, 1991; Nelson Le-Gall, 1992). The third stage requires that the teacher observe, monitor, and facilitate students' learning (Hertz-Lazarowitz, 1992).

Stage 1: Managing Work Routines

Three types of routines are recommended: social rules, signals, and group roles. Social rules help teachers and students manage work routines within a context of student self-discipline. In the training workshops, some examples of social rules are presented to the teachers. Then they are asked to suggest examples of social rules that are relevant to their cooperative classroom climate and/or to the needs of their particular students. Creating social rules and checking their implementation is a continuous process within the workshop and in the classroom. Social rules that are mastered by the participants, such as "take turns" and "listen to each other," are taken off the list, and new required social rules, such as "explore more than one idea or answer," are added. Social rules are a dynamic assessment of group function for effective classroom management and are constantly reformulated (Gibbs, 1987).

Other classroom-management techniques include nonverbal teacher-student communication such as the "zero-noise signal" and other signals. Teachers are encouraged to develop a repertoire of nonverbal signals for class management. These are adapted easily for students of all age levels (Dishon & O'Leary, 1984; Slavin, 1990).

The workshops present essential group roles and describe the functions for each role, such as recorder, reporter, and materials manager. The purpose of these roles is to ease teachers' management responsibilities, regulate group activities, and increase student participation. In addition, samples of discourse strategies and behaviors for each role are presented. Teachers expand and apply their own strategies by role-playing specific situations that call for these functions. Teachers experiment with these roles in their classrooms in the very early stages of CL implementation.

Stage 2: Discourse for Helping and Cooperation

After the basic elements of classroom management have been acquired, teachers learn to observe and develop students' attitudes, skills, and vocabulary for helping and cooperation. Four interactive constructs are central to effective classroom cooperation: facilitating content, facilitating process, helping, and displaying a positive attitude. Once students have had sufficient practice with roles in stage 1, they can practice becoming content and process facilitators. The content facilitator asks the group questions such as "Is there another definition for democracy?" and "Is this the only possible answer?" The process facilitator asks questions such as "Did everybody understand it?" "Do we have another opinion?" and "Has everyone had a turn?"

The vocabulary of helping is taught by first using metaphors to describe what helping looks like. Next, "helping" is defined within a context of "peer helping." There are a variety of activities that can be used to bring awareness of the variety of helping and hindering behaviors. Teachers and students also create metaphors about what helping "looks like," what helping "is not," and what being positive "sounds like" and then develop vignettes or skits of group work and role-play the discourse and helping behaviors. Next, teachers suggest their own true-to-life situations and in this way gain insight into their students' cooperative and noncooperative behaviors. Debriefing questions are used to help students connect helping to learning. The discourse of "positive attitude" is learned through situational role playing. Both negative and positive examples of approaching and dealing with a variety of classroom and groupwork situations are role-played. Farivar and Webb's (1991) manual on helping behavior is an excellent source to illustrate methods of how to fill the role of the helper as well as of the one being helped.

Stage 3: Teachers as Observers and Planners of Their Classrooms

In the third level of classroom management, teachers become observers and planners of their classrooms and study their own classroom culture.

They learn to study their classrooms through the model of the Six Mirrors of the Classroom (Hertz-Lazarowitz, 1992). This model assists teachers to become aware of the major dimensions of their classrooms as a basis for creating genuine cooperation and learning. Teachers observe and redesign their classrooms by relating to the following six features or dimensions:

1. The *physical organization* of the classroom should be flexible enough to promote interaction within and between groups, to enable students' movement in the classroom, to include learning and investigation centers, and to enable student-teacher interaction.

2. The *learning tasks* include activities that incorporate a division of work among the students in each group, an integration of students' ideas to produce a group product that reflects high-level creative work by all students, and accountability for individual learning.

3. *Teacher communication* emphasizes multilateral forms of teacher-student and student-student interaction. Teachers carefully combine the use of individual, small-group, and whole-class instruction.

4. *Teacher instruction* gives students responsibility for engagement in group learning.

5. *Social skills* development helps students become effective cooperative team members.

6. *Academic cognitive skills* development helps students become active learners using higher-order thinking, investigative, and creative skills (Hertz-Lazarowitz, 1992).

The six-mirror model provides teachers with a set of concepts for understanding the classroom context and for facilitating students' social and academic development. In various Teachers Learning Community sessions, teachers learn how to observe their videotapes, analyze the six dimensions (mirrors) of the classroom, take notes while they monitor small groups at work, and use their observations as a base for planning their interaction with the groups. With time and experience, teachers progress through the stages of development from classroom managers to architects of their own classrooms.

Becoming Competent with Simple and Complex Cooperative Learning Strategies

After teachers have experienced several workshop sessions with simple CL strategies and have tried them in their classrooms, they are asked to form groups, according to their grade level or subject-matter specialty, that will plan lessons. This typically begins around the fourth week of implementation. Teachers are asked to define their objectives and projected outcomes, choose CL strategies, design the learning tasks and activities for individuals, pairs, and groups, and define assessment procedures for the learning products.

After experimenting with several simple CL strategies, teachers and children will need additional challenges, in integrating and using a variety of CL structures, methods, and models. More complex CL methods can be introduced, such as Cooperative Integrated Reading and Composition (Stevens, Madden, Slavin, & Farnish, 1987) and Group Investigation (Sharan & Sharan, 1992). Teachers find CIRC and Group Investigation effective for relating the study of novels to topics in social studies and science because these methods accommodate an interdisciplinary curriculum that can be geared toward students' personal interests.

There appears to be a gradual sequence for applying CL methods in the classrooms. The sequence follows our recommendation to proceed from simple to complex CL structures and from structured methods to less structured and more open methods. Group Investigation is accepted and implemented much more easily at a later stage than if it is used as the first method of cooperative learning that teachers employ. Observing these principles will decrease failures in implementing and retaining CL methods in the school. One major pitfall of implementation is that many CL trainers promote only one CL method and miss the opportunity to create a more comprehensive teaching repertoire that borrows the best practices from several schools of cooperative learning.

Teachers as Curriculum Developers for Cooperative Learning

Developing materials and curricula is one of the major challenges confronting those who seek to implement CL. At the beginning of a CL project, it is advisable to use prepared materials so that teachers need not be concerned about developing lessons and can concentrate on implementing cooperative learning. Rarely are teachers happy with these materials, and they soon find it necessary to modify them or develop their own materials.

School districts generally do not recognize time for materials development as a necessary part of in-service teacher training or of teachers' workload (Fullan & Stiegelbauer, 1991). One way to overcome this obstacle is to have an external expert develop materials for teachers to pilot. Then, based on teacher feedback, materials are rewritten or adjusted. It is easier for teachers to comment on materials that are being developed than to prepare the materials themselves.

Different schools create their own mechanisms for working on curriculum development. Grade-level teams of teachers can develop curricula for their Group Investigation units with the assistance of trainers, or teachers can collect examples of lesson plans and curricula as a basis for developing their own. In other circumstances, resource teachers can develop the materials during the summer and give them to the teachers to pilot-test during the year in order to suggest revisions to be made the following summer. The curriculum issue in implementing CL has yet to be dealt with adequately (Barth, 1990; Fullan & Stiegelbauer, 1991). If schools are shifting to interdisciplinary curricula, they will need to allocate time for their teachers to redesign curricula and adapt them for cooperative learning.

THE PROCESS OF TRAINING AND IMPLEMENTATION

Theories of staff development and teacher professional growth emphasize that teacher isolation is the most serious impediment to effective implementation of instructional innovations. Paradoxically, teachers are trained in groups and then expected to implement what they learned in isolation. Therefore, Teachers Learning Communities are developed and integrated into the CL workshops and process of implementation.

The general principles of training and implementation are the following: (1) use interactive models of coaching, training, and follow-up support systems; (2) implement CL simultaneously with the collaborative teacher support system; (3) institutionalize the Teachers Learning Communities (TLCs); and (4) work within a conceptual framework of developmental stages for teachers (Fullan & Stiegelbauer, 1991; Joyce & Showers, 1988; Schon, 1987; Sharan & Hertz-Lazarowitz, 1982).

Interactive Models of Training, Coaching and Follow-up Support Systems

Teachers are first shown the research on transfer of skills to the classroom, and they discuss what can happen when teachers attempt to implement a complex model such as CL. The environmental factors that affect teachers during the year of implementation are presented (Calderón, in press). Teachers are then asked to identify barriers during the year that might impinge upon implementation or enhance it. This helps them see the need for peer assistance at critical times. They can predict when they will need more help from one another and when they will need support or new information from the trainers.

The initial training as well as all follow-up sessions incorporate a variety of interactive activities. Teachers experience various content and teaching strategies and techniques by participating in the trainers' demonstrations. The training cycle consists of a concrete experience followed by debriefing, questions about application, reflection, and planning how to modify or adapt the specific activity to the classroom. Sometimes there are minilectures of no more than twenty minutes, followed by a personal-journal or learning-log entry, sharing with one's partner, whole-group sharing, discussion, and elaboration.

The concept of a community of learners is practiced by communicating to teachers that both trainers and teachers can build new and relevant instructional approaches to problems of teaching and learning. Constant monitoring of groups is conducted by trainers to make sure every teacher is participating and to gauge the climate of each group.

Implementing CL Simultaneously with Collaborative Teacher Support Systems

The fundamental assumption of our implementation model is that cooperative learning in small groups is not only for students but also for teachers. The authors' recent research on mentoring beginning teachers shows that CL structures are very effective in building collaboration among teachers. Teachers that form collaborative teams generally implement cooperative learning at a higher level. This combination of CL implementation with peer collaboration helps teachers make the connection between teaching students and being a learner within the teachers' community. Moreover, it creates the organizational framework for long-term retention of collaborative work in the school.

Teachers as a Learning Community: Institutionalizing Teacher Support Systems

During the first week of in-service training sessions, teachers form study groups or TLCs to reflect, assess, and transfer what they learned to their classrooms. They study theory, practice with their peers, exchange ideas, and develop group lessons. They continue with their TLC meetings every week.

The Teachers Learning Community (TLC) concept is introduced during the first week's training session when teachers are grouped in triads to plan lessons. They first work on individual selections for ten minutes, then take turns (twenty minutes each) getting help from their colleagues to further refine their lessons. The next half day of the workshop is devoted to presentations of their lessons. They use the workshop participants as students to demonstrate key segments. The feedback for the lessons is based on principles of peer coaching that were introduced earlier in the peer-coaching segments.

The peer-coaching cycle is introduced in the initial phase of implementation as part of the TLC. The preconference is explained and role-played, and a simple technique for observation and for giving feedback is also presented and rehearsed. As teachers continue to practice peer coaching, more sophisticated observation techniques are introduced as well as note-taking and recording strategies for the observations. Unfortunately, it is very difficult to convince program implementors that training in peer coaching cannot achieve its goal by providing just an initial workshop with follow-up practice and implementation. Peer coaching entails a set of skills that require considerable training time throughout the first two years in order to develop and be effective.

After the initial one- or two-week in-service sessions, the task of ensuring teacher practice and competence with CL strategies begins. The TLCs should begin functioning the first week of school, although actual peer coaching can be postponed until the third week of school when classroom composition is settled. It is the role of the trainer to focus attention on TLC and peer-coaching activities. Otherwise, teachers will keep postponing until "we have time." Without a firm commitment to this aspect of the program, the innovation will deteriorate rapidly and disappear by the end of October or the beginning of November. Teachers will either stop using CL or, worse yet, become accustomed to certain undesirable behaviors that lead them to say that CL does not work (Calderón, in press; Hertz-Lazarowitz & Fuchs, 1987).

The most effective TLC model consists of organizing the following activities at the start of the training: (1) a forty-minute weekly common preparation period to plan lessons or discuss problems and solutions; (2) a resource-teacher visit twice a month to do classroom demonstrations on CL, observe and coach the classroom teacher, or answer questions about CL; (3) brag-a-bunch lunches where teachers bring their students' latest products to show to other teachers; (4) two-hour sessions once or twice a month after school, with refreshments, where teachers share, discuss, reflect, practice, test new ideas, and motivate each other (in all of these activities, teachers are encouraged to bring students' products and to describe how they were produced); and (5) creative mentoring. For example, an experienced teacher, Norma, invited a new teacher to move into her classroom, along with her students, for two weeks to teach with CIRC. First, she modeled the various instructional strategies while the new teacher observed, then they took turns team teaching, and finally the new teacher taught all the students while Norma observed.

As teachers continue with the five activities for four to six months, they enter what we call phase 2 of TLC. They learn how to (1) devote more time to collegial planning and problem solving; (2) conduct more in-depth study of their students' behaviors and outcomes; (3) enhance their own learning by pursuing graduate studies, reading, or other training; and (4) become role models and trainers for other teachers and discuss these experiences in their TLCs.

1. Teachers devote more time to collegial planning and problem solving. They go beyond planning a single activity and take it upon themselves to modify lessons, create books via computers, and create other helpful means for enhancing their students' learning. They invest more time in developing curricula for their own

classrooms, and they exchange their ideas more readily. The TLC meetings become a think tank for teachers.

2. Teachers conduct more in-depth study of their students' behaviors and outcomes. Students become the focus of this second phase. Teachers have learned how to talk about students' social and academic behavior, and they become more specific in describing their students. It becomes easier for teachers to identify students who are shy or aggressive. Teachers are generally more prepared to give groups of students responsibility for helping their less adjusted peers become effective group members. The teachers now carefully study student outcomes as measured through classroom performance along with scores derived from statewide standardized tests. They diagnose their students individually and plan learning strategies to help them master test criteria. They do so not by teaching to the test but rather by integrating needed skills into CL. One of the greatest accomplishments at this stage is that teachers no longer see skill building as isolated drills.

3. Teachers enhance their own learning by pursuing graduate studies, reading, or other training. In the TLC meetings, they exchange ideas and reflections about what they have learned in all spheres, such as university courses, conferences, and training sessions. Ideas from these experiences are typically integrated into a holistic approach to CL.

4. Teachers become role models and trainers for other teachers. As the teachers who practice cooperative learning become a bonded community of learners, other teachers in the school and in the district may gradually view them as role models. They willingly open their classrooms for teachers and administrators to come and observe. In the TLC meetings, they consult with each other on how to improve demonstrations for other teachers. They also plan workshops and training activities for other teachers.

While the role of the trainer is to facilitate the TLC functions and reflect with teachers about each stage of development, the principal also has a significant partnership in the TLC. The role of the principal is to encourage the teachers to set up their support systems and to facilitate TLCs. Principals help teachers by restructuring schedules where needed to enable common preparation times, participating in classroom observations as a coach when CL is being practiced, and scheduling daylong follow-up in-service sessions at least every two months. The most critical role of the principal is to develop a creative plan for releasing teachers for peer coaching. At this phase, teachers can observe each other in short ten- to fifteen-minute blocks. The principal can help free the participating teachers from their classroom duties for these short observations by organizing assemblies, giving students reading time in the library, or taking over a class herself or himself. Some principals organize parents' and teachers' (PAT) programs where parents are instructed on how to manage CL classes while teachers coach one another.

Stages of Professional Development: Teachers Implementing Change

Calderón (in press) identified five stages that teachers go through as they attempt to implement CL. At each stage, certain problems and milestones either propel teachers to demonstrate a higher stage of implementation or convince them to stop using CL. What is worse, such problems can cause them to stagnate at a low level of implementation.

Fullan and Stiegelbauer (1991) found that development in the three dimensions of materials, teaching approaches, and beliefs is essential if the intended outcome is to be achieved. They and other investigators (Hall & Hord, 1987) also found that it is possible to adopt superficial changes by endorsing certain goals, using specific materials, and even imitating certain behaviors without understanding the principles and rationale of the change. Teachers can go through the motions and "put on a good show" even for supervisors, but the skills, beliefs, and understanding are actually at stage one or two. The strategies for each stage of implementation serve as guidelines to help change agents assist teachers to reach the highest levels of implementation (Figure 18.2).

CHALLENGES OF IMPLEMENTATION

A school faces many challenges when it is working toward becoming a cooperative learning school. In this section of the chapter, we present the challenges that are most relevant to the school that works with this model of implementation. We also discuss and present ways in which schools have tackled these challenges successfully.

No One Believes That It Takes So Much Time and Energy

Too often school principals and teachers think that a one-week workshop and a few follow-up sessions are enough to enable teachers and students to function effectively with cooperative learning methods. Supervisors may expect to see cooperative learning functioning perfectly two to three months later. They may not always value the many creative adaptations teachers need to make in their old instructional repertoire. They cannot accept the notion that teachers might even get worse before they get better (Joyce & Showers, 1988). Because CL changes all classroom dimensions, it is a multifaceted change. Administrators must allow the time for quality implementation.

It takes at least one year to accumulate practical experience and for the TLC support system to function, and it takes two to three years to begin to see measurable student and teacher growth (Duran, in press). On the one hand, teachers may be ready to learn and try CL because they recognize

Figure 18.2
Teacher Researchers: Empowerment for Stages 1–5

STAGE 1 - Creating Awareness, Enthusiasm	STAGE 2 - Regrouping, Survival, Maintenance	STAGE 3 - Enhancing Teaching Skills
• Motivational session: create a vision	• Motivational session: create a mission	• Motivational session: create a passion
• Present information and demonstrate simple CL teaching methods	• More workshop sessions on classroom management, new simple CL techniques	• Add 4-5 Cooperative Learning strategies and revisit old ones
• Bring experienced teachers to talk about the innovation and the best ways to implement it	• TLC sessions on problem solving	• Anchor classroom management techniques
• Demonstrate classroom management techniques with heterogeneous class of students	• Jigsaw articles on CL and discuss implications • Sessions on integrating content and CL strategies	• Revisit concept of heterogeneous grouping • Help refine system for turning in scores/grades
• Hold practice sessions where teacher observes a demo, and experiences the new methods	• Demonstrate and have teachers practice observing their students and taking notes	• Do more lessons integrating content and CL • TLC sessions on special problem students
• Hold problem solving sessions where teachers work on: student adaptation, management, discipline problems, letting go of old "teaching" habits, integrating new learnings, student assessment	• Revisit how to conduct debriefing of process and content with students • Dispel myths about grading CL activities • Discuss ways to deal with that one student who doesn't want to cooperate	• Workshop on student-student interaction • Workshop on authentic assessment • Coaching workshop on refining communication and feedback strategies; assign coaching tasks to try and experiment with
• Present information on building Teachers Learning Communities (TLCs); forecasting transfer problems; peer-coaching; collaborative problem solving; observation, data gathering, feedback and communication skills	• Present mini session on the concept of student centered interactive learning • Check to see how much peer-coaching and peer-observation is occurring; do follow-up session on coaching	• Conduct session where teachers analyze selected segments of own classroom video recordings
• Session on teacher appraisals in CL classrooms		

Figure 18.2 (Continued)

STAGE 4 - Revisiting, Relearning	STAGE 5 - Beyond the Classroom
• Motivational session: rethink the vision	• Motivational session: Recharge the passion-the teacher as a researcher and change agent
• Sessions to examine the macro and micro pieces of the innovation	• Sessions to examine creative variations of the CL methods, techniques & strategies
• Workshops on more complex CL methods such as Group Investigation	• Workshops on more complex CL methods
• Workshops on higher order thinking and questioning strategies, scaffolding discourse	• Jigsaw articles on research on CL and related topics (Language Minority Issues; reading, writing, authentic assessment)
• Jigsaw articles on CL and related methodologies	• Graduate research courses
• TLC sessions on reorganizing parts of the CL method	• Workshops on innovation implementation, school change, site-based management
• TLC sessions on sharing student assessment measures, techniques, student products	• TLC sessions to analyze students' on-going performance
• TLC sessions to analyze own video tapes	• TLC sessions to analyze own video tapes
• Two-week sessions to rewrite curricula and integrate CL	• Workshops on conducting workshops
• Parties to celebrate instructional, curricular and student outcome successes	• Two-week sessions to write/revise curricula
	• Parties to celebrate instructional, curricular, student outcomes, teachers' professional accomplishments and organizational successes

its potential for student gains. On the other hand, teachers are faced with competing trends such as teaching for tests and new instructional fads every year. However, when teachers become empowered professionals, they scrutinize new fads and integrate relevant new ideas and skills into their CL repertoire.

Cooperative learning can be successfully adopted and implemented if the school gives it time to mature. Projects that allow for three to five years of implementation produce quality changes in many facets of schooling, such as teachers' professional growth, school climate and morale, participation in decision making, student social and emotional growth, and student academic achievement. Schools that internalize the philosophy of CL are very creative in finding ways to connect other innovations to their system.

Challenges for Successful Collaboration among Teachers

Teachers are often afraid to do peer coaching. They are not accustomed to opening their classrooms to colleagues. They fear that they are going to be judged and evaluated. Thus the elements of peer coaching have to be very thoroughly integrated into the TLC meetings so that they help to ease the teachers into peer coaching. By starting with brief meetings where they share student products, teachers first learn to be comfortable with each other and to gradually build the trust that will lead to peer coaching. Teachers find ways of subverting peer coaching when they are told they have to do it, but when they are allowed to grow into it, they find creative ways of doing it. Teachers visit their colleagues down the hall for a few minutes during their lessons or call them to "see how my students are working with CL." Visits within schools are particularly helpful for teams of novice teachers.

Gradually, collaborative planning and peer coaching become part of this phase of implementation. The teachers learn a lot about their own teaching and their colleagues' teaching because videotaping and viewing of own videotapes is introduced. However, individual differences need to be respected, and some teachers like being videotaped less than others. Some prefer to have several visitors, others only one at a time. We encourage teachers to form their own collegial help unit (Sharan & Hertz-Lazarowitz, 1982) so they can interact professionally with peers with whom they feel most comfortable. Yet we build high expectations for the progression toward more independence and quality of collegial norms. We need to accommodate for these subtle, yet significant differences.

REFERENCES

Barth, R. (1990). *Improving schools from within: Teachers, parents, and principals can make the difference*. San Francisco: Jossey-Bass.

Calderón, M. (1991a). Benefits of cooperative learning for Hispanic students. *Texas Researcher Journal, 2*, 39–57.

Calderón, M. (1991b). Cooperative learning builds communities of teachers. *Journal of Teacher Education and Practice, 6*, 75–79.

Calderón, M. (in press). Mentoring and coaching minority teachers. In R. De Villar, C. Faltis, & J. Cummins (Eds.), *Cultural diversity in schools: From rhetoric to practice*. Buffalo: SUNY Press.

Dishon, D., & Wilson O'Leary, P. (1984). *Guidebook for cooperative learning*. Holmes Beach, FL: Learning Publications.

Duran, R. (in press). Cooperative learning for language minority students. In R. De Villar, C. Faltis, & J. Cummins (Eds.), *Cultural diversity in schools: From rhetoric to practice*. Buffalo: SUNY, Press.

Farivar, S., & Webb, N. M. (1991). *The helping behavior activities handbook*. Los Angeles: UCLA Graduate School of Education.

Fullan, M. G., & Stiegelbauer, S. (1991). *The new meaning of educational change.* New York: Teachers College Press and the Ontario Institute for Studies in Education Press.

Gibbs, J. (1987). *Tribes, a process for peer involvement.* Santa Rosa, CA: Center Source Publications.

Hall, G. E., & Hord, S. (1987). *Change in schools: Facilitating the process.* Albany: SUNY Press.

Hertz-Lazarowitz, R. (1989). Cooperation and helping in the classroom: A contextual approach. *International Journal of Educational Research, 13,* 113–119.

Hertz-Lazarowitz, R. (1992). Understanding interactive behaviors: Looking at six mirrors of the classroom. In R. Hertz-Lazarowitz & N. Miller (Eds.), *Interaction in cooperative groups: The theoretical anatomy of group learning.* New York: Cambridge University Press.

Hertz-Lazarowitz, R., & Fuchs, I. (1987). *Cooperative learning in the classroom* (in Hebrew). Haifa: Ach.

Johnson, D. W., & Johnson, F. (1991). *Joining together: Group theory and group skills* (4th ed.). Englewood Cliffs, NJ: Prentice Hall.

Johnson, D., & Johnson, R. (1989). *Leading the Cooperative School.* Edina, MN: Interaction Book Co.

Joyce, B., & Showers, B. (1988). *Student achievement through staff development.* White Plains, NY: Longman.

Kagan, S. (1992). *Cooperative learning.* San Juan Capistrano, CA: Resources for Teachers.

Little, J. W. (1982). Norms of collegiality and experimentation: Workplace conditions of school success. *American Educational Research Journal, 19,* 325–340.

Nelson Le-Gall, S. (1992). Children's instrumental help-seeking: Its role in the social acquisition and construction of knowledge. In R. Hertz-Lazarowitz & N. Miller (Eds.), *Interaction in cooperative groups: The theoretical anatomy of group learning.* New York: Cambridge University Press.

Schmuck, R. A., & Runkel, P. J. (1988). *The handbook of organizational development in schools* (3rd ed.). Palo Alto, CA: Mayfield.

Schon, D. (1987). *Educating the reflective practitioner.* San Francisco: Jossey-Bass.

Sharan, S., & Hertz-Lazarowitz, R. (1982). Effects of an instructional change program on teachers' behavior, attitudes, and perceptions. *Journal of Applied Behavioral Science, 18,* 185–201.

Sharan, Y., & Sharan, S. (1992). *Expanding cooperative learning through group investigation.* New York: Teachers College Press.

Slavin, R. E. (1990). *Cooperative learning: Theory, research, and practice.* Englewood Cliffs, NJ: Prentice Hall.

Stevens, R. J., Madden, N. A., Slavin, R. E., & Farnish, A. M. (1987). Cooperative Integrated Reading and Composition: Two field experiments. *Reading Research Quarterly, 22,* 433–454.

19

Cooperative Learning and School Organization: A Theoretical and Practical Perspective

Shlomo Sharan and Hanna Shachar

SCHOOL ORGANIZATION AND INSTRUCTIONAL CHANGE

Adoption and dissemination of cooperative learning in schools entails distinct and far-reaching changes in prevailing instructional methods, values, and attitudes. Many investigators agree that one of the primary impediments to change in instruction is to be found in the school's organization and norms and is not only a function of the resistance of individual teachers to the process of change (Elmore, 1987; Fullan & Stiegelbauer, 1991; Conley, 1988; Sarason, 1982, 1990; Sharan & Sharan, 1991). Because such changes are notoriously difficult to implement in schools, it is imperative to analyze and clarify the nature of the relationship between classroom instructional methods and the school's organizational structure.

This chapter considers the essential features of change in classroom instruction required for implementing cooperative learning methods and how these changes, in turn, are dependent upon policies and decisions to be made at the schoolwide organizational level. We argue that genuine change in the former is in fact dependent upon change in the latter. The discussion offered here is intended to indicate some of the specific changes at the level of schoolwide staff organization that affect classroom practice (Cuban, 1990; Elmore & associates, 1991; Hawley, 1988; Murphy, 1991).

Demonstrating positive effects of cooperative learning methods on student outcomes, as the existing research has done (Johnson, Maruyama, Johnson, Nelson, & Skon, 1981; Sharan, 1990; Slavin, 1983, 1990) is a necessary but not sufficient condition for carrying cooperative learning into the reality of schooling now or in the future (Hawley, 1988; Sarason, 1990). Consultants who seek to have schools adopt and implement cooperative learning must bring about significant changes in staff organization if real change in classroom teaching is to be accomplished. The limiting effects of schools' bureaucratic structure on teachers' instructional behavior has been noted by many investigators of school organization (Conley, 1988; McNeil, 1986; Sarason, 1990).

CLASSROOM INSTRUCTION AND SCHOOL ORGANIZATION

Direct whole-class instruction is still the single most prevalent form of teaching practiced in schools today, particularly at the secondary school level. This style of classroom teaching has proven exceedingly resistant to change even in the face of concerted efforts to introduce alternative forms of instruction (Cohen & Spillane, 1992; McNeil, 1986; Sarason, 1982, 1983, 1990; Sharan & Hertz-Lazarowitz, 1982; Sharan & Sharan, 1991).

The structure and organization of the "presentation-recitation" form of classroom teaching bear an essential relationship to the bureaucratic model of organizations. Moreover, it appears that the classroom-school organizational relationship, in a sense, protects this method from attempts to supplant it or even change its basic character.

We do not wish to imply that changing the school's organizational structure from a bureaucratic one, with a low level of participation in decision-making processes of all people in the school, to one based primarily on an open-systems model, with a high level of participation, would necessarily produce a more progressive or group-centered, rather than teacher-centered, form of instruction. Teachers must develop the attitudes and skills related to cooperative small-group forms of instruction in order to implement them, even when the school's organization invites teacher participation in decision making and supports change. Given the opportunity to make their own decision as to their preferences for instructional methods, teachers might not opt for the adoption of cooperative learning. But if and when teachers favor cooperative learning methods, a lack of coordination between the organizational requirements of these methods and the bureaucratic features of the school as a whole will undermine teachers' efforts and eventually make it too difficult for them to maintain their practice of the cooperative learning methods. Just why this is so is the subject of the discussion that follows.

Figure 19.1 presents scales for assessing three basic features of classroom instruction and of school organization in two different organizational models: a low-participation bureaucratic approach and a high-participation systems approach. First we discuss traditional frontal teaching as a low-participation bureaucratic organization and then proceed to examine the same features of classroom instruction as they appear with cooperative

Figure 19.1
Classroom and School Organizational Features with Low versus High Levels of Participation in Decision Making

	Low-level participation							High-level participation		
Behavior	1	2	3	4	5	6	7	8	9	10
Work Design and Tasks	1	2	3	4	5	6	7	8	9	10
Space/ Time Organization	1	2	3	4	5	6	7	8	9	10

learning as a high-participation systems organization. We then show how these features are repeated at the school level.

The same three scales describe classroom-level features and school-level features. Different classrooms and schools manifest these dimensions of instruction and organization in varying degrees, so that they can be located at different points along each of the three scales in a manner relevant to their organizational level. We predict that the location of a particular classroom on the three scales will correspond highly to the location of the school along the same scales applied to the schoolwide level.

THE CLASSROOM

Direct Whole-Class Instruction as a Low-Participation Bureaucratic Organization

Classroom teaching practiced in most public schools of Western society can be placed toward the left-hand side of the three scales appearing in Figure 19.1. These three dimensions, as they are manifest in the traditional presentation-recitation model of teaching, reflect the critical features of the bureaucratic model of organization. These dimensions or features are (1) behavior of teachers, administrators, and students; (2) work design and tasks; and (3) space/time organization.

Behavior of Teachers, Administrators, and Students

Administrators and teachers determine the content of the study tasks and materials to be presented in the classroom and the quantity (and hence the pace) at which given subject matter is to be presented, as well as the criteria for judging the quality of the output by the students. The pace of instruction and criteria of assessment are uniform for the class as a whole.

The teacher mediates between the materials and the students, and between the students themselves. Thus the definition of the work to be performed and the rate at which it is to be carried out are decisions made by superiors who then inform the workers what they are to do. This is one of the central features of the top-down hierarchical organization with low-level participation of students and teachers in deciding about the nature of their work in the classroom.

Student behavior is controlled by rules and regulations determined by the school and/or by the teacher. Students are perceived as occupying the lowest rung in the organizational ladder, and they are expected to implement their superiors' instructions both in their interpersonal behavior and in their educational activities in the school. They rarely can affect classroom policy, and they are not invited to select study tasks, affect the pace of instruction, or play a role in setting the criteria of evaluation. Consequently, the students are placed in a relatively passive role regarding the degree of control they exercise over their school and classroom environment, and over the content and process of learning itself (Goodlad, 1984; Sarason, 1983, 1990). For students, and in some respects for teachers as well, the classroom is a tightly controlled bureaucratic organization.

Communication in traditionally taught classrooms is primarily unilateral (from teacher to students) during the "presentation" stage of a lesson and bilateral during the recitation and question-and-answer stage. Teachers generally ask students many questions about the material that was presented, or studied outside of the classroom, to check students' knowledge. Students are asked to respond to teachers' questions in serial fashion, in keeping with the view of the classroom as an aggregate of individuals, each one of whom relates individually to the teacher-manager. Communication is initiated by the teacher, and only rarely during a lesson does a conversation occur among peers (Hertz-Lazarowitz & Shachar, 1990; Weinstein, 1991).

Work Design and Tasks

Students in the class are addressed as an undifferentiated audience. The teacher presents the entire audience with the same information so that curricular materials are standardized for given subject matter. The expected products of the students' efforts to learn the required material are predetermined according to standard criteria. Students can exercise little or no discretion over the selection or design of learning tasks or over the products they must produce.

Space/Time Organization

The physical layout of the classroom, including the placement of furniture, is intended to facilitate the efficient transmission of information from teachers to all students in the class simultaneously. The expectation is that the physical structure of the class is relatively permanent and need not be altered as conditions of learning change.

Students are expected to carry out their learning tasks while spending the greatest portion of their time in school at their desks. Some investigators have observed that seatwork occupies fully 70% of instructional time (Weinstein, 1991). In many schools, even the library is used only rarely. The assumption is that students will not have to meet with peers in their class for purposes of planning or coordinating their work, since these functions are carried out at the managerial level, that is, by the teacher. Hence no significant changes in classroom structure are anticipated, and no flexibility in this dimension of instruction in the classroom appears to be required, not to speak of utilizing resources outside of the classroom, such as those found in the surrounding community, for purposes of learning (Sarason, 1983). Constraints of class scheduling, that is, the fifty-minute hour after which students in secondary schools proceed to a different subject and teacher, exert enormous pressure on teachers to have students avoid moving around during the class session. Thus traditional teaching schedules based on the principle of "one class–one teacher" (Sarason, 1982), as well as the very physical placement of the furniture in classrooms, embody the basic principles of low-participation bureaucracy.

Loose Coupling and Tight Coupling in Schools

What we are suggesting emphasizes the limited applicability of the theory of school organization as a loosely coupled system (Weick, 1976). This theory is readily misinterpreted to mean that events at one level in a school have relatively little effect on events at another level. In the realm of the schools' expectations for students' mastery of given materials, and of the method teachers employ to carry out their instructional responsibilities, centralized control (by the school administration or by the district) is a powerful mechanism for maintaining predictability and uniformity. Many important facets of schools are relatively tightly coupled, such as the nature of formal control of curriculum, the quantity of material to be delivered to students, and the regulation of teachers' and students' whereabouts through the schedule of classes. These chains of regularities exist alongside the relative lack of connection between school structure and instructional technology, and between the technology and learning outcomes, which were the phenomena addressed by loose-coupling theory (Meyer & Rowan, 1983). The relatively tight coupling of curricular requirements and of teachers' and students' behavior is a salient feature of the school's bureaucratic mode of functioning (Conley, 1988; Sarason, 1982).

Cooperative Learning as a High-Participation System

The perspective being presented here states that the methods of cooperative learning, and Group Investigation in particular, reflect the principles of an open system that involves a high level of members' participation in decision-making processes. That theoretical orientation emphasizes the importance of (1) the relationship between members of the system rather than viewing the organization as comprised of a collection of people who interact only rarely; (2) the multilateral flow of information among members of the system rather than the relative isolation of individuals performing the same or specialized tasks; (3) a horizontal rather than hierarchical organization of the setting (i.e., interactive small groups rather than top-down directives), such that people with diverse talents and skills contribute to each other's work and growth; and (4) reliance on feedback to correct current functioning and to plan future activities (Banathy, 1992). Cooperative learning classrooms would be placed toward the right-hand side of the three scales that appear in Figure 19.1.

Behavior of Teachers, Administrators, and Students

Teachers guide students, encourage them to ask questions about the topics they chose to study, and assist them in planning and making decisions about what and how they will study. Teachers serve as facilitators of student learning, help them organize into small groups, help them plan the subtopics of the unit to be studied, help students identify and locate resources of various kinds, and advise them on the preparation of a synthesis of group members' work for presentation.

The pace of learning emerges from the groups' activities and from the demands of the tasks that were undertaken by the students with the teacher's guidance. The pace of learning is not determined solely by administrators through the medium of a predetermined curriculum or by standardized tests. The teacher has an obligation to follow broad guidelines for educational goals set by the district or state, but these need not mandate specific contents or quantities of material to be "covered."

Communication flows between students in small groups (i.e., it is multilateral) unmediated by the teacher, and between the teacher and small groups of students. Students refer to each other's ideas and suggestions. Teachers coordinate communication between groups. The range of content in students' communications is not constrained by the need to recite before the entire class or to respond to specific questions.

Work Design and Tasks

Students play an active role in identifying specific subtasks to be studied within broad guidelines provided by the teacher. Students decide how they will proceed to study the topics chosen. Tasks are designed to invite co-operation among group members and to encourage individual contributions that could reflect personal abilities and interests. Students' cooperative planning of study topics and procedures implies a classroom atmosphere of latitude for different groups to pursue study topics in a variety of ways and to achieve goals that may not have been anticipated (Sharan & Sharan, 1992).

Learning tasks are designed to foster cooperation among group members. That means that different aspects of, or perspectives on, the topic are to be studied by different students or by subgroups of students, rather than having everyone study all aspects of the topic at the same time. The final products of these efforts incorporate the synthesis of information and ideas contributed by group members. Consequently, the content of the groups' products are not specifiable in advance, and teachers do not feel constrained to achieve uniformity in students' academic outcomes.

Space/Time Organization

The classroom structure is flexible and changes with the nature of the learning tasks and with the nature of the interaction required by the students' activities. Teachers must judge the amount of space needed for small groups of students to interact effectively and not to be either too distant or too close to one another.

Class scheduling is also flexible, subject to changing needs of instruction. Teachers confer to alter the class schedule to fit their classrooms' progress in learning.

Coordinating the Three Features for Change

Change in one or two of the dimensions presented here occurs frequently in classrooms, and many teachers think that by so doing they are in fact implementing cooperative learning. However, such piecemeal changes only result in the ultimate failure of the cooperative learning classroom to function effectively. More important, it also means that the traditional classroom remains largely intact and is not transformed into an open-systems organization. Each of the three features forms an important part of the high-participation classroom, and all of the parts are interrelated. For real change to occur, it must affect all three features in the manner designated here. Otherwise, what is thought to be a change will simply be more of the same (Sarason, 1982, 1990).

Many teachers encounter difficulty in conducting cooperative learning classes because one or more of the three features are omitted. Typically, learning tasks are not designed for intergroup cooperation but, like most curricular formulations, are directed at the individual student (even though the teacher is instructing an entire classroom). A group cannot function if its task is designed on the basis of the assumption that it is simply a physical aggregate of individuals sitting around a table. When students are expected to work in groups, but they are asked to engage in a study task directed at them as individuals, the group rapidly disintegrates into its component parts. Teachers then conclude that students cannot work together. This is only one example of the need to coordinate all three dimensions of classroom teaching and learning in order to have groups of students pursue cooperative learning productively.

Equally important is the change in teacher and student behavior that must occur if the desired results of cooperative learning are to be achieved. Teachers' behavior must change from primary presenter of information to resource person, facilitator of students' learning processes, and coordinator of interaction within and between groups in the classroom. These changes are a prerequisite for transforming students from passive players in classroom events to active participants in determining their work, carrying it out, and synthesizing information and ideas in cooperation with classmates (Graves & Graves, 1985; Johnson & Johnson, 1987; Sharan & Sharan, 1992; Slavin, 1990).

THE SCHOOL

Schools as Low-Participation, Bureaucratic Organizations

Readers interested in the various arguments as to whether schools are or are not bureaucracies in terms of Max Weber's original definition are referred to authoritative presentations of the relevant literature regarding that debate (Abbott & Caracheo, 1988; Campbell, Fleming, Newell, & Bennion, 1987, pp. 72–78). However, when the scales describing school features (Figure 19.1) reflect the use of centralized control for reducing ambiguity and increasing regularity and predictability in the organization, and thereby reducing teachers' (and students') participation in decision-making processes, they indicate typical patterns of bureaucratic organization and functioning.

Behavior of Teachers and Administrators

The content and scope of the curriculum are largely determined by school authorities, and not by the teachers or students. Nor are the subject matter that is studied in classrooms and the pace of instruction a function of the students' interests or activities in school.

School authorities, usually at the district or state level, frequently administer examinations to assess student achievement. Such tests are uniform by subject matter for all students at given grade levels, thereby constraining the teacher's latitude for changing instruction to meet the needs of specific groups of students. Standardized testing or expectations for achievement also impose conformity to formal criteria of performance.

The imposition of a set curriculum requires that teachers transmit large quantities of academic subject matter to students within given periods of time. Teachers experience considerable pressure to forge ahead with their presentations as rapidly as possible in order to meet their "production schedule." In-depth investigations by students of study topics cannot be driven by consideration of quantity "covered" per unit time, as if "more is better" (Harvey & Crandall, 1988; Murphy, 1991; Sizer, 1984). The unavoidable consequence of "coverage" constraints of this kind is teachers' conformity to traditional instructional norms.

Communication is typical of the top-down bureaucratic organization. It is consistent both with the hierarchical conception of authority and with the notion of instructional efficiency that prevails in secondary schools. Communication between the administration and teachers is almost invariably at teachers' meetings or through written memoranda.

Communication among colleagues in schools is, first and foremost, among members of the same disciplinary department, and, to a lesser extent (and usually in informal contexts), with other members of the staff. This organizational embodiment of subject-matter specialization is a typical feature of bureaucracy in schools.

Most schools have little or no committee work where small groups of teachers communicate on an ongoing basis about school matters, and where teachers assume responsibility for problem solving and decision making on the basis of authority delegated to them by the principal (Runkel, Schmuck, Arends, & Francisco, 1978; Schmuck & Runkel, 1985; Sharan & Shachar, 1990). This situation means that communication in schools is very limited in content and structure compared to the wide breadth of topics that schools confront daily. As long as the regulation of instruction by the prevailing class schedule proves to be effective because instruction is tailored to fit neatly into the rooms and time frames controlled by the schedule, it will not be necessary for teachers to confer in order to alter the school's uniform space/time allocations required by alternative instructional methods.

Work Design and Tasks

The teachers' task is to instruct all students in a similar way: They are to teach the same thing (by subject) in the same way to all students at the same time and for the same amount of time. The only exception to this rule is when students are categorized by a special criterion (such as gifted, retarded, disturbed, or learning disabled).

Teachers' instructional work, in terms of who, what, and when they will teach, is largely determined by administrators. How to teach is generally taken for granted by the educational hierarchy (haven't teachers already completed their professional training?) but is governed to a large degree by schools' informal norms. In addition to the relative absence of teachers' influence on the content and process of instruction, they do not have a voice in determining school policy in regard to classroom membership and composition, the length of class periods, the school's pedagogical priorities, determining in-service training needs, the adoption of innovations, and other matters. Like students, teachers are obliged to follow a substantial corpus of instructions (Cohen & Spillane, 1992). Their discretionary power seems limited to selecting specific curricular contents from a narrow range of options offered by the mandated curriculum and to affecting ongoing transactions with students within the confines of the classroom lesson.

Teachers' primary focus is on classroom instruction. They are rarely expected or invited to devote time and attention to schoolwide matters of policy, including teaching methods, the duration of instructional units, curricular continuity across subjects and across the students' years in school, and school-community relations. Hence the low-participation nature of the teachers' role reinforces the school administration's perception of teachers as workers rather than as professionals (Cuban, 1990; Elmore & associates, 1991; Johnson, 1991; Lieberman, 1988; Sykes, 1983, 1991).

Space/Time Organization

In terms of the physical distribution of teachers within the school building, school organization is largely based on the fundamental axiom of "one class–one teacher" (and, we must add, "one subject"). This organizational principle, considered by the bureaucratic code to be a primary criterion of organizational efficiency, is one of the major sources of the infamous "isolation" of teachers during the implementation of their work in schools, just as students in the traditional classroom are constrained to remain isolated from one another despite their physical proximity. Teachers can exercise little or no discretion in forming coalitions with colleagues for instructional purposes or for obtaining advice or feedback on their instructional activity (Lortie, 1975; Sarason, 1982).

Moreover, the distribution of teachers to classes and of classes to time slots in the school schedule remains almost unalterable during the course of the year, except for emergencies. Teachers' whereabouts and activities in the school and their interaction or collaboration with other teachers are controlled by the class schedule set in advance by the school administration. Class scheduling is thus almost a purely administrative act uncoupled from the nature of the processes it controls, with little or no opportunity for teachers to change the schedule on the basis of collective decisions or in light of feedback about ongoing events. Class scheduling generally bears no essential relationship to the professional needs of the teachers, such as obtaining feedback and assistance from colleagues, or to the learning needs of the students. These conditions have manifold implications for students' learning and for teachers' personal and professional well-being, development, influence on school working conditions, and so forth (Goodlad, 1984; Lortie, 1975; Rosenholtz, 1988; Sarason, 1982, 1983).

Schools Organized as High-Participation Systems

Schools as high-participation systems that parallel the classroom features of cooperative learning would be placed toward the right-hand side of the three scales appearing in Figure 19.1. The kind of organizational super-structure necessary to sustain cooperative learning obviously differs considerably from the bureaucratic model. School organization ranked to appear on the right side of the three scales embodies the basic principles of open-systems theory and is not dominated exclusively by the tenets of bureaucracy, which is a low-participation system (Clark, 1985; Hoy & Miskel, 1987; Weick, 1985).

Behavior of Teachers and Administrators

Administrators involve teachers in an ongoing process of setting school policy and curriculum, working together in instructional teams to implement an integrated curriculum, setting principles for evaluating students, deciding how to adjust class scheduling to differentiated methods of instruction, coordinating students' learning experiences in different classrooms, and including parents in various aspects of school life. Teachers' participation is authentic, and not merely lip-service, only when the administration delegates authority to teachers to make decisions rather than implementing directives and seeks to resolve the basic tension between the professional and bureaucratic dimensions of school organization (Abbott & Caracheo, 1988; Campbell et al., 1987; Cohen, 1991; Corwin, 1969; Elmore, 1987; Elmore & associates, 1991; Murphy, 1991; Sarason, 1990).

Teachers initiate programs and classroom and staff learning activities. They engage in ongoing assessment of school functioning and in critical analysis of the school's instructional and organizational practices. Teachers function as learners in the process of improving instruction, both at the classroom level and at the level of schoolwide organization, such as class scheduling appropriate for different subject-matter and student needs (Fullan, 1991).

Schools that encourage cooperation and collegiality among teachers generally succeed in having their students reach higher levels of academic achievement than do students in schools with limited cooperation among teachers (Chubb & Moe, 1990; Rosenholtz, 1988). Furthermore, a basic principle of human organization is that relatively complex technologies can be sustained only by relatively sophisticated organization (Morgan, 1986). Cooperative learning is generally considered to be a more complex form of instruction than the traditional frontal-didactic approach. Greater sophistication in instructional process requires support from a more complex organization of the teaching staff, and the "one-class, one-teacher" rule is no longer adequate. Teachers conducting classroom instruction with small cooperative groups need the advice, support, and cooperation of their colleagues, as well as ongoing discussions of topics needing interclass coordination. Colleagues are teachers' primary resource for assistance in maintaining complex forms of instruction (Cohen & Spillane, 1992; Cohen, 1986; Rosenholtz, 1988; Sharan & Hertz-Lazarowitz, 1982).

Channels for communication are created to allow free exchange of information among colleagues. Communication is within teacher teams engaged in team teaching and cooperative problem solving, between teams to foster coordination, between team coordinators and the administration, and between teacher teams and students. Teacher teams are not formed solely on the basis of a given discipline, so that cross-departmental communication is ensured.

Work Design and Tasks

Teachers identify topics of concern to the school as a whole that require attention. These topics serve as a basis for data gathering, analysis, and program planning on the part of the teaching staff. Schoolwide tasks for teachers are designed to make systematic cooperation among teachers an inherent part of their job definition and of the official expectations of their normative professional function (Cohen, 1991; Darling-Hammond, 1988; Little, 1988; Lieberman, Saxl, & Miles, 1988; Runkel et al., 1978; Schmuck & Runkel, 1985; Sharan & Shachar, 1990; Sykes, 1983).

Space/Time Organization

Teacher teams are involved in planning the use of the school's space, time, and resources. Various settings within the school or in the environment can perform multiple functions, such as learning and teaching teams, conducting observations, and school-community activities. Teacher teams overcome the "time-slot" character of traditional school schedules.

The High-Participation Systems Model and Teacher Professionalism

Teacher cooperation and participation in decision making is not a panacea and can even lead to collective support for nonaction or for sanctioning the status quo (David, 1991; Fullan, 1991; Little, 1988, 1990). It is certainly not the case that a particular style of school management will invariably lead to the adoption of cooperative and investigatory methods of classroom teaching and learning (Flinders, 1988; Fullan, 1991; Hawley, 1988).

Nor will teachers be able to adopt cooperative learning in their classrooms unless they acquire competence in this form of instruction, independent of their relative empowerment in a setting that practices school-based management (Guskey, 1986; Hawley, 1988). The building of teacher professionalism in schools requires visionary leadership as well as long and arduous work, including acquisition of organizational knowledge and interactive skills (Cohen, 1991; Jacobson & Conway, 1990; Murphy, 1991; Raywid, 1991; Sykes, 1991). Teachers can gain the required competence to serve as effective members of teacher teams engaged in problem solving, decision making, program implementation, and ongoing evaluation only if these activities form an integral part of their normative function in the school.

Implications for Change

These remarkable parallels between direct frontal teaching, with its relatively low level of student participation, and the bureaucratic model of organization, with its relatively low level of teacher participation in decision making, are not fortuitous. The conception presented here emphasizes the effect of the continuity between teachers' experience in the school as a social setting, where uniformity and standardized expectations of learning, thinking, and behaving are imposed on teachers by official directives and by informal norms, and the nature of teachers' instructional behavior in the classroom (Murphy, 1990; Sarason, 1972, 1990).

Again, we do not wish to imply that progressive forms of instruction would necessarily be adopted by schools if teachers had the power to decide how to teach based on their instructional preferences. Sarason observed: "The assumption that teachers can create and maintain those conditions which make school learning and school living stimulating for children without those same conditions existing for teachers, has no warrant in the history of man" (Sarason, 1972, pp. 123–124; see also Sarason, 1990, p. 147). Schools generally require teachers to conform to an entire range of behavioral regularities regarding the implementation of their instructional work. Can teachers for whom this environment is the norm of schooling possibly appreciate and be willing to implement, on a relatively permanent basis, a method of instruction whose fundamental features are irreconcilable with those of the school as a whole (Sharan & Sharan, 1991)? What aspects of the teachers' experience of schooling would lead them to think, feel, and appreciate the importance of changing their well-established patterns of teaching that are harmonious with their school environment and to adopt a strikingly different pattern of instructional behaviors? And isn't such a result even less likely considering the fact that the new method's legitimacy, in their own eyes and in the eyes of their superiors and colleagues, is far from unequivocal?

The significance of the classroom-school organizational parallelism is particularly apparent when we try to change the prevailing presentation-recitation method of instruction and supplant it, to some noticeable extent, with alternative methods. At that juncture, the bureaucratic organization of the school, through its various mechanisms of administrative control, not only proves to be hospitable to direct whole-class teaching, which is fundamentally a low-participation, bureaucratic form of instruction, but it also impedes and often precludes the adoption of significant instructional innovations that seek to increase participation of students and teachers dramatically (Abbott, 1969). Many investigators of schooling have noted the limitations of frontal teaching and the consequences of the bureaucratic model of school organization for teaching and learning, particularly in respect to the nature of the knowledge acquired in schools and the norms of instruction observed by teachers (Elmore, 1987; Goodlad, 1984; McNeil, 1986; Sizer, 1984).

Coordinating School and Classroom Levels for Implementing Change

The main conclusion to be drawn from this discussion is that both the school and classroom levels must operate on the basis of the same organizational model if real change in classroom instruction is to be achieved. Too often, attempts to implement an instructional innovation such as cooperative learning are made at the classroom level only, leaving the school organizational level uncoordinated and incongruent with events in the classroom.

Doubtless, providing in-service training for a group of teachers, some of whom may then employ cooperative learning, probably in the short term, is far less demanding and complicated than trying to introduce basic changes in the school's organizational regularities. What we have tried to demonstrate here is that a "mixture of models," such as classroom teaching with cooperative learning based on a high-participation open-systems model in a school whose organizational norms and regulations are based on a low-participation, bureaucratic model, will not support basic changes in instruction. Indeed, we predict that such changes, even if they are introduced into a given school, will be short-lived. Only a relatively high level of congruency between the classroom and school organizational models and coordination of the three basic features within each level provide the basis for anticipating that the changes will become institutionalized (Huberman & Miles, 1984; Sarason, 1990).

REFERENCES

Abbott, M. (1969). Hierarchical impediments to innovation in educational organizations. In F. Carver & T. Sergiovanni (Eds.), *Organizations and human behavior*. New York: McGraw-Hill.

Abbott, M., & Caracheo, F. (1988). Power, authority, and bureaucracy. In N.

Boyan (Ed.), *Handbook of research on educational administration* (pp. 239–257). New York: Longman.

Banathy, B. (1992) *A systems view of education.* Englewood Cliffs, NJ: Educational Technology Publications.

Campbell, R., Fleming, T., Newell, L., & Bennion, J. (1987). *A history of thought and practice in educational administration.* New York: Teachers College Press.

Chubb, J., & Moe, T. (1990). *Politics, markets, and America's schools.* Washington, DC: Brookings Institution.

Clark, D. (1985). Emerging paradigms in organizational theory and research. In Y. Lincoln (Ed.), *Organizational theory and inquiry: The paradigm revolution.* Newbury Park, CA: Sage Publications.

Cohen, D., & Spillane, J. (1992). Policy and practice: The relations between governance and instruction. *Review of research in education, 18,* 3–49.

Cohen, E. (1986). *Designing groupwork.* New York: Teachers College Press.

Cohen, M. (1991). Key issues confronting state policymakers. In R. Elmore & associates (Eds.), *Restructuring schools: The next generation of educational reform* (pp. 251–288). San Francisco: Jossey-Bass.

Conley, S. (1988). Reforming paper pushers and avoiding free agents: The teacher as constrained decision maker. *Educational Administration Quarterly, 24,* 393–404.

Corwin, R. (1969). Professional persons in public organizations. In F. Carver & T. Sergiovanni (Eds.), *Organizations and human behavior.* New York: McGraw-Hill.

Cuban, L. (1990). Reforming again, again, and again. *Educational Researcher, 19,* 3–13.

Darling-Hammond, L. (1988). Policy and professionalism. In A. Lieberman (Ed.), *Building a professional culture in schools.* New York: Teachers College Press.

David, J. (1991). Restructuring in progress: Lessons from pioneering districts. In R. Elmore & associates (Ed.). *Restructuring schools: The next generation of educational reform* (pp. 209–250). San Francisco: Jossey-Bass.

Elmore, R. (1987). Reform and the culture of authority in schools. *Educational Administration Quarterly, 23,* 60–78.

Elmore, R., & Associates (Eds.). (1991). *Restructuring schools: The next generation of educational reform.* San Francisco: Jossey-Bass.

Flinders, D. (1988). Teacher isolation and the new reform. *Journal of Curriculum and Supervision, 4,* 17–29.

Fullan, M. (1991). Staff development, innovation, and institutional development. In N. Wyner (Ed.), *Current perspectives on the culture of schools* (pp. 181–201). Brookline, MA: Brookline Books.

Fullan, M., & Stiegelbauer, S. (1991). *The new meaning of educational change.* New York: Teachers College Press.

Goodlad, J. (1984). *A place called school.* New York: McGraw-Hill.

Graves, N., & Graves, T. (1985). Creating a cooperative learning environment. In R. Slavin, S. Sharan, S. Kagan, R. Hertz-Lazarowitz, C. Webb, & R. Schmuck (Eds.), *Learning to cooperate, cooperating to learn* (pp. 403–436). New York: Plenum Press.

Guskey, T. (1986). Staff development and the process of teacher change. *Educational Researcher, 15*, 3–12.

Harvey, G., & Crandall, D. (1988). A beginning look at the what and how of restructuring. In C. Jenks (Ed.), *The redesign of education: A collection of papers concerned with comprehensive educational reform* (pp. 1–37). San Francisco: Far West Laboratory for Educational Research and Development.

Hawley, W. (1988). Missing pieces of the educational reform agenda: Or, why the first and second waves may miss the boat. *Educational Administration Quarterly, 24*, 416–437.

Hertz-Lazarowitz, R., & Shachar, H. (1990). Teachers' verbal behavior in cooperative and whole-class instruction. In S. Sharan (Ed.), *Cooperative learning: Theory and research* (pp. 77–94). New York: Praeger.

Hoy, W., & Miskel, C. (1987). *Educational administration* (3rd ed.). New York: Random House.

Huberman, A., & Miles, M. (1984). *Innovation up close*. New York: Plenum Press.

Jacobson, S., & Conway, J. (Eds.). (1990). *Educational leadership in an age of reform*. New York: Longman.

Johnson, D., & Johnson, R. (1987). *Learning together and alone* (2nd ed.). Englewood Cliffs, NJ: Prentice Hall.

Johnson, D., Maruyama, G., Johnson, R., Nelson, D., & Skon, L. (1981). Effects of cooperative, competitive, and individualistic goal structures on achievement: A meta-analysis. *Psychological Bulletin, 89*, 47–62.

Johnson, S. (1991). Redesigning teachers' work. In R. Elmore & associates (Eds.), *Restructuring schools: The next generation of educational reform* (pp. 125–151). San Francisco: Jossey-Bass.

Lieberman, A. (Ed.). (1988). *Building a professional culture in schools*. New York: Teachers College Press.

Lieberman, A., Saxl, E., & Miles, M. (1988). Teacher leadership: Ideology and practice. In A. Lieberman (Ed.), *Building a professional culture in schools* (pp. 148–166). New York: Teachers College Press.

Little, J. (1988). Assessing the prospects for teacher leadership. In A. Lieberman (Ed.), *Building a professional culture in schools* (pp. 78–106). New York: Teachers College Press.

Little, J. (1990). The "mentor" phenomenon and the social organization of teaching. *Review of Research in Education, 16*, 297–351.

Lortie, D. (1975). *Schoolteacher*. Chicago: University of Chicago Press.

McNeil, L. (1986). *Contradictions of control: School structure and school knowledge*. New York and London: Routledge.

Meyer, J., & Rowan, B. (1983). The structure of educational organizations. In J. Meyer & W. Scott (Eds.), *Organizational environments* (pp. 71–97). Beverly Hills: Sage Publications.

Morgan, G. (1986). *Images of organization*. Newbury Park, CA: Sage Publications.

Murphy, J. (1990). Helping teachers prepare to work in restructured schools. *Journal of Teacher Education, 41*, 50–56.

Murphy, J. (1991). *Restructuring schools*. New York: Teachers College Press.

Raywid, M. (1991). Rethinking school governance. In R. Elmore & associates

(Eds.), *Restructuring schools: The next generation of educational reform* (pp. 152–205). San Francisco: Jossey-Bass.

Rosenholtz, S. (1988). *Teachers' workplace*. New York: Teachers College Press.

Runkel, P., Schmuck, R., Arends, J., & Francisco, R. (1978). *Transforming the school's capacity for problem solving*. Eugene: University of Oregon, College of Education.

Sarason, S. (1972). *The creation of settings and the future societies*. San Francisco: Jossey-Bass.

Sarason, S. (1982). *The culture of the school and the problem of change* (2nd ed.). Boston: Allyn & Bacon.

Sarason, S. (1983). *Schooling in America: Scapegoat and salvation*. New York: Free Press.

Sarason, S. (1990). *The predictable failure of educational reform*. San Francisco: Jossey-Bass.

Schmuck, R., & Runkel, P. (1985). The *handbook of organizational development in schools* (3rd ed.). Palo Alto, CA: Mayfield.

Sharan, S. (Ed.). (1990). *Cooperative learning: Theory and research*. New York: Praeger.

Sharan, S., & Hertz-Lazarowitz, R. (1982). Effects of an instructional change program on teachers' perceptions, attitudes, and behavior. *Journal of Applied Behavioral Science, 18*, 185–201.

Sharan, S., & Shachar, H. (1990). *Organization and staff management in schools* (in Hebrew). Tel Aviv: Schocken.

Sharan, S., & Sharan, Y. (1991). Changing instructional methods and the culture of the school. In N. Wyner (Ed.), *Current perspectives on the culture of schools* (pp. 143–164). Brookline, MA: Brookline Books.

Sharan, Y., & Sharan, S. (1992). *Expanding cooperative learning through group investigation*. New York: Teachers College Press.

Sizer, T. (1984). *Horace's compromise: The dilemma of the American high school*. Boston: Houghton Mifflin.

Slavin, R. (1983). *Cooperative learning*. New York: Longman.

Slavin, R. (1990). *Cooperative learning: Theory, research, and practice*. Englewood Cliffs, NJ: Prentice Hall.

Slavin, R., Sharan, S., Kagan, S., Hertz-Lazarowitz, R., Webb, C. & Schmuck, R. (Eds.). (1985). *Learning to cooperate, cooperating to learn*. New York: Plenum Press.

Sykes, G. (1983). Public policy and the problem of teacher quality. In L. Shulman & G. Sykes (Eds.), *Handbook of teaching and policy* (pp. 97–125). New York: Longman.

Sykes, G. (1988). Inspired teaching: The missing element in "effective schools." *Educational Administration Quarterly, 24*, 461–469.

Sykes, G. (1991). Fostering teacher professionalism in schools. In R. Elmore & associates (Eds.), *Restructuring schools: The next generation of educational reform* (pp. 59–96). San Francisco: Jossey-Bass.

Weick, K. (1976). Educational organizations as loosely coupled systems. *Administrative Science Quarterly, 21*, 1–19.

Weick, K. (1985). Sources of order in underorganized systems: Themes in recent organizational theory. In Y. Lincoln (Ed.), *Organizational theory and in-*

quiry: The paradigm revolution (pp. 106–136). Newbury Park, CA: Sage Publications.

Weinstein, C. (1991). The classroom as a social context for learning. *Annual Review of Psychology, 42,* 493–525.

20

Cooperative Learning and the Teacher

Shlomo Sharan

THE COMMON GROUND OF TEACHING

Cooperative learning is a group-centered and student-centered approach to classroom teaching and learning. Yet in no way does this statement detract from the decisive significance of the teacher's role in the conduct of classroom learning. Research on teaching, more often than not, concentrates on the learner and only secondarily on the teacher. Far too little is known about teachers' instructional behavior, its patterns and effects, and how these may vary in different organizational environments. Much still remains to be understood about teaching if we are to make real progress in improving learning.

The chapters in this book depict distinctly expanded roles, responsibilities, and behavioral repertoires for teachers in cooperative learning classes compared to the behavioral patterns typical of traditional methods of teaching. Not that traditional whole-class teaching necessarily excludes all of the behavioral patterns required by cooperative learning. Nevertheless, the teacher's modes of operation in the cooperative classroom differ significantly from those generally displayed and necessitated by traditional instruction.

This chapter focuses mainly on the characteristic features of the teacher's role when instruction is conducted with cooperative learning methods. However, we must not forget that all forms of teaching entail several fundamental expectations from teachers that are not dependent upon the method they employ to perform their role or upon the specific content taught. These expectations may seem obvious and not in need of repetition. Yet, because many teachers experience difficulty in meeting these expectations, they must be stressed as forming the bedrock professional expectation directed at all teachers, namely, to evidence interest in the students' welfare and progress in school, intellectual, social, and emotional. To encounter teachers who are relatively indifferent to their personal condition in school can, and often does, have devastating consequences for students' motivation to learn and for their self-esteem as students and even as people. Students quickly discern a lack of caring, empathy, or interest on the part of teachers and react accordingly. No method of instruction, including forms of cooperative learning, can mask teachers' basic emotional and attitudinal orientation toward students (Noddings, 1992; Sarason, 1985). Keeping this premise in mind, we turn to those aspects of the teacher's behavior that are more typically required in the cooperative learning classroom than in classes taught with traditional whole-class teaching.

CLASSROOM LEARNING AND AFFECT

Most classrooms are not known for their free-flowing affective climate. Many observers frequently complain about the affective sterility they encounter in schools (except on the playground or during recess). This is particularly true in secondary schools. Cooperative learning and regular teamwork with colleagues, through peer interaction and communication, invite a much broader range of affective behavior on the part of students and teachers than is typically found in traditional school settings. The freer expression of feelings lends vitality to classroom learning and to work in school that teachers must learn to recognize and appreciate. It can be a source of satisfaction to students and teachers alike. But, like many other aspects of human behavior, it can also give vent to conflicts and unpleasant confrontations.

The almost-exclusive emphasis in teachers' professional preparation on a cognitive orientation toward teaching and learning and on solo teaching behind the classroom door may leave some teachers ill prepared to deal with the freer expression of emotion in school. Yet making teaching and learning into the active pursuit of knowledge by small groups of students stimulates much more expression of emotion. The same is true on the school level when teachers' work involves systematic problem solving and decision making in collaboration with colleagues. Relating to this kind of school atmosphere must be part of teachers' professional repertoire.

PARTICIPATIVE DECISION MAKING, MOTIVATION, AND EFFECTIVENESS

Cooperative learning methods strive to have students assume a high degree of responsibility for their own learning, rather than perceiving learning as imposed by others. It is a basic psychological truth in our society that people are more likely to assume responsibility for their own behavior when they are given the opportunity to exercise that responsibility. On the other hand, those who give orders to others often remain responsible for their implementation, even if they do not carry them out themselves. Those who are hired or feel coerced, in whatever manner, to perform the labor involved rarely have a sense of personal responsibility for carrying out the requisite acts beyond the specified requirements of the job. In traditional whole-class teaching, teachers give the orders and students are expected to do what they are told.

By contrast, group-centered learning is facilitated by having student groups participate in regulating their own activities in the classroom, including the conduct of learning. Student participation in the planning of learning is recommended as the primary means for cultivating students' personal and collective responsibility and motivation for learning (De-Charms, 1976; Deci & Ryan, 1985; Dewey, 1943; Sharan & Sharan, 1992; Sharan & Shaulov, 1990).

It follows that cooperative learning entails significant decentralization of decision making in the classroom, empowering students to play a role in directing their academic behavior and work in school. This decentralization of decision making and empowerment of students necessarily imply some alteration in the centrality of the teacher in the management of the classroom in general and in the process of instruction in particular (Cohen, 1986).

Moreover, if genuine change in the centrality of the classroom teacher is to take place and to be sustained in a school, a parallel change must occur in the principal's role, widely recommended as an essential ingredient of school restructuring. In decentralized organizations, leadership takes precedence over management, which is to say that the aim of the formal leadership is to facilitate the work of all groups in the organization so they can perform their work with maximum benefit and effectiveness. Leadership is not primarily concentrated on ensuring that regulations are followed. Maximum effective functioning can be achieved when the various groups of teachers and students in the school provide constant information to the leadership about ongoing events and conditions affecting their work. In return, they expect to receive support from the principal to help them fulfill their roles in the best way they can.

At the school level, this approach can translate into a policy for the principal to form and maintain the operation of teacher committees or teams devoted to ongoing problem solving and decision making about schoolwide topics of concern to the teaching staff. These include instructional policy and coordination of different teachers' instructional efforts in terms of curricular content and instructional methods. Through direct contact with team coordinators, the principal is constantly informed of the teams' activities, their decisions and programs, the conditions needed to carry out these programs, and the progress that remains to be accomplished. Through this contact with team coordinators (who are not necessarily the subject-matter coordinators of the school), principals can lead their schools toward achieving their educational goals.

At the classroom level, this approach means that teachers do not engage primarily in the transmission of information to students according to predetermined criteria of quantity and pace of instruction, or in maintaining discipline. Rather, their main role is to facilitate the constructive and productive academic work of teams of students who participate in the planning of the content and procedures of their investigative efforts. Knowledge is sought out by the learners' effort to solve problems or find enlightened responses to serious questions.

Decentralization of decision making, by the principal or by the teacher, and active participation in problem solving by teachers and students form one pole of a continuum of which centralized decision making and limited participation form the opposite pole. Furthermore, these same processes equally affect the school and the classroom as interrelated organizational systems (Banathy, 1991).

In this conception, decentralization and high participation are not only powerful motivators of teachers' and students' behavior, but also a major predictor of their task performance. High participation in decision making and high involvement in learning are less likely to occur when the student group is of very large size, such as the entire classroom of thirty to forty or more students taught at the same time by one teacher, or where the school's scheduling does not structure frequent and systematic face-to-face meetings among teachers devoted to schoolwide educational topics. Isolation of students from one another during learning, virtually unavoidable in the traditional whole-class format of instruction, and of teachers during teaching reduces their overall effectiveness. Such isolation can be prevented by a variety of organizational arrangements that sustain collective learning and professional growth through interaction with peers and the giving and receiving of feedback (Elmore & associates, 1991); Epstein, 1988; Lieberman, 1988; Rosenholtz, 1989; Schmuck & Runkel, 1985; Schmuck & Schmuck, 1992; Shachar & Sharan, in press; Slavin, 1990).

DECENTRALIZATION OF DECISION MAKING AS A PREVENTIVE STRATEGY

The variety of cooperative learning methods and applications presented in this volume reflects the range of needs arising from the decentralization of instruction. Since cooperative learning methods cultivate direct communication among peers, teachers are relieved of a significant part of the control function that traditional instruction requires of them. Redefinition of the students' role in cooperative learning is a mirror image of the redefinition of the teacher's role that occurs when cooperative learning is practiced competently. This redefinition frees teachers to invest a greater portion of their attention in students' learning instead of in discipline. To date, no systematic research has documented the manifestations or degree of disciplinary problems in the cooperative classroom. All accounts have it that such problems decline dramatically. If that is substantiated by subsequent research, it means that cooperative learning performs a significant preventive function from which both teachers and students benefit greatly. Cooperative learning prevents the emergence of cycles of negative feelings and behavior among teachers and students that affect attitudes toward, and gratification from, teaching and learning (Schmuck & Schmuck, 1992). It prevents negative perceptions of school as a workplace or as a place for learning, and instead it cultivates a sense of acceptance, of belonging, and of efficacy on the part of teachers and students. Cooperative learning prevents boredom, which is one of the truly destructive maladies affecting schooling in our society (Sarason, 1983). The preventive effects of cooperative learning can foster more positive involvement in learning than the investment of considerable resources in remedial programs.

TEACHER PROFESSIONALISM

Cooperative learning methods help teachers become more learner centered and less tied to the transmission of prescribed subject matter. It also helps teachers become less concentrated on themselves as presenters of information and less concerned with how they present themselves. Greater concentration on students' learning needs is indicative of increased professionalism on the part of teachers. Indeed, one of the most decisive measures of professionalism in most of the human-service professions is the practitioner's ability to attend closely and with empathy to the needs of the client and not to be highly invested in the presentation of self. Since this is admittedly difficult for many people to achieve, the acquisition of concepts, insight, and skills that foster this "decentered" level of functioning is distinctly beneficial to both practitioner and client. Research found that teachers feel more efficacious when they use cooperative learning methods because it affords them the means by which they can "reach" many more students and engage them in learning, unlike traditional forms of instruction where a significant portion of the class remains peripheral to the learning process. Many more students in the cooperative classroom become engaged in learning, in part because teachers significantly limit their own centrality and domination of the classroom process. Instead of constant questioning and talking, teachers encourage students to talk to one another (Harel, 1992; Hertz-Lazarowitz & Shachar, 1990).

Subject-matter-oriented educators are likely to find this thesis paradoxical. How can less attention to subject-matter presentation lead to increased teacher efficacy and to increased student achievement? Yet that is precisely the kind of psychological logic that bureaucratic logic is unlikely to fathom. This is not to say that teachers who employ cooperative learning are released from careful preparation of subject-matter resources for their students, and that they should not pay attention to the quality of the substance students study. In fact, one of the impediments to the large-scale dissemination of some cooperative learning methods is the schools' relative lack of exciting resources for the pursuit of information in many content areas. The chief purveyor of knowledge in the world, the schools, is often a pauper in knowledge resources. Whatever be the richness of the resources available at any given site, cooperative learning cannot be implemented reasonably well without adequate attention to the resources teachers will make available to students for learning. That approach is still a far cry from having teachers invest their energies primarily in their preparation of subject matter for the students, instead of enabling students to proceed by actively pursuing information relevant to their studies.

It is no surprise that teachers' main attention is focused on the preparation of their own presentations to the students, rather than on the students themselves. The school as an organization is built around the teacher, not around the learner, contrary to public claims made by schools. What the teacher is to do, when, and to whom are the primary elements on which the school bases its entire program. Whatever students might need or find interesting rarely stands at the center of the school's organizational plans (Sarason, 1993a). To this extent, schools impede the professionalization of teachers by keeping the teachers as the central focus of the system. This is another observation about traditional schooling that is certain to be viewed as a paradox by many students of education. Only when our attention is directed at what teachers are to do for and with the students do the students become the main object of our professional thinking. The truly professional teacher knows how to build the classroom system around the learners instead of keeping herself or himself on center stage (Banathy, 1991; Sarason, 1983, 1993b).

GOAL CLARIFICATION

Teachers who use cooperative learning methods are called upon to assist groups of students to set goals for themselves in order to direct their collective and individual efforts. Goal clarification is one of the most constructive ways teachers can facilitate productive work by student groups. The group's goal also defines the relationships between its members in terms of who does what and when, as well as setting the criterion for groups to assess their own progress. Goals also make it possible for groups to benefit from their members' heterogeneity by directing their diverse personal talents, interests, and knowledge toward the accomplishment of the collective purpose. "A shared commitment to common purpose makes diversity tolerable, and the clearer and stronger the commitment, the more diversity can be tolerated and made a source of strength" (Thelen, 1981, p. 132).

REFLECTION ON GROUP PROCESS

Most of the authors in this volume underscore the need to have group members identify the problems they experience when they are working together by "processing" the group's behavior. Such processing paves the way for improved effectiveness and productivity by making group members aware of how they behave and what they think would improve their work in the group (Graves & Graves, 1985; Johnson & Johnson, 1987).

Helping groups process their behavior is not a traditional role for teachers. To do so requires that teachers, first and foremost, learn to see groups of students, rather than thinking about them exclusively as individuals. Teachers are rarely given any preparation needed for considering small groups of students as social structures that emerge from interactions among their members, and not just as a collection of personalities. Teachers can lead groups to define and interpret their collective goals and their patterns of working with one another. To do so, they must understand that a group goal is one that is recognized and accepted by its members, not a purpose that was assigned by the teacher. Even if a group signs up to study a particular topic, it will have to clarify to itself several times precisely what it intends to do and how it plans to accomplish its goal. Group members must have opportunities to express their preferences as part of the group's collective goal. Moreover, groups' goals change with time and experience, and the teacher's need to help the group clarify its goal is reactivated. In the Group Investigation method, for example, each stage in the group's progress entails some change in the teacher's role, as well as in the reciprocal relationship between the teacher's and the students' roles (Sharan & Sharan, 1992, p. 95).

GROUP INFLUENCE ON MEMBERS' BEHAVIOR

Just as groups frequently need the teacher's help to redefine their goals and procedures and to process their relationships with one another, so too the groups will need assistance to deal successfully with disruptive behavior on the part of this or that student. When teachers truly perceive groups, not individuals, as the functional units of learning in the cooperative classroom, they will recognize that the occasional misbehavior of some member should be dealt with by the group itself without having the teacher intervene and separate that individual from the group as a form of punishment. Helping groups clarify behavioral norms with their members will contribute to the groups' development and make it possible for them to operate with greater skill and effectiveness for their own benefit. It will also prevent groups from making a scapegoat out of any particular member for whatever reason. Students should not be made into "problem children" (Thelen, 1981). Their behavior is a problem for the group. An approach such as this is fully consistent with the method described in this volume for having cooperative learning make a significant contribution to students' moral development (chapter 9).

TEACHERS AS OBSERVERS

The teachers of cooperative classrooms must constantly observe how groups work. Observation replaces the traditional role of presenting information. Observation will indicate to the teacher when groups' activities are more or less educative, when groups are learning or have become bogged down in unproductive labor. The latter condition emerges in most groups at one time or another, as anyone knows who has participated in the work of committees. At such times, the teacher should intervene and assist groups to redirect their energies and procedures and to redefine their goals. Facilitative intervention requires astute assessment of a group's state, of the nature of the interactions among group members, and of the emotional climate of the group, whether it is supportive or not of each member's work and thinking.

The way in which a teacher intervenes in a group's work will be directed by how the teacher thinks about the group's progress and where the group should be at any given time in carrying out its plan of work. Of course, this assessment of the group's stage of operation will differ from one cooperative learning method to the next, or it will differ as a function of the particular model of cooperative groupwork that the teacher envisions. Almost invariably, intervention in a group's work will seek to review the group's movement forward toward its goal as set forth in its plan or in the teacher's mental model. The teacher should not simply tell the group how to reorganize or what it should do next. A more effective way is to question the group members about how they see the group's problems and help them suggest ways to overcome them (Cohen, 1986; Thelen, 1981).

APPLYING DIFFERENT METHODS WHEN APPROPRIATE

This book presents a wide range of cooperative learning methods and applications. It should be obvious that no one method is appropriate for each and every instructional goal or purpose. No one method is recommended for achieving all of the following goals: teaching reading and writing skills, studying specific information related to a particular topic, cultivating concepts that cut across academic disciplines, engaging students in the systematic search for information and in synthesizing information from a variety of sources, and planning and conducting experiments or demonstrations. Different cooperative methods should be selected for achieving these different goals (Graves & Graves, 1985; Kagan, 1985). Also, teachers certainly must make use of teaching methods other than cooperative learning when the circumstances require them, such as short lectures, individualized methods of instruction, and others.

Choice of the instructional method appropriate for given aspects of classroom teaching and learning rests with the teacher. There can be no substitute for teachers' broad grasp of the different methods available and how they serve different needs and goals. This book encourages an eclectic approach, recommending not only that different cooperative methods be used for different goals, but even that several methods be combined and integrated, each one addressing that feature of the curriculum for which it is most appropriate.

For example, a teacher integrating several cooperative learning methods may choose to follow the CIRC procedure for language arts development in the early part of the day, with students grouped by reading levels. Later on in the day, the students regroup, based on their interest in a subtopic they are investigating, as part of a Group Investigation of a broad unit. Some groups may be involved in brainstorming procedural plans, while others may be conducting a summary discussion. The teacher may ask all groups to read some specific material and discuss it, using the Jigsaw structure. Cooperative learning methods provide teachers with enormous flexibility and variability that can sustain students' involvement in learning activities over long periods of time.

COOPERATION AMONG TEACHERS

Almost all of the authors whose work appears in this volume emphasize the critical importance of teachers' cooperation for mutual assistance in planning, implementing, coordinating, and evaluating their work with cooperative learning methods. No classroom is a self-contained unit, even though the prevailing bureaucratic organization of schools, particularly at the secondary level, would make it seem so. The sustained use of cooperative learning in the classroom ultimately demands a high degree of coordination among teachers on a variety of topics, such as curricular continuity, the physical structure of the classroom, the continuity of students' experiences, and expectations regarding instruction. Teachers must agree that cooperative learning is a legitimate approach to instruction at their school, and that it is school policy to support its implementation. Otherwise, teachers will feel that they are bucking the system or their colleagues, and they will gradually or rapidly abandon their use of cooperative learning methods. Moreover, the need for curricular redesign necessary for transforming study topics initially directed at individuals into projects or tasks for groups makes demands on teachers' time and energy that can only be met by cooperation among teachers. Finally, since cooperative learning is a more sophisticated form of instruction than whole-class direct teaching, teachers will require feedback and support from colleagues (Sharan & Hertz-Lazarowitz, 1982; Sharan & Sharan, 1991).

Schoolwide coordination of curricular and instructional policy is not regularly an inherent part of teachers' professional repertoire. Many teachers are likely to perceive this role as foreign to their professional training and status, a role that cannot legitimately be expected of them. There is a growing awareness that change in teachers' professional role at the school level is a prerequisite for affecting the practice of instruction in the classroom (Darling-Hammond, 1988; Elmore, 1991; Murphy, 1991, Sarason, 1990; Sykes, 1991).

Teaching and learning in school automatically arouse mental images of solo occupations (Sarason, 1982; chapter 19 in this volume). As a general principle, it is unreasonable to anticipate that teachers will understand and seek to implement cooperation among students when there is no counterpart in their own experience as teachers (Sarason, 1972).

THE PRINCIPAL

Just as teachers must adopt a new set of images regarding the nature of instruction in the classroom, principals are being called upon to alter their conception of their role as organizational leaders. They must begin viewing the teaching staff as engaged in an ongoing process of problem solving, decision making, and coordination across subject disciplines and grade levels. That change is necessary to facilitate the needed change in teachers' roles from information transmitters in single classrooms to members of interacting teams for the improvement of the school as a whole. Students cannot be helped to function cooperatively in teams by teachers who are solo practitioners, and teachers cannot cooperate with colleagues to set and implement school instructional policy when principals relate to them as a collection of individuals whose decision-making responsibility ends at the classroom door.

NEW ROLES FOR TEACHERS: A SUMMARY

The role of the teacher in the cooperative learning classroom and school is expanded considerably compared to the role designated by traditional instruction and school organization. This expanded role includes the following functions, although not all of them will appear in each and every cooperative learning method:

1. Conceive of the classroom as a system of small groups as the functional learning units.

2. Redesign curricular materials to be appropriate for group-centered learning that requires cooperation instead of being aimed exclusively at individuals.

3. Identify and locate a wide variety of resources for learning beyond textbook-related assignments.

4. Involve student groups in planning their topics of study and the process of their work.

5. Monitor groups to assure free exchange of information, mutual helping, and maximum participation by all members within the group.

6. Help groups to reflect on the interactions among their members and to receive feedback from one another on their performance as group members, in order to enable groups to develop and become more congenial and effective.

7. Select the cooperative learning methods most appropriate for the curricular materials to be studied. Combine or integrate two or more methods as circumstances require to afford students the best possible means for pursuing the study of subjects at hand.

8. Advise student groups on the selection of creative means for organizing and presenting their work to their peers and to the teacher for evaluation.

9. Participate in one or more teams of teachers who plan and implement cooperative learning methods in their classrooms, as well as engage in problem solving and decision making about instruction on a schoolwide basis.

By performing these functions, teachers will gradually move their classes along the path of development where, eventually, students can operate as a community of inquirers (Thelen, 1981). This means that students will have acquired norms of mutual assistance and constructive participation in the pursuit of knowledge as an intellectual and social value.

REFERENCES

Banathy, B. (1992). *A systems view of education*. Englewood Cliffs, NJ: Educational Technology Publications.

Cohen, E. (1986). *Designing groupwork*. New York: Teachers College Press.

Darling-Hammond, L. (1988). Policy and professionalism. In A. Lieberman (Ed.), *Building a professional culture in schools*. New York: Teachers College Press.

Dewey, J. (1943). *The school and society*. Chicago: The University of Chicago Press.

DeCharms, R. (1976). *Enhancing motivation: Change in the classroom*. New York: Irvington, Halsted-Wiley.

Deci, E., & Ryan, R. (1985). *Intrinsic motivation and self-determination in human behavior*. New York: Plenum.

Elmore, R., & Associates (Eds.). (1991). *Restructuring schools: The next generation of educational reform*. San Francisco: Jossey-Bass.

Epstein, J. (1988). Effective schools or effective students: Dealing with diversity. In R. Haskins & D. MacRae (Eds.), *Policies for america's public schools: Teachers, equity and indicators* (pp. 89–126). Norwood, NJ: Ablex.

Graves, N., & Graves, T. (1985). Creating a cooperative learning environment: An ecological approach. In S. Slavin, S. Sharan, S. Kagan, R. Hertz-Lazarowitz, C. Webb & R. Schmuck (Eds.), *Learning to cooperate, cooperating to learn*. New York: Plenum.

Harel, Y. (1992). Teacher talk in the cooperative learning classroom. In C. Kessler (Ed.), *Cooperative language learning* (pp. 153–162). Englewood Cliffs, NJ: Prentice-Hall.

Hertz-Lazarowitz, R., & Shachar, H. (1990). Teachers' verbal behavior in cooperative and whole class instruction. In S. Sharan (Ed.), *Cooperative learning: Theory and research*. New York: Praeger.

Johnson, D., & Johnson, R. (1987). *Learning together and alone* (2nd ed.). Englewood Cliffs, NJ: Prentice-Hall.

Kagan, S. (1985). Dimensions of cooperative classroom structures. In R. Slavin, S. Sharan, S. Kagan, R. Hertz-Lazarowitz, C. Webb, & R. Schmuck (Eds.), *Learning to cooperate, cooperating to learn*. New York: Plenum Press.

Lieberman, A. (Ed.). (1988). *Building a professional climate in schools*. New York: Teachers College Press.

Murphy, J. (1991). *Restructuring schools*. New York: Teachers College Press.

Noddings, N. (1992). *The challenge to care in schools*. New York: Teachers College Press.

Rosenholtz, S. (1989). *Teachers workplace*. New York: Teachers College Press.

Sarason, S. (1972). *The creation of settings and the future societies*. San Francisco: Jossey-Bass.

Sarason, S. (1982). *The culture of the school and the problem of change*. Boston: Allyn and Bacon (2nd edition).

Sarason. S. (1983). *Schooling in america: Scapegoat and salvation* New York: The Free Press.

Sarason, S. (1985). *Caring and compassion in clinical practice*. San Francisco: Jossey-Bass.

Sarason, S. (1990). *The predictable failure of educational reform*. San Francisco: Jossey-Bass.

Sarason, S. (1993a). *Letters to a serious education president*. Newbury Park, CA: Sage.

Sarason, S. (1993b). *The case for change: Rethinking the preparation of educators*. San Francisco: Jossey-Bass.

Schmuck, R., & Runkel, P. (1985). *Handbook of organizational development in schools*. (3rd ed.). Palo Alto, CA: Mayfield.

Schmuck, R., & Schmuck, P. (1992). *Group processes in the classroom* (6th ed.). Dubuque, IA: Brown.

Shachar, H., & Sharan, S. (In press). Talking, relating, achieving: Effects of cooperative learning and whole-class instruction. *Cognition and Instruction*.

Sharan, S., & Hertz-Lazarowitz, R. (1982). Effects of an instructional change project on teachers' behavior, attitudes and perceptions. *Journal of Applied Behavioral Science, 18*, 185–201.

Sharan, S., & Sharan, Y. (1991). Changing instructional methods and the culture of the school. In N. Wyner (Ed.), *Current Perspectives on School Culture*. Cambridge, MA: Brookline Books.

Sharan, S., & Shaulov, A. (1990). Cooperative learning, motivation to learn, and academic achievement. In S. Sharan (Ed.), *Cooperative learning: Theory and research* (pp. 173–202). New York: Praeger.

Sharan, Y., & Sharan, S. (1992). *Expanding cooperative learning through group investigation*. New York: Teachers College Press.

Slavin, R. (1990). *Cooperative learning: Theory, research and practice*. Englewood Cliffs, NJ: Prentice-Hall.

Sykes, G. (1991). Fostering teacher professionalism in schools. In R. Elmore & Associates (Eds.), *Restructuring schools: The next generation of educational reform*. San Francisco: Jossey-Bass.

Thelen, H. (1981). *The classroom society*. London: Croom-Helm.

Selected Bibliography

Anderson, M. (1989). *Partnerships: Teambuilding at the computer.* Arlington, VA: Ma-Jo Press.

Andrini, B., with Kagan, S. (1990). *Cooperative learning and math: A multi-structural approach.* San Juan Capistrano, CA: Resources for Teachers.

Aronson, E., Blaney, N., Stephan, C., Sikes, J., & Snapp, M. (1978). *The Jigsaw classroom.* Beverly Hills, CA: Sage Publications.

Artzt, A., & Newman, C. M. (1990). *How to use cooperative learning in the mathematics class.* Reston, VA: National Council of Teachers of Mathematics.

Brody, C. & Davidson, N. (Eds.)(1998). *Professional development for cooperative learning: Issues and approaches.* Albany, NY: State University of New York Press.

Brubacher, M., Payne, R., & Rickett, K. (Eds.) (1990). *Perspectives on small group learning.* Oakville, Ontario: Rubicon.

Cohen, E. G. (1986). *Designing groupwork: Strategies for the heterogeneous classroom.* New York: Teachers College Press.

Davidson, N. (Ed.). (1990). *Cooperative learning in mathematics.* Menlo Park, CA: Addison-Wesley.

Davidson, N., & Worsham, T. (Eds.). (1992). *Enhancing thinking through cooperative learning.* New York: Teachers College Press.

Gibbs, J. (1978). *Tribes, a process for peer involvement.* Santa Rosa, CA: Center Source Publications.

Graves, N., & Graves, T. (1988). *Getting there together: A source book and guide for creating a cooperative classroom.* Santa Cruz: Cooperative College of California.

Graves, N., & Graves, T. (1990). *What is cooperative learning? Tips for teachers and trainers* (2nd ed.). Santa Cruz: Cooperative College of California.

Hertz-Lazarowitz, R., & Miller, N. (Eds.). (1992). *Interaction in cooperative groups: The theoretical anatomy of group learning.* New York: Cambridge University Press.

Johnson, D., & Johnson, R. (1987). *Learning together and alone* (2nd ed.). Englewood Cliffs, NJ: Prentice Hall.

Johnson, D. W., & Johnson, R. (1992). *Creative controversy: Intellectual challenge in the classroom.* Edina, MN: Interaction Book Company.

Johnson, D. W., Johnson, R., & Holubec, E. (1992). *Advanced cooperative learning* (2nd ed.). Edina, MN: Interaction Book Company.

Kagan, S. (1992). *Cooperative learning: Resources for teachers.* San Juan Capistrano, CA: Resources for Teachers.

Kessler, C. (Ed.). (1992). *Cooperative language learning.* Englewood Cliffs, NJ: Prentice Hall Regents.

Madden, N. A., Slavin, R. E., & Stevens, R. J. (1986). *Cooperative Integrated Reading and Composition: Teacher's manual.* Baltimore, MD: Johns Hopkins University, Center for Research on Elementary and Middle Schools.

Male, M., Johnson, D., Johnson, R., & Anderson, M. (1986). *Cooperative learning and computers: An activity guide for teachers.* Santa Cruz, CA: Educational Apple-cations.

Mastny, A., Kahn, S., & Sherman, S. (1992). *SCIENCE TEAMS: Lessons in environmental science and cooperative learning.* New Brunswick, NJ: Rutgers University Consortium for Educational Equity.

McCabe, M., & Rhoades, J. (1992). *The cooperative classroom: Social and academic activities.* Bloomington, IN: National Education Service.

Orlick, T. (1978). *The cooperative sports and games book.* New York: Pantheon Books.

Orlick, T. (1981). *The second cooperative sports and games book.* New York: Pantheon Books.

Pedersen, J., & Digby, A. (Eds.). (in press). *Cooperative learning in secondary schools: Theory and practice.* New York: Garland.

Putnam, J., & Burke, J. (1992). *Organizing and managing classroom learning communities.* New York: McGraw-Hill.

Reid, J., Forrestal, P., & Cook, J. (1990). *Small group learning in the classroom.* Concord, Ontario: Irwin Publishing.

Robertson, L., Regan, S., Freeman, M., & Contestable, J. (1993). *Number power: A cooperative approach to mathematics and social development.* Menlo Park, CA: Addison-Wesley. Five books for grades 2 through 6.

Schmuck, R., & Runkel, P. (1985). *The handbook of organizational development in schools* (3rd ed.). Palo Alto, CA: Mayfield.

Schmuck, R. A., & Schmuck, P. A. (1992). *Group processes in the classroom* (6th ed.). Dubuque, IA: Wm. C. Brown.

Sharan, S. (Ed.). (1990). *Cooperative learning: Theory and research.* New York: Praeger.

Sharan, S., Hare, P., Webb, C. D., & Hertz-Lazarowitz, R. (Eds.). (1980). *Cooperation in education.* Provo, UT: Brigham Young University Press.

Sharan, S., Kussell, P., Hertz-Lazarowitz, R., Bejarano, Y., Raviv, S., & Sharan, Y. (1984). *Cooperative learning in the classroom: Research in desegregated schools.* Hillsdale, NJ: Lawrence Erlbaum Associates.

Sharan, Y., & Sharan, S. (1992). *Expanding cooperative learning through group investigation.* New York: Teachers College Press.

Slavin, R. (1983). *Cooperative learning.* New York: Longman.

Slavin, R. (1986). *Using Student Team Learning* (3rd ed.). Baltimore, MD: Johns

Hopkins University, Center for Research on Elementary and Middle Schools.

Slavin, R. (1990). *Cooperative learning: Theory, research, and practice.* Englewood Cliffs, NJ: Prentice Hall.

Slavin, R. E., Leavey, M. B., & Madden, N. A. (1986). *Team Accelerated Instruction—Mathematics.* Watertown, MA: Mastery Education Corporation.

Slavin, R., Madden, N., Dolan, L. & Wasik, B. (1996). *Every child, every school: Success for all.* Thousand Oaks, CA: Corwin Press.

Slavin, R., Sharan, S., Kagan, S., Hertz-Lazarowitz, R., Webb, C., & Schmuck, R. (Eds.). (1985). *Learning to cooperate, cooperating to learn.* New York: Plenum Press.

Solomon, D., Watson, M., Schaps, E., Battistich, V., & Solomon, J. (1990). Cooperative learning as part of a comprehensive program designed to promote prosocial development. In S. Sharan (Ed.), *Cooperative learning: Theory and research.* New York: Praeger.

Stahl, R. (Ed.). (1993). *Cooperative learning in the social studies: A handbook.* Menlo Park, CA: Addison-Wesley.

Stanford, G. (1977). *Developing effective classroom groups.* New York: A. & W. Visual Library.

Thelen, H. (1981). *The classroom society.* London: Croom Helm.

Weissglass, J. (1990). *Mathematics for elementary teaching: A small-group approach for teaching.* Dubuque, IA: Kendall-Hunt.

Author Index

Abbott, M., 325, 328, 331
Adams, M., 179, 191
Allen, J., 198, 209
Amabile, T., 147, 155
Ames, G., 72, 80
Anderson, M., 269, 279, 349, 350
Archambault, R., 98, 113
Arends, J., 326, 334
Armbruster, B., 202, 210
Aronson, E., 35, 37, 50, 202, 210, 349
Artzt, A., 349

Baker, L., 202, 210
Banathy, B., 323, 328, 332, 339, 341, 346
Barnes, D., 137, 155
Barth, R., 304, 309, 316
Bartlett, J., 293, 298
Battistich, V., 154–56, 351
Bejarano, Y., 199, 200, 204, 210, 350
Bellanca, J., 293, 296, 298
Bennett, B., 293, 298
Bennett, C., 293, 298
Bennion, J., 325, 332
Berger, J., 84, 95
Bever, T., 204, 211
Blaney, N., 50, 202, 210, 349
Bohm, D., 213, 225

Bowering, G., 225
Brandt, R., 159, 175
Breen, M., 198, 210
Brewer, M., 149, 155
Bridge, C., 184, 192
Brown, A., 159, 170, 175, 202
Brown, C., 184, 192
Brown, D., 154, 155
Bruner, J., 173, 176
Burke, C., 179, 192
Burke, J., 286–87, 289, 299
Burns, M., 251, 253, 264

Caine, G., 284, 298
Caine, R., 284, 298
Calderon, M., 304, 309, 316
Campbell, R., 325, 328, 332
Campione, J., 159, 175
Canale, M., 200, 206, 210
Caracheo, F., 325, 328, 331
Carr, E., 160, 175
Carrell, P., 203, 210
Carrithers, C., 204, 211
Catanzarite, L., 86, 96, 159
Center for Special Education
  Technology, 271, 279
Chall, J., 179, 191
Clark, D., 328, 332

Cocking, R., 100, 113
Cobb, P., 247, 266
Cohen, B., 84, 95
Cohen, D., 319, 327, 332
Cohen, E., 84–86, 88–89, 95–96, 144,
    149, 155, 159, 175, 329, 332, 338,
    343, 346, 349
Cohen, M., 328–30, 332
Collins, B., 73, 80
Conley, S., 318–19, 322, 332
Contestable, J., 256, 265
Continuous Electron Beam
    Accelerator Facility Manual, 233,
    244
Conway, J., 330, 333
Cook, C., 214, 225
Cook, J., 36–37, 50, 214, 225
Cooperative Learning magazine, 285,
    295, 298, 299
Corwin, R., 328, 332
Costa, A., 284, 286, 296, 298
Coughlin, E., 112–13
Crandall, D., 326, 333
Crookes, G., 206, 210
Cross, B., 226, 244
Crowley, P., 179, 192
Cuban, L., 318, 326, 332
Cunningham, J., 185, 191

Dainutis, J., 214, 225
Danks, J., 204, 210, 332
Darling-Hammond, L., 329, 332, 345–
    46
Davey, R., 189, 190–91
David, J., 329, 332
Davidson, N., 247, 264–65, 349
DeAvila, F., 91, 96
DeCharms, R., 338, 346
Deci, E., 338, 346
Dees, R., 247, 265
Delucchi, K., 154, 156
Derry, S., 170, 175
Deshler, D., 173, 175
Deutsch, M., 52, 64, 80
Dewey, J., 67–68, 80, 338, 348
Dias, P., 216, 225
Digby, A., xiii, 350
DiPietro, R., 199, 210

Dishon, D., 293, 299, 316
Dishner, E., 190, 192
Dole, J., 184, 191
Doughty, C., 199, 210
Dowdy, S., 214, 225
Duffy, G., 170, 176, 184, 191
Duncan, S., 91, 96
Duran, R., 313, 316

Ebmeier, H., 12, 18
Ellis, E., 159, 173, 175
Elmore, R., 318, 326, 328, 331, 332,
    339, 345–46
End, L., 204, 210
Epstein, J., 339, 347
EQUALS, 255, 265

Farivar, S., 305–6, 310
Farnish, A., 25, 29, 33, 179, 203, 211,
    308, 317
Fleming, T., 325, 332
Flinders, D., 329, 332
Fogarty, R., 296, 298
Forrestal, P., 36, 37, 50, 214, 221,
    225, 350
Francisco, R., 326, 334
Freeman, M., 250, 256, 265
Fuchs, I., 304, 317
Fullan, M., 97, 152, 304, 308–9, 313,
    317, 329, 332

Gallimore, R., 114, 156
Gardner, H., 85, 96
GEMS, 255, 265
Gibbs, J., 284, 304–5, 317
Gickling, E., 22, 32
Good, T., 12, 18
Goodlad, J., 321, 328, 331–32
Goodman, K., 178, 179
Goodman, Y., 178, 179
Gottlieb, J., 22, 32
Grabe, W., 202, 210
Graves, D., 28, 32
Graves, N., 99, 113, 283, 290–91, 293,
    295, 298, 325, 342, 344, 347, 349
Graves, T., 99, 113, 283, 290–91, 293,
    295, 298, 325, 342, 344, 347, 349
Greene, D., 147, 155

Grouws, D., 12, 18
Guskey, T., 330, 333

Hall, G., 304, 313, 317
Hare, P., 37, 50, 113
Harel, Y., 340, 347
Harper, G., 159, 175
Harris, K., 173, 175
Harste, J., 179, 192
Harvey, G., 326, 333
Hawley, W., 318, 329–30, 333
Heid, M., 263, 265
Hertz-Lazarowitz, R., 30, 37, 50, 113, 210, 244, 304–5, 307, 309, 317, 333–34, 340, 345, 349–51
Heymsfeld, C., 179, 192
Hibbard, K., 288, 296, 298
Hildebrandt, C., 153, 156
Holubec, E., 51–52, 54–55, 57, 224, 227, 350
Horak, V., 21, 32
Hord, S., 304, 313, 317
Howe, A., 214, 220, 225
Hoy, W., 328, 333
Huberman, A., 331, 333
Huhtala, J., 112–13
Hutcheon, L., 212, 225

Jacobson, S., 330, 333
Janis, I., 68, 80
Johnson, D., 51–52, 54–55, 57, 59–60, 62, 64–65, 67, 71–73, 75–76, 80–81, 144, 154–56, 158–59, 175, 192, 200, 210, 227–28, 244, 263, 265, 268, 279, 293, 295, 303–4, 317–18, 325, 333, 342, 347, 349–50
Johnson, D. D., 181, 192
Johnson, F., 65, 81, 317
Johnson, L., 293, 298
Johnson, R., 51, 54–55, 57, 59–60, 62, 65, 67, 71–73, 75–76, 81, 144, 154–56, 158–59, 175, 210, 227–28, 244, 263, 265, 268, 279, 293, 295, 298, 303–4, 318, 325, 342, 347, 349–50
Johnson, S., 327, 333
Johnston, B., 214, 225
Jones, B., 160, 175
Joyce, B., 97, 113, 309, 313, 317

Kagan, M., 99, 116, 119, 125, 133
Kagan, S., 37, 50, 113, 116, 119, 123, 125, 129–30, 132–33, 168, 175, 227, 232, 244, 251, 269, 279, 293, 295, 298, 317, 334, 344, 347, 350–51
Kahn, S., 227, 244, 350
Karsenty, G., 227, 244
Karweit, N., 5, 19
Kelley, T., 106, 113
Kessler, C., 350
Kreidler, W., 295, 298–99
Kroll, D., 247, 265
Kussell, P., 210, 350
Kyle, W., 227, 244

Lazarowitz, R., 227, 244
Leavey, M., 22, 31, 33
Leechor, C., 89, 96
Lepper, M., 147, 155
Levine, T., 205, 210
Levita, I., 279–80
Leyser, Y., 22, 32
Lieberman, A., 327, 329, 333, 339, 347
Little, J., 304, 317, 329, 333
Long, M., 199, 206, 210
Lortie, D., 327–28, 333
Lotan, R., 86, 89, 96, 159, 175
Lyman, F., 234, 244, 295, 299

McCabe, M., 293, 299, 350
McNeil, L., 319, 331, 333
McTighe, J., 234, 244
Madden, N., 22, 25, 29, 30–33, 179, 192, 308, 317, 350
Maheady, L., 159, 175
Male, M., 267, 279, 350
Mallette, B., 159, 175
Maruyama, G., 51, 318, 333
Marzano, R., 106, 113, 157, 159, 175
Mastny, A., 227, 244, 350
Mevarech, Z., 279, 280
Meyer, J., 322–33
Miel, A., 111, 113
Miles, M., 52, 65, 329, 331, 333
Miller, N., 149, 155, 349
Miller, R., 21, 32
Miskel, C., 328, 333
Moe, T., 328, 333

Moore, D., 185, 191
Moorman, C., 293, 299
Morgan, G., 328, 333
Mosenthal, P., 179, 192
Moshman, D., 173, 176
Murphy, J., 318, 326, 328, 330, 333, 345, 347
Murray, F., 72, 80

Naisbitt, J., 284, 299
National Assessment of Educational Progress, 172, 192
National Council of Teachers of Mathematics, 245–46, 254, 265
Nelson, D., 51, 65, 318, 333
Nelson Le-Gall, S., 305, 317
Newell, L., 325, 332
Nicholls, J., 147, 155
Noddings, N., 337, 347
Nunan, D., 198, 206

O'Leary, P., 304, 306, 316
Oakes, J., 22, 32
Ogle, D., 160, 175
Oickle, E., 5, 19
Okebukola, P., 5, 18
Olsen, R., 104, 113
Olshtain, E., 205, 210
Orlick, T., 296, 299, 350

Palinscar, A., 169, 175
Payne, R., 349
Pearson, P., 181, 184, 191, 192
Peck, M., 287, 299
Pedersen, J., xiii, 350
Perrault, R., 5, 18
Pica, T., 199, 210
Pickering, D., 159, 175
Porter, P., 199, 210
Presseisen, B., 157–58, 176
Pressley, M., 173, 175
Putnam, J., 286–87, 289, 299, 350

Raviv, S., 210, 350
Raywid, M., 330, 333
Readence, J., 190, 192
Regan, S., 256, 265
Reid, J., 36–37, 50, 350

Resnick, L., 157, 176
Rhoades, J., 293, 298
Robertson, L., 256, 265, 350
Roehler, L., 170, 184, 191
Rogoff, B., 142, 155
Rosenholtz, S., 328, 334, 339, 347
Ross, G., 173, 176
Rowan, B., 322, 333
Runkel, P., 304, 317, 326, 329, 334, 339, 347
Russell, S., 242, 244
Ryan, R., 338, 346

Sarason, S., 318–19, 321–22, 324, 327–28, 330–31, 334, 337, 340–41, 347
Saxl, E., 329, 333
Schaps, E., 154–55, 351
Schmuck, P., 99, 113, 210, 284, 286, 299, 340, 347, 350
Schmuck, R., 50, 99, 113, 210, 286, 299, 304, 317, 326, 329, 334, 339–40, 347, 350–51
Schneidwind, N., 295, 299
Schon, D., 309, 317
Schumaker, J., 173, 175
Schwab, J., 293, 299
Seliger, H., 199, 210
Serra, M., 263, 265
Shachar, H., 199, 211, 222, 321, 326, 333–34, 339–40, 347
Sharan, S., 32, 37, 50, 98, 112–13, 137, 155, 158, 176, 199, 200, 203–4, 210–11, 214, 222, 225, 240, 244, 304, 308–9, 317–19, 324–26, 342, 345, 347–48, 350–51
Sharan, Y., 98, 112–13, 137, 155, 158, 176, 200, 204, 210–11, 214, 222, 240, 244, 304, 308, 317–19, 324–25, 329, 330, 334, 338, 342, 345, 347–48, 350
Shaulov, A., 100, 113, 199, 211, 338
Shaw, V., 130, 133
Sherman, A., 234, 242, 244
Sherman, L., 5, 18
Sherman, S., 227, 234, 242, 244, 350
Short, E., 173, 176
Showers, B., 304, 309, 313, 317
Sigel, I., 100, 106, 113
Sikes, J., 50, 202, 210, 349

Sizer, T., 326, 331, 334
Skon, L., 318, 333
Slavin, R., 4–6, 19, 21–22, 24–25, 29, 30–33, 37, 50, 158, 176, 178–79, 192, 199, 200, 202–3, 211, 244, 306, 308, 317–18, 325, 334, 339, 348, 350–51
Smith, F., 179, 182
Smith, K., 51, 54, 65, 67, 81
Snapp, M., 50, 202, 210, 349
Snider, B., 154, 156
Solomon, D., 153–56, 351
Solomon, J., 154, 156
Spiegel, D., 179, 192
Spillane, J., 319, 326, 332
Spolsky, B., 193, 195, 197, 199, 200, 206, 211
Stahl, R., xiii, 351
Stanford, G., 284, 296, 299, 351
Stanne, M., 268, 279
Steiner, J., 205, 210
Stephan, C., 50, 202, 210, 349
Stern, D., 279–80
Stern, H., 198, 211
Sternberg, R., 85, 96
Stevahn, L., 293, 298
Stevens, R., 25, 29–30, 32–33, 179, 192, 203, 211, 308, 317, 350
Stiegelbauer, S., 304, 308–9, 313, 317
Swain, M., 199, 206, 210–11
Sykes, G., 327, 329–30, 334, 345, 348

Tarone, E., 197, 211
Tharp, R., 114, 152, 156

Thelen, H., 98–99, 106, 112, 114, 156, 343, 346, 351
Theobold, J., 22, 32
Thomas, M., 5, 18
Tierney, R., 190, 192
Todd, F., 137, 155
Townsend, D., 204, 211
Tuck, P., 154–55

Watson, D., 179, 192
Watson, G., 52, 65
Watson, M., 153–56, 351
Webb, C., 37, 50, 350
Webb, N., 247, 266, 305–6, 316
Weick, K., 322, 334
Weil, M., 98, 113
Weinstein, C., 321–22, 335
Weissberg-Benchell, J., 173, 176
Whimbey, A., 232, 244
Whimbey, L., 232, 244
Willensky, J., 212–13, 225
Winograd, P., 184, 192
Wood, P., 173, 176
Wood, T., 247, 266
Woodward, V., 179, 192
Worsham, T., 113, 349

Yackel, E., 247, 266
Yager, S., 154, 156

Zelditch, M., 84, 95

Subject Index

Accountability: individual, with computers, 271; in STAD, 3–4; in the structural approach, 118, 129

Accuracy: in speaking a second language, 195; with nonnative speakers and teacher-led discussions, 199

Activities: and lessons, 122, 124; and the structural approach, 119–121

Activity card, in Complex Instruction, 87

Administrative cooperative teams, at the district level, 62

Administrators: as administers of achievement tests, 323; as determiners of curriculum, 320, 322, 325; as determiners of teachers' work, 323, 326; set school schedules, 322, 327

Affect, in the classroom, 327

Affective climate, and classroom learning, 337

Assigning competence, in Complex Instruction, 86–87

Attribute wheel, 236

Authentic assessment, and a sense of community, 292

Authentic learning, in language arts, 178

Authentic materials, in language arts, 178, 180

Authority: delegation of, to teachers, 326; hierarchical conception of and school organization, 326; and postmodern teaching of literary text, 212

Bartholomew and the Oobleck, integration of science and literature, 237

Basal-reader, 178, 180

Base group: in Jigsaw, 40–41; in The Learning Together approach, 51–52, 54–55, 57

Base scores, for STAD, 7

Behavioral psychology, 179

Big Four multifunctional framework, in the structural approach, 123

Boredom, prevention of, 340

Brainstorm, in science teams, 232

Bureaucracy: as impediment to instructional innovation, 331; and low level of teacher participation in decision making, 319–322, 325–328,

330; and whole-class instruction, 320–322

Centralized control, of school organization, 322
Certificates, as rewards in STAD, 3
Change agent, role in cooperative learning, 302
Change: adoption and dissemination of cooperative learning, 318; impediments to, 318; and school organization, 318, 331
Checker, in science teams, 228
Clarifier, in science teams, 230
Class-building. See Teambuilding
Classification, by science teams, 229
Classroom: management skills, 304; observations for monitoring implementation in, 305; six mirrors of, 307; social rules in, 305; stages of management skills for the, 305–307
Classroom instruction: as bureaucratic organization, 320; and school organization, 319
Classroom physical structure: as fixed, 322; as flexible, 322, 324; reflects school's organization, 322
Climate building: of cooperation, 284, 304; examples of, 286, 292
Closure, of a lesson in science teams, 231–232
Co-op Jigsaw, 123
Coach, in science teams, 237
Cognitive development, through cooperative learning, 157–159
Cognitive literacy strategy, 160; applying, 171; extending, 172; four stages of, 166; and framing, 169–170, 173; and orienting, 168
Cognitive psychology, and language arts, 179
Collaboration: begin with simple, 227; in CDP, 137, 141–142, 144, 148
Collaborative activities: response to literature, 214; for teaching reading, 178
Colleagues, as resources, 329

Collegial support groups, and Learning Together, 51, 60–62, 64
Color-Coded Co-op Cards, 123
Communication, 177; in bureaucratic school, 326, 329; of limited content in bureaucratic school, 326; with peers, 180; and real life, 178; in a second language, 204; strategies, 180–181; strategies in a second language, 197; in traditionally taught classrooms, 321; and work in schools, 321
Community: belonging to, 286; building a, 284, 289; caring, 152, 285; classroom, 284; definition of, 286–287; developing, 289; of inquirers, 98; lack of, 285; of learners, 35, 284; school as, 286–287; sense of, 283; sense of in CDP, 150
Competing demands on teachers, and implementing cooperative learning, 285
Competition, 145; absence of, 146, 151; reduction of, 146, 149
Competitive artificial reward economy, 35
Complex technology (methods of instruction), and sophisticated school organization, 328
Composition of teams in STAD, 7–8
Conclusion, reached by science teams, 228–229
Concurrence seeking, 67–68, 71–73
Conflict: absence of as indicator of apathy, 66; cognitive, 159; constructive management of, 77, 79; and cooperation, 66–68, 75–77; and interpersonal liking, 71, 73; management of, in the learning community, 295; as promotor of higher-level reasoning, 66, 73; skills for, 80; suppression of, 67, 70; and task involvement, 72. See Controversy, academic
Confusion, productive, 151
Constructed meanings, 221

Content, of second language learning, 179, 195
Contextuality, 213
Contract, between students and teachers, 214–215
Controversy, academic: and advocacy, 70–71, 74, 79; and cognitive rehearsal, 74–75; and critical thinking, 73, 79; elements of constructive, 76; and erroneous information, 71; example of, 68; and exchange of expertise, 72; and fun, 71; and individual accountability, 78; and perspective taking, 75; and problem solving, 71, 76; structured, 67, 71; structuring, 66, 77–78; synthesizing, 76
Cooperation: among students for planning, 323, 324; among teachers, 328–329; invited by the learning task, 324
Cooperative behaviors: in Complex Instruction, 88; norms, 87–88
Cooperative classroom designs for computer use, 271–279
Cooperative computer lesson, 268; ingredients of, 268
Cooperative Integrated Reading and Composition (CIRC), 25–28, 308. See also Writing
Cooperative learning: and bureaucratic school organization, 318, 331; in mathematics, 21, 30–31, 246; methods as a comprehensive instructional repertoire, 308; as a multifaceted change, 313; and a second language, 199; simple, complex and creative structures of, 304, 308; strategies, simple 250; and teaching reading, 177. See also Research
Cooperative learning structures: in Learning Together, 54; with math, 256
Cooperative lesson structure, in Learning Together, 54
Cooperative planning, 102, 104
Cooperative school, 30–31; and cooperative learning in the classroom, 60–63; and decision making groups, 62; and Learning Together, 51, 59–64
Cooperative writing, with computers, 272. See also Writing
Coordination: between school organization and cooperative learning, 319–338; inter-class to sustain cooperative learning, 329; with peers, 322; of three dimensions of change, 324, 331
Curriculum: for Complex Instruction, criteria, 91; redesign by teachers, 344; for STAD, 7; TAI and CIRC, 21
Curriculum-free methods, of cooperative learning, 20

Database, use with computers, 276
Debate, among students, 67
Debriefing: and teachers' metacognitive skills, 304, 309; in workshops and training sessions, 304–306
Decision making: decentralization of, 338–339, 345; as a preventive strategy, 339; teachers' participation in, 337–339
Delegation of authority: to students, in Complex Instruction, 87–88; to teacher committees, 326, 328
Design elements, in the structural approach 123–124
Development, ethical and social, 137, 142–143, 147–148
Developmental appropriateness, 148
Deviant behavior, dealing with in the learning community, 295
Dialogue: brainstorming as, 215; and divergent thinking, 213, 215
Direct instruction: and student talk, 89; and teaching reading, 171, 179
Discrete items, in learning a second language, 195, 197, 207
Discussion, 213; and convergent thinking, 213; fishbowl format for, 219; of poetry, 216; as restructuring

of the classroom, 213; and the
"roles in groups" technique, 219; in
small groups, 220; taping of, 219
Disequilibrium or conceptual conflict,
74, 75; as motivation to learn
others' position, 74–75; as
motivation to obtain information,
74. *See also* Conflict; Controversy,
academic
District office, role in implementation,
303
Diversity, and communication, 158–
159
Diversity of the student body: in
Complex Instruction, 82; valuing in
the learning community, 286–290,
296. *See also* Heterogeneous classes
Divided resources: in Learning
Together, 58. *See also* Task
Domain-specific learning and
cooperative approaches, 21
Drawing conclusions, as reading skill,
186

Eclectic, approach to teaching reading,
180
Eclecticity, and postmodernism in
teaching literature, 212
Effective instruction, 123
Element deck, for creating structures,
119
Elementary mathematics instruction,
with cooperative learning, 250
Elements of structures, 116–117, 121,
123–124
Empowerment, of students, 338
Encourager/praiser in science teams,
228
Ending the classroom community, 297
Epistemic curiosity, 74, 75–76
Equal participation, in structural
approach, 118, 127
Evaluating fact or opinion, 189
Evaluation: criteria for in literature,
215; observation of performance as,
107, 110–111; of presentations, 110;
of projects by students and teachers,

109; by students, 108; summary
discussion of, 109
Expectation states theory, 84
Expectation to teach, and higher levels
of cognitive organization, 159
Expectations for competence, 84, 86–
87; by the group, 86
Experiential activities, in second
language learning, 200
Experimentation, by science teams,
229, 235
Exploring community, for common
projects, 292

Fable, a postmodern, 217–220
Facilitating group work, with math,
249
Faculty meetings, 60, 62
Feedback: from colleagues, 345; from
peers, 159, 174; in teaching and
school organization, 327
Flashcard Game, in the Structural
Approach, 119, 130
Focused discussions, and Learning
Together, 54
Following directions, and reading,
188–189
Formal cooperative learning, and
Learning Together, 51–52, 55
Forming community, 289
Four Corners: as a math game, 256; as
strategy for studying science, 232
Friendship, inter-racial, in STAD, 5
Functions, for oral production, 197

Games, for math, 251
Gatekeeper, in science teams, 227
Generalizing, tasks for reading, 184
Generic cooperative learning method,
STAD, 5
Getting acquainted, and a sense of
community, 289
Goal interdependence, and Learning
Together, 56, 58
Goals: of CDP approach, 147;
clarification, 341; coordinating, 106;
different methods for different, 343
Grading for effort, in STAD, 18

Grammar, in learning a second language, 197–198, 200–202
Graphic organizer, and science, 235
Group: intervention in work of, 342–343; and Learning Together, 51–52, 54, 56–60; and members' behavior, 342; process, 342; processing behavior of, 342; as a social structure, 342
Group Discussion method, and a second language, 204–205, 207–209
Group dynamics movement, 99
Group in CDP: duration, 150; membership, 149; roles, 144–146; size, 138, 149
Group Investigation: and choice, 103, 104; interpretation in, 100; intrinsic motivation in, 100; and knowledge, 98–99; locating resources for, 112; as open-systems organization, 323; in science, 230; a social-intellectual process, 100, 111; for studying bubbles in science classroom, 240; for studying pH in science classroom, 242; and teaching literature, 214, 222–224; variety of resources for, 101. See also Learning process; Stages of Group Investigation; Teachers
Group problem solving, and math instruction, 247, 252, 255, 259–261
Group product: grading of, 49; with Jigsaw, 48
Group projects and investigations, on math, 262

Hands-on science study, and cooperative learning, 227, 229, 231
Heads Together, for studying math, 250
Helping, students' and teachers' vocabulary for, 306
Heterogeneity, 149
Heterogeneous classes, 82; cross-role team with Jigsaw in, 34–35; programs for TAI, CIRC, 20; and student roles, 88; and teacher roles, 89

Heterogeneous groups, 130–131; in academic controversy, 77–78; and computers, 268; for science study, 227; and second language, 199, 202, 205–208
Hit the target, math game, 253
Home groups: in Jigsaw 35–37, 40, 42–49; for studying science, 227
Homogeneous grouping, and second language, 205
How to learn, strategies and processes of, 157
Hypothesis, for science teams, 229

Identity, whole-group, and a sense of community, 290–291
Implementation: challenges of, 308; of cooperative learning, 304–307
Improvement, record of in the learning community, 296
Inclusion, in community, and cooperative learning, 287
Individual, and society, 222
Individual accountability, and Learning Together, 53, 56, 58
Individual improvement score, in STAD, 6–7, 13–14, 17
Individuals Interview Partners, 120
Inference, as process skill for studying science, 229
Informal cooperative learning: elements of, 54–55; and Learning Together, 51, 54–55, 57
Input, in second language learning, 198
Inservice training, and organizational factors, 303
Instructional conversations, 152
Instructions for conducting controversy, 78–79
Integration: of language skills, 206; in second language learning, 193–195
Intelligence, multidimensional, 85, 92
Interaction: and CDP, 141–143, 148, 153; effective, 99; in Group Investigation, 99; for learning a second language, 197; and nature of language learning, 195; ongoing,

287; oral, 197, 204; quantification of in the structural approach, 115; simultaneous, 126–127, 131; skills, 208; as a social context for learning, 99; in the structural approach, 115; structured by teachers, 284; and training students, 202, 204–206

Interdependence: in Jigsaw groups, 34, 37, 39, 43, 49; in literature classrooms, 221; reward, in Learning Together, 56; as a source of conflict, 66

Interdisciplinary: curriculum, for cooperative learning, 308; instruction, 297

Interest groups, on the basis of subtopics, 103

Interest teams, 130

Interpersonal, and CDP: environment, 146; skills, 144, 146, 150, 153; values, 141, 147, 150

Interpretation: independently by the student, 216; of meaning by the literature teacher, 216; of a particular poem, 219. See also Group Investigation

Introducing a lesson (cooperative mathematics), 248

Investigation: carrying out of, 105; as orientation, 98

Jigsaw, examples: character study, 44–45; excursions, 45–47; problems in working together, 40–41; staff development with, 42–44

Jigsaw method, 34; assessment and evaluation, 43, 48; with computers, 276; discussion for pairs, 38; and extrinsic reward structure, 37; focus groups, 36, 40–41, 44, 46–48; four generic stages of, 35, 37; Jigsaw I, 37; Jigsaw II, 37, 44; and learning a second language, 202–204, 208–209; and math, 261; pressure of accountability with, 43; problems with contrived interdependence, 49; and subject matter specialization,

35–37, 44; and task specialization, 47

Knowledge, of second language: functional 195–197; linguistic, 197; strategic, 197

Learning community: cooperative, 285; problems of, 288, 292

Learning difficulties, and Integrated Strategies Instruction, 160

Learning environment, and reading, 181

Learning process, in Group Investigation, 97, 103, 105, 107, 108, 109, 111

Lesson designs, with structures, 122–124

Line up activities, as a math problem, 256

Listening comprehension in second language learning, and Jigsaw, 204

Loose coupling and tight coupling: of the curriculum, 322; of school organization, 322

Mainstreaming: with STAD, 6; and TAI, 22, 30–31

Management, in the structural approach, 115, 130–132

Many pieces problems, in math, 255, 261

Materials, for science study, 227, 230

Materials manager, in science teams, 227, 230

Meaning, in response to poetry, 216

Meaningful learning, and CDP, 144–145, 147, 149

Measurement, in science teams, 229

Mental math, 251

Menus, for math problems, 253

Metacognition: modeling of, 184, 189–191; and second language, 202; strategies, and cooperative learning, 158, 168, 170; and thinking aloud, and reading, 189–191

Monitor, in science teams, 233

Monitoring phase of lesson: in CDP, 150–151; role of teacher in, 151–152

Motivation: in CDP, avoidance of
extrinsic, 145, 151; deemphasis of
extrinsic, 147; improving, with
STAD, 14; intrinsic, 137–138, 141,
145–151; as main idea of STAD, 3–
4; match between goals and, 199;
and second language, 199. *See also*
Group Investigation
Multi-ability, classroom, 87;
curriculum for, 83, 85; status
treatment, 85–86; tasks, 91–95
Multiple viewpoints, in CDP, 149, 151
Multiplicity, and postmodernism, in
literature, 212
Mystery equation, math game, 254

Natural learning, and reading 178–180
Negotiation: of criteria for formative
evaluation, 214; as a natural part of
learning, 223; process of, 215; by
students of curriculum, 214
Norms of learning, in STAD, 4, 8
Novels, investigation of, 223
Numbered Heads Together: 119, 128–
130; in math, 258; in science teams,
232

Observation, by science teams, 229
Open-ended tasks: in Complex
Instruction, 87, 91; of learning tasks
in CDP, 142–143, 146, 148, 153
Open systems organization: and
cooperative learning, 323–324;
features of, 323; and high teacher
participation in decision making,
319, 323, 328, 331
Outreach, to help other settings, 296
Overview, of science lesson, 230

Pace of instruction: and coverage of
academic material, 326; as a
function of groups' activity, 323; set
by administrators, 325; as uniform
for entire class, 320–321
Paired activities: and academic
controversy, 68, 78–79; in CDP
approach, 144, 147, 151; check, in
CIRC, 27; check, with math

problems, 144, 147, 151; check, in
the structural approach, 119; in
Jigsaw, 39, 46; and Learning
Together, 55; with math, 251; for
problem solving in math, 252; for
problem solving in science teams,
232; reading in CIRC, 25–27; in
STAD, 4, 12
Partner interview, about math
problems, 252
PASS (preview, ask and answer,
summarize and search for errors),
160; "A" step of PASS, 161; and
creating new strategies, 173; "P"
step on PASS, 161; "S" step of
PASS, 162; writing, 162–165
Pattern, as goal of science study, 229
Pedagogy, for second language
learning, 200
Peer, evaluation, 215, 224
Peer interaction in Complex
Instruction: and learning, 82, 88, 93;
and motivation, 82; rates of, 94
Peer support: in Jigsaw, 47; in STAD,
6, 8
Performance, follows understanding,
in CDP approach, 142
Personal responsibility, for learning,
338
Planning: guidelines for, 107; and
investigations, 222
Planning learning activities, with
Jigsaw, 47; with math and
cooperative learning, 248
Policy, unaffected by teachers, 321
Portfolios, with Jigsaw, 49
Positive interdependence: for groups
with computers, 270; and Learning
Together, 51–52, 58; in the
structural approach, 125, 128–129
Postmodernism, in the literature
classroom, 212
Predicting outcomes, in reading, 186–
187
Prediction, made by science teams,
229
Presentations to class, in STAD, 6.

See also Stages of Group
Investigation
Principal investigator, in science
teams, 227
Principal's role: decentralization of
338; in implementing cooperative
learning, 300–301; and innovations,
95; leadership and management in,
338, 345; and teacher committees or
teams, 338; and teacher support
groups, 312
Problem for investigation: criteria,
112; students' questions about, 112
Problem solver, in science teams, 233
Problem solving, and cooperative
learning with computers, 268, 274
Procedure, in science study, 230
Process, as nonnegotiable part of
curriculum, 215
Process skills, for studying science, 229
Processing group functioning: in
science lesson, 230; when working
with computers, 271
Productive functioning, as a learning
community, 294
Products of cooperative learning: not
specifiable in advance, 324; not
uniform for entire class, 324
Professionalism: and attention to
client, 341, 345; impeded by school
organization, 341–345; of teachers,
336, 340
Programmed instruction, and
cooperative learning, 21
Promotive interaction, and Learning
Together, 58

Questions in Group Investigation:
students', 103, 104; and subtopics
for investigations, 107
Quiz, 11, 13–14, 17–18; scoring of, 4;
by students of one another, 4, 13

Random groups, in the structural
approach, 130
Reading comprehension, and second
language, 197, 202–204
Reading expert, profile of student, 184

Reading groups, in CIRC, 26
Recitation-presentation teaching
methods, 97
Reconstituted groups 35–37
Recorder, in science team, 227
Reflecting on group process, in Jigsaw,
36, 40–41, 48
Reflection: in CDP, 140–141, 144, 152;
on cooperative learning experiences,
154; encouraging through PASS,
160; on studying math, in
cooperative groups, 249
Reflectivity, about the creative act,
213
Regularity, sought in studying science,
229
Relevant and irrelevant details, in
reading, 186–187
Repetition, and cooperative tasks, 153
Research: on Circ, 21, 25, 29; on
cooperative learning with math, 247;
on TAI, 24–25
Research question, for science teams,
229
Resources, students as, in Complex
Instruction, 84
Response: as an approach to
literature, 223; journals for students'
readings of poetry, 216, 223
Restructuring, and rescheduling
classes, 288
Rewards: and Learning Together, 58;
in STAD, 3–4, 6–8, 11, 12–17
Risk taking, and good reading, 179
Roles: and Learning Together, 55–56,
58; of students working with
computers, 274, 279. See also
Teachers
Rotation learning centers, 123
Roundrobin, 117–118, 123, 128; for
teambuilding in science, 228, 237
Roundtable: with math problems, 257,
258; for teambuilding in science,
228, 237
Rules, to control behavior, 321

Scales, to assess class and school
organization, 319–320, 323

Schedule of activities for STAD, 11
Scheduling: and bureaucracy, 322; for different subjects and students, 324; flexible, 324; to overcome, 329; as time-slots to control instruction, 326; as uncoupled from processes, 327
School, as purveyor of knowledge, 341
School and classroom organization: continuity betweeen, 319, 330; as high participative organizations, 323
School factors: and implementation, 302, 309; participation in training, 303, 309
School reform, and TAI, CIRC, 31
Scientific inquiry, not limited to subjects labeled "science," 98–99
Scores, calculating for, in STAD, 4, 11, 14
Secondary mathematics instruction, with cooperative learning, 256
Self-reflection: and the learning community, 286, 288, 293, 295; and teambuilding, 289, 291
Sequence chain, for organizing ideas in science, 236
Set-up (introduction) phase, of CDP lesson, 150
Signal: quiet, 142; zero noise, 306
Simulation, and second language learning, 209
Skills: academic, in CDP, 153; social, and Learning Together, 52–53, 56, 59; social, in the structural approach, 115, 132; teaching of social, when working with computers, 270; of younger and older students in CDP, 149, 153
Social Focus, 146
Software: learner-centered, 267; recommendations for, 268
Space/Time Organization, 321–322, 329
Spelling, in CIRC, 27
Spokesperson, in science teams, 227
STAD (Student Teams-Achievement Divisions): absence of competition in, 3; and achievement, 3–4;

appropriate for well-defined subjects, 4; components of, 6–7; for learning a second language, 200–202; research on, 3–6; as a series of design elements, 123; and six stages for learning a second language, 200–202, 204, 207–208; and social studies, 3–6; worksheets for, 5–6
Staff development, for Complex Instruction, 92
Stages of Group Investigation: Stage 1, class determines subtopics, 101–103; Stage 2, groups plan investigations, 101, 103–105; Stage 3, groups carry out the investigation, 101, 105; Stage 4, groups plan presentations, 101, 107–108; Stage 5, groups make presentations, 101, 108–109; Stage 6, teachers and students evaluate their projects, 101, 109–110
Status problem in Complex Instruction: and learning problems, 85; and participation, 83–84; treatment of, 85–86; and unequal influence, 84
Story-related activities, 26
Strategies, and reading skills, 179
Structural approach, principles of, 115, 125. See also Design elements
Structured natural approach, 132
Structures, 115–119; choice of as a function of objectives, 118–119; creating, 119; modifying, 119; and related constructs, 115; understanding, 116, 119; usefulness of, 116, 118
Student talk, rates of, 94. See also Talk
Students: as an audience, 321; as center of classroom system, 341; cooperation among, 324; expected to obey rules, 321; as experts, 106; isolation from one another, 339; and motivation to learn, 336–337; participation in planning, 338; in a passive role, 321, 325; peripheral to

learning process, 340; and seatwork, 322
Students as resources, in Jigsaw, 35
Success, equal opportunity for in STAD, 3–4
Summarizing, and reading, 185
Synthesizing, and reading, 184–185

Talk: in Group Investigation, 106; in second language learning, 204; quality of students', 199
Talking Chips, 119
Task: for cooperative learning, 325; in second language learning, 198, 202, 205–206, 208
Task sheets, for Jigsaw, 42, 44, 48
Teachers: attitudes related to instructional change, 318; and caring, 337; centrality of, 338–339; changes in roles of, 336, 342, 345; competence in Learning Together method, 55, 61, 63–64; and conformity, 326, 330; control function of, 339; cooperation among, 344; and coordination of curriculum by, 344; coordinators of group interaction, 323; and curriculum for cooperative learning, 308; efficacy of, 340; expectations from, 336; expertise in Learning Together, 57, 59–64; as facilitators of learning, 323, 338; grasp of different methods, 344; as initiators and decision makers, 319, 321, 323, 325–330; intervention in groups in CDP method, 142; isolation of, 339; isolation of and bureaucratic school organization, 327; isolation and cooperative learning, 309; lack of professionalism, 327; limited discretional power of, 327; as mediator in teaching reading, 180; and mentoring of new teachers, 310–311; as observers, 306–308, 311; and peer-coaching cycle, 310, 316; as planners, 306, 309–312; and preparation of learning resources, 341; as questioners of students, 321;

role in CDP, 148, 150–152; role in Group Investigation, 97, 103–105, 107, 108, 109, 111; role in implementation, 301; as role models and trainers, 311; role in STAD, 6–7, 13; role in teaching math with cooperative learning, 247; and school organization, 341; support system and cooperative learning, 309, 310; as transmitters of information, 97; use of different methods, 343–344; as workers and not professionals, 327
Teachers in Complex Instruction: collaboration among, 95; expertise, 93–94; feedback to, 93–95; higher-order thinking, 90; role of, 86, 89–90; and team meetings, 95
Teachers Learning Community (TLC), 310–313, 316; phase 1 of, 303, 310; phase 2 of, 311
Teachers of language, and response to students, 195
Teaching groups, with TAI, CIRC, 23
Team, recognition in STAD, 6, 11–14
Team Assisted Individualization (TAI): combines motivation and peer-assistance, 21; for grades 4–5, 22; principal elements of, 22–24; for social effects, 22
Teambuilding, 115; activities for science teams, 228; aims of, 129; as primary function of structures, 119, 129; with teachers, 304; when working with computers, 269
Team discussion, 117–118
Team learning with STAD, as alternative to traditional instruction, 3–8
Team roles, in science teams, 230
Team scores, in TAI, CIRC, 24
Team teaching: and communication among teachers, 329; with new teachers of cooperative learning, 311
Team word webs for studying science, 235
Teammates, 4–6, 11–13, 23
Teams, for STAD: changing

composition of, 9, 11, 18; for classroom organization, 3, 5; 4 or 5 members per, 4; goals of, 3; recognitions for, 6–7, 11, 13–14; steps in composing, 8

Teams: ethnicity, achievement levels and sex in, 22; 4 or 5 members, in TAI, CIRC, 22; in the structural approach, 115, 127–132; steps for study methods of, in CIRC, 23–24; and students' active participation, 127–131

Tests, in CIRC, 27

Text, in learning a second language, 197

Textuality, in literature, 213

Think-ahead (activation processes), of PASS, 160, 163–164

Think-back (consolidation processes), of PASS, 160, 165–166

Think-during (on-line processes), of PASS, 160, 164–165

Think-Pair-Share: to clarify thinking in science teams, 234; with math, 250, 258

Think-Pair-Square, 123

Think-Pair-Write, 251

Think-Write-Pair-Square, 123

Think-Write-Roundrobin-Share, 123

Three-Step Interview, 117–118; with math problems, 257; in science classroom, 234

Time: for developing learning materials, 308; for quality implementation of cooperative learning, 300, 313

Timekeeper, in science teams, 227

Top-down hierarchical organization, and the nature of work in schools, 321

Training: group roles in, 306; interactive models for, 309

Tutoring, by team members, in STAD, 3, 6

Values: in CDP, 137, 141, 153; of fairness, 137, 143, 147, 153; of helpfulness, 147; of responsibility, 137, 150

Variables, in the study of science, 229

Vertical groupings, for continuity, 297

Videotaping, of one's own and of colleague's teaching, 307, 316

Vocabulary, 181; building activities, 182; categories of basic, 182; in second language, 207–208; usage and cooperative learning, 181

Whole language, 178–180; complemented by direct instruction, 179

Whole-Class: approach, 214–215; and setting an agenda, 220; and small groups, 220; teaching to, 214

Whole-class activities: with Jigsaw, 39; with math, 256

Whole-class instruction: and bureaucratic organization, 319–320; as resistant to change, 319

Whole-class units, in TAI, 24

Work environment, cooperative for teachers, 285

Work required: as an approach, 215; in the literature class, 215

Worksheet, decreased attention to, 246

Workshop, classroom as, 214

Wrap-up: in CDP, 140, 147, 150–151; and reflection on group process, 154

Writing: in CIRC, 27–28; as thinking on paper, 162. See also Cooperative Writing

About the Editor and Contributors

SHLOMO SHARAN is professor of educational psychology at the School of Education, Tel Aviv University, Tel Aviv, Israel, where he has been teaching since 1966. He is the author of many books, research studies, and articles on cooperative learning and on school organization and development. He is the editor of *Cooperative Learning: Theory and Research* (1990) and coauthor with Yael Sharan of *Expanding Cooperative Learning through Group Investigation* (1992).

MARIA V. BALDERRAMA is a doctoral candidate at Stanford University School of Education. She is currently interested in how middle schools work with Mexican immigrant children.

YAEL BEJARANO heads the Department of English as a Foreign Language at the Open University of Israel, Tel Aviv, Israel. She is involved in teacher training, cooperative learning in English as a second language, and second-language testing.

MARK BRUBACHER heads the Department of English at York Memorial Collegiate. A past president of the Ontario Council of Teachers of English, he is coeditor of *Perspectives on Small Group Learning: Theory and Practice* (1990).

MARGARITA CALDERÓN is an associate professor in the Department of Educational Leadership, University of Texas, El Paso. She is engaged in teacher training for ESL and cooperative learning in many states and countries and is the director of the Teachers' Learning Community Center in El Paso.

JUDY CLARKE is a member (1993–1996) of the executive board of the International Association for the Study of Cooperation in Education (IASCE) and is vice-principal at the Dr. Marion Hilliard Senior Public School in Toronto, Ontario.

ELIZABETH G. COHEN is professor of education and sociology at the School of Education, Stanford University, where she directs the Program for Complex Instruction. She is the author of *Designing Groupwork: Strategies for the Hetero-*

geneous Classroom (1986) and of many articles in journals and books. She has concentrated much of her research effort on the problem of status differences in heterogeneous classrooms.

RUTH COSSEY is a doctoral candidate at Stanford University School of Education, where she is studying the sociology of math education. She was a developer of the Family Math program at the University of California in Berkeley and is president-elect of the Northern California Council of Mathematics.

STEFAN DASHO is Senior Staff Developer at the Child Development Studies Center in San Ramon, California. He has conducted classroom ethnographic research and staff development in classroom socialization and cooperative learning.

NEIL DAVIDSON is a professor in the Department of Curriculum and Instruction at the University of Maryland, College Park. He is currently the president of the International Association for the Study of Cooperation in Education (IASCE) and has edited *Cooperative Learning in Mathematics* and *Enhancing Thinking through Cooperative Learning* (with Toni Worsham).

ROBERTA L. DEES is associate professor of mathematics at the University of Illinois, Chicago. She has taught for twenty-eight years in a wide range of educational settings. She is codirector of the college preparatory mathematics program, a high school intervention program using cooperative learning.

EDWIN S. ELLIS is associate professor of special education at the University of Alabama in Tuscaloosa. He is the author of many books and articles on cognitive strategy training and learning disabilities.

R. KEVIN FELDMAN is a program specialist for Sonoma County Schools in California and an instructor at Sonoma State University. He specializes in teaching cooperative learning, learning strategies, self-esteem, and effective communication to teachers, parents, and other adults.

LIANA NAN GRAVES is an educational consultant, artist, writer, and anthropologist who has taught from preschool to graduate school. She is coeditor of *Cooperative Learning Magazine* and serves on the executive board of IASCE and of the California Association for Cooperation in Education.

DAVID W. JOHNSON is professor of educational psychology, and ROGER T. JOHNSON is professor of curriculum and instruction at the University of Minnesota in Minneapolis. The Johnson brothers are codirectors of the Cooperative Learning Center at the University of Minnesota, as well as coauthors, with colleagues, of numerous books, research studies, articles, and curricula in cooperative learning. They have conducted training institutes for teachers and administrators in cooperative learning in many countries. Among their many well-known books are *Learning Together and Alone* and *Cooperation and Competition: Theory and Research*.

MIGUEL KAGAN is a graduate of the University of California, San Diego, and is coauthor of *Advanced Cooperative Learning: Playing with Elements*. He works at Kagan Cooperative Learning Company.

SPENCER KAGAN directs the Kagan Cooperative Learning Company in San Juan Capistrano, California. Formerly a professor of education and psychology at the University of California at Riverside, he has published research studies on cooperation in different cultures and is the author of the well-known text *Cooperative Learning*, which has appeared in many editions.

SYLVIA KENDZIOR is director of staff development at the Developmental Studies Center, San Ramon, California. She has many years of experience as an elementary school teacher and early child educator.

RACHEL HERTZ-LAZAROWITZ is associate professor of educational psychology at Haifa University, Haifa, Israel. She is coauthor, with Ina Fuchs, of *Cooperative Learning in the Classroom* (in Hebrew), and coauthor, with Shlomo Sharan, of *Cooperation and Communication in Schools* (in Hebrew). The volume *Interaction in Cooperative Groups* (1992) was edited by Rachel Hertz-Lazarowitz and Norman Miller.

RACHEL A. LOTAN is a senior research scholar at Stanford University School of Education and associate director of the Program for Complex Instruction there. Her current interests include the design and development of multiple-ability group activities for the heterogeneous classroom.

NANCY A. MADDEN is principal research scientist at the Center for Research on Effective Schooling for Disadvantaged Students, The Johns Hopkins University. She is coauthor, with Robert Slavin and colleagues, of many books, research studies, and articles on cooperative learning, mainstreaming, and special education, as well as on reading, writing, and mathematics instruction. Among the books she has coauthored is *Effective Programs for Students at Risk* (1989).

MARY MALE is professor of special education at San Jose State University. She is author of a series of books on the use of computers in the classroom with diverse populations, including exceptional children. She has been a consultant on technology for school districts throughout the United States.

RYDER PAYNE is the coauthor of a series of language texts, *Language for Living*, and coeditor of *Perspectives on Small Group Learning* (1990) with Mark Brubacher and Kemp Rickett. He is studying the use of collaborative learning strategies in multicultural, inner-city schools for the city of York, Ontario, Canada.

LAUREL ROBERTSON directs the Cooperative Mathematics Project at the Developmental Studies Center, San Ramon, California. This project, supported by the National Science Foundation, develops *Number Power: A Cooperative Approach to Mathematics and Social Development*, a curriculum for kindergarten through grade 6. She is also a member of the board of directors of IASCE.

HANNA SHACHAR is an Assistant Professor in the Department of Education and at the Institute for Promotion of Social Integration in Schools, at Bar Ilan University, Ramat Gan, Israel. She directs the implementation of cooperative learning projects in schools. With Shlomo Sharan she is coauthor of *Language and Learning in the Cooperative Classroom* (1988) and *Organization and Staff Management* (1990, in Hebrew).

YAEL SHARAN is coordinator of in-service teacher training for the Israel Educational Television Center in Tel Aviv, Israel. She is the author, with Shlomo

Sharan, of *Expanding Cooperative Learning through Group Investigation* (1992) and *Small-Group Teaching* (1976), as well as numerous articles and chapters in books on cooperative learning.

SHARON J. SHERMAN is the leader of the Science Education Program at Princeton University's Plasma Physics Laboratory. She is coauthor of *Basic Concepts of Chemistry, SCIENCE TEAMS: Lessons in Environmental Science and Cooperative Learning*, and other books and articles on science education and cooperative learning.

PETER SHWARTZ is a curriculum and materials developer at the Developmental Studies Center in San Ramon, California. He has designed and taught supplemental reading programs and trained teachers to teach them and he collaborated on writing *Taking Books to Heart: How to Instill Love of Reading in Your Child*.

ROBERT E. SLAVIN is currently director of the Early and Elementary School Program at the Center for Research on Effective Schooling for Disadvantaged Students at the Johns Hopkins University. He has authored and coauthored more than 120 articles and 11 books, including *Educational Psychology: Theory into Practice* (1986, 1991) and *Cooperative Learning: Theory, Research, and Practice* (1990). He is one of eleven recipients in the United States of the New American School Development Corporation grants for developing innovative schooling.

DANIEL SOLOMON is director of research at the Developmental Studies Center, San Ramon, California. He is the author of *Children in Classrooms: An Investigation of Person-Environment Interaction* (1979), as well as many research articles and chapters on the San Ramon Child Development Project described in this volume.

PATRICIA E. SWANSON is a doctoral candidate at Stanford University School of Education, and a Former bilingual English-Spanish teacher. Her current interests include teacher education and linking educational theory to classroom practice.

MARILYN WATSON is director of programs at the Developmental Studies Center, San Ramon, California, and program director of the Child Development Project at the center. She has conducted research on the development of children's social cognition and behavior and on the educational role of the family.

JENNIFER A. WHITCOMB is a doctoral candidate at Stanford University School of Education. She is a former English teacher interested in curriculum in heterogeneous classrooms and in what teachers learn from writing case studies of their teaching.

ARYEH WOHL is educational director of the Center for Educational Technology in Israel. He has taught at Tel Aviv, Ben-Gurion, Hofstra, and St. John's Universities. He is presently engaged in writing a course of study on the principles and practice of the teaching of reading for the Open University of Israel.

ESTHER KLEIN-WOHL is a doctoral candidate at the University of London's Institute of Education. She is coordinator for curriculum development in ESL reading comprehension for the Open University of Israel, Tel Aviv, Israel.